MW00464948

MINICOMPUTER SYSTEMS

Structure, Implementation
and Application

MINICOMPUTER SYSTEMS

Structure, Implementation
and Application

(OVER)

CAY WEITZMAN

TRW Systems Group

PRENTICE-HALL, INC.   *Englewood Cliffs*, New Jersey

Library of Congress Cataloging in Publication Data

WEITZMAN, CAY.
　Minicomputer systems.

　Includes bibliographies.
　1. Miniature computers. 1. Title.
TK7888.3.W43　　001.6′4′044　　74–9516
ISBN　0–13–584227–1

ⓒ 1974
by PRENTICE-HALL, INC.
Englewood Cliffs, New Jersey

10 9 8 7 6 5 4 3 2 1

PRENTICE-HALL INTERNATIONAL, INC. *London*
PRENTICE-HALL OF AUSTRALIA PTY, LTD., *Sydney*
PRENTICE-HALL OF CANADA, LTD., *Toronto*
PRENTICE-HALL OF INDIA PRIVATE LIMITED, *New Delhi*
PRENTICE-HALL OF JAPAN, INC., *Tokyo*

Printed in the United States of America

to Ruth

CONTENTS

PREFACE

Thousands of magazine articles have been published, and hundreds of seminars and conferences have been given concerning various aspects and virtues of minicomputers and the benefits various users have derived from them. Seldom do you find anyone complaining about his system, problems incurred in converting to a minicomputer system, or the purchase of hardware elements that do not serve their intended purpose in the system.

A large number of users still "design" their system based on some vague notions or past experience with "the same type of equipment" from a hardware manufacturer, while others look solely at the convenience of converting from an outdated existing system to a new one, with a minimum of conversion problems, regardless of whether the new or even the old equipment does the job. Others, again, may select a particular system based on the idea of being able to expand it to an "undefined size" or, perhaps, because the chairman or president of the company likes the "looks" of the system CRT or the color of the equipment.

To insure success, the user must not only take the time to determine what the system must accomplish *for him* but also have a fundamental working knowledge of the qualitative and quantitative design approaches to minicomputer systems evaluation, selection and interfacing, and hardware, software, and firmware integration. Quick, poorly supported decisions coupled with lack of knowledge of the various details of minicomputer systems analysis and design will in all probability result in an unsatisfactory selection or solution to the problem.

My purpose is, therefore, to give the system designer and/or user an overview of latest minicomputer hardware and software technology, tools, procedures, and approaches used in evaluating and designing minicomputer systems as well as guidelines as to how to implement, maintain, and support these systems. The material herein follows closely the course-outline of a successful seminar given at UCLA called "Minicomputer Systems—State-of-the-Art, Design, Implementation, and Application."

Chapter I contains an overview of minicomputers; Chapters 2 through 4 survey the various hardware, "firmware," and software elements making up a minicomputer system; while Chapter 5 explores various system design approaches. Chapter 6 provides examples of various minicomputer systems, with basic design rules and easy-to-understand formulas. Chapter 7 explores some common problems the user of a minicomputer system is faced with; and Chapter 8 provides a look at future trends in the minicomputer system field.

Several problems and exercises have been included at the end of the book to give the reader some insight into the kinds of questions that the system designer is faced with during the design process.

I wish to acknowledge numerous contributions to this book. Much of the "know-how" and experience reflected in this book has been gained through participation in numerous proposal efforts, system designs, developments, and installations in my work as an "in-house consultant" at System Development Corporation, in Santa Monica, California.

Information on various minicomputers, miniperipherals, and software programs has been borrowed from a large number of manuals, a list of which would be too long to include here.

I am grateful to all my colleagues at System Development Corporation, as well as to various minicomputer and miniperipheral manufacturers, for their cooperation.

In particular, I wish to thank Sal Aranda, Paul Atkinson, Irwin Book, George Cady, Ron Citrenbaum, Gerry Cole, Paul Cudney, Roy Gates, Irwin Granat, John Luke, Lorimer McConnell, Ted Peng, Janis Sekera, Bill Schasberger and Monroe Spierer for their support and criticism of various sections in this book.

I also want to thank my secretary, Kathy Kibbey, for her infinite patience and unending support, without whom this book would not exist.

Finally, I want to thank my wife for her understanding and encouragement, making it all come true.

Cay Weitzman

MINICOMPUTER SYSTEMS

Structure, Implementation
and Application

1

INTRODUCTION TO

MINICOMPUTERS

1.1 COMPUTING, CLASSES OF COMPUTERS, AND THE MINICOMPUTER

The Birth of the Mini

Starting in the mid-1940s with the programmable vacuum-tube computer that was developed to compute ballistic firing tables, the growth of computers has been extremely rapid both in capability and quantity. Early vacuum tube technology limited computer memories to thousands of words and memory access time to hundreds of microseconds. The vacuum tube type of machine was made obsolete in the late 1950s by the transistorized computer. Solid-state technology enabled a rapid increase in logic capability and complexity. A transistorized computer could be made more powerful, less expensive, smaller in size, more reliable, and with less power dissipation than its earlier counterpart, the vacuum tube computer. An upper limit of tens of thousands of instructions per second was now expanded to hundreds of thousands of instructions per second. The transistorized computer that was first developed under military requirements for smaller physical size, extremely high reliability, and low power dissipation, soon found its way into the commercial marketplace. The second-generation computer shared many of the earlier first-generation peripherals such as magnetic tape drives and magnetic drums with more cost-effective storage devices such as fixed and moving head disks.

The next quantum jump was also made possible by advancements in solid-state technology, with much of the research and development again supported by the military and designed to reduce the physical size and power dissipation, as well as to improve the reliability of aerospace computers. Space-age requirements for highly reliable, compact navigational and guidance computers for the Minuteman missile, as well as various manned and un- manned spacecraft, accelerated the development of integrated circuit tech- nology,* so that by the mid-1960s, the third-generation computer had found its way into the commercial computer market.

Third-generation machines range from the 16-bit process control com- puters such as the IBM 1800 and the CDC 1700, the 24-bit CDC 3000 series of business and commercial machines, and the 32-bit Scientific Data Systems (now Xerox) Sigma 5 and 7 real-time computers to the large-scale 60-bit CDC 6000 series of scientific "number crunchers." The change from second- to third-generation peripherals was related to throughput and capacity rather than new types.

Sometime in the early 1960s it was realized that a large number of applications did not require the full capability of complex machines at the lower end of the computer spectrum. The rapidly declining cost of integrated circuits, coupled with demand for low-cost, limited-capability data processors, brought about the minicomputer. It is difficult to pinpoint the exact year that the minicomputer originated. Small airborne computers using a 16- or 18-bit word format had been developed by the early 1960s, and a transis- torized 12-bit, second-generation, low-cost machine was introduced on the commercial market a few years later. It was not until integrated circuits had become commercially available that the minicomputer market exploded. A first step toward greater complexity in integrated circuit design was taken in the mid-1960s with the dual flip-flop on a chip. Rapid expansion in tech- nology brought the first medium-scale integrated (MSI) circuit to the com- mercial market in 1967 with more than 12 functions per chip, and later in the 1960s the first large-scale integrated (LSI) circuit, with more than 100 functions per chip, became available. Since that first 12-bit mini was marketed in 1965, the mini has acquired many more applications in data processing.

The transition from third to fourth generation is hard to pinpoint. It may have started with the introduction of militarized computers using MSI circuits in the late 1960s or with the advent of LSI circuits in microminia- turized aerospace computers such as the Bunker Ramo BR-1018 or the CDC 469 in the early 1970s. The fourth generation incorporated changes in storage technology in addition to microminiaturized logic technology.

---

* Integrated circuit technology started in the early 1960s with the development of a complete logic function such as a single gate or a flip-flop on a single chip, where each function consisted of two or more basic passive and active elements such as resistors, capacitors, and diodes, as well as transistors.

Fourth-generation computers use solid-state computer memory, replacing or complementing the earlier core technology (as in many of the IBM 370 series of machines). Fourth-generation computers are based on virtual memory and firmware technology as well as on multiprogramming and multiprocessing. None of the latter technologies are, of course, unique to the fourth generation; they were found in one form or another as early as the second generation. It is the wide acceptance of these techniques that truly separates the fourth-generation machines from their predecessors. A time chart for computer technology that ranges from the first to the fourth generation is shown in Figure 1-1.

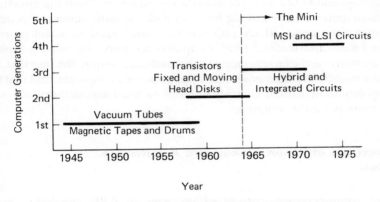

Figure 1-1   Time chart of computer technology

The cost relationship between computers and their peripherals as well as hardware and software from the first to the present generation has continually been changing. The cost of computer hardware is currently being reduced by about an order of magnitude every six years. Advancements in solid-state technology have brought the cost of minicomputers down by almost one order of magnitude in less than a decade. The cost of minicomputer peripherals has also been decreasing, although at a slower pace than the cost of minicomputers. From an initially limited set of minicomputer peripherals where many devices were "borrowed" from expensive larger-sized systems, a new class of *miniperipherals* has emerged. Many of these peripherals are specifically designed for the mini in terms of cost and capability. Typical miniperipherals are the cassette tape unit, the minidisk, the cartridge disk, the miniprinter, and the low-cost cathode-ray tube (CRT) terminal. In spite of these relatively low-cost electromechanical devices, a total system cost imbalance still exists however, because the cost of electro-mechanical devices in peripherals has been declining at a slower rate than the batch-fabricated microcircuits used almost entirely in the central processing unit (CPU).

A cost differential also exists between minicomputer system hardware and software. This is explained by the hardware cost being linked to technology and technological advances which continually brings cost down, while software or programming cost for the most part depends on programmer salaries, which are forever increasing. Furthermore, applications software is user-oriented and, in most instances, individually tailored to the user's particular application—in contrast to general-purpose minicomputers, which can be produced in large numbers for different users. In addition, the tools for mass-producing software have traditionally been nonexistent or, at best, lagging behind the tools for hardware production. With the growth of the minicomputer market and the heavy inroads the minicomputer has made into applications areas, which until now have used more powerful general-purpose small- and medium-sized computers as tools, the mini is rapidly replacing many of the larger, more costly machines, despite the fact that the applications software is generally a more expensive development, and that the mini, by definition, cannot compete in terms of word and memory size with larger, more powerful computers.

The Spectrum of Power, Throughput, Architecture, and Cost

Most computers are categorized in terms of CPU capability, word length, memory capacity, speed, input/output (I/O) capability, complexity of the interface, reliability, maintainability, and supplied software.

The word lengths of most available computers range from 8 bits to 64 bits. (The exception is the microprogram word size, which can stretch up to 64 bits per word or more—see Similarities and Differences Among Several Microprogrammable Minicomputers in Chapter 2.) Minicomputer word lengths vary between 8 and 18 bits, with the most popular word length being 16 bits. The lower range of the more powerful third- and fourth-generation machines is based on word size of 16, 18, 20, or 24 bits. Intermediate-sized machines use a word size ranging from 24 to 36 bits, whereas larger machines use word sizes starting at 32 bits (many operate on double words or more). The purchase cost of small computers ranges from $50,000 to $300,000, medium-sized computers from $200,000 to $1 million, and large computers from $500,000 up to $8 million. "One-of-a-kind" supercomputers cost from $2 million up. In the early 1970s, minicomputer cost ranged from $50,000 down to a few thousand dollars, depending on the amount of memory and the number of options. The relative cost versus word size for the entire range of commercial computers is shown in Figure

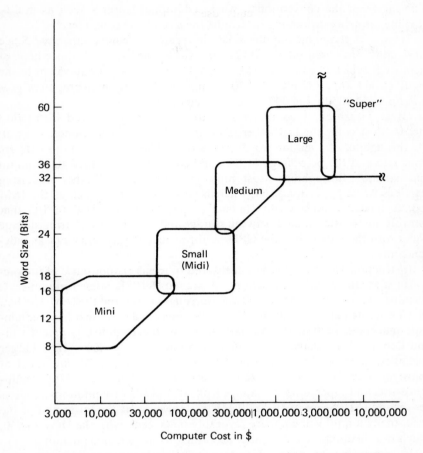

Figure 1-2 Cost of mini- to super computer systems (ILLIAC-IV, TI-ASC, CDC STAR-100, PEPE, IBM 370/195, CDC 7600)—early 1970s

1-2 (this excludes military computers, which often cost three to five times as much as their commercial counterparts).

Memory capacity is to some degree a measure of computer "size." The most popular and widely used family of computers, the IBM 360/370 series, where memory is measured in terms of 8-bit bytes although the machines use 32-bit words have memory ranges from 4000 bytes (1000 words) to 4 million bytes (1 million words). Machines with a maximum of 16,000 words are generally considered small (360/20 to 360/30), and machines limited to a maximum of approximately 128,000 words are considered to be of medium size (360/50, 370/145). Computers with memories of 500,000 words up are considered large. The truly large supercomputers usually have an architecture differing from the conventional, where additional features such as multi-, pipeline, or array processing determine the size of the computer.*

How does the minicomputer relate in terms of memory capacity? Since most minis are based on 16-bit (2-byte) words, the practical upper limit of memory is typically 64,000 bytes or 32,000 words, which is equivalent to the small 16,000-word (32-bit), 360/30, computer. (A few minicomputers provide up to 64,000 or 124,000 words of memory.)

Other measures of computer size are I/O throughput and instruction speed. Most computers, whether mini or medium-sized machines, have an I/O throughput of 1 million words per second. The qualifiers in this case are word size and the percentage of the total computer being used to maintain this maximum throughput. Most minicomputers inhibit all other processing activities while performing I/O, whereas small computers, such as the IBM 360/30, have an independent channel or processor dedicated to I/O that controls the transfer of data between storage and the I/O unit, sharing storage cycles with the CPU while the CPU performs its data processing tasks independently.

Instruction speed is generally measured in terms of thousands of instructions per second or kilo-instructions per second (KIPS). Some medium-scale machines, such as the IBM 360/50, the Burroughs 4700, and the IBM 370/145, have been rated at 170, 220, and 330 KIPS, respectively, while other medium-scale machines, such as the Xerox Sigma 7 or the Digital Equipment Corporation PDP 10, have been rated at approximately 400 KIPS. Larger machines, such as the Honeywell 6070 or the Univac 1108, are rated at approximately 500 and 600 KIPS, respectively. The truly large multiprocessors and supercomputers range from 1000 KIPS or million-instructions per second (MIPS) up to 10 or 20 MIPS. However, at the lower end of the scale, many a mini will compare favorably in "speed" with the IBM 360/50, which is a medium-scale computer according to our previous definition.

In summary, the most obvious distinction between minis and other digital computers is in cost, word size, and complexity of the I/O mechanism. Other common features that distinguish a minicomputer are their small physical size and limited processing capability; however, the mini often makes up for the latter in microprogramming and higher throughput capabilities.

——

* The multiprocessor is a system of central processing units, memories, and I/O devices, all under the control of a central executive controller written in software, where every memory unit and I/O device in the system is available to every processor. The pipeline or *vector* processor manipulates string arrays where operands are processed simultaneously and sequentially in microsteps, several operands always being in the pipeline in various stages of processing. The array processor contains a large number of processing elements operating synchronously under the direction of a single central *host* or *instruction* unit.

System Categories and Applications

Initially, data processing was used to compute ballistic trajectories and later simple scientific and business-oriented problems in a sequential batch mode. Some of the more important newer areas in which it is used are text manipulation, management information systems, manufacturing and process control, data communications, and data base management. Many of these

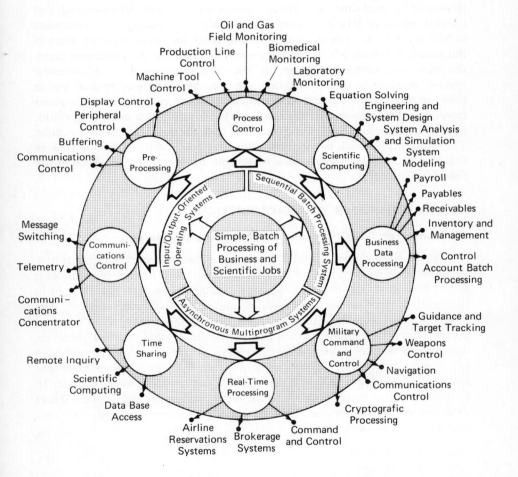

Figure 1-3 Computer systems application development, starting from sequential batch processing of business and scientific jobs, grew from sequential, asynchronous multiprogramming and I/O-oriented operating systems into time sharing, real-time processing, process control, communications, and several other types of computing systems

computer applications are based on multiprogrammed, time-shared, real-time systems.

The sequential batch and control-function-oriented systems generally use small- to medium-sized computers, while the multiprogram systems use large computers. The smaller systems typically require much man power *per job*, while large systems require very little man power per job.

The three basic systems—I/O-oriented, sequential batch, and asynchronous multiprogram systems—are used in various control applications, time sharing, real-time processing, military and commercial command and control, business data processing, and scientific computing. The expansion of the three basic system categories into eight major application areas is illustrated in Figure 1-3. Although used in all eight major application areas, the present minicomputer system fits best the description of the I/O-oriented system. Regardless of the fact that the mini by itself is of limited use in time sharing and command and control environments, most minisystems have proved to be cost-effective solutions for control, data communications, and limited-capacity business processing and scientific number crunching. The variety of functions performed by minicomputers is summarized in Figure 1-3. Detailed descriptions of several minicomputer applications are found in Chapter 6.

1.2 MINICOMPUTER CHARACTERISTICS

Minicomputer Definitions and the Minicomputer Jargon

The question "What is a mini?" may have been answered in terms of how minis differ from larger nonmini systems, such as in limited physical size, 8- to 18-bit word size, limited processing capability, low cost, limited built-in diagnostic and error-checking features, and limited software support. The minicomputer, with few exceptions, has been nothing more than a system component with a limited range of peripherals, limited support software, and limited support from the manufacturer. However, many changes have taken place in the early 1970s, particularly in the area of peripherals and software. Let us now examine the areas of commonality among minis. In general, minicomputers have the same basic elements found in their larger counterparts. Hence, minicomputer system parameters generally fall into one of the following areas:

- Processor
- Memory
- Input/Output
- Software
- Peripherals
- Size, expandability, and flexibility

As a rule the central processor is a single-address,* binary machine where negative numbers are expressed as two's complement and the word size ranges between 8 and 18 bits. The number of general-purpose hardware registers typically ranges from one to eight, and hardware multiply-and-divide is available as an optional feature. Floating-point arithmetic, decimal arithmetic, searches, and 8-bit byte-manipulating instructions, which are found in small- and medium-sized machines, are seldom available in the mini processor. The basic differences among various minicomputer processors, such as number and type of registers, available instruction sets, instruction decoding techniques, interrupt handling, and bus arrangement, will be discussed in detail in Chapter 2.

Most minicomputers use core memory; however, some provide a solid-state memory with a faster cycle time but with the problems of volatility and generally higher cost. Core memories have cycle times ranging from approximately 600 nanoseconds to over 1 microsecond. The solid-state memories have access times in the low hundreds of nanoseconds. The memory increments for the majority of minis are either 1024, 4096, or 8192 words, and the maximum memory size for most minis is 32,000 words, although some minicomputer memories can be expanded to 128,000 words (note that 16 bits allow only direct addressing to 64,000 words, or, for byte addressing, 32,000 2-byte words). Many minicomputer memories feature both parity check and memory protect, although these may be optional features.

The input/output section is an integral part of most minicomputers. Unlike most larger machines, the minicomputer I/O is limited to two or three schemes: processor-program-controlled I/O through one or more hardware registers in the CPU, direct memory access (DMA) with memory cycle stealing but without intervention from the processing unit, and, finally, the less common method of direct multiplexed memory access (DMC). The first scheme is the slowest and ties up the entire CPU, while DMA is the fastest and is usually used for block transfer to and from a disk or other external high-speed device. The interrupt structure of a mini is an integral part of the I/O section. The interrupt structures are generally of two kinds: single-level, no priority systems which reserve one storage location for the current program address, and multilevel systems which reserve several storage locations as pointers to different interrupt servicing routines. The higher-level interrupts can interrupt lower-level interrupts. The details of various priority controls are also discussed in Chapter 2. Some of the earlier minis use single-level interrupt, while most minis today use the multilevel.

---

* Some two-address minis are becoming available, such as the Digital Equipment PDP-11 and Interdata 70.

Software for minicomputer systems can be divided into several classes:

- *Program development software* needed by the user to develop his programs for particular applications.
- *Input/output software routines* for the system hardware and peripherals. These packages are generally defined by the characteristics of the respective hardware.
- *Applications software*, which is related to the task that the system is to perform and which is therefore unique to the particular system.
- *Operating system software*, also called the executive or system monitor, which tells what to do, when to do it, and what to do it with or to.

The minicomputer development software consists of editors, assemblers, debugging and utility routines, and one or several compilers such as BASIC or FORTRAN. Some minicomputer manufacturers offer both core resident and disk operating systems and, in some cases, magnetic tape operating systems. The subject of minicomputer software is treated in greater detail in Chapter 4.

Generally, the medium-sized and large machine peripherals are not interfaced with minis. A few exceptions exist, such as the IBM 2314 disk unit with close to 30 megabytes of storage and several 600-lines-per-minute line printers. Minicomputer output devices are usually confined to low- and medium-speed card and paper tape punches and character printers. Several low-speed line printers have been designed especially for the mini. Input devices are also limited to alphanumeric keyboard terminals, CRT terminals, and low- and medium-speed card and paper tape readers. The most commonly used storage devices are cassette and low-speed seven- or nine-track IBM compatible tape drives and 2.5- to 5-megabyte moving head disk drives. Peripherals, such as graphic displays, optical character readers, and computer output microfilm and voice-output devices, are not typically used with a mini unless the mini serves as a controller interfaced to a larger machine. The details of various peripherals are discussed in Chapter 3.

Today's mini is normally 19 inches wide, mounted in a rack. The trend has been toward large-sized circuit boards with the entire CPU on one board, 16,000 words of core on another board, and one or more peripheral controllers on a third board. These circuit boards all slide into the same enclosure, and when it is filled to capacity an expansion chassis can be added with an internal power supply for its boards. Although the large-board approach is quite common, other packaging methods have been used for minis.

Most minis are constructed with a plug-in front panel which can display register contents and which provides auxiliary switches and lights for register input and display for the programmer.

The flexibility and ease of expansion in a mini is often provided in terms of memory exchangeability. When faster memories become available, the old memory can simply be removed and replaced by a newer, faster one. In addition, with denser packaging technology, a 4000-word circuit board can be replaced by a single 8000-word board and later on by a single 16,000-word board without having to resort to an expansion chassis. Many minicomputers also provide complete interchangeability between boards and board positions in the computer.

The Minicomputer as a Systems Element

The minicomputer should be viewed by the systems designer as a small but nevertheless important element in the total system. The most common minicomputer systems are either man-machine- or machine-machine-oriented. The former consist of data acquisition, process control, and time sharing and problem-solving systems, while the latter are either peripheral or remote terminal communications control systems. Data acquisition systems require limited or no feedback to the process from the operator. These systems convert process information derived in analog or digital forms to computer-understandable information through a sensor-data input interface. After appropriate computer processing the information is displayed to the human operator in a form understandable to him. This type of system is shown in Figure 1-4. The process control system, which usually requires a large amount of feedback, contains, in addition to the elements of the data acquisition system, a computer-readable input interface from the operator for the

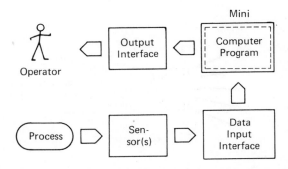

Figure 1-4 Data acquisition system, limited or no feedback, man-machine interface

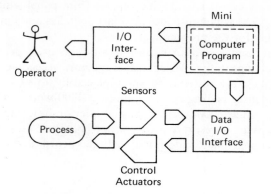

Figure 1-5 Process control system, large amount of feedback, man-machine interface

operator's control response as well as control activators on the process side of the computer to effect control of the process. In some instances, the closed loop is limited to the process and the computer, excluding the operator. This type of system is shown in Figure 1-5.

The time-sharing and problem-solving system is limited to interaction between the user-operator and the computer. The computer is generally connected to an auxiliary storage device such as a magnetic tape or disk drive where parts of a data base are stored. The time-sharing or problem-solving system is shown in Figure 1-6.

The machine-machine-based minicomputer system shown in Figure 1-7 uses the mini as a peripheral control or communications preprocessor and buffer in order to relieve the larger computer from tedious and time-consuming tasks such as error checking, polling, line buffering, hand shaking, and other protocol-related processing.

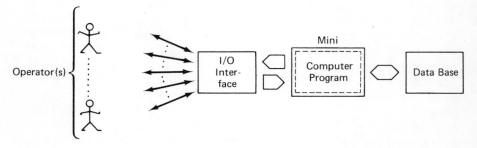

Figure 1-6 Interactive time-sharing, business data processing or problem-solving system, man-machine interface

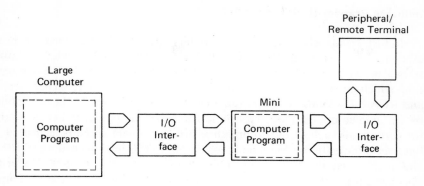

Figure 1-7 Peripheral or remote terminal control system, machine-machine interface

In addition to the above-mentioned external man-machine or machine-machine interfaces and system I/O problems, the designer must concern himself with the internal subsystem boundaries such as interfaces between various elements within the computer and interfaces between the computer, peripheral controllers, peripherals, data lines, and peripheral and communications software. In selecting a minicomputer that meets functional performance requirements, the designer must make sure that all internal considerations have been considered and that all boundary problems have been solved. For instance, a typical problem encountered in interfacing a nonstandard printer to a minicomputer involves the size of the buffer in the printer controller, the bit-serial or parallel controller interface, the hardware/software protocol on each side of the boundary, the electronic compatibility of devices, and the adaptability of existing software to the new printer, and so forth.

Many systems will eventually reach the point of saturation in terms of throughput and other performance limitations. The designer must therefore allow for flexibility and growth in his initial design in order to save the system user at a future date from having to replace most or all of the system elements. The minicomputer selected should be modular in terms of both hardware and software in addition to being compatible with a large number of other potential system elements. For example, the memory should be expandable, faster memory should be usable when available, and if it is not available it should be possible to add DMA and a real-time clock as well as other features at a later date. An important consideration in this case is the capability of retrofit or change without having to interrupt the system operation for the time required to ship the computer back to and from the factory. More information on minicomputer systems and system trade-offs is given in Chapter 5.

Industry Standards and the Mini

Industry-wide standards for computers are either ill-defined or non-existent. In most cases, the computer giant, IBM, has created its own standards, which to a great extent have, in turn, been adopted by the competition, which consists of large computer manufacturers such as CDC, Xerox, and RCA (now Univac). These same IBM standards have also been adopted by the minicomputer industry. These transformed standards are generally for peripherals such as 132-column line printers, where speed is measured in lines per minute (lpm). Medium speed is 300 to 600 lpm, according to IBM, and high speed is 1100 up to 2000 lpm. The 80-column IBM Hollerith punched card is still one of the most widely used I/O media in the computer industry. However, the IBM System/3, 96-column card has not made inroads into the minicomputer industry. Paper tape devices, being at the low end in terms of cost of I/O devices, are very popular in the minicomputer industry. Medium-speed paper tape punching is in the range of 50 to 75 characters per second, while the medium-speed paper tape reader range is from 100 to 300 characters per second. (One character is typically defined by 5 to 8 bits.) The IBM compatible magnetic tapes are either seven- or nine-track systems recorded on tape $\frac{1}{2}$-inch wide. Each parallel group of bits thus recorded constitutes one character or byte. The number of bits recorded per inch of tape (bpi) on each track is referred to as recording or packing density. Standard IBM densities range from 200 to 6250 bpi. The writing (recording)/reading speed varies from 4 inches per second (ips) to 200 ips. Most minicomputer seven- or nine-track tapes have a read/write speed between 10 and 45 ips.

Low-capacity disk drives, such as those IBM is using in the System/3 (Model 5440), have also been adopted by the minicomputer industry. The similarities between the IBM removable or fixed disks and the minicomputer IBM-like, disk drives are often superficial. The actual interchange of disks between IBM disk drives and minicomputer disk drives may not be as simple as that for magnetic tapes and IBM and minicomputer tape drives.

The minicomputer industry seems to be close to a standard of its own in the area of magnetic cassette tapes. A cassette is generally defined as a tape container in which the tape can be driven in either direction and in which data can be read or written onto the tape without removing the tape from the container. The most popular digital cassette makes use of the standard Philips audio cassette. The above "standards" are only in terms of input/output media and, perhaps, formats. The only other significant standard has been imposed by the communications industry on the computer industry. This standard relates to actual hardware interface character formats and code as well as hand shaking or protocol between two devices that are interfaced to each other. An additional standard, also imposed by the communications industry, is the transmission rate. The rate generally pertains to digital bit-serial transmission of characters that either consist of actual data or are used only for control, such as *end-of-text, start-of-text, acknowledge*, and *not-acknowledged*.

Typical low-speed data rates are either 110 bits per second (bps), 150 bps, or 300 bps (10, 15, and 30 characters per second, respectively). Medium-speed transmission ranges up to 2400 bps, while high-speed transmission extends beyond 50,000 bps.

The actual equivalence between data transmission rates, card reader/punch, paper tape reader/punch, and line printer speed is shown in Figure 1-8.

Bits Per Second	Characters Per Second, 1 Char. = 8-11 Bits	Characters Per Minute	Words Per Minute, Word = 6 Char.	Cards Per Minute 80-Col. Card	Boxes Per Hour, 1 Box = 2000 Cards	Lines Per Minute 132 Char./Line	Pages Per Hour, 1 Page = 63 Lines
110	10	600	100	7	—	4	4
150	15	900	150	11	—	7	7
600	60	3,600	600	45	2	30	30
1,000	100	6,000	1,000	75	2	46	40
1,200	120	7,200	1,200	90	3	50	50
1,300	130	8,000	1,300	100	3	60	60
1,500	150	9,000	1,500	112	3	70	70
1,800	180	10,800	1,800	135	4	80	80
2,000	250	15,000	2,500	188	4	80	80
2,100	270	16,000	2,700	200	6	120	120
2,400	300	16,000	3,000	225	7	140	130
4,000	500	30,000	5,000	375	11	230	220
4,200	530	32,000	5,300	400	12	240	230
4,800	600	36,000	6,000	450	13	270	260
5,300	660	39,600	6,600	495	15	300	290
10,600	1300	79,200	13,000	990	30	600	570
19,400	2400	145,000	24,000	1800	54	1100	1050
40,800	5100	306,000	51,000	3080	92	2300	2200
64,000	8000	480,000	80,000	6000	180	6000	5700

Figure 1-8   Speed conversion table

Who Makes What in the Minicomputer Industry

The minicomputer industry started as an outgrowth of modular computer circuit board manufacturing. The Digital Equipment Corporation and what was to become the Computer Control Division of Honeywell started from a broad base of low-cost module manufacturing to become two of the giants in the minicomputer field. They were later joined by Hewlett-Packard, Varian,

Data Machines, Interdata, and Data General, and a multitude of smaller firms. The minicomputer industry can presently be divided into four major segments: the main-frame manufacturers, the peripheral manufacturers, the software suppliers, and the turn-key system suppliers.

By 1970, some 40 to 50 companies had entered the minicomputer manufacturing field. The majority of machines were either 8-, 12-, or 16-bit computers, and the variations in design were mostly in the area of instruction sets. The competition has, since then, forced many of these manufacturers out of business, and the variations in the majority of types of machines presently sold are limited to less than a dozen. The trend among the five or six manufacturers that control the largest segment of the minicomputer main-frame market is to manufacture their own peripherals, such as disk drives, drums, and cassette tape drives as well as the software drivers and hardware controllers for their complete line of peripherals.

The second largest segment of the minicomputer market consists of peripheral manufacturers of devices such as line printers, card readers, paper tape readers and punches, disk drives, plotters, CRT terminals, and keyboard terminals. Several manufacturers also produce plug-to-plug-compatible* computer memories for various minicomputers. A subset of this group of manufacturers has also emerged. This "peripheral" manufacturer buys the "end" peripheral, such as a disk or a card reader, from the peripheral manufacturer and develops his own hardware/software controller. He then sells the entire system, including the disk or card reader as the case may be, to the end user. His system may be an improvement on the comparable system sold by the main-frame manufacturer in that his peripheral control software requires less main-frame memory or his system sells for substantially less.

The third segment of the market consists of the software supplier who may be providing a more efficient higher-level language or a general-purpose modularized applications package that can be run on a particular (widely used) minicomputer. Many such packages exist for the DEC PDP-8 and PDP-11 as well as for the Data General Nova. In some cases, end users have developed software applications packages for their own system and have tried later to recover some of the cost of developing this software. Large software companies, such as Computer Sciences, Planning Research, System Development Corporation, and Informatics, generally do not sell off-the-shelf software but perform minicomputer software development for a customer on a contractual basis. This is, of course, also true of the many small independent software companies who can favorably compete with the "biggies" because of their low overhead.

---

* Plug-to-plug means that the hardware itself is physically compatible; unplug one and plug in the other.

The fourth segment of the market comprises the independent turn-key system suppliers who compete head-on with the main-frame manufacturers. This last type of supplier is generally at a disadvantage since he must purchase a large part, if not all, of the hardware from the hardware manufacturer. The "value added" in this case is the applications software and the intimate knowledge of the applications area. Some of the problems faced by this "buy-and-tie" supplier are the size of the particular market and the question of being able to amortize his development costs over a reasonable number of sales. The advantage to the end user of purchasing a complete system from this type of supplier lies in the predictability of the total cost of the system, including hardware, software, system integration, test, installation, and maintenance. If problems are encountered, there is only a single vendor involved, which completely eliminates the problems of "finger pointing" that are common to this industry.

1.3 WHAT THE MINICOMPUTER CAN AND CANNOT DO

The Range of the Mini—Upper and Lower Boundaries in Size and Capability

The mini has been defined as an 8- to 18-bit word-size machine with a memory ranging from 1000 to 32,000 words. In spite of limited accuracy, low speed for double-precision arithmetic operations, and lack of floating-point hardware, many new minis include microprogramming capability, multiple I/O access features, and rather extensive instruction repertoires, providing powerful programming capability that often approaches that of small- and medium-sized computers.

The upper boundary or next quantity jump in terms of performance is the *midi* or small computer. The midis are generally manufactured by the large computer manufacturers such as IBM, Control Data Corporation, NCR, and Xerox. The IBM 1800 and 1130 as well as System/7 and System/3 are considered midis or small computers. Similarly, the CDC 1700 and the Xerox Model 530 belong to the latter class of machines.

Why is the IBM 1800 labeled a small computer and the Data General Nova 800 considered a mini? Both are 16-bit machines and the Nova has a cycle time that is five times faster than the IBM 1800. The answer in this case lies in the abundant software, the breadth of support, and the cost of the IBM machine, which is in the $50,000 to $150,000 range, compared to the less extensive software and support as well as the low cost of the Nova, which ranges from $5000 to $20,000, almost one order of magnitude less. Furthermore, the Nova is a desk-top machine, while the 1800 is physically large, housed in a freestanding enclosure. Most significantly, however, the

Characteristics	Programmable Calculator	Minicomputer	Midi or Small Computer
Maximum memory word size	100	32,000	256,000
Maximum number of bits per word	64	18	24
Higher-level language	Hardware: BASIC	Software: FORTRAN BASIC ALGOL RPG	Software: FORTRAN BASIC ALGOL RPG COBOL
Function	Dedicated	General-Purpose	General-purpose
Display I/O, and recording devices	Built-in	External peripherals	External peripherals
Speed	Slow	Fast	Fast
Programming	Manually from integral keyboard	Assembly or higher-level language	Higher-level language
Required user knowledge of machine-level operation	None	Extensive	Limited
Applications	Dedicated program solving Limited data acquisition	Limited time sharing Problem solving Data Acquisition Process Control Peripheral Control	Simultaneous limited time sharing and batch processing Multiprogramming Data acquisition Process control Extensive problem solving
Cost	Very low	Low	High

Figure 1-9 Comparison of programmable calculator, minicomputer, and midicomputer characteristics

IBM 1800, unlike the Nova, contains a number of error detection features so that any attempt by the program to read from a memory storage location having incorrect parity or to write a word having incorrect parity will result in an internal interrupt. Once an error is detected, retries or other error recovery procedures can be initiated.

Most midicomputers are significantly more powerful (and expensive) than minis. Midis usually contain double-precision instructions and floating-point hardware as well as external I/O processors and, in many cases, multiple memory ports. They also allow memory to be expanded to 256,000 words. Word size for midis ranges from 16 to 24 bits, and, most significantly, midis have the capability of running background batch programs while concurrently responding to multilevel multiple real-time external events. Many small computers are also upward compatible with larger systems. At the low end of the scale, the mini is bound by the controller and the programmable calculator. The controller is generally a minicomputer with a nondestructive memory and performs a predetermined, nonalterable. control function in a system. Examples of such machines are the Honeywell 116 and the DEC PDP-16. The controller is dedicated to a single application and, as its name implies, performs a control function. The calculator, on the other hand, is designed for jobs that fall between the slide rule and the computer. The calculator is designed for solving complex equations, is quite slow, and has limited internal memory. It differs from the computer in that it allows the user to do his programming from an English language keyboard where each key represents the code of one function of a program. The calculator usually contains a built-in display for calculated results and sometimes a small printer. Therefore, the calculator does not require any peripherals, and, unlike the mini, no experience is required by the first-time user. However, the calculator is far less versatile than the mini and can be considered a complement to rather than a competitor of the mini.

A summary of various features for calculators, minis, and midis is shown in Figure 1-9.

Alternatives to the Mini

Application dictates the available range of alternatives to a minicomputer. In areas where the mini serves as a control element—such as device control, numerical machine control, and process control—as well as for manufacturing and laboratory testing, instrumentation monitoring and analysis, and other forms of data acquisition, the alternatives to the mini are the hard-wired controller and the programmable controller. The former is designed to perform a device-specified action and may, for that reason, be a one-of-a-kind design. The programmable controller is more like the mini. As already mentioned, it consists of an off-the-shelf, small fixed-program processor with a limited amount of read/write memory used for data storage, not programs, and a read-only memory which contains the instructions.

The choice between these alternatives depends on the complexity of the job to be performed as well as the magnitude and complexity of expected future changes. The hard-wired solution is obviously less desirable in a dynamic environment where frequent system changes take place. The non-recurring development cost of the hard-wired controller should also be weighed against the cost of software development for the minicomputer.

In the area of simulation and scientific equation solving, the trade-off is between the analog and digital computer. The analog computer is generally not competitive with the mini in terms of cost. Here again, processing requirements such as speed and accuracy will dictate the choice of hardware. The analog and hybrid computers are slowly disappearing, although the problems of economically sensing all source information digitally are still not solved.

Simulation, scientific equation solving, data base management, and business data processing may be performed on a dedicated "stand-alone" mini as well as on a larger in-house general-purpose data processing system. Of course the processing can also be performed at an outside service bureau* or with a corporate seller of excess computer time. The dedicated minicomputer approach is generally cost-effective in terms of relatively light but evenly distributed workloads, while the large in-house data processing facility, whether used in a batch or time-sharing mode, may be the preferred approach where data processing requirements are infrequent and vary greatly in job size. As a rule, the dedicated mini eliminates problems of availability, scheduling, continuous sales expenses of excess time, and unforeseen system crashes caused by unrelated jobs performed by other users. The advantages of the large machine are, again, the wider range of peripherals, the larger amount of CPU and peripheral storage capacity, and the facilities for writing programs in larger numbers of higher-level languages such as PL/1 and COBOL. No simple rules exist for choosing among the various alternatives; however, each application must be individually analyzed in terms of development cost, schedule capability, performance, operational cost, and user convenience.

1.4 ECONOMIC INCENTIVES

Computer Automation and Changes in Industry Structure

Rising labor and material costs have created major problems of cost control for management in many manufacturing industries. In addition to

---

* The service bureaus purchase or lease computer equipment and hire staffs of programmers, analysts, and operators. They offer computer services to users who prefer not to obtain equivalent equipment directly. A service bureau may also offer time-shared services to outside users by virtue of input/output remote terminals connected to its facility over telephone lines. In some instances, the service bureau and time-sharing vendor are considered two separate entities.

the cost problem, to remain competitive manufacturers have been forced to install machines and equipment with a high degree of complexity. These two factors, more than anything else, have forced industry into computer automation at an unprecedented rate. Adding to these factors the fact that, unlike the medium- and large-sized commercial computers, the typical mini is capable of withstanding the typical industrial control environment, the mini is the ideal tool for low-cost production control. This industrial environment often lacks air conditioning and air filtering. With the rapidly declining cost of the mini, it is now being used in smaller and smaller plants. In small factories it is quite common today to have minicomputers perform process and manufacturing control, inventory control, cost control, and labor control; in larger factories, minicomputers feed some of the information for further processing into central computers. The small satellite computer that is capable of performing limited data processing as well as providing communications control has strengthened the centralized control function in industries with widely dispersed facilities.

The widespread acceptance of the so-called smart or intelligent* terminal for small business/accounting operations has brought the power of the computer to medium- and small-sized business firms. (The intelligent terminal is discussed in greater detail in Chapter 6.) The small business data processing center capability has enabled smaller businesses to adopt methods of order entry, invoicing, and inventory control that they would otherwise not have been able to afford, and it has enabled medium-sized businesses to reduce their accounting and keypunch-personnel overhead.

Money-Saving Potential and the Mini

The effect on profit through the use of electronic data processing has been defined by Paul Rau† as the difference between the benefits received from using a system, where the benefits are equivalent to the cost differential of using a computer and performing the same functions without a computer, and the sum of the development and operational costs. The development and operational costs include the cost of hardware and software as well as programming maintenance, supplies, data preparation, and clerical support. Assuming that the benefits for a particular application are equal regardless of whether a stand-alone mini, a time-sharing service, a service bureau, or a large computer is used, the effect on profit can be maximized only by reducing either the development or the production cost or both.

As previously mentioned, the cost of an in-house minicomputer system and the cost of a larger computing facility differ substantially. The cost of

---

* *Smart* and *intelligent* refer to small minicomputer-based stand-alone or remote terminal systems connected to a central large computer facility over telephone lines.

† P. Rau, "Evaluating the EDP Function," *Datamation*, September 1972, 72–73.

hardware for a minicomputer is, of course, significantly lower, but in some instances this may be less significant because of the relatively lower cost of software development on a large machine. The cost advantages may, however, still be on the side of the mini, since many minicomputers offer cross-assemblers; i.e., the assembly can be performed on a large machine and the program run later on the mini. However, the running costs of a self-contained in-house computing system, whether a mini-based or a larger system—including maintenance, setting up, and choosing auxiliary and peripheral equipment—have an adverse effect on cash flow that use of a time-sharing service or service bureau does not. (We shall discuss maintenance further in Chapter 7.) The cost of software can also vary considerably depending on the data processing approach. Not all the software from a large computer manufacturer is free, nor is it free from the minicomputer manufacturer. The cost of software from a time-sharing service is included in the service charge and may be even more difficult to evaluate.

One big disadvantage of owning a system concerns equipment obsolescence and replacement. When dealing with a service bureau, the user can simply cancel unsatisfactory service, but when the equipment is owned outright, the user is stuck with it. The user should, however, keep in mind that time-sharing service is weighed down by the cost of communications lines over which he has no control and by terminal charges while the user is on-line but not computing. These two costs can amount to half or more of the total charge for the use of a time-shared computer. Additional disadvantages of using service bureaus are turnaround times between batch jobs and, to some extent, the inconvenience of long waits or of not being able to access a remote time-sharing computer when the system is operating close to its maximum capacity.

The realization that a large number of programs running on time-sharing systems are less than 200 words long prompted the development of low-cost minicomputer-based time-sharing systems. These types of dedicated, in-house, time-sharing systems are presently manufactured by many of the large minicomputer manufacturers (and some small ones), including Digital Equipment Corporation, Hewlett-Packard, Data General, and Wang. Some of them are purely core resident, using a minimum of four teleprinter terminals. The original two choices of big cash outlay or service bureau charges have thus been augmented by various configurations of mini time-sharing terminals.

The medium- or large-scale system user is often confronted with the problem of having to upgrade his system. In spite of computer families with upward compatible systems, the transition cost can often be significant. They include, in addition to shipment and installation charges, the cost associated with the software/hardware conversion. In this case the minicomputer may serve as a viable solution to the system upgrading. The mini can share the load with the original system and perform some of the smaller jobs. The cost of the mini system may also be significantly less than the cost differential between the old and new large-scale systems, and, most importantly, no significant conversion problems are incurred.

Purchase, Lease, or Rental of a Mini

Once the potential user has decided on the minicomputer he wants to use, there are several options available to him for hardware acquisition: he can either purchase the computer, lease it through a third party, or (with the exception of a few manufacturers), if he is part of a university, rent it from a minicomputer manufacturer. The exception made to universities is based on the often limited budget of schools, which does not allow an outright purchase.

The purchase of minicomputers, unlike larger computer systems which can be acquired on an installment basis with interest paid to the manufacturer, is based on outright purchase. Minicomputer purchase is generally financially the most attractive alternative when sufficient cash is available. The total hardware cost equals the difference between initial purchase cost, maintenance cost (except for warranty period), cost of money on purchase price, insurance cost and the total of the residual value, full investment tax credit, and the tax advantage of accelerated depreciation.

The primary argument voiced in favor of rental is the issue of obsolescence. Obsolescence may be physical obsolescence, which generally is higher for the minicomputer peripherals than for the CPU; technical obsolescence as a result of a high rate of technological change in the minicomputer field; and economical obsolescence. This last factor is largely dependent on limitations in system expandability and growth to the point where it no longer can be reconfigured or readapted to meet the user's new requirements effectively.

The matter of manufacturer leverage is purely academic when the equipment is leased through a third party. In this case, pressure can seldom be applied to gain the desired support from the manufacturer. Withholding payment can only gain manufacturer attention when he is the direct recipient of the money. (One of the most important criteria for selecting hardware is the reputation of the vendor in backing up his products.)

The methods used for determining third-party monthly rates for minicomputers are usually based on full payoff in the lease period, which could be anywhere from 3 to 8 years or a lease term of 13 to 66 months, where after full payoff the lessee has the option of annually renewing the lease at a rate such as 3% per year. Some lease agreements give the user the option of purchasing the minicomputer at the end of the lease period for a certain percentage of the fair market value. This option must, however, be negotiated before the lease is signed. Needless to say, all rates fluctuate with the prime rate. Partial payoff is quite unusual in the minicomputer field and could reflect the concern of the lessor or manufacturer with problems of technical obsolescence. The question of obsolescence is generally of lesser significance in the large computer manufacturing industry, where large investments in software generally prevent the industry from making frequent replacements of acquired computer systems. This trend may spread to the minicomputer industry with the growth in complexity and quantity of minicomputer software.

The Used Mini

The rapid growth of the minicomputer industry has created a market for used minis. The used minis may be returned, leased machines, production line leftovers, surplus machines from original equipment manufacturer's inventory, or computers from older systems.

The hazards of buying a used mini are the availability or nonavailability of service and spare parts, particularly if the minicomputer line is discontinued by the manufacturer or, worse yet, if the manufacturer has gone out of business. The original manufacturer may "refurbish" the used mini and extend a 30-day warranty, but buying the mini from an independent seller usually means that the equipment must be purchased on an as-is basis.

Used minis can be purchased from the large minicomputer manufacturers, used-computer dealers, or the original owner. The last usually advertises his used mini in various trade journals. In some cases, the used mini is sold by the minicomputer manufacturer, where the used mini is taken as a trade-in on a new machine.

The advantages of the used mini are immediate delivery, debugged and proved software and hardware, and, in most cases, interfaced operational peripherals. The main advantage is, of course, cost. A used mini, depending on its age and general condition, can often be purchased at less than half the cost of a comparable new computer. In addition, like the used car, the used mini generally depreciates at a slower rate since the large initial depreciation is absorbed by the first owner.

The purchaser of the used mini should assure himself of the operability of the system, since a defective used machine could turn out to be extremely expensive to repair. Lack of adequate documentation may also make the used-mini approach more costly than purchasing a brand new computer from an original manufacturer.

Other items the purchaser of a used mini must concern himself with are available cables, connectors, power supplies, accessories, special nonstandard logic additions or changes, installation cost, and availability of interfaces for needed peripherials. These and other factors can easily make up for the 50% "savings" of the used machine.

In summary, don't buy a used mini until you have explored all the alternatives.

REFERENCES

ASMUS, P. L., "The Calculator and the Engineer—Part 1 (Try It on the Calculator)," *Electronic Design 20*, September 28, 1972, 57–60.

—— and J. A. MURPHY, "Programmable Calculators," *Modern Data*, October 1971, 42–49.

CHAPIN, N., *Computers, A Systems Approach*, Van Nostrand Reinhold Company, New York, 1971.

FIELDS, S. W., "Calculator Has Full Basic Capability," *Electronics*, November 6, 1972, 133–135.

FORD, M. A., "Buying the New Minicomputer," *Modern Data*, September 1972, 52–54.

LANE, R. L., "How To Buy a Used Minicomputer," *Computer Decisions*, October 1972, 42–43.

LINTON, L. A., and J. L. WAINTRAUB, "Minicomputers: A State-of-the-Art Survey," *Digital Design*, September 1972, 18–42.

OLLIVIER, R. T., and A. L. LINTON, "Revolt Within the Rack," *EDN*, July 15, 1969, 51–53.

RAU, P., "Evaluating the EDP Function," *Datamation*, September 1972, 72–80.

SMITH, L. W., "The Calculator and the Engineer—Part 3 (Expand Programmable Calculators)," *Electronic Design 22*, October 26, 1972, 62–66.

STORER, T., "Minicomputers: An Introduction," *IEEE Computer Group News*, July/August 1970, 2–7.

TERHOST, K., and T. BUDLONG, "The Calculator and the Engineer—Part 2 (Programmable Calculator Languages)," *Electronic Design 21*, October 12, 1972, 74–76.

2

Minicomputer Hardware

2.1 MINICOMPUTER ARCHITECTURE

The architecture of a mini is the key to its performance and an indication of its relative utility and power. Machine architecture has a direct bearing on its operating characteristics, such as speed and efficiency, how instructions are carried out, and how easy or difficult it is to program the machine.

The following units are the basic building blocks in a mini:

- Memory
- Arithmetic and logic processor
- Control
- Input and Output (I/O)

The above subunits are interconnected by several lines which provide paths for data, control signals, and computer instructions. These lines are commonly called buses. A common minicomputer is based on the subunit-bus structure shown in Figure 2-1.

The memory, also referred to as the main storage unit, stores actual data as well as instructions that tell the control unit what to do with the data. The arithmetic/logic processor temporarily stores data received from memory and performs calculations and logic operations on this data. The arithmetic/logic processor contains one or more registers, which, in turn, contain the data being operated on as defined by the instruction.

The control unit, as its name implies, controls the flow of data in the system, fetches instructions from memory, and decodes the instructions in one or more instruction registers. The control unit executes instructions by enabling the appropriate electronic signal paths and controlling the proper

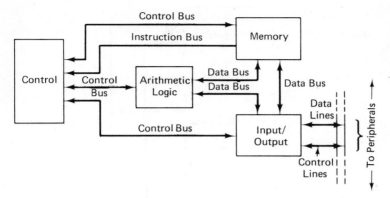

Figure 2-1   Minicomputer subunit organization

sequence of operations performed by the arithmetic/logic and input/output units. Finally, it changes the state of the computer to that required by the next operation.

The input/output unit provides the interface and, in some systems, buffering to peripherals connected to the computer, transferring data to and receiving data from the outside world.

The control unit and the arithmetic/logic processor units with buses and registers are referred to as the central processing unit (CPU). The earliest, and still the most widely used, architecture is based on the CPU talking to the memory over a high-speed memory bus and to all external devices over an I/O bus, as shown in Figure 2-1.

Some of the more recently introduced minicomputers such as the DEC PDP-11 and the Lockheed SUE treat the memory as an external device and communicate with it over the same I/O bus, just as they would with an external peripheral device. Interface registers act exactly the same as core memory registers. There is, therefore, no need for special I/O instructions. The full power of the entire instruction set can thus be used in manipulating the interface registers (we shall discuss this further under Registers). The subsystem based on this architecture (also called the INFIBUS, UNIBUS, or MONOBUS structure) is organized as shown in Figure 2-2. The single-bus organization offers several advantages over the more conventional minicomputer architecture. In the PDP-11, the data bus is asynchronous and therefore not clocked. The CPU is therefore completely independent of memory timing, allowing for faster memory modules to be incorporated into the system at a later date without requiring a comprehensive redesign of the CPU. The single bus also permits the user to mix various speed memories in the same system. Furthermore, it permits a considerable amount of standardization to be applied in the interface design. The interface itself

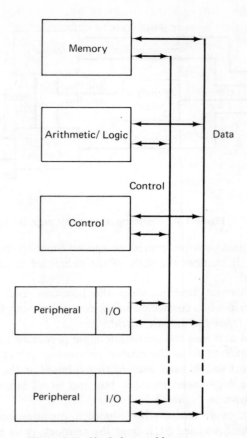

Figure 2-2   Single-bus architecture

is somewhat more complex because of the universality of the single bus. However, the real strength of the unibus lies in simplified functional programming for control applications. The merits of this approach are discussed in greater detail in DMA and the Single Bus Mini.

For a better understanding of the strengths and weaknesses of various design approaches and system architectures, the basic building blocks and their structure are described in the following sections.

Memory

Normally, memory is measured in units of 1024 words referred to as 1K. A 4K mini, therefore, designates a minicomputer with 4096 words of memory. Most minicomputer manufacturers specify memory in terms of words. A word may contain either 8, 12, 16, or 18 bits. However, in some instances mini manufacturers use the word *byte* to define memory size (a la IBM). A byte is generally equivalent to 8 bits with few exceptions (some foreign minicomputer manufacturers use a 6-bit byte format). An 8K byte machine may therefore be equivalent to a 4K or an 8K word machine, depending on the word size of the mini. To add to the confusion, some minicomputers talk about 16-bit half-words, where full-word size is equivalent to 32 bits. In this case, the memory, registers, and I/O are built around a half-word format, although a large number of instructions are full-word (or 32 bits). (The apparent reason for this designation is to attain compatibility with the IBM 360/370 instruction format.)

Words in minicomputers are expressed either in octal (radix of 8) or hexadecimal (radix of 16) values. The octal system assigns numerical values to pure binary forms, which are divided into groups of 3 bits, each group representing a single octal digit. The hexadecimal system groups the binary digits into sets of 4 bits. The relationship among binary (base 2), octal (base 8), decimal (base 10), and hexadecimal (base 16) is listed in the table shown in Figure 2-3. In number conventions used throughout this book, octal numbers are prefixed with 8, hexadecimal numbers are prefixed with 16 and decimal numbers have no prefix.

Magnetic core is presently the most commonly used memory element in minicomputers largely because of low cost. Minicomputer memory ranges from 1K to 128K words, with core memory speeds typically ranging from 0.6 to 2 μsec. Core memory is organized into 4K, 8K, or 16K modules usually,

Binary	Octal	Decimal	Hexadecimal
0000	0	0	0
0001	1	1	1
0010	2	2	2
0011	3	3	3
0100	4	4	4
0101	5	5	5
0110	6	6	6
0111	7	7	7
1000	10	8	8
1001	11	9	9
1010	12	10	A
1011	13	11	B
1100	14	12	C
1101	15	13	D
1110	16	14	E
1111	17	15	F

Figure 2-3 Relationship between binary, octal, decimal, and hexadecimal numbers

although 1K and 2K modules are also available for use in dedicated original equipment manufacturer (OEM) applications requiring very small programs.

Several minicomputer manufacturers, among them Data General Corporation, Texas Instruments, and Digital Equipment Corporation, presently offer semiconductor memory for applications requiring high memory speed. Present semiconductor memory speeds range from 0.2 to 0.4 μsec. Part of the speed advantage lies in the fact that the information in a semiconductor memory remains unchanged after a read operation and, unlike core, therefore does not require a *write* following a *read*. The disadvantage of the bipolar memory, in addition to its present high cost, is its volatility. System power failure will result in total loss of memory contents (unless a battery is used for power backup).

Several minicomputers are available with one or two optional bits per memory word. One of these extra bits serves as a parity check to detect read errors and interrupts the computer immediately upon detection of a parity error. The second "extra" bit, also called the memory protect bit, is used to protect selected memory sections and prohibit writing into these sections

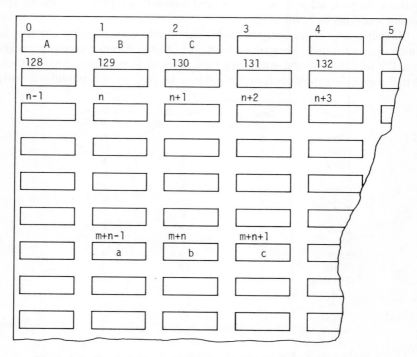

Figure 2-4 Part of memory, showing word locations (addresses) and contents (instructions or data)

except when the system is in a restricted supervisory mode. These optional bits are also used by some manufacturers to extend the addressing range of the machine. This feature is discussed under Central Processing Unit.

Some of the more powerful minicomputers offer two-port memory access. The two memory ports allow simultaneous access to different memory modules (4K or 8K) from multiple locations (such as the CPU and an external device). This arrangement also allows the interconnection of two CPUs through memory.

In the following section, memory will be treated in a generalized form wherein memory cell content is arbitrarily designated as A, B, C, or a, b, c, regardless of word length or number of bits per word, and where the location or address may be any bit pattern arbitrarily indicated by $n-1$, n, $n+1$ or $m+n-1$, $m+n$, $m+n+1$, regardless of a particular minicomputer memory size or implementation of addressing structure (Figure 2-4). Each rectangle or box (shown in rows and columns in Figure 2-4) is a memory cell. A cell may contain any bit pattern written into it, while the location or *address* of the respective cell is fixed and predetermined by the designer of the machine. A memory can be likened to a number of mailboxes where each box has its name associated with it while the contents may vary depending on what is placed into it.

Central Processing Unit

BASIC MECHANIZATION

The basic elements in the CPU are the instruction register, the decoder, the control unit, the program counter, the adder and comparer, the accumulator, and the status register. The block diagram in Figure 2-5 illustrates how these elements are interconnected.

A typical minicomputer processing cycle can be divided into two subcycles:

- Instruction or fetch cycle
- Execution cycle

The following chain of events takes place during the fetch cycle:

1. The control unit logic fetches memory address n from the program counter.
2. The decoder decodes this address.
3. The control unit logic fetches the contents A of memory word n addressed.

4. The control unit logic interprets memory word n as an instruction (not data) and loads instruction A into the instruction register.
5. The control unit logic increments the program counter by 1 for the next cycle. (The counter therefore acts as a memory pointer.)
6. The control unit fetches the contents of instruction register A and decodes the instruction.

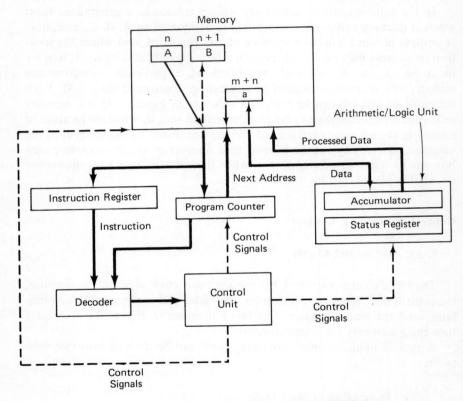

Figure 2-5   Basic minicomputer mechanization

The control unit is now ready to implement the second subcycle, the execution cycle. The steps followed in the execution cycle depend on the type of instruction to be executed. One of the most common instructions is addition or ADD. A typical ADD instruction is based on the following sequence of steps:

1. A piece of data arbitrarily designated a stored in memory location m+n is added to the contents of the accumulator.

Assuming that the previously stored quantity in the accumulator is b, the new amount after addition will be a+b.

2. The new contents of the accumulator is stored in location m+n, which will now contain a+b.

The status register varies in size and complexity depending on minicomputer architecture. As a minimum, two single-bit registers are used, where the first one stores the overflow from the accumulator. The overflow bit is generated when a number is added to the number already stored in the accumulator, resulting in a number exceeding the maximum capacity of this register. For example, assuming that the initial binary number in the accumulator is 100111000110 (2502) and the number stored in location m+n is 110100100101 (3365), the result of the addition is

$$
\begin{array}{r r}
  100111000110 & 2502 \\
+ \ 110100100101 & 3365 \\
\hline
  1011011101011 & 5867
\end{array}
$$

However, the largest number that can be stored in this 12-bit register is 111111111111 (4095). The thirteenth bit is therefore an overflow bit, also called a *carry bit*.

The second single-bit register is often called the *test* or *link* register. This register is used to test the condition of the accumulator. An all-zero value in the accumulator will result in a 1 in this register.

Many of the latest minicomputers contain a status register which includes the carry or overflow bit and the test bit. In addition, indicators are available in the status register, which allows the programmer to check out the program in terms of register and processor status at various execution times.

The previous description of a typical instruction cycle indicates that even the most simpleminded instruction will require at least two separate memory fetches. Since each fetch generally requires a full memory cycle, it can be seen how memory speed is one important element in determining the "speed" of the minicomputer. Other parameters are the instruction set and the addressing power of the mini.

ADDRESSING

It is clear from the previous discussion that many of the key operations in a mini are based on addressing memory and moving information between memory and registers. The addressing features of a minicomputer are consequently of paramount importance, determining its overall capability.

For a direct memory addressing capability, the following relationship between number of bits and the size of the addressable memory exists:

Bits	Direct Address of Number of Words in Memory (in decimal notation)
6	64
7	128
8	256
9	512
10	1,024
11	2,048
12	4,096
13	8,192
14	16,384
15	32,768
16	65,536

As previously mentioned, one of the primary definitions of a mini-computer is word size. An 8-bit mini could therefore, for all practical purposes, address a maximum of 256 words; a 12-bit machine, 4096 words; and a 16-bit computer, 65K words.* [In most machines, the first bit is used to denote positive or negative value (plus or minus).] The addressing range of a typical 16-bit mini is therefore limited to 32K words (2^n, where $n = 15$ is equal to 32,768).

Most minicomputers only use a fraction of the available bits in the word for direct addressing since the majority of instructions require addressing only to a limited number of words such as 256 or 512. From this discussion it can be concluded that at least two different types or modes of addressing are needed: one for addressing all 4096 words in a 12-bit machine and all 65K words in a 16-bit machine as well as one for addressing a subset of total memory in respective machines. It is also obvious that in the latter case direct addressing is possible only if more than one word is used for the instruction, which implies that in addition to the instruction code and address, the instruction must contain information indicating the address mode. Hence, a basic instruction contains three fields:

- Instruction or operation code (OP code) field
- Address mode field
- Address field

---

* Note that some 16-bit machines which include two extra bits for parity and memory check use these extra bits in an extended addressing mode to directly address 128K words or 256K bytes.

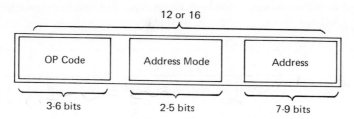

Figure 2-6 Basic instruction set format

The basic instruction format for a 12- or 16-bit word mini is therefore as shown in Figure 2-6. This format is said to have a limited addressing range (128 to 512 words). An extended addressing range instruction is based on the double-word format shown in Figure 2-7. The two types of formats are also called *short form* and *long form*, respectively.

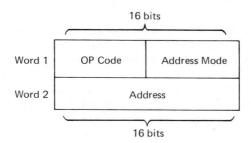

Figure 2-7 Basic double-word format

Several minicomputers restricted to the short form are *paged*. The DEC PDP-8/I and PDP-8/L are typical 12-bit word-paged computers. In these machines the memory is segmented into 32 (decimal) word blocks or pages where each page contains 128 words. The instruction has the format shown in Figure 2-8.

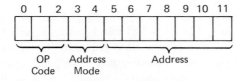

Figure 2-8 PDP-8 word format

Two bits in the address mode field will obviously allow for four addressing modes:

Bit 3	Bit 4	
0	0	The operand is in page 0 at the address, specified by bits 5–11.
0	1	The operand is in the current page at the address, specified by bits 5–11. The current page is the page containing the instruction being executed as determined by bits 0–4 of the program counter. [Note that the 5 bits (0–4) in the program counter plus the 7 bits in the memory reference instruction (5–11) permit addressing of 4096 memory word locations.]
1	0	The absolute address of the operand is taken from the contents of the location in page 0, designated by bits 5–11. The absolute address is a 12-bit number used to address any location in memory.
1	1	The absolute address of the operand is taken from the contents of the location in the current page, specified by bits 5–11.

A 1 in bit location 3 indicates that indirect addressing is used. The difference between direct and indirect addressing is illustrated in Figures 2-9 and 2-10, respectively. Hence, indirect addressing is the only way a program can access a memory location outside an instruction's own page or page 0 in a paged machine. Without this feature, each subroutine or program module would have to be sufficiently small to fit within the boundary of a page. Increasing the page size beyond 256 words may be impossible in a 12-bit word machine, while too large a page size, such as 2048 or 4096 words, in a 16-bit word machine may be wasteful from a programming standpoint. The page boundary restriction has, however, been circumvented in some machines by using program-relative paging. In this mode, the address bits of an instruction represent the displacement of the addressed memory word from the program counter. Program-relative paging is usually implemented in terms of a forward or backward range of up to half a page in each direction. Program-relative paging is illustrated in Figure 2-11. Note that x and y can be different values as long as they are less than half the maximum relative page size. The program counter is, of course, incremented by 1 during the execution of an instruction.

Relative addressing is also used in nonpaged minis. The Data General Nova can address to +127 or −128 words either relative to the program counter or relative to one of two base registers. The base register is also called the memory pointer. The latter addressing method is similar to the previously discussed program-relative paging method. Base-relative addressing in contrast to program-relative paging can, however, also be used

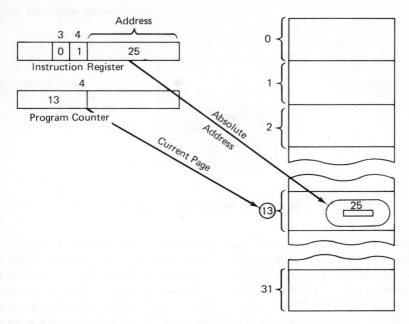

Figure 2-9 Current page direct addressing

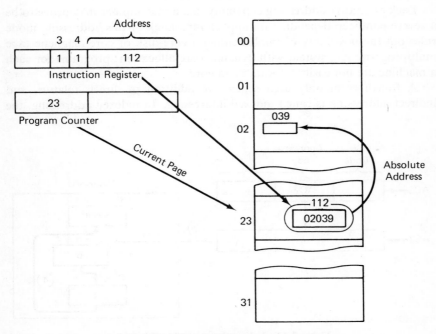

Figure 2-10 Current page indirect addressing

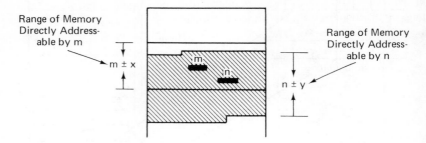

Figure 2-11 Program relative paging

in an indirect mode. Indirect base-relative addressing provides the effective address, as shown in Figure 2-12. The addressing mode in this example is indirect relative. The displacement n in register AC3 is added to the contents of base register AC2 (also called the memory pointer). Memory location m+n becomes the effective address. However, since the addressing mode is also indirect, the result stored in location m+n will be in memory location p. Several levels of indirect addressing are possible. p may contain the effective address q, which in turn contains the result, etc.

Lack of relative addressing capability in a minicomputer may prove to be a severe handicap depending on application. Lack of this addressing mode rules out the possibility of implementing a core-disk or core-magnetic tape multiprogramming system with dynamic core allocation; programs for such a machine are not easily relocatable in core.

A fourth commonly used scheme in addition to direct, relative, and indirect addressing is called indexed addressing. In indexed addressing, the

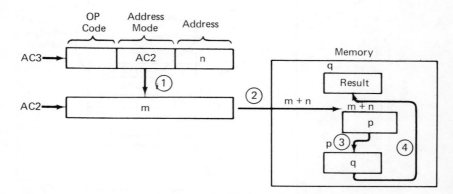

Figure 2-12 Indirect base-relative addressing

contents of an index register (located either in core memory, which adds one extra cycle time to each indexed instruction, or implemented as an active-element storage register) are added to the address field to arrive at the effective address in memory. There are two ways to perform indexed addressing:

- Postindexing
- Preindexing

These two methods differ only when an indirect address is being calculated. Also, of the two, postindexing is more frequently used. Both methods differ in the sequence of operations. In postindexing, the following sequence of events take place:

1. The memory location specified by indirect address is found (all indirect addressing steps are performed first).
2. The contents of this memory location (final address) are added to the contents of the specified index register (if more than one index register exists in the mini).
3. The new contents of the index register (effective address) now point to the memory location which contains the desired information.

This sequence is illustrated in Figure 2-13. $n+p$ is thus the effective address, and A is the desired information at this address.

In the preindexing scheme, the specified indexing is performed prior to fetching of indirect address. The sequence is performed in the manner

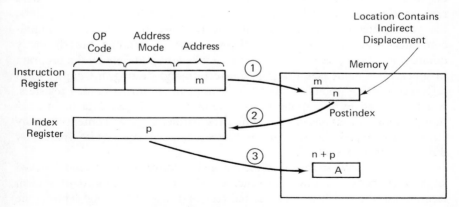

Figure 2-13 Postindexing sequence

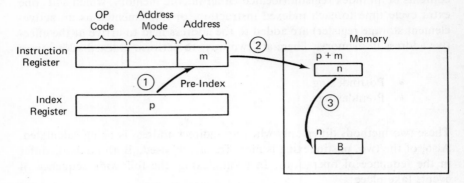

Figure 2-14   Preindexing sequence

shown in Figure 2-14:

1. The contents (p) of the index register base are added to the instruction-supplied base address (m).
2. The sum of the index register contents (p) and address (m) now point to the memory location which contains the indirect address (n).
3. The indirect address (n) points to the location which contains the desired information (B).

Some minicomputers offer base-relative addressing using a base address register as an alternative to preindexing. As previously described, the address displacement in the instruction word is added to the contents of a base register to provide the effective address. In most applicable minicomputers, the two addressing modes are equivalent. However, in larger, nonmini-computer systems, indexing and base register addressing are distinctly different functions; base registers are generally accessed only by the program in supervisory mode (see Program Correction and Testing in Chapter 4) to reference starting points of various programs in contrast to index registers, which are used by the applications programmer to access data or instructions within various programs. While the former register contents usually remain unchanged, index register contents are changed quite frequently during program execution.

So far, we have discussed direct, paged, relative, indirect, and indexed addressing modes. A powerful scheme based on combinations of several techniques is called base-relative, indirect, indexed addressing. This mode allows one instruction to address any one data item from any one of a number of tables. The sequence is as follows:

1. Add the contents (n) of the base register to displacement m stored in the instruction address field. n+m now points to one of a number of address storage locations in a base address table.
2. The contents q of one of the index registers specified in the instruction contains the displacement, which is added to the base address P of one of the tables. The desired information A is thus located in the memory location with the address P+q.

This sequence is illustrated in Figure 2-15.

Some of the less common addressing modes among minis are immediate and list-sequential addressing. Immediate or literal addressing is usually used to define constants by placing the operand in the address field of the instruction or in a second word of a double-word instruction. This feature eliminates the need for an addressing field.

List-sequential or autoindexed addressing uses list pointers or index registers for addressing list data. Autoindex registers keep track of the sequence when handling list data. They increment automatically in steps of one or two, pointing to the next word or byte in the list. The PDP-11 reserves one of its eight registers for the pointing function. This register (6) is also called the stack pointer. A *stack* is simply a list of sequential memory locations. A *push-pop* stack implies the capability to easily access the contents of the list in a *last in-first out* manner (LIFO). Obviously, all minicomputers have some capability of creating lists (or stacks) in memory. However, since registers can be incremented or decremented faster than core locations, the list-sequential addressing mode is very efficient in accessing sequential data such as characters or data strings, for instance in I/O processing. In the PDP-11, stacks are used primarily for arithmetic operations on tabular data, subroutine processing, and interrupt processing, discussed in Input and Output (I/O).

Minicomputers such as the PDP-11 and Interdata 70 also offer double-operand addressing. This feature permits register-to-register or register-to-storage operations using a single instruction. A typical double-operand instruction word looks as shown in Figure 2-16. An ADD instruction, for example, would add the contents of register 2 to register 1 and store the result in register 2.

The PDP-11 double-operand addressing mode uses the instruction word format (Figure 2-17). The source and destination addresses can each be any combination of modes, such as indexed, absolute, or relative. Each operand may be anywhere in core storage, in one of the general registers, or in a peripheral device register. As an example, a MOV instruction will move the source operand to the destination location as defined by instruction register

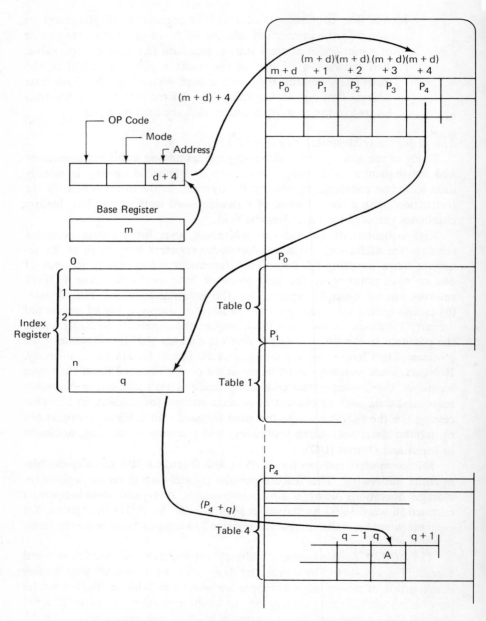

Figure 2-15 Base-relative, indirect, indexed addressing sequence

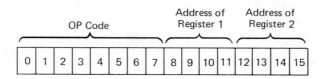

Figure 2-16 Double-operand addressing format

bits 7, 8, 9 and 13, 14, 15, respectively. If one or both of the source and destination operands are registers, for example, no time would be required for the source address derivation and/or the destination address derivation.

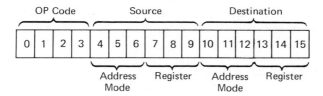

Figure 2-17 PDP-11 double-operand address format

REGISTERS

Most of what happens in a minicomputer program gets done in registers. Table 2-1 lists the types of registers discussed in the context of addressing

Table 2-1. Registers Usable by Program

- Accumulator
- Index register
- Base register
- Program status register
- Stack pointer or autoindex
- Temporary storage register

which are accessible to the programmer. Every mini has at least one accumulator, but only a single register used as an accumulator will impose a severe restriction on the data flow in the machine. Programs become shorter and execute faster when the number of registers is increased. The amount of registers in a mini is thus a measure of its power. However, the number of registers in a 16-bit word single-address machine is generally limited to only 4 or 8. The reason for this is simple. For an instruction to specify one of eight registers, 3 bits must be reserved in an instruction word. Since most minis typically use 6 or 7 bits to calculate memory displacement, 4 bits for OP code, and 3 bits for addressing mode, only 2 or 3 bits remain for specifying one of four or eight registers, respectively.

Of four registers, it is quite helpful to have at least two index registers. This permits keeping multiple indexes in registers rather than shuffling them in and out of core (some minicomputers are built with registers in core). A machine which is designed with multiple general-purpose registers is obviously more powerful than a mini where each register is limited to performing only a single task, such as accumulator extension for multiply and divide, indexing, base addressing, memory access, memory buffering, and status accounting.

The system designer is well advised to examine not only the flexibility of the available registers in a mini but also the *actual* number of *accessible* registers in a mini. Some manufacturers include a large number of status bits and temporary, nonaccessible registers in their total register complement.

THE INSTRUCTION REPERTOIRE

OP Code Field, Instruction Groups, and Size of Repertoire.   As previously indicated, a basic minicomputer instruction is usually divided into three fields: OP code, address mode, and address. The address mode field, depending on the number of index registers, direct and indirect addressing, and absolute as well as relative addressing, requires from 3 to 5 bits. This leaves from 11 to 13 bits for the OP code and address. This may seem like far too few bits to handle both the OP code and the address fields. However, by separating memory and nonmemory instructions, a significant number of instructions can be included into a minicomputer instruction repertoire.

Nonmemory instructions have been divided by the manufacturer of the NOVA minicomputer into two groups:

- Arithmetic and logical functions
- I/O instructions

Arithmetic instructions typically perform functions such as ADD and SUBTRACT, while logical instructions perform Boolean operations such as AND, OR, and EXCLUSIVE OR. Some minicomputers include bit test instructions.

I/O instructions are typically associated with moving data between registers and peripherals as well as controlling peripherals. The memory and nonmemory group instruction formats for the Nova are as shown in Figure 2-18. These formats allow 12 OP codes for memory reference instructions and close to 200 for nonmemory instructions. Had the computer

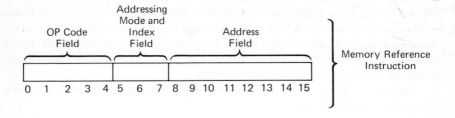

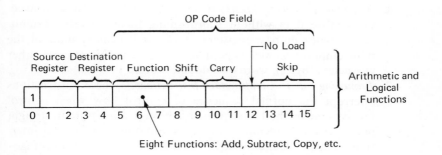

Eight Functions: Add, Subtract, Copy, etc.

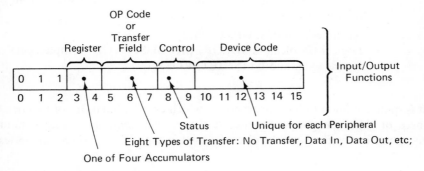

Figure 2-18 Memory and nonmemory instruction formats (Data General Nova)

designer limited himself to memory reference instructions alone, the upper limit for OP codes would have been 32 (bits 0–4).

Most minicomputer instruction sets, however, are less extensive than 200. A very large instruction set may be a detriment rather than a plus. With a large instruction set, only a relatively small subset will be used frequently, while esoteric instructions will generally be ignored. An occasional use of an instruction may result in misinterpretation, thus extending program debugging time. On the other hand, the more powerful the instruction set is, the faster and more program-efficient a processor will be, independent of cycle time. Increased size and complexity of the instruction set may, of course, result in some degree of overlap among the instructions, and the more instructions there are the more expensive is the system.

Functional Categories. The instructions can be classified into three major functional categories:

1. *Information-Moving (Data-Moving) Instructions:* These instructions move data without transforming them between accumulators, index or base registers, stacks and memory units of the minicomputer, as well as peripherals. Data in this case are either characters (bytes), words, or double words.
2. *Branching and Conditional Instructions:* These instructions interrupt the normal sequence of control flow when control involves the method of sequencing through a program in straight line, decision branching, looping, subroutine linkage, and interrupt handling. Conditional instructions are provided for testing— to change a program's operation.
3. *Transformational (Operator) Instructions:* These instructions operate on data. The types of operators show considerable variation between various minis, which may have some or all of the following types of instruction:

   Arithmetic (add, subtract, multiply, divide)
   Logical (Boolean AND, OR, EXCLUSIVE OR, complement)
   Word, byte, and bit (SHIFT, ROTATE)

It is quite common to have instructions which are combinations of two or all three of these categories. Several of the more commonly available minicomputer instructions will be discussed within each of these three categories.

Instructions: What They Are and What They Do. The most common information moving instructions are LOAD and STORE. A LOAD instruction specifies a memory word location or address from which the contents is placed into a specified register. In the Data General Nova, the LOAD instruction LDA, AC, D, X loads accumulator AC with the contents of the memory cell specified by the effective address E, which is made up of the displacement D and index X. This is illustrated by the following example:

LDA 3, 21, 2

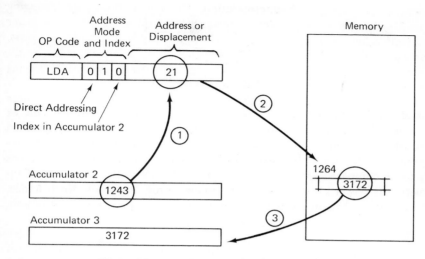

Figure 2-19 Data General Nova LDA instruction sequence

The following sequence will now take place (Figure 2-19):

1. The effective address (D or displacement 21) is added to index 1243 stored in accumulator 2. The effective address is thus $1243 + 21 = 1264$.
2. The contents 3172 stored in memory location 1264 are loaded into accumulator 3.

A STORE instruction stores the contents of a register in a specified memory location. Some minicomputers provide load and store instructions for both full words (16 bits) and bytes (8 bits). The latter feature is extremely useful in applications involving data handling in byte units, particularly in data communication applications.

Typical byte instructions are INTERCHANGE BYTES OF A (ICA), INTERCHANGE BYTES OF A AND CLEAR LEFT BYTE (ICL), INTERCHANGE BYTES OF A AND CLEAR RIGHT BYTE (ICR), CLEAR LEFT BYTE OF A (CAL), and CLEAR RIGHT BYTE OF A (CAR).* ICA will obviously switch bytes in accumulator A (Figure 2-20). Instructions such as LOAD BYTE and STORE BYTE† will allow the programmer to load or store half the contents of a register. Texas Instrument's

---

* Prime 200, Prime Computer Inc.
† SPC 16/40, General Automation.

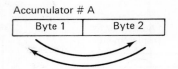

Figure 2-20   Byte interchange

Model 980A minicomputer has several complex byte instructions. One of them is CLC. This byte instruction compares one consecutive, specified byte string in memory to a second byte string in memory. The first "byte-comparison-not-equal" terminates the instruction, and the number of bytes left to be compared are stored in a register (Figure 2-21). This type of instruction is powerful in terms of shortening a program which, for instance, may require a checking of incoming messages versus prestored information.

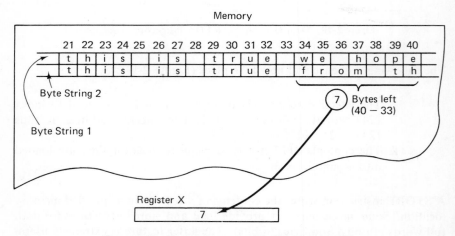

Figure 2-21   Byte string operation (TI Model 980A)

It is therefore performing a control and monitoring function, rather than moving data.

The most commonly available control and conditional instruction types are

- JUMP
- BRANCH
- SKIP
- TEST
- COMPARE

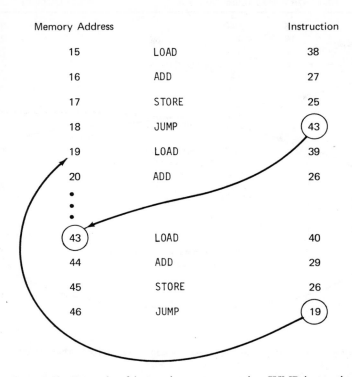

Memory Address		Instruction
15	LOAD	38
16	ADD	27
17	STORE	25
18	JUMP	43
19	LOAD	39
20	ADD	26
43	LOAD	40
44	ADD	29
45	STORE	26
46	JUMP	19

Figure 2-22 Example of instruction sequence using JUMP instructions

JUMP. JUMP instructions consist of commands which direct the program to a nonsequential address for execution of the instruction located there. An example of this is shown in Figure 2-22. The execution sequence is thus 15, 16, 17, 18, 43, 44, 45, 46, 19, 20 . . . . The JUMP instruction is commonly used to jump to subroutines. The subroutine is a set of instructions which can be executed several times by the same program as well as other programs. A subroutine may perform a function such as taking a square root of a number, multiplying or dividing two numbers, and computing a certain interest rate.

Subroutine JUMP instructions, also called JUMP-AND-MARK or JUMP-AND-STORE, direct the program to a nonsequential jump address, store the contents of the program counter there, and then execute the instruction following the jump address.

Using the previous example with a subroutine JUMP, we obtain Figure 2-23. The JUMP-AND-STORE instruction stores its return linking address, (memory location 19) in memory location 43, whereupon the program

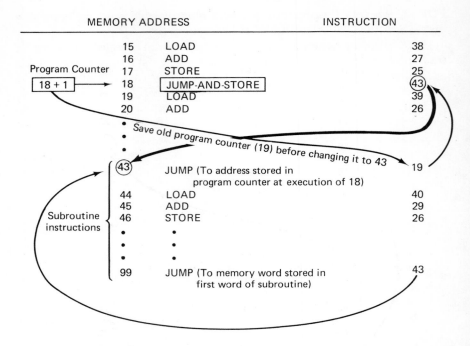

MEMORY ADDRESS   INSTRUCTION

Figure 2-23 Instruction   sequence   using   the   JUMP-AND-MARK
instruction

counter is set to 43. The subroutine instructions are now executed, and when
the JUMP TO 43 instruction stored in location 99 is reached, the program
will again execute a jump to 19. The main program execution will now
continue.

This instruction is of critical importance in real-time processing since it
will allow automatic reentry to the main program upon execution of the
subroutine. The subroutine call is therefore reentrant since a subroutine can
be called by another program or by itself. This also means that a single copy
of a subroutine can he shared by several programs in the computer.

Several minicomputers offer a large variety of conditional JUMP and
JUMP-AND-STORE instructions where jumps are executed depending on
whether a particular register is zero or is not zero or whether various other
conditions are or are not met.

BRANCH.   BRANCH and JUMP instructions tend to be synonymous in
most minicomputers. There are exceptions to this rule however. In the

PDP-11, the JUMP instruction provides more flexible program branching than is provided with the BRANCH instruction.

BRANCH instructions in this computer are range-limited in terms of transfer of control within memory and also restricted in terms of the available addressing modes.

SKIP. SKIP instructions are generally conditional. After a function has been performed, the result can be tested to see whether or not to conditionally skip the next instruction in sequence. SKIP can be made if the carry bit is zero or nonzero, if the result is zero or nonzero, if either the carry or the result or both are zero, if both the carry and the result are nonzero, etc. The skip instruction is often used for looping, as shown in Figure 2-24. In

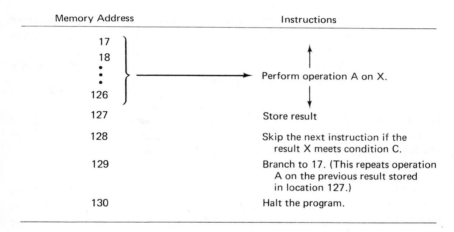

Figure 2-24 Instruction sequence with SKIP instruction

this example, a certain operation such as decrement 100 by 2 will be performed 50 times until condition C is met, where C is equivalent to a zero in location 127.

Hence, several minicomputers provide for loop control with an instruction that increments or decrements a memory register and skips or branches when a word arrives at a specific value (zero in the previous example).

The SKIP instruction can also be used in process control, or a process monitoring system, where a skip or branch occurs depending on the condition or setting of status bits in the status register. The status bits are generally set, depending on the results of previous instructions, such as if the result was zero or negative, if the operation resulted in a carry from the most significant bit (bit 15 in a 16-bit word since bit 16 almost always is reserved for the sign bit), or if the operation resulted in the arithmetic overflow.

TEST AND COMPARE. Several other conditions are provided for testing to change a program's operation. These include relationals such as *greater than, greater than or equal to, equal to, less than or equal to,* and *less than.*

All minicomputers provide one or more numeric sign conditionals. This primarily includes testing for less than zero, equal to zero, or greater than zero. The method of testing varies between minis. In some computers explicit COMPARE instructions exist, while in others the compare is always done automatically by the hardware, and a flag or status bit is set.

The General Automation SPC-16 provides three types of compare instructions:

1. Compare the contents of a register with a word in memory.
2. Perform an arithmetic operation between or a logic operation in the contents of two registers, such as add contents of registers A and B, and set a status bit to reflect the answer.
3. Add, Subtract, or perform a logic operation on the contents of a register and a constant (literal).

In all of the above operations, the numerical result of the addition, or whatever the operation may be, will be discarded, leaving the contents of memory or registers unaltered.

Arithmetic.   All computers provide binary arithmetic capability. Some computers designed expressly for business applications have decimal arithmetic. Most minis provide ADD and SUBTRACT instructions and some of the new minis also offer MULTIPLY and DIVIDE either as an optional or as a standard feature.

Just having an ADD or a SUBTRACT instruction is obviously not enough in most applications. In some machines, an ADD instruction can only add registers to one another. Some add memory to registers, while a few minis add memory to memory, register to register, and register or memory to I/O registers. In a minicomputer with stack processing capability, the PDP-11, the top two elements can be added and replaced with their sum. The top element of the stack can also be increased by the contents of the address field (source address), in the instruction word.

Logical.   The logic instructions in a large number of minicomputers include AND, OR, and EXCLUSIVE OR. Typically, these instructions allow the programmer to "and" or "or" the contents of a specified memory location with the contents of a register.

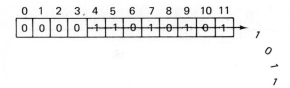

Figure 2-25 Register contents using shift operation

The AND or OR function is performed between each bit in the register and the corresponding bit of the effective memory address, where the result typically replaces the previous contents of the register.

Shift. SHIFT instructions are provided in almost all minicomputers in some form or another. SHIFT instructions may shift the contents of a register one or more steps at the time, either to the left or the right. The high- (or low-) order bit is lost with each shift (Figure 2-25). A right shift is equivalent to dividing by 2, while a left shift is equivalent to multiplying by 2. In some minis, the number of shifted positions can be specified in the instruction. The shift is said to be arithmetic if the vacated high-order bit location is loaded with the value of the sign bit, thus propagating the sign bit to the right. When the vacated bit locations are filled with zeros, the shift is logical (the sign bit is not propagated). The shift may also be rotational, in which case the bits shifted out of the register are loaded one at a time into the opposite end of the register. A 16-bit register which stores two bytes, byte a and byte b will, upon rotational shifts, contain these bytes in reverse order (Figure 2-26).

Some rotational SHIFT instructions allow circular or rotational shifts to be made through a status bit or a link bit. A circular shift through the status bit may also allow branching through the status bit as shown in Figure 2-27. The above example may thus be equally well considered an information- or data-moving instruction, since the contents of the register is read out through the status bit.

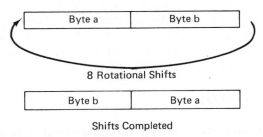

Figure 2-26 Register contents after eight rotational shifts

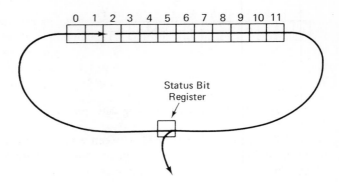

Figure 2-27   Circular shift with branching through the status bit register

Instructions, Applications, and Throughput.   The basic minicomputer instructions discussed so far are as follows:

1. Data moving: LOAD, STORE
2. Branching and conditional: JUMP, BRANCH, SKIP, TEST, COMPARE
3. Transformation: ARITHMETIC, LOGICAL, SHIFT

This list is by no means exhaustive. Several variations exist within each group, and many other types of instructions are available. The problem of evaluating the instruction sets of various minis is therefore very complex. In general terms, it can be concluded that powerful branching and conditional instructions, as well as logical instructions, are important in process control and monitoring applications. Data-moving instructions, and particularly byte instructions, are valuable in telecommunications and message-switching environments, and an extensive arithmetic instruction set is important when solving scientific problems.

The *number* of instructions in a minicomputer is by itself not a sufficient criterion for evaluating a machine. Considerations must also be given to memory space used by the program as well as the execution speed. The latter characteristics are, of course, a function of memory speed, individual instruction execution time, addressing capability, and the number and type of available registers. In addition, the I/O structure plays an important part in the overall throughput of the total system.

Input and Output (I/O)

Input-output embraces methods for transferring data and commands between internal storage, such as memory and CPU registers, and external devices, such as peripherals, auxiliary storage devices, and telecommunications terminals. Key elements determining the I/O capability of a mini are the I/O speed, the number and types of I/O schemes available in a system, and the priority control facility built into the computer that allows various external devices to interrupt the normal sequence of instruction executions.

The majority of minicomputers provide one or more of the following I/O capabilities:

Low Speed:
- Sequential I/O under program control (software) using standard I/O bus
- Interrupt-initiated I/O with or without data multiplex control

High Speed:
- Auxiliary processor or selector channel with direct memory access
- Direct memory access (DMA) channel cycle stealing I/O

The proper selection of I/O method is generally dictated by the requirements of the external device.

The recording of instrument readings typically requires very low-speed transfer rates, such as 1 to 100 decimal or binary numbers per second. The data transfer may be requested by the computer at regular intervals or initiated by the instrument when a change in conditions occurs.

A Teletype transmits data asynchronously at 10 characters/sec in a bit-serial fashion where the transmission is initiated by the operator when he hits a key.

Data from low-speed peripherals, such as a card reader, a paper tape reader, or a cassette recorder, are typically transferred upon demand from the computer, while data received over telephone lines may be unscheduled and must be serviced on a demand basis in order not to lose the information.

Data arriving at high speed from devices such as a disk or magnetic tape unit may be requested by the computer or transferred on demand by the peripheral device.

LOW-SPEED PROGRAM-CONTROLLED I/O

Low-speed transfers are typically handled under program control where each word or data unit is transferred through either a separate I/O register or through another of the internal registers, such as the accumulator, into memory, each transfer requiring one or more instruction execution cycles. Instructions within the CPU initiate the transfer of data between the peripheral and the accumulator and between the accumulator and memory.

This type of transfer is in some minicomputers performed by a direct input/output channel, which typically consists of an 8-bit address bus, a 16-bit input bus, several strobe lines, timing pulses, up to 16 interrupt signal lines, an external sense and system reset line, and various terminator voltages.*

Since each peripheral generally has its unique set of input/output rules or conventions, a level shifter-signal converter will be required between the peripheral and the minicomputer output channel to provide the appropriate coupling. Such a unit is called a device controller. Most minicomputers provide a set of standard device controllers uniquely designed for a selected (and usually) limited number of peripherals. The system designer must therefore design his own device controller in case he wants to use a peripheral which is not on the minicomputer manufacturer's price list.

Peripherals communicating with the mini under program control are generally connected to the channel through a common I/O bus. Each I/O device controller connected to this I/O bus is equipped with circuitry that recognizes the operation codes that are addressed to the device. Each controller is also equipped with circuitry that appends a device identification code to the response message from the particular responding peripheral. In some systems, the device addresses are explicitly given (typically over an 8-bit address bus); in other systems, each device is associated with a distinct time slot simplifying the decoding circuitry. The latter scheme is called time multiplexing, and the I/O channel is called a multiplexer channel.

The I/O instruction† has the following format (Figure 2-28). The I/O instruction is thus typically divided into three basic fields:

1. Op code (I/O instructions for CPU)
2. Device command (send/receive data, test status, etc.)
3. Device selection (device code to all peripherals)

Each I/O data transfer requires a substantial number of I/O instructions. The maximum data transfer rate over the programmed party line I/O channel

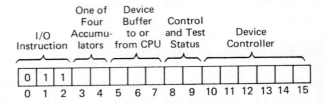

Figure 2-28   I/O instruction format

---

* Raytheon 706
† Data General Nova

is thus limited by the program overhead of the I/O devices requesting service. The I/O bus data rates for most minicomputers range from 20 to 50K words/sec. The most significant drawback of this approach is, however, that the CPU must continuously poll the peripherals for data inputs when the data transmission is *not* initiated by the CPU.

Through the use of interrupt driven processing, more time is made available to the CPU to perform non-I/O-type operations.

Interrupt-Initiated, Low-Speed I/O. Typically when a peripheral device interrupts the processor, the computer is directed to a memory address specified by the interrupting device and executes the instruction at that address. Normally, the instruction of the interrupt address causes a jump to the interrupting peripheral's I/O service subroutine. The computer returns to the original program through an appropriate JUMP instruction at the conclusion of the interrupt service routine.

The interrupt service routine must therefore save the contents of working registers, the status register, and the program counter. Prior to this, the following sequence of events has occurred:

1. Signaling of interruption from the peripheral or external device to the processor.
2. The interrupt may be disabled or masked depending on present activity. (It is possible that the system designer intentionally wants certain interrupts to be ignored during a certain period of program execution.) The interrupt will in this case be enabled as soon as the period of interrupt suppression or disabling is terminated by the software.
3. The interrupt processing may also have to wait until the end of the current instruction's execution. This wait period could equal the duration of the longest instruction executable on the system.

The total instruction *wait time* including the necessary *save and restore* of machine status is usually a good indicator or *figure of merit* of the minis interrupt processing speed. Of equal importance, determining the flexibility and efficiency of interrupt-initiated I/O of a mini is the basic technique employed to implement it.

The most primitive method of implementing interrupt service is through the use of a polling table. This technique is based on all peripherals being connected to a single common interrupt line. When an interrupt is allowed, the software program will poll each device according to the polling table to

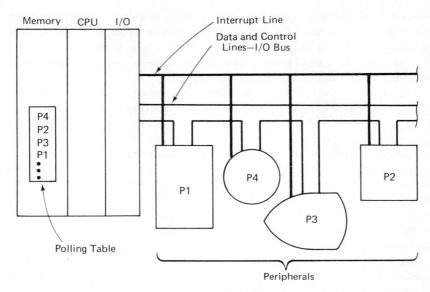

Figure 2-29   Interrupts, using a polling table

determine where the interrupt emanated. The priority of a particular device is determined by its position in the polling table (Figure 2-29).

A second commonly used interrupt scheme is similarly based on a single common interrupt line. I/O devices are connected, in a daisy-chain arrangement, to the I/O bus. Any number of devices can simultaneously request an interrupt. The device nearest the CPU has the highest priority and obtains access first. Further interrupts from other devices are automatically being inhibited while the current one is being processed. The interrupt go-ahead signal from the CPU is relayed to a lower-priority device in the chain, in order. The CPU can alter the priorities by inhibiting interrupts selectively. When the interrupt-requesting device responds to the go-ahead signal its device controller will store the starting address of its interrupt service routine in the program counter. This action will also identify the particular interrupting device. This scheme is shown in Figure 2-30.

A third equally common method of interrupt control is based on individual interrupt and go-ahead lines for each peripheral device. Contention is generally resolved on a priority basis determined by internal CPU hardware/software control (Figure 2-31).

The latter interrupt scheme is the fastest of the three but increases the number of lines in the interface. The basic trade-off, in this case as well as in the case where address and data lines are shared, is among more complicated interface, slower data transfer, and fewer number of lines per cable and fewer I/O cables.

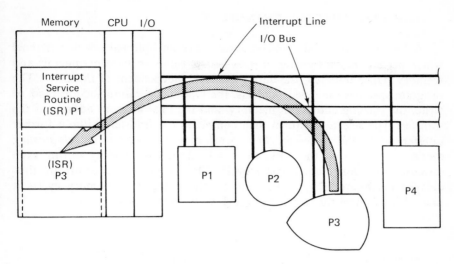

Figure 2-30 Interrupts, using a service routine

Multiplexed word or byte-oriented I/O can be performed both in a program-controlled or interrupt-initiated I/O mode. Some multiplexor channels, such as in the Interdata 70, allow for automatic as well as burst mode I/O in addition to the two previously discussed schemes. The last two methods transfer some of the CPU functions to the channel hardware in the multiplexor, providing for higher data transfer rates (165K words/sec for burst mode operation in the Interdata 70).

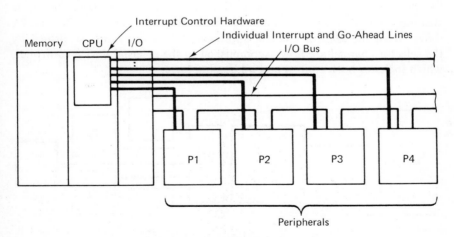

Figure 2-31 Individual interrupt lines

HIGH-SPEED SELECTOR CHANNEL I/O

A limited number of minicomputers offer an optional selector channel which permits block transfer of data between one or more peripherals and memory. Once initiated, the data transfer is independent of the CPU. The program specifies the device address, the type of operation such as read or write, the starting address in memory, and the final memory address of the transfer. The selector channel then completes the transfer, without further interference by the processor. The operation is performed in a *cycle-stealing* mode, meaning that the CPU must wait accessing memory during each selector-to-memory data transfer cycle. CPU memory operations are thus delayed correspondingly, depending on the number of memory cycles it must "share" with the selector channel, which has priority.

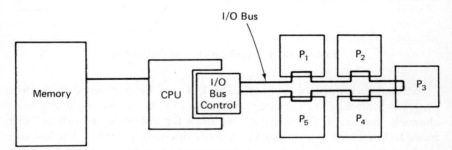

Figure 2-32   Sequential I/O under program control

Direct Memory Access.   Direct memory access (DMA) is quite similar to the selector channel approach. Both approaches are based on cycle stealing, and both types of channels have priority over the CPU. DMA differs from the selector channel approach in that functions performed by the selector channel are now accomplished in the external device controller, which includes both control and addressing logic.

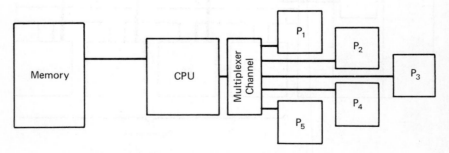

Figure 2-33   Interrupt-initiated, multiplexed I/O

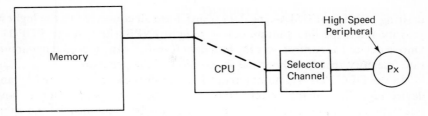

Figure 2-34   High-speed selector channel I/O

Since most minis have only one memory bus, transfers via DMA suspend processing of the processor, as the processor and DMA try to access memory simultaneously. The effective internal processing time can thus be easily computed for DMA, where, for instance, data are transferred between a disk storage device and memory.

In a 1-μsec memory cycle minicomputer, a 200,000-word/sec disk transfer rate implies that the computer is available for processing only 80% of the time. (The maximum DMA transfer rate is a reciprocal of the memory cycle time.)

The DMA function in most minis is implemented in one of two ways:

1. The DMA channel shares data and address lines with the programmed I/O section.
2. The DMA channel uses an autonomous set of buses.

The latter scheme is more complex and costly since it uses a different set of logic and control circuits but is superior because of added flexibility of I/O operations. Both of the basic I/O schemes are illustrated in Figures 2-32 through 2-35.

DMA and the Single-Bus Mini.   In the single-bus-structured machine, as discussed in Section 2.1, the DMA as well as program control and interrupt-initiated transfers are all performed using the same bus. External devices

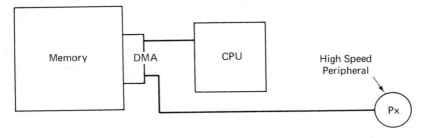

Figure 2-35   Direct memory access I/O

desiring high-speed DMA-type data transfer are all connected to the highest-priority interrupt line [nonprocessor request (NPR) line in the PDP-11]. Once a device has control over the bus, data transfers can proceed at maximum rate (memory speed) without the supervision of the processor.

In the DEC PDP-11, noninterrupt I/O transfers can be requested by any device regardless of the current state of the interrupt system. Hence, both interrupt and noninterrupt I/O processing can be combined in the same program. The latter computer maintains an automatic stack for interrupt processing, where higher-level requests can interrupt the processing of lower-level interrupt service and automatically return control to the lower-level interrupt service routines, when the higher-level servicing is completed.

When a higher-level interrupt occurs, the lower-level interrupt program status is thus stored in the stack on a last in-first out basis, and the new device service routine location is *vectored* by the latest interrupt.

The single-bus system interrupt scheme is illustrated in Figure 2-36. Note that several sublevels exist which makes this scheme analogous to a combination of the single common interrupt line and the individual interrupt line systems previously described.

In summary, the pros and cons of program-controlled and DMA transfers are given in Figure 2-37. Recapitulating this section, the I/O

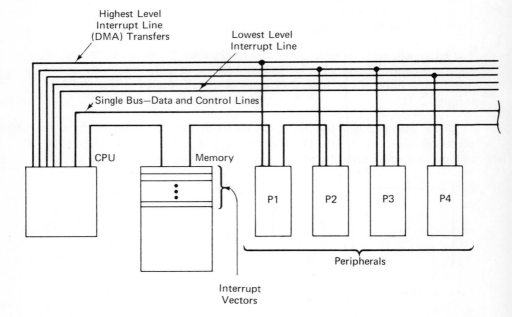

Figure 2-36 Single-bus interrupt scheme

	Pros	Cons
I/O under program control	Less hardware and less cost (depending on whether DMA is optional). Software choice of future action since each data unit transferred can be examined on an individual basis.	Low data rates High software overhead reduces available data processing time.
I/O—DMA	Can accommodate high data rates and block of data. Small software overhead	More complex hardware and higher cost (direct or indirect). Only block transer is efficient as a rule. Special multiplexors are required for several devices sharing the DMA channel

Figure 2-37   Pros and cons of various basic I/O schemes

capabilities of a mini are defined by the following terms:

- I/O word length (byte, word, double-word)
- Number and types of I/O channels
- Maximum word transfer rates
- Types, levels, and sublevels of priority interrupts
- Response time to interrupts (latency)
- Number and type of I/O instructions
- I/O efficiency in terms of cycle stealing

Special Features

All minicomputers offer a host of special features, some of which are mandatory for normal operation while others may be required, depending on the intended application.

One of the most vital of these features is power failure protection, in some systems called power fail safe. This facility provides for a safe shutdown of the computer, without destruction of the contents of its main storage or hardware registers whenever power fails. Power fail safe is generally combined with an automatic restart capability which enables the computer to automatically get back into operation when power is restored. This complete cycle can be visualized in terms of the sequence of operations· shown in Figure 2-38. When the power drops below a predetermined level, an internal interrupt is thus generated which initiates the power fail service routine. This interrupt must, of course, have priority over all other interrupts in the system.

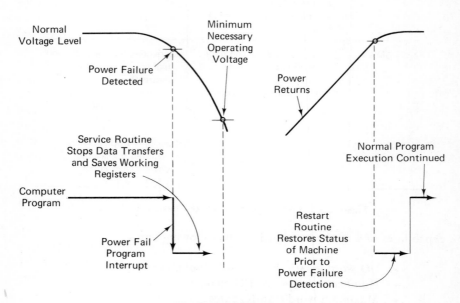

Figure 2-38   Power fail-restore sequence

Internal interrupts, or interrupts controlled and generated by the CPU, are used for a host of functions such as memory protection and memory parity check. A memory protection feature prevents unauthorized or unintentional program access to, or modification of, protected areas of memory. When a program is either overflowing into a protected segment or area from an unprotected area, writing or jumping into a protected segment, or executing an I/O or a HALT instruction in an unprotected segment, an internal interrupt will occur and a subroutine will be executed which performs an error analysis and correction. This subroutine is generally user-written.

All real-time systems require a real-time clock (RTC). Such a device provides immediate access to current timing information and is used to control and synchronize operations in process control data acquisition and time-sharing systems. Several types of clocks are available, the most common being the line frequency clock, which measures time intervals at line frequency (50 or 60 Hz) and causes an internal interrupt every 16.6 or 20 msec, depending on line frequency. In some minicomputers, such as the Nova, the clock frequency can be selected through a bit setting in the instruction. Four frequencies are thus available: ac line frequency, 10 Hz, 100 Hz, and 1000 Hz. Several systems include a clock counter or interval timer which either indicates the amount of time that has elapsed since the occurrence of a significant event or triggers an interrupt signal when a predetermined interval of time has elapsed. The latter feature allows for automatic start and stop of devices, or instrument reading, according to a preset schedule in a process control environment.

The clock can be used in scheduling processes for time sharing, allowing a program or a user a limited amount of time on the computer. The interval timer can be used as an alarm clock to prevent a part of the software from remaining in an endless loop caused by software failure by providing a time-out interrupt. It can also serve as an hardware error-checking tool to provide a time-out in case an external device does not respond within an expected time interval. The time-out interrupt may initiate a subroutine which transmits an alarm message to the operator indicating which device may have failed.

Almost all minicomputers offer at least one special arithmetic hardware feature such as hardware multiply and divide. Although essential in many scientific applications, floating-point arithmetic capability is offered in very few minicomputers. One of the exceptions is the Interdata 70, which provides both fixed- and floating-point registers as well as instructions. Several minicomputers lacking the latter feature provide software routines which allow the user to perform floating-point arithmetic. These subroutines seem to be relatively time-consuming, however.

A limited number of commercial minicomputers offer special macro instructions which perform squaring, square root, exponential, or decimal arithmetic operations. Floating-point arithmetic, as well as powerful macros which eliminate software subroutines and thus save both time and memory space, are implemented in firmware through microprograms in most, if not all, of the more recent minicomputers.

2.2 MICROPROGRAMMING AND THE MINI

Microprogramming is a computer design technique which has been around since the early 1950s. The large computer manufacturers such as IBM, RCA (when still in the commercial computer manufacturing business), and Honeywell implemented this technique already in several of their third-generation machines. Minicomputer manufacturers adopted this technology in the late 1960s and several minis were introduced based on this feature, such as the Spiras-65; the Interdata Models 3, 4, and 5; and the Digital Scientific Meta 4. More recently, the Micro 1600, the Modcomp family of computers, the Hewlett-Packard 2100A, and the Varian 73 have been introduced. Several other minicomputers use microprogramming internally where the user is deliberately denied access to alter or increase the existing instruction set.

Microprogramming; How Does It Work?

As we recall from the first part of this chapter, the typical minicomputer architecture (or building blocks) consists of the memory, the arithmetic and logic processor, the control, and the input/output section. As pointed out, computer programs are stored in the memory section.

To execute a program, a specified sequence of instructions is extracted from the memory and fed to the control unit, while data words are routed between memory and the arithmetic and logic units of the I/O. The control unit timing is closely synchronized to the memory cycle speed, and the execution period of each instruction is usually some multiple of memory clock rate. These submultiples of the memory clock rate or *time period pulses* are routed throughout the computer to ensure the appropriate sequence of operations. The control functions performed by specialized, hard-wired, fixed logic circuits are typically scattered throughout the computer.

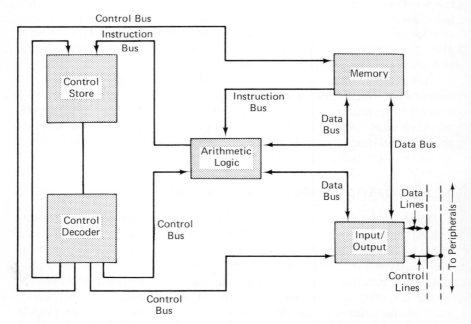

Figure 2-39 Microprogrammed minicomputer mechanization

Microprogrammed minicomputers differ from the conventional machines primarily in the design of the control unit. Instead of hard-wired fixed logic, the control unit of a microprogrammed machine is designed as a stored program element which in some respects functions in a fashion similar to that of the total machine and can be viewed as a computer within a computer.

The control unit in a microprogrammed mini is divided into two functional units, the control store and the control decode. The control decode is typically relatively simple and straightforward and operates and controls all elements of the computer system including two levels of memory, main storage and the high-speed control store. The latter is also called the *control memory*, the *read-only store* (ROS), and the *read-only memory* (ROM). A microprogrammed minicomputer is thus mechanized in the manner shown in Figure 2-39. The control store ROM contains the stored sequence of control functions or microprograms called *firmware*, which corresponds to conventional computer sequences called *programs* or *software*, which are stored in the main memory.

Conceptually, the microprogram control store and decoder interact with the part of the computer which is microprogram-controlled in the manner shown in Figure 2-40:

①   The memory location of the instruction is defined by the address register.

②   The instruction is fetched from the memory and placed in the instruction register.

③   The OP code of the instruction that is stored in the instruction register is decoded.

④   The required microprogram address is placed in the ROM memory address register, which serves as micro location counter.

⑤   The first output word or micro instruction from the ROM is gated to the micro instruction register in the control decoder.

⑥   The contents of the micro instruction register is decoded and, based on the result, one or more operations are carried out in the mini.

⑦   If the result of the operation is incomplete based on status information, the contents of the micro location counter is advanced and the next micro instruction will be read into the micro instruction register and, in turn, decoded.

When the operation is completed, the cycle will repeat. A new instruction is requested by advancing the address in the address register and the micro-location counter is reset for the next sequence of micro instructions.

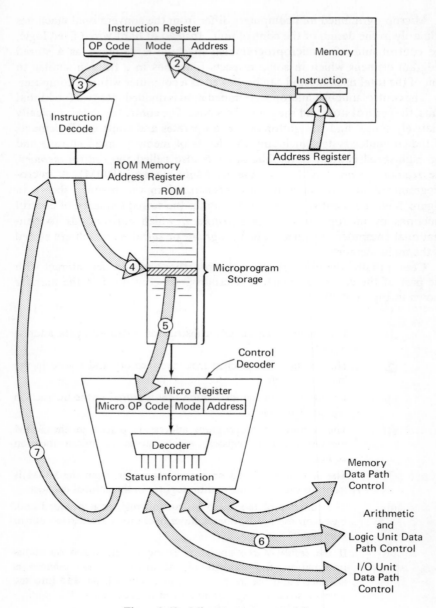

Figure 2-40 Microprogram control flow

The fixed read-only memory typically operates at higher speed than the regular core memory, performing between 5 and 10 micro instructions in a microsecond. Such a sequence of micro instructions may, for instance, include the loading of a register with the contents of an addressed memory word, the shift of the new register contents left by 1 bit, and, finally, the skip of next instruction if the bit shifted out of the register was a 1. This operation is obviously equivalent to at least three conventional instructions, such as

- LOAD REGISTER
- SHIFT RIGHT ONE BIT
- SKIP ON CARRY BIT SET

A microprogrammable computer can, therefore, perform certain operations at considerably higher speeds than a conventional mini. However, unless a very large number of micro instructions are available, the specifically tailored microprogrammed machine is optimized to perform a relatively narrow set of tasks. The main reason for this lack of flexibility lies in the use of ROM. The term ROM reflects a read-only memory which is not electrically alterable. (Some compromise designs exist which allow the user to alter several words in a period of minutes; others permit the user to program his ROM, called programmable ROM or PROM.)

Electrically alterable microprogram stores with reasonable write times are called writable-control storage (WCS) units. Several significant advantages exist in using writable-control storage: Since microprogramming in ROM requires one physical address location to be dedicated to each actual instruction of the microprogram, significant microprogramming activities cannot be efficiently accommodated with ROM. This limitation precludes the use of overlays of different subroutines sharing the same address assignments. However, using writable-control storage allows the microprogrammer to have alterable programs via microprogramming, as do other programmers using software. With a writable-control store, a microprogram which totally requires perhaps 10,000 words of control store can fit into a machine processing 2000 control storage words, where the most frequently used routines are paged in and out of the WCS. A writable-control store also permits the use of dynamic microprogramming whereby a control storage word can be dynamically altered while the microprogram is running. Additional instruction can thereby be generated using micro instructions. These additional instructions can later be implemented by the microprogram on a dynamic basis. The read/write store will also permit the user to prepare and debug his own microprograms.

On the negative side, considerable cost is involved in terms of time for a microprogrammer to familiarize himself with the machine architecture, logic design, and microcode generation in order to write, debug, and implement microprograms. Improper or unauthorized changes will, of course, "bomb" the whole system. Also, complete system compatibility between the operating system (see Chapter 4) and the machine language instruction set may be lost through inappropriate microcoding. Furthermore, once microprogrammed instruction changes or additions are made, the original software will have to be modified to recognize the new function codes.

Similarities and Differences of Several Microprogrammable Minicomputers

Most of the early microprogrammed computers used relatively long micro instructions—90 bits in the IBM 360/50 and 100 bits in the 360/65. Based on this scheme, each bit is used to cause some specific action to occur, and very few micro instructions per microprogram are required since a large number of operations can be performed in parallel. The disadvantage of this approach lies, for one thing, in terms of cost, since many of the available bits in each instruction are unused, thus wasting storage space in the control store.

Furthermore, it turns out that programming based on instructions using 90 or 100 bits/word becomes extremely complex and time-consuming. An additional drawback of these giant size micro instructions is their inherent inflexibility. (Microprogramming by users of IBM 360 machines is, of course, not permitted.) Many of the minicomputer designers that have incorporated microprogramming capability into their machines have rejected this "horizontal" microprogramming in favor of more primitive, shorter word length micro instructions, with less built-in sequencing and with the ability of using many more of the system's resources simultaneously. The latter scheme resembles more closely the conventional method of programming, where the micro instruction word lengths vary from 12 bits in the Canadian Automatic Electric Systems AES-80 Microprocessor to 32 bits in the Spiras 65. This short word length microinstruction scheme is called *vertical microprogramming*.

Very little standardization exists among minis in terms of micro instruction word lengths and formats. Some salient features of typical user microprogrammable minis will be described to illustrate the gross "disparity" between various design approaches.

The Microdata Micro 1600 is a byte-oriented 8-bit word mini with 16-bit microwords. The control store can be implemented as ROM, PROM, or alterable read-only memory (AROM). ROM is low cost and recommended for volume production of field-proved firmware. PROM permits microprograms to be installed at the factory or in the field with fast turnaround time and low initial setup costs for use in low-production volume. AROM is intended for a dynamic microprogramming environment or where the firmware can be debugged in a real-time environment before implementation into the more permanent ROM.

The control store/decoder architecture is based on the previously described systems approach with minor deviations (Figure 2-41). The contents of the U register are used to modify the output of the ROM. This permits dynamic microprogram modification and changing of operation codes and file register designators. The system includes 30 general-purpose 8-bit file

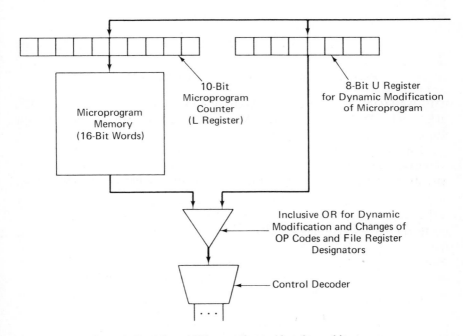

Figure 2-41   Micro 1600 control store/decoder architecture

registers, which under program control are assigned functions such as I/O buffer registers, accumulators, index registers, and program counters.

The Micro 1600 is an example of a typical vertical microprogramming machine, and as such, the micro instruction formats closely resemble the conventional minicomputer instructions. The 16-bit microcommand repertoire contains some 70 micro instructions based on three command formats: literal, operate, and generic commands. Literal, also called *immediate*, instructions specify in the address field an actual number, not the address in memory where the number will be found. The literal instructions for the Micro 1600 have the format shown in Figure 2-42. The operate class of commands is based on the format shown in Figure 2-43. Finally, generic commands or commands with common characteristics such as NO

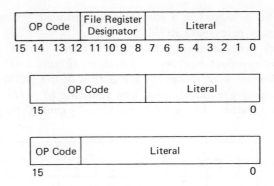

Figure 2-42   Literal microinstruction formats for Micro 1600

OPERATION, ENABLE COMMUNICATION RATE GENERATORS, RETURN, DISABLE REAL-TIME CLOCK, and HALT all have the format shown in Figure 2-44.

The Micro 1600 serves as basis for several macro processors such as the 1600/10, 1600/20, and 1600/21. The latter machines have a standard instruction set which is based on the many-for-one or macro instructions de-

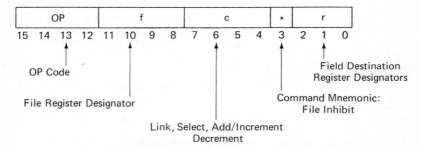

Figure 2-43   Operate commands (Micro 1600)

veloped through the built-in firmware of the basic machine. As an example, the Micro 1600/21 computer contains a set of 107 instructions, each one implemented through microprogramming, where the microprogram is permanently stored in the ROM. The system architecture and instruction set is thus "frozen," and the user implements his software just as in a conventional minicomputer with hard-wired control.

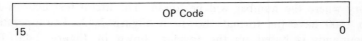

Figure 2-44   Generic commands (Micro 1600)

Hewlett-Packard, in their 2100A computer, has taken a slightly different approach in microprogram design. HP's micro instruction is 24 bits wide and divided into six *micro orders* or segments, where each micro order is decoded to activate one or a set of control lines to perform a given function. A control decode can thus simultaneously activate six separate control functions. This approach is actually a hybrid between vertical and horizontal microprogramming. The 2100A micro instruction has the format shown in Figure 2-45. A typical three micro instruction sequence may thus look as shown in Figure 2-46. Three operations are thus initiated by a micro instruction stored in ROM location 0140 and two operations initiated from 0141 and 0142, respectively.

The "special" field is of particular interest in the case of the 2100A. Functions in this field are used as controls to allow the 2100A to more easily emulate its predecessor, the older HP 2114, 2115, and 2116 series of minicomputers. Emulation means that the 2100A can run software programs of earlier, slower, and less efficient machines. The 2100A has, in fact, been optimized to emulate the older HP minis and is for that reason a different

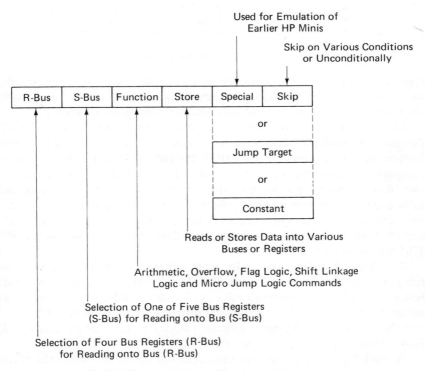

Figure 2-45 Micro instruction formats (HP 2100A)

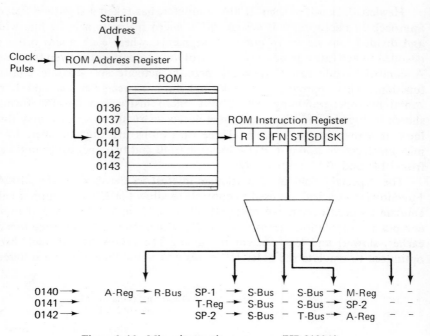

Figure 2-46 Micro instruction sequence (HP 2100A)

type of hybrid microprogrammable mini. Not all instructions are decoded
and executed at the microprogram level; the control unit is based partly
on firmware and partly on hard-wired nonmicroprogram control.

One of the earlier microprogrammable minicomputers was originally
designed as emulator—not of earlier machines made by the same manufacturer but of machines made by IBM, the IBM 1130 and 1800. This minicomputer, designed by Digital Scientific, called the Meta 4, can emulate the
two IBM computers, providing higher performance with extra features such
as floating-point capability and register-to-register instructions not found in
the emulated machines. In addition to being able to emulate the IBM 1130
and 1800, Meta 4 can also emulate the IBM 2314 disk controller and the IBM
2703 transmission control unit.

The Meta 4 differs drastically from other microprogrammable minicomputers in the design of its ROM. The ROM is mounted on circuit
boards in the form of removable adhesive-bonded metallic *bit-patch* patterns,
representing bit positions in sequential instructions. A bit patch is binary 1
and the absence of a bit patch indicates binary 0. Each board contains 32
32-bit double words or a total of 1024 bits.

A much higher bit density has been achieved by Varian, where the microprogram storage is truly a read/write memory or WCS. The density on a

TS	AF/MS	MT	FS	TF	SF	GF	MR	AB	IM	LB	L4	RF	FF	MF	CF	WR	SC	VF	WF	XF	SM	BB	AA

Figure 2-47 Varian 73 micro instruction word format

Varian 73 WCS board is 32,768 bits, or 512 64-bit words. The micro-programming structure of this mini is horizontal with one of several word formats containing 24 fields. Each field consists of a limited number of bits used for a subset of instructions, such as LOAD, PROGRAM COUNTER, SHIFT COUNTER, KEY REGISTER, and OPERAND REGISTER. (See Figure 2-47.) Although gigantic in its own right, the Varian 73 micro instruction set is limited to only a miniscule subset of all possible word structures (2^{64}, or approximately 10^{19}).

The Varian 73 differs in several respects from the previously described microprogrammable minis in terms of architecture. This machine is based on a mix of both horizontal and vertical microprogramming schemes and uses three writable-control stores, two with a 16-bit word length and a third with 64-bit words. In addition, one WCS uses a subroutine stack which provides a call and return capability for micro instruction subroutines. Up to 16 addresses for branches can be stored in the stack, which operates in a push-and-pop mode (see page 41). The Varian 73 microprogram WCS decode configuration looks as shown in Figure 2-48. The memory WCS

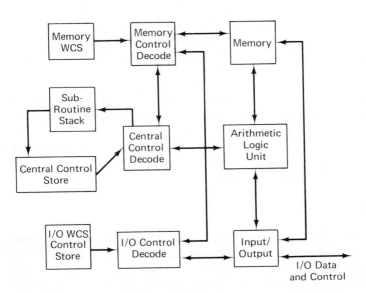

Figure 2-48 Varian 73 microprogram WCS decode configuration

consists of two 16-word, 16-bit-per-word arrays and the I/O WCS control store consists of a 256-word, 16-bit register array. The central control store consists of a 512 64-bit word ROM which contains the standard instruction set required to emulate the Varian 73 predecessor's (the Varian 620/f) instruction set. Up to three additional WCS 512 word pages can be added to the central control store, where each page is contained on a single board.

The user of a microprogrammable machine is well advised to seriously consider his objectives, such as emulation of an older, in-house machine; tailoring a mini for a specific application; or purchasing built-in, future expansion capability in terms of an expanded instruction set. The trade-offs in each case are based on cost, schedules, and required manpower. Technical factors affecting the choice of a microprogrammable mini also include the ease of microprogramming the machine, the available microprogramming tools, and the power and expansion features of the machine. Alternatives to microprogrammable machines are special-purpose machines or machines which belong to a "family" of computers.

2.3 MINIFAMILIES AND SPECIAL PURPOSE MACHINES

The Family Concept

The concept of computer *families* was introduced by the large main-frame manufacturers such as IBM, RCA, Univac, and Control Data in the 1960s. The IBM System/360-370 is probably the largest existing family of computers. The characteristics of a family are a common data format (the 8-bit byte), a common instruction set, and the capability of running the same higher-level software, regardless of where the machine fits within the family. The family members differ from each other in terms of the range of available memory, the number of I/O channels, the execution speed of the machine, and the types of peripherals that can be interfaced to the computer. Another characteristic feature of the family is upward compatibility. Software written for a 360/30 can be run on a 360/40, 360/50, 360/65, etc., but the reverse is not true. Similarly, a Model 2301 drum storage on the 360/65 could be attached to a 360/85 but not to a 360/30.

Minifamilies

The same concept has been applied to minicomputers. A minicomputer family differs, however, in some respects from the larger machine families. The size of the minicomputer family is more modest than IBM's 360/370 and could be called a *minifamily*. Two different types of minifamilies exist presently and both also differ from the IBM type of family.

The Data General Nova family members differ mostly in terms of packaging and memory speed, all other features being practically identical. The Nova is available with either 2600-, 1200-, 1000-, or 800-nsec core memory or 300-nsec semiconductor memory. The Nova chassis is available with either 4, 7, 10, or 17 card slots, where one slot is occupied by the CPU. The Nova minicomputer family members are compatible both upward *and* downward in terms of software and peripherals.

Digital Equipment Corporation has taken a slightly different approach from Data General in terms of minifamily design. The PDP-11 series of machines, starting with the PDP-11/03, resembles IBM's 360/370 family in terms of upward compatibility and increase in memory size. The PDP-11/05, 11/10, 11/15, and 11/20 can be expanded only to 32K words of memory, while the 11/40 and 11/45 memories can be expanded to 124K words. In addition, the 11/40 provides an optional 32-bit floating-point arithmetic capability, while the 11/45 provides a 64-bit floating-point arithmetic capability.

Another illustration of increased capability is, for example, internal speed. The *move time* for register-to-register transfers varies as follows:

PDP-11/03 PDP-11/05 PDP-11/10	3.1 μsec
PDP-11/15 PDP-11/20	2.3 μsec
PDP-11/40:	0.9 μsec
PDP-11/45:	0.3 μsec

However, the PDP-11 family resembles the Nova family of minis in terms of peripherals; any member of the family can handle the full set of peripherals, being I/O-signal- and program-compatible.

Although not unique to the minifamily, a large number of the available peripherals are manufactured by the main-frame manufacturers, in this case Data General and DEC. The pros and cons of "nonstandard" peripherals are discussed in greater detail in Chapter 3.

Minicomputer families have also been produced by Honeywell, Hewlett-Packard, Digital Equipment Corporation, Varian, Interdata, Modular Computer Systems, Microdata, Raytheon, and Lockheed. The Interdata series or family of machines, the Models 50, 55, 70, 74, 80, and 85, differs from the Nova and PDP-11 families in that each model is designed for a group of special-purpose applications. The Model 50 is a data communications processor with 88 general-purpose instructions and 26 data communications instructions, while the Model 55 is dual-processor communications system where one CPU handles I/O while the other CPU performs the data processing. The instruction set for the Model 55 contains 227 instructions.

The Model 74 is the least expensive general-purpose processor in the Inter-data family, while the Model 70 covers the medium-performance range and the Model 80 covers the high-performance range. The main difference between the 70 and 80 is in instruction execution time, the 80 being two to six times faster than the 70. The applications orientation in the 50 is achieved through microprogramming.

Special-Purpose Machines

Where the requirement for upward or downward compatibility does not exist and when it is clearly uneconomical and impractical for the user to microprogram his machine for a specific application, several applications-oriented minicomputers are available for use in such diverse areas as business data processing, data communications, and industrial control.

Minicomputers such as Clary Datacomp 404 (with the CPU built into the pedestal of a Model 33 Teletype), Hetra S-1, Bit 483, and Qantel V are all capable of performing decimal arithmetic on variable length operands and feature business-oriented software. A variable length operand in the Bit 480 is determined by a word mark in the most significant byte (Figure 2-49).

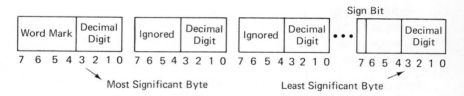

Figure 2-49   Variable word length (Bit 480)

Each byte contains one decimal digit in its four low-order bits. The sign of the operand is indicated in the high-order bit of the least significant byte of the operand. Thus, decimal numbers in ASCII or any similar code can be added or subtracted with no conversion.

In addition to decimal addition and subtraction, the Bit 483 includes a *simultaneous edit* feature. With this feature the programmer can perform decimal arithmetic operations without having to worry about manipulating dollar signs, commas, and decimal points. Hence, simultaneous edit performs an addition as follows:

$$
\begin{array}{r}
\$01.43 \\
+\ \$21.37 \\
\hline
=\ \$22.80
\end{array}
$$

The Qantel V has an explicit set of instructions for character manipulation similar to the IBM 360 instruction set and includes MOVE CHARACTER, MOVE ZONE, MOVE NUMERIC, EDIT, UNEDIT, PACK, and UNPACK.

Data communications is an area which requires highly specialized computer functions. Many machines designed to efficiently perform data communications processing functions—such as converting bit streams into characters and vice versa, and performing data buffering, line handling, code conversion, terminal control, and the like—are available on the market. Some of them, like the Intercomputer i-50, are specifically designed to perform this function, while others, being members of a minifamily, are "reconfigured" in terms of firmware, such as the previously mentioned Interdata 50 and 55.

Finally, several minicomputers, although general-purpose from the point of view of internal architecture, provide special interfaces or are ruggedized or miniaturized to perform in a "hostile" environment. These machines may have to be located outdoors and thus subjected to wide temperature variations or to be operated on a factory floor, truck, ship, airplane, or missile, each environment imposing its own peculiar restrictions on the machine.

2.4 HARDWARE DESIGN

One of the definitions of a minicomputer is small physical size. Most minicomputers, in addition to being compact in size, also offer great flexibility in terms of the particular functional configuration as well as future growth and expansion. All these features generally contradict the goal of low cost, another characteristic of the mini. Low cost and modularity of hardware are, however, achieved through volume production, use of common parts, highly automated manufacturing and test procedures (automatic component insertion and computerized testing of subassemblies), as well as simple design approaches in terms of packaging.

Packaging for Modularity and Expandability

The electronic parts, such as transistors, capacitors, resistors, integrated circuits, and crystals, are generally mounted on printed circuit (PC) boards. In the earlier minicomputer designs, the PC boards were usually relatively small, typically 5 by 6 in., and a CPU could consist of some 30 or 40 boards. Because of the desirability of locating a larger segment of memory on a single board and maintaining a standard board size, PC boards have been growing in size to 10 or 15 by 18 in. Some minicomputers, such as the Data General

Nova, use a single PC board for the CPU, another PC board for the 16-bit word size core, and a third PC board for up to four I/O channels.

The advantage of the single board CPU lies mainly in the simplicity and ease of maintaining the system. A failure anywhere in the CPU requires only a single card change and thus only a single card to be stored as CPU spare. Most manufacturers are still using simple two-sided boards, but higher packaging densities and increased use of LSI is forcing some manufacturers into using multilayer boards based on three and four discrete layers (DEC, PDP-11/45). Multilayer boards have, of course, been used in military and space applications requiring high packaging densities and where size is more important than cost. The cost of board is, obviously, proportional to the number of layers.

The PC boards in a mini are mounted inside a chassis or card guide frame. The card guide can hold one or more CPU's memory and I/O boards which slide into it, depending on the particular mini, from the side, top, or rear and either horizontally or vertically. The cards, when inserted into the chassis, plug into a backplane or motherboard on which horizontal or vertical pin connectors (depending on the orientation of the cards) are mounted. The "other side" of the motherboard provides paths for power and signal lines either through metal etches or wires wrapped around pins which connect to the respective connectors on the reverse side.

The circuits mounted on the PC boards are powered from a supply which may be mounted into a separate chassis (Varian 73) or internally in the same chassis as the CPU memory and I/O boards. A typical assembly looks as shown in Figure 2-50. In this chassis, cards are mounted vertically, which

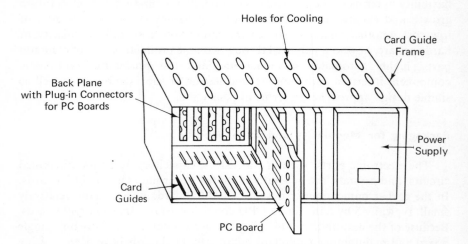

Figure 2-50 Typical minicomputer hardware assembly

may eliminate the requirement for forced-air cooling from a fan. A fan helps the mini to run cooler but may itself reduce the reliability of the system since it is an electromechanical component.

Most minicomputers include a control panel, which in some systems consists of a plug-in PC board. The operator's control panel includes two- or three-position toggle switches and light indicators. The control panel typically provides switches and corresponding indicators to enter and read out data from selected working registers. Some panels include start and stop switches, a single step mode switch, and an I/O reset switch. In the case where the computer is equipped with boot load or an automatic bootstrap into memory of the initial loader, the panel provides a switch which allows initiation of this action.

In some process control operations where the mini is loaded from a remote location or where the operation is fully automatic and no interference by an operator is required or expected, the console may be left out. Several manufacturers therefore make the front panel optional (Texas Instruments' 980A and Computer Automation's Naked Mini). Lockheed Electronics goes as far as offering both circuit boards, a power supply, a motherboard, and a front panel as optional features (the SUE). The user can thus buy any one or all of these components to build a system which best satisfies his requirements.

Almost all minicomputer manufacturers offer additional flexibility in terms of expansion capability. The user may either purchase his chassis in one of several sizes, depending on the amount of electronics that must be incorporated into the system, or expand into additional enclosures—expansion chassis—depending on projected future growth requirements. The expansion chassis generally includes its own power supply and mounts either directly on the main chassis connecting to it through a PC-board-type connector, or through a cable. In order to accommodate the interrupt system, most systems require minor wiring changes or additions by the user when new circuit boards are added to or removed from the original configuration.

Minicomputer Reliability

As a rule, the minicomputer is the most reliable element in a computer system, mostly because very few electromechanical components are used. The statistical mean time between failure (MTBF) is measured in several thousands of operating hours for most commercial minis. (Assuming the operating hours per day in a 5-day week, this is equivalent to perhaps half a year to a full year of continuous use without a failure.) Hardware most likely to fail, when a failure occurs, are cooling fans, switches or light indicators on the front panel, or semiconductor elements that are subjected to high currents and/or voltages, typically in the power supply.

The MTBF of a mini is often a function of how closely to its design limits a mini is being operated. Most minicomputer designs are based on the use of low-cost, commercial components which operate with relatively narrow temperature limits, typically 50 to 120°F. A minicomputer continuously operated in a 120°F environment will therefore exhibit higher failure rates than if the same unit was operated at 70°F. (Other problems, such as transient memory failures, may also occur at high temperatures, since core memory circuits are analog in nature and designed to run in an optimum operating condition which is normal room temperature, or 72°F.)

Many applications may require the minicomputer to be used in a hostile environment. It may be used on a factory floor where iron dust and, in some cases, even iron filings are present. These types of contaminants obviously present a hazard to computers using magnetic core memory.

Some environments may be highly explosive. A typical example is a hospital operating area, which may contain ether. Sparks emitted from mechanical relays or switches may easily set off an explosion.

Computers monitoring or controlling various outdoor processes, as in oil refineries or subways, may be subjected to humidity, moisture, or even rainwater. Condensation moisture or liquids may corrode some parts or cause shorts on circuit boards or backplanes.

The answer to these and other similar problems are the ruggedized minis. Ruggedized commercial minicomputers are functionally identical to their nonruggedized counterparts but are designed to perform reliably during severe environmental conditions. A part of the typical specifications for a ruggedized mini includes the following information (PDP-11R20):

Temperature:	0 to 50°C (operating)
Maximum altitude:	10,000 ft (operating)
	50,000 ft (not operating)
Shock:	5 G, 11 msec (operating)
	15 G, 11 msec (not operating)
Vibration:	5–9 Hz, 1-in. double amplitude
	9–500 Hz, 4 G
Humidity:	95% relative humidity
Reliability (MTBF at 25°C):	22,000 hr (CPU)
	33,000 hr (power supply)
	11,000 hr (memory)

To meet these specifications, the computer uses sealed front panel switches, a welded chassis, heavy-duty chassis slides, heavy-duty connectors, and protection against the effects of humidity and corrosive environments. The last is generally accomplished by coating all circuit boards and critical elements with a thin layer of varnish.

In addition, several ruggedized minis are designed to operate in environments which may subject the computer to electrical disturbances. Motors being turned on and off or reversed can produce momentary spikes of thousands of volts. The ruggedized minis are also shielded therefore against electromagnetic interference (EMI) through the use of shielding material, such as gaskets, RFI stripping, all-metal enclosures, and screening material for indicator lamps. In addition, adequate high-voltage and -current filters are inserted between the line and the minicomputer power supply.

The ultimate in reliability is achieved using military-specified minicomputers. A limited number of commercial minicomputers (Data General Nova and Honeywell DDP-516) have been repackaged and ruggedized to meet stringent military standards. These computers are generally smaller and lighter in size than their commercial counterparts and require less power to operate. The cost of these minis is, however, at least three times that of the same nonruggedized commercial unit.

If no other reason exists for selecting a military-specified mini than the desire to increase the MTBF by perhaps an order of magnitude, the user should seriously consider a less costly alternative such as the use of two standard machines, operating in parallel. However, if the environmental constraints are severe, the military-specified mini may offer the best solution. Typically, a militarized mini can withstand case temperatures ranging from -55 to $95°C$, 15-G shocks without shock mounts, and 300-G shocks with shock mounts (Rolm 1602).

REFERENCES

FORBES, B., "Computer Architecture for Instrumentation," in *Proceedings of the 1971 Computer Designer's Conference*, ed. D. Pritchard, Industrial and Scientific Conference Management, Inc., Chicago, Ill. 1971, pp. 55–60.

FOSTER, C. C., *Computer Architecture*, Van Nostrand Reinhold Company, New York, 1970.

HAAVIND, R. C., "The Many Faces of Microprogramming," *Computer Decisions*, September 1971, 6–10.

KAENEL, R. A., "Minicomputers—A Profile of Tomorrow's Component," *IEEE Transactions on Audio and Electroacoustics AU-18*, December 1970, 354–379.

McDERMOTT, J., "Suddenly, Everybody is Building Microprogrammal Computers," *Electronic Design*, November 25, 1971, 23–28.

ROBERTS, W., "Microprogramming Concepts and Advantages as Applied to Small Digital Computers," *Computer Design*, November 1969, 147–150.

SANFORD, R. C., "Novel Computer Organization Results in Design for a Maxi-Mini," *EDN*, October 15, 1972, 39–44.

SOUCEK, B., *Minicomputers in Data Processing and Simulation*, John Wiley & Sons, Inc. (Interscience Division), New York, 1972.

STORE, H. S., *Introduction to Computer Organization and Data Structures*, McGraw-Hill Book Company, New York, 1972.

3

MINICOMPUTER PERIPHERALS

3.1 DEFINITION AND CHARACTERISTICS

Miniperipherals are characteristically relatively small in size and can be placed on a tabletop or rack-mounted, together with the minicomputer. The only exceptions to this are medium-speed line printers, which usually are freestanding or pedestal-mounted. Also, analogous to the price relationship between minicomputers and their larger relatives, miniperipherals are less expensive than medium- and large-scale computer peripherals. It is, however, possible to connect almost any standard-, small-, medium-, or large-sized computer peripheral to a minicomputer if cost factors are ignored.

Miniperipherals, in comparison with standard peripherals, are generally at the low end of the performance scale, mostly because of economic reasons. It obviously does not make sense to put a $100,000 printer or a $200,000 disk or drum on a $3000 minicomputer, where the mini could wind up giving full time service to the peripheral. In fact, in systems using a large number of miniperipherals, the cost of the minicomputer is relatively small.

Recently, several low-cost miniperipherals have been developed mainly to alleviate this cost imbalance, such as the flexible *floppy* cartridge disk* and the cassette tape storage.

A large number of miniperipherals are presently available, with a bit-serial EIA Standard RS-232B or C interface, which makes it simple and economical to connect the device in question to almost any minicomputer without having to resort to special hardware interface design. The only limiting feature of this method of interfacing is the relatively low throughput that can be achieved. Devices typically interfaced in this manner are generally

---

* A floppy disk is made of Mylar, the same material that is used for magnetic tape.

limited to interactive terminals, paper tape readers, low-speed card readers, and low-speed line printers.

3.2 INTERACTIVE DEVICES

Various input and output devices are actually one and the same; that is, a keyboard terminal can generally be used both for input and output to a minicomputer. Relatively few devices are either strictly input or strictly output. Of the former, data collection devices, such as optical character or special badge readers and the like, are capable only of reading data into a system; representative of the latter type are line printers and plotters.

A large group of the combination input and output devices are termed interactive. With few exceptions, interactive terminals are either of the keyboard/printer or the keyboard/display variety.

Hard-copy Terminals

An interactive hard-copy terminal keyboard/printer or teleprinter is defined as a device which includes an alphanumeric keyboard, produces hard-copy output, and can transmit to as well as receive digital information from a local (or remote) minicomputer. In general, teleprinters are categorized by equipment configuration into three classes: receive-only (RO), keyboard send-receive (KSR), and automatic send-receive (ASR).

Further breakdown depends on printing technique, such as impact or nonimpact, character format, degree of portability, and print speed. Beyond these basic features are a whole host of additional points of comparison discussed in the following section.

The RO terminals, in the strictest sense of the above teleprinter definition, do not belong to the category of devices called interactive hard-copy terminals, since they simply receive and print data. However, the RO terminal is, in general, considered a *subset* of a KSR line, where the keyboard has been removed and the opening covered with a metal plate or similar item. KSR devices do, of course, employ keyboards, while ASR devices include both a keyboard/printer console and paper tape punch and reader or cassette tape module (Figure 3-1).

TERMINAL FEATURES AND PRINTING CHARACTERISTICS

Of two basic printing techniques, impact printing is presently the most widely used, mostly because of its low cost, but is receiving increased competition from nonimpact-type teleprinters. The former type uses mechanical pressure to force an ink-filled ribbon against the paper, to form a character.

Figure 3-1 Twin-cassette hardcopy terminal (Courtesy Texas Instruments Incorporated.)

Special paper is not required, which reduces operational costs. However, impact printers tend to be noisier than nonimpact devices, and the impact mechanism is subject to wear. Impact printers employ two techniques for forming characters: On-the-fly-type printers force paper against selected characters with hammers; character fonts may be mounted on a drum (Teletype), wheel (Diablo), spherical printball (IBM), chain (GE and Memorex), or typebar (Conn. Technical) (see Figure 3-2). The other technique is based on dot-matrix printers that create the characters in a 5×7 or 7×9 dot-matrix array. Both types give anywhere in the range from three to six copies in addition to the original. Dot-matrix types cut down on the mechanical parts required and are potentially cheaper for higher-speed use.

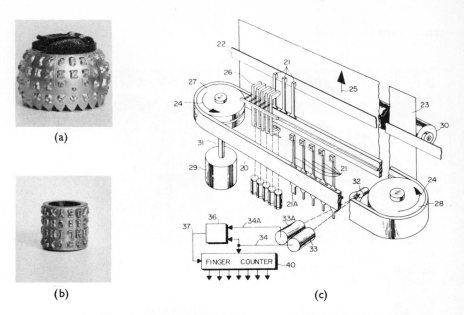

(a)

(b)

(c)

(d)

Figure 3-2 Various hardcopy terminal printer impact devices: (a) IBM-printball, (b) Teletype® terminal print-drum, (c) GE Terminet print chain, (d) Diablo character wheel, (Used with permission of the manufacturers)

A 5 × 7 dot matrix produces a relatively poor-quality uppercase character and is unacceptable in many applications requiring lowercase characters.

Nonimpact printers may use thermal, electrosensitive, or electrostatic techniques. While nonimpact teleprinters eliminate the need for changing ribbons and ink rollers, they cannot, in most cases, provide multiple copies and, with the exception of electrostatic types, require special paper. Most nonimpact teleprinters for minicomputer applications use the thermal printing technique. The nonimpact-type teleprinters are thus quiet, faster, lighter in weight (portable), and, since they have less moving parts, more reliable (up to one order of magnitude) than impact-type devices.

Additional printing characteristics to consider include the number of characters per line and the number of available characters. Typical line lengths are 72 or 80 characters, although several teleprinters provide 118, 132, and even 156 characters/line. With the ASCII code,* 64 characters are available, which include uppercase alphabetics with numerics and control characters, while the full ASCII set provides both uppercase and lowercase characters.

Several teleprinters allow tabulation to be performed up or down and left or right, to draw graphs, to write equations, or to assist in ordinary printing functions. Vertical or horizontal tab stops are made with the touch of a switch or by control signals from the minicomputer. In many applications, a *break* key is a desirable feature. This feature will allow a user to interrupt the minicomputer when the computer is not expecting the user to input data. The importance of such a feature can be illustrated by an example. Suppose that the user has invoked the minicomputer to perform a particular task and that the computer begins printing what obviously will be a lengthy job. When the user discovers that he has asked for the wrong thing, he wants to stop the computer before it has finished printing. Break key to the rescue!

Most impact-type printers provide a choice of either friction or pin feed of the paper. Friction feed makes it easier to handle variable form widths, although pin feed platens are necessary for multiple copy forms. Some teleprinters offer optionally split platens with double pin feed, which allows for the typing of material independently on two separate forms. This feature is highly desirable in business-oriented minicomputer applications. Other useful options for nonportable teleprinters include an accumulator shelf for

---

* The most common code used to represent characters with bytes is the American Standard Code for Information Interchange (ASCII). This code used either 6 or 7 bits for data representation. The 7-bit code is called full ASCII, extended ASCII, or USASCII. An eighth bit for parity check is usually added to full ASCII. Six-bit ASCII excludes lowercase characters. A second, relatively widely used code, generally associated with IBM-related equipment, is Extended Binary Coded Decimal Interchange Code (EBCDIC). Minicomputers almost exclusively use ASCII code.

taking fanfold paper, as well as margins and tab stops (without having to remove paper or shut off the terminal).

OPERATIONAL CHARACTERISTICS

The Teletype Model 33 is the terminal most commonly used by mini-computer manufacturers. The Model 33 is limited to uppercase characters, 80 characters/line, and prints at only 10 characters/sec (cps). However, its relatively poor operational and printing characteristics are offset by its low cost. The Teletype Model 33 has an interface based on a current loop, which permits the user to connect the device to a mini over a relatively long distance—up to several hundred feet. The current-loop interface does not, however, permit the Model 33 to be remoted from the mini over telephone lines using a Standard EIA RS-232 voltage level telecommunications interface without a current-loop to voltage-level converter.

Most teleprinters operate at speeds of 15 and 30 cps with a few of them offering optional speeds up to 60 and 120 cps. Several teleprinters offer switch-selectable speeds, which may be advantageous when the terminal is used in other than minicomputer applications.

Increased transmission speeds generally increase error rates. An asynchronous transmission format, in addition to start and stop bits, also includes a parity bit for error checking. Some terminals, in addition to error checking, also provide error-correcting capability. The latter usually consists of an automatic retransmission request, in case a parity error is detected by the hardware.

OPERATOR AND HUMAN ENGINEERING FACTORS

In addition to tab features previously discussed, important operator considerations are the type of teleprinter keyboard to be used, the keyboard arrangements, and the tactile feedback from the keyboard. Two basic keyboard formats are available: the familiar typewriter configuration and the block keyboard configuration with separate numerical and control functions. Some teleprinters cover up part or all of the line being printed by the print head or a ribbon, which may irritate the operator. With many units it is difficult to reload the paper or change the print ribbon. As with most peripherals, it is important that the device be tested by the user or operator as part of the selection and system design process before a commitment is made for purchase.

DEVICE SELECTION

A typical teleprinter selection decision tree is shown in Figure 5-16. To augment this process, it is highly desirable that the systems designer assign

Selection Criteria

1. Terminal features	Print mechanism (impact/nonimpact)
	Character font
	Number of copies
	Options (cassette, paper tape, etc.)
2. Printing characteristics	Number of characters per line
	Paper width
	Pin or friction feed
	Split platen
3. Operational characteristics	Speed(s)—switch-selectable
	Upper- and lowercase
	Interface (EIA, TTY, other)—code
	Error detection and/or correction
	Portable/mobile/fixed
	Terminal under computer control
	Accumulator shelf (for fanfold paper)
4. Operator factors and	Tab control
human engineering	Vertical/horizontal
	Local/remote
	End-of-line warning
	Fixed
	Variable
	Keyboard arrangement
	Typewriter keyboard
	Block-type keyboard
	Separate numeric pad
	Separate function keys
	Tactile feedback from keyboard
	Audio feedback from keyboard
	Coverup of printed line by ribbon, etc.
	Ease of reloading paper and changing ribbon
5. Service considerations	Service and maintenance cost
	Paper cost
	Response time
6. Manufacturer	Stature and reputability
7. Cost	Unit cost
	Cost of options
	Quantity discounts
8. Other	Noise
	Reliability
	Physcial size and weight
	Power

Figure 3-3 Checklist for teleprinter

priorities to features such as impact or nonimpact, cost, and speed. A checklist should, as a minimum, include the selection criteria shown in Figure 3-3.

Interactive Alphanumeric Display Terminals

Interactive alphanumeric display terminals differ from teleprinter terminals mainly in not being able to produce a hard copy (unless a printer is connected to the terminal) and of their often extensive editing and block transfer of the edited message to the minicomputer capabilities. Several alphanumeric display terminals offer various graphic capabilities in addition to color. Some interactive alphanumeric displays even permit simultaneous display of video from a TV camera and alphanumeric data from a minicomputer.

There are two main types of display terminals; the stand-alone and the clustered display. The stand-alone display terminal incorporates all control features together with the display into a single enclosure, while the clustered or multistation terminal system uses a central controller which typically drives 8 or 16 displays. The latter type is cost-effective only when a large quantity of displays are used in close proximity to each other. Several manufacturers, at this writing, regard the cost break as being at approximately 16 terminals, each terminal located less than 50 ft from the controller.

The display itself is generally based on the cathode-ray tube (CRT), although the relatively new plasma display, using a gas discharge technique, may become a contender for a low-priced compact display.

DISPLAY CHARACTERISTICS AND TERMINAL FEATURES

The CRT display terminal typically consists of

- CRT display unit
- Keyboard
- Refresh storage and control
- Character generation
- Communications interface

A block diagram of terminal elements is shown in Figure 3-4.

Distinguishing features of displays include the size of the display area, the number of characters per line and lines per display, the number of different characters that can be displayed, and the character generation technique. Most low-cost display CRTs are between 10 and 14 in. diagonal and display a maximum of approximately 2000 characters. The characters are usually formed by a 5×7 dot matrix, although a few displays offer higher-resolution characters formed by a 7×9 dot matrix. As with the dot-matrix-type

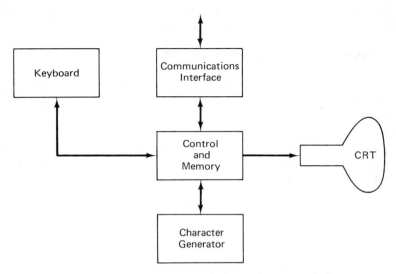

Figure 3-4 Block diagram of a CRT display terminal

teleprinter, a 5 × 7 dot matrix is probably adequate for most minicomputer applications, where the display of lowercase characters is not required.

Although some CRT terminals are based on storage tube technology, the large majority are refreshed, from a local memory, 60 times/sec. This may, in some cases, result in interference from fluorescent lighting when the terminal and lights do not operate at quite the same frequency. The storage tube permits the display of both alphanumerics and vectors but cannot be selectively erased or edited. In addition, storage displays have poor contrast ratios and relatively low light output. The main advantage of the storage tube, as its name implies, is the capability of the tube to store the information, thus eliminating the need for a refresh memory.

Refresh memories in nonstorage tube displays are generally large enough to store a screenful of data plus a few characters for logical control. Some terminals offer a paging capability where the memory is organized to hold more data than can be displayed on the screen at any one time. The stored data can be displayed on command, a "page" at a time, or rolled back and forth in front of the display "window" or viewing area. A program listing on a CRT is normally limited to 24 lines, while with paging a 100-line program can be stored and displayed.

It should be noted that the maximum number of displayable characters does not necessarily coincide with the maximum number of character positions on the screen. The latter approach allows the manufacturer to supply a smaller refresh memory. However, from a user and programming standpoint, a one-to-one correspondence between character positions on the CRT and the display memory is generally preferred.

OPERATIONAL CHARACTERISTICS

Important operational capabilities in display terminals include editing and communications with the minicomputer. A characteristic feature of CRT displays is the cursor. A cursor marks the position on the screen where the next character will be read or written from memory. The cursor can be moved up, down, left, right, and, in some systems, to the top left-hand corner. The cursor implementation varies from a blinking character or a blinking square, positioned on top of a character, to a solid underline or a set of brackets on top and underneath a character. Most operators prefer the solid to the blinking cursor, since the blink feature becomes irritating after extended periods of terminal usage. In some systems, the solid cursor starts blinking when the system detects a parity error. Several CRT terminals provide the computer with information and control to continually "sense" the location of the cursor and reposition it under software control.*

Edit keys add or delete information from the display based on the cursor position. The most common edit features are replace, insert, and delete. This allows for character/line deletion and/or insertion. The delete function is sometimes expanded to DELETE AND ERASE. DELETE moves the preceding words on a line or lines up to contract the text, while ERASE or CLEAR clears the word(s) or line(s), leaving the area cleared blank. Additional editing features are roll/scroll, partial transmit, split screen, selective blink, tabulation, format control, and audible alarm. The roll/scroll is the ability to roll data off the top of the screen, line by line, after the last character of the last line has been entered. (The top line is obviously also lost in the local memory unless the paging feature is included in the display terminal.)

Several CRT terminals can be operated either in a *teletype mode*, where each character, when entered from the keyboard onto the screen, is simultaneously transmitted to the minicomputer, or in a *block mode*, where the entire message can be composed and edited off-line on the screen before it is transmitted in full to the computer. Partial transmit means that part of the information on the screen can be operator-selected for transmission, leaving other data not transmitted. The latter feature is a time (and memory) saver in applications that require that forms be filled out and where a requirement for transmission of the "fixed" form itself does not exist. If the left or right half of the screen can be locked out for the display of only a fixed message and the cursor cannot be moved into this area, then the controller

---

* This feature is of great value, for instance, in minicomputer-based computer-aided instruction (CAI) where the cursor is automatically moved to a specific line or question on the screen based on the type of answer given by the student to the preceding question.

has split screen capability. In contrast, the *field protect mode* uses *delimiters* or special transparent characters to define any areas on the screen that are locked out and prevents data from being entered into or removed from the protected area.

Selective blink allows portions of the message to be made to flash to attract the attention of the operator. The tabulation feature is generally the same as that found on teleprinters, being able to jump to a preset position. Format control allows the line length to be determined by the operator. An audible alarm can alert the operator to the approach of the end of the line or other predetermined programmed conditions. When the screen is blank, the alarm or beep is also used to inform the operator that the computer is processing a message.

The time to transmit 1800 characters to or from a display terminal at teletype speed (110 bps) is 3 min. At 1200 bps this time period is reduced to 15 sec; at 2400 bps the total transmission is 6 sec. The value of high-speed interface is, therefore, quite obvious, particularly in applications requiring transmission of large-character-sized displays. Many terminals offer both the Teletype current loop, the EIA RS-232C standard, and a character-parallel, nonstandard, line interface. In addition, the bit-serial transmission may be switch-selectable between 110 and 9600 bps.

However, to economize on the interface hardware, several displays featuring synchronous data transmission capability include start and stop bits on each character (we shall discuss this further under Transmission Media, Speeds, Methods, and Modes). The start and stop bits, required only in asynchronous transmission, are highly undesirable in synchronous transmission, since the minicomputer must strip off the redundant bits, incurring undesirable software overhead.

Two additional features bear mentioning: Several terminals provide optional interfaces to RO-type printers which may be used to provide hard copy of selected portions of the transmitted data and cassette tape storage devices, which can be used to expand the internal storage capacity of the CRT terminal. The portable CRT terminals are the most recent additions to the terminal group of equipment. The portables, like their teleprinter counterparts, include a built-in coupler which permits the user to dial the computer, insert the telephone receiver into the coupler, and be on-line with the computer (for more on couplers, see Section 3.4).

OPERATOR AND HUMAN ENGINEERING FACTORS

Important features from a human engineering point of view are the accessibility (and availability) of adequate adjustments for display brightness and focus. All operator switches should be located in front of the CRT and be easy to recognize by the operator. The front of the CRT should be

Figure 3-5   Comparative in-house analysis at SDC of several CRT display terminals, from left to right: Conrac, Beehive, Hazeltine, and Lear Siegler

made of a material which cuts down glare, and the unit should be quiet operationally and also run cool. In addition, the presentation on the CRT should be flicker-free and linear without any waviness in the lines, and the characters should be adequate in size for normal viewing. The most direct way to test visual and operational characteristics is to perform an in-house evaluation, as shown in Figure 3-5.

DEVICE SELECTION

The device selection should consider the features discussed above, in addition to cost, quantity discount, maintainability, vendor support, reliability, physical size, weight, noise, and power requirements. A checklist which provides some of the important features to be considered in CRT display selection for minicomputer systems is shown in Figure 3-6.

3.3 LOW- AND MEDIUM-SPEED I/O DEVICES

Except for minis built into dedicated systems, minicomputers require some means of loading a program into the computer memory. The least expensive approach from a hardware point of view is to use the ASR Model 33 Teletype. The main drawback of this method is speed; at 10 characters/sec, it takes approximately half an hour to load or dump (readout) 8000 words of

1. Terminal features	Stand-alone or clustered
	If clustered, number of units per controller
	Options (hard copy, cassette)
2. Display characteristics	CRT size
	Characters per line, lines per display
	Character positions
	Character generation technique
3. Edit features	Roll/scroll
	Characters per line, insert/delete
	Format control
	Full cursor controls
	Tabulation
	Selective blink
	Partial transmit
	Audible alarm
	Remote cursor positioning
	Split screen/field protect
4. Communications features	EIA and current-loop interface
	Full and half-duplex
	110, 300, 600, 1200, 2400, 4800, and 9600 bps
	Parallel interface
5. Other	Dimensions, weight (if portable)
	Power
	Price (purchase and lease)
	Maintenance cost

Figure 3-6   Checklist for CRT terminal selection

core, twice that time to list a 1000-instruction assembly language program (see Chapter 4) with comments, and several minutes to output a table of data which may take the mini seconds to calculate. An improvement of at least one order of magnitude is achieved using a paper tape reader.

An alternative to the paper tape reader is the cassette tape, where the tape can be prepared off-line using an ASR cassette tape teleprinter or a display terminal, coupled to a cassette tape device. A third quite common approach is to use a card reader, where the cards are prepared using a keypunch.

In special applications, inputs to the mini are made using various types of optical readers or, in control and laboratory environments where analog voltages or relay pulses are monitored, analog- or syncro-to-digital converters or voltage level shifters.

The most commonly used output-only peripheral is the line printer. Other types of output-only peripherals are plotters and voice synthesizers or recorders. Each of these types of devices will be described in greater detail.

Paper Tape Readers and Perforators

The type of tape read by paper tape readers may be paper, paper-Mylar, or metalized Mylar. Most tapes are 1 in. wide, utilizing a row of eight holes for coding purposes. Most, if not all, paper tape readers require a special-purpose controller for minicomputer interface. This controller must be designed in a manner which prevents damage to the paper tape if, for any reason, power is removed from the minicomputer before the paper tape device. Most minicomputers provide an off-the-shelf controller to one or more paper tape units.

OPERATIONAL CHARACTERISTICS

Minicomputer paper tape perforators punch tape between 50 and 150 characters/sec, and paper tape readers read between 50 and 1000 characters/sec. Most readers operate in both an asynchronous start-and-stop mode and a synchronous block mode. Start-and-stop reading is generally limited to a maximum of 300 Hz. Some paper tape readers may produce chatter and vibrations at some lower frequency, resulting in rapid failure. Bidirectional reading may be advantageous in some applications in addition to fast rewind, which is useful when the tape is scanned for data blocks or a field-separating character.

OPERATOR AND HUMAN ENGINEERING FACTORS

The disadvantages of using paper tape are numerous. The tape lacks the flexibility of 80-column cards, it is subject to tear, it is awkward to handle even when fanfolded, and it is only machine-readable. In addition, many minicomputer paper tape readers are designed with fanfold tape storage bins that are too small, often resulting in jamming or tangled paper. Also, devices combining paper tape reading and punching nevertheless require operator intervention when the punched tape must be read back into the computer. The only reason the paper tape has survived as an I/O medium, and is still widely used, is its relatively low cost compared to other I/O devices. This position is, however, rapidly being eroded by the introduction of reliable cassette tape units which have read and write error rates approaching that of the paper tape.

DEVICE SELECTION CRITERIA

The systems designer, having decided on the use of a paper tape reader and/or punch, should consider factors such as the availability of an interface and controller to his minicomputer, the construction of the device in terms of modularity, the degree of use of electronics rather than mechanical components in the system, and the ease of loading the unit. Unless the device reads fanfolded tape, a spooler, which rerolls tape during reading and leaves it immediately ready for reuse, is highly desirable.

A device selection checklist for paper tape readers and perforators is shown in Figure 3-7.

1. Operational features	Speed (cps)
	Asynchronous or synchronous operation
	Bidirectional or unidirectional
	Can read paper and Mylar tape
	Fast rewind
2. Design characteristics	Fanfold paper
	Spooler
	Supply and takeup reel
3. Other	Rack-mountable
	Power supply included
	Low noise perforator
	Oversized easy-to-remove chad container for perforator

Figure 3-7 Paper tape/punch selection checklist

Card Readers

The punched card is still the predominant off-line batch data entry medium in small- and medium-sized computer systems. This does not mean that card equipment is not used with minicomputers. On the contrary, a large number of low-cost card readers are presently available, competing favorably with paper tape devices. Cards are generally easier to edit than paper tape and can, of course, be directly read by people. The disadvantage of using cards is the fact that the combination of keypunch equipment and card reader is generally more expensive than paper-tape-generating equipment and the paper tape reader. In addition, systems using card readers usually still require an interactive terminal such as a Teletype. An IBM keypunch varies in price between $2000 and $4000 depending on available features. This compares with approximately $1500 for an ASR Model 33.

OPERATIONAL CHARACTERISTICS

Low-cost minicomputer card readers typically operate at reading rates between 200 and 600 cards/min (cpm). As indicated in Figure 1-8, 200 cards/min (based on 80-column Hollerith cards) is equivalent to a paper tape reading rate of 270 cps. Although the 96-column IBM System/3 card has been on the market for several years, it appears as though the minicomputer market prefers to stay with the older, 80-column card.

Card readers transfer cards from an input reader hopper through a read station to a stacker bin. Input hoppers and output stackers typically have room for 500 to 1000 cards. Some high-speed readers operate at up to 1500 cpm, and the hopper and stacker are accordingly larger, with a capacity of up to 2500 cards. Several minicomputer card readers are available with two output stackers. The cost of high-speed readers is generally disproportionately high for use in minicomputer systems. This is particularly true for card punches. Most minicomputer manufacturers therefore do not include the cost of a card punch interface on their standard price list.

Several low-speed card readers are available for use at sites remote from the minicomputer. Most of these devices operate over phone lines at tele-type speed, which is 10 or 15 characters/sec or, 7 to 11 80-column cpm, although at least one higher-speed device is available operating at 120 characters/sec (approximately 30 cpm).

The mark sense card reader can read 80-column punched cards as well as cards which are prepared with a common pen or pencil. The main ad-vantage of this reader is that keypunching can be eliminated and data directly read into the computer.

OPERATOR AND HUMAN ENGINEERING CHARACTERISTICS

All card readers perform the following sequence of operations:

- Pick a single card at a time from the input hopper
- Transport the card past a read station
- Stack the card in one or more output stackers

Problems are sometimes encountered in picking the card; two or more cards may stick together because of humidity or various other conditions, or the mechanism may fail to pick a card. The card may be skewed or mis-aligned when transported past the read station and thereby damaged during the read operation, or the transport mechanism may bend or otherwise mutilate the card. In addition, the lack of a positive drive may cause the stack operation to jam. Any or all of these problems may reduce the efficiency of the card-reading operation.

Important features, from an operational point of view, are therefore automatic shutoff if a data error, pickup error, or card jam occurs; automatic stop if the hopper is empty; and the capability of loading and unloading while the unit is running without causing pick failures, data errors, or stacker jams.

Many card readers exhibit an intolerable noise level, not even when reading but also when the reader is on a standby basis, with power on. It

1. Operational characteristics	Card rate (read and/or punch)
	Card capacity (hopper and stacker)
	Card specification
	Operational noise level
	Load/unload while running
	Automatic shutoff
2. Reliability maintainability	MTBF > 2000 hr
	Ease of replacing light source
	Diagnostic test points
3. Interface	EIA RS-232C or parallel interface
	Controller to desired minicomputer

Figure 3-8 Partial checklist for card equipment

therefore behooves the potential user to test the reader before a commitment is made to incorporate it into the system. A checklist for card readers/ punches is shown in Figure 3-8.

Digital Cassette Recorders

The digital cassette recorder provides the systems designer with an alternative to paper tape and card devices. The main advantages of cassette tape over paper tape and punched cards are its low cost, compact size, ease of loading into a reader, and superior editing capability. The major disadvantage of the cassette tape is the relatively low data reliability—for some recorders, depending on recording technique, up to one bit error per 1 million recorded bits (5 to 10 errors/cassette). A large number of improvements have, however, been made in cassette recorders since the first units were introduced in the late 1960s. The maturity of the digital cassette recorder is indicated by the fact that most major minicomputer manufacturers now offer a fully integrated cassette recorder, including software, in their standard products line. As a matter of fact, in 1972, Univac, the first of the large mainframe manufacturers, introduced a digital cassette recorder on the OEM market.

Some confusion still exists in terms of the difference between cassette and cartridge recorders. Technically both are the same kind of device, but industry has chosen to call the Philips-type cassette a cassette and any other type of cassette a cartridge. Another distinction exists in the fact that cassette recorders were originally designed for audio applications, while cartridge devices were, from their inception, designed for computer-based digital systems. Most cartridge recorders therefore offer vastly superior performance characteristics compared to the cassette recorder and compete with the IBM-type, seven- or nine-track, 0.5-in. recorder rather than with the 0.15-in. cassette. (Various cartridge systems are discussed in Section 3.4.)

TECHNICAL CHARACTERISTICS

The Standard Philips cassette consists of a small plastic container, approximately $2\frac{1}{2}$ by 4 in., in which two flangeless reels are mounted. The 0.15-in.-wide, 300-ft-long tape is available to the transport through an opening along one side of the container. The reel hubs can be engaged by drive shafts mounted in the transport. To understand the inherent limitations of cassette recorders, the various methods of operation should be understood.

The performance of the recorder is closely related to its electromechanical design. Three fundamentally different design approaches are presently used, each including a large number of variations. The most common type of tape drive mechanism is based on the use of the capstan and pinch roller. The tape is moved at constant velocity past a read/write head (Figure 3-9) by a capstan, which consists of a small rotating cylinder. The tape is forced against the capstan by a pinch roller. In some systems, two capstans are used, each permanently rotating in opposite directions.

The direction of tape motion depends on which of the two pinch rollers is activated, thereby clamping the tape against the respective capstan. Some

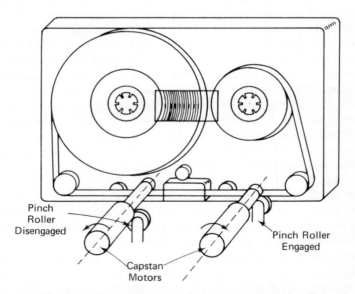

Figure 3-9 Cassette recorder using capstan and pinch roller

systems keep the tape permanently in touch with the capstan and start and stop the tape motion by turning the motor on and off, driving the capstan. The major drawbacks of the capstant/pinch roller systems are tape slippage, uneven tape motion, dirt being ground into the tape, tape wear, and the tape becoming accidentally wrapped around the capstan.

A second approach becoming increasingly popular is the reel-to-reel drive which uses reel motors to move the tape. The reel-to-reel systems use either complex servo control both for constant tension and tape speed or a ratio recording technique that allows for reading and writing, regardless of tape speed. The latter approach, allowing the reel motor to run at constant speed, thus eliminating devices used to regulate tape speed, keeps the less reliable mechanical parts to a minimum and relies more heavily on electronics (Figure 3-10). The latter method will cause the tape velocity to vary as the moving tape winds around the hubs within the cassette, increasing the

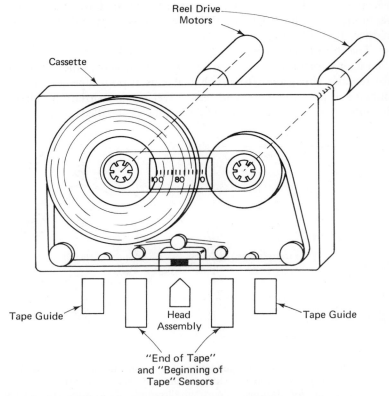

Figure 3-10 Cassette recorder using reel-to-reel drive

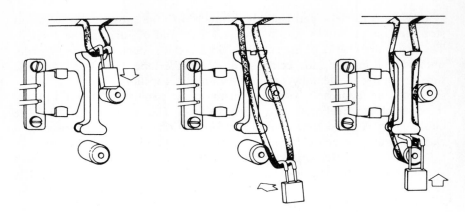

Figure 3-11 Cassette tape mechanisms (Courtesy Bell and Howell Electronics and Instruments Group, Pasadena, Calif.)

effective hub diameter. To reduce variations in tape speed, some manu-facturers limit the length of the tape to less than 300 ft, which, in turn, reduces the storage capacity of the cassette.

The third type of cassette recorders, generally with the best performance characteristics but also with the highest cost, pulls the tape out of the cassette for reading, thus eliminating such problems as poor tape guidance, tape edge damage, rapid tape wear, and reel-to-reel tension variation. These types of recorders vary widely in the way the tape is handled outside the cassette.

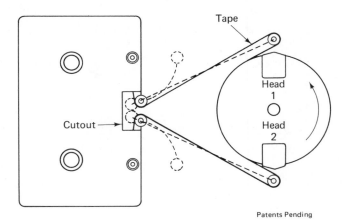

Patents Pending

Figure 3-12 Idlers that hold tape in position against the rotating head assembly are shown in light solid lines; dashed lines indicate idlers in position for loading (Courtesy Electronic Processors, Englewood, Colorado)

The Dicom 440 uses two vacuum columns similar to large computer reel drives, approaching their performance. Bell and Howell's Model 240 pulls the tape out of the cassette with mechanical "fingers" and drops the tape loop over a capstan. The third most complex system, the Electronic Processors, Inc. (EPI) WRV-200 series tape drive, not only pulls the tape out, but holds it stationary against one side of a rotating drum that carries two separate heads past the tape. Once the stationary section of the tape is read, the tape is moved forward for the next *scan*. The latter technique is borrowed from the helical scan used in video recorders (Figures 3-11 through 3-13). All these high-performance devices trade cost for lower error rates and less tape wear. A decision to use one of these units should not be made until a cost performance comparison is made with cartridge and other types of high-performance storage devices.

Cassette drives are based either on continuous or incremental recording. Both types of recording are performed bit-serially on one or two tracks. So-called continuous recorders write serially onto the tape in groups of bits (typically 8 or 16). The groups of bits are organized into words which, in turn, are structured into records. A record may range from two to several thousand words. Again, the records are grouped into files, which range from two to hundreds of records (usually limited by the length of the tape).

Words are recorded in a synchronous manner (see Section 3.5), and records are separated by interrecord gaps, typically 0.5 to 1 in. long.

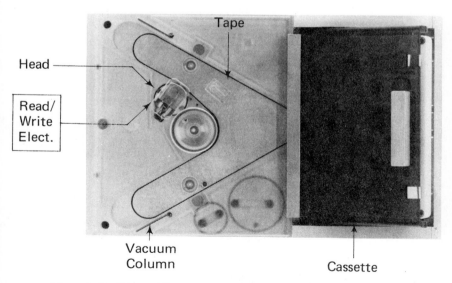

Figure 3-13 Dicom 440 vacuum cassette tape system (Courtesy Dicom, Sunnyvale, Calif.)

Synchronous cassette recorders can record up to 700,000 characters/tape depending on the number of records and, consequently, the number of interrecord gaps as well as the density of recording (bits per inch).

Incremental cassette tape drives record data by starting and stopping the tape for each bit or character, thereby eliminating the need for large gaps. The latter recording method eliminates the requirement for buffering and simulates the asynchronous operation of a teleprinter or CRT terminal. The incremental cassette recorders generally use lower-density recording techniques, thus limiting the cassette storage capacity to the range of 50,000 to 100,000 characters/cassette.

Several continuous recorders can be run in a character incremental mode with transfer rates ranging from 10 to 400 characters/sec. The very low-transfer-rate devices are designed for use with data communications equipment and teleprinters operating at 10, 15, 30, 60, and 120 cps. These devices are available with a bit-serial, instead of a parallel interface. The bit-serial interface may be either a Teletype 20-mA current loop or EIA, RS-232C-compatible.

1. Operational characteristics	ECMA/ANSI standards
	Recording density (bpi)
	Fast forward/reverse search
	Transmission speed (read/write)
	Maximum rewind time
	Maximum number of characters that can be recorded
	Number of tracks per side
	Incremental/continuous
	Error-checking features
	Bidirectional read/write
2. Interfaces	Current-loop, EIA, RS-232C, parallel
	Interface and controller for specific mini
3. Other	Number of recorders per unit (2, 3, 4, 5, etc.)
	Status information to computer (beginning/end of tape, reading, writing, parity error, ready, etc.)
	Automatic power shutoff
	Automatic stop
	Adequate front panel controls
	For asynchronous transmission; selectable bit rates
4. Reliability	MTBF
	Error rates (soft and hard)
5. Maintainability	Frequency of required cleaning of read heads, etc.

Figure 3-14   Partial checklist for cassette recorders

Typical control functions are commands such as READ, FORWARD, REWIND, BACKSPACE N BLOCKS, FORWARD SPACE N BLOCKS, WRITE, and WRITE END OF FILE. Parallel interface generally includes separate control lines for the recorder, while serially interfaced recorders are controlled either by separate control lines or by standard ASCII control characters using the bit-serial, common data, and control line.

Important cassette tape characteristics are defined by cassette capacity, record file and tape lengths, recording technique, number of tracks, recording density, error detection capability, interrecord gap length, character transfer rate(s), maximum rewind time uni- or bidirectional read/write capability and available interface(s). Very few, if any, cassette recorders have identical performance characteristics. In spite of the earlier ECMA (European Computer Manufacturers Association) and the more recent ANSI (American National Standards Institute) cassette standard, most manufacturers prefer to design for what they consider to be the broadest user market. The ECMA/ANSI standards are based on synchronous (continuous) recording with a single track of 800-bpi recording, and with all the 8-bit ASCII characters strung together end to end. Furthermore, the tape length must be a minimum of 282 ft and the interrecord gap between 0.7 and 19.7 in., with a pre- and postamble* for each record. The error checking must be performed by a cyclical-redundancy-check character (CRCC). The latter feature has, however, been included in the Nova cassette (which otherwise does not meet the above standard). In this device, the read head reads the data shortly after it has been recorded (read after write) and calculates a CRCC checkword. At the end of a block of data, the read checkword is compared against the one written on the tape. If they match, the recording is error free.

OPERATOR AND HUMAN ENGINEERING CHARACTERISTICS

As previously pointed out, the main weakness of the cassette recorder has been high error rates in recording and data output. To minimize problems with error rates, either some of the performance characteristics, such as high transfer rates and cassette capacity, must be compromised, or the user must be willing to pay a higher price for the device. Most of the more recent designs incorporate read-after-write capability with CRCC. This, together with the fact that high performance, certified digital cassettes are used, will reduce soft error rates typically to one in 10^7 and hard error rates to one in

---

* When a message block is recorded on a magnetic tape (or a disk), it is usually preceded by a fixed number of bits or characters called a preamble, which initializes and synchronizes the read electronics. The message block is also followed by a fixed number of bits or characters called a postamble. The latter is used to turn off the write electronics.

10^8. Soft errors are generally caused by dust particles on the tape and corrected by rereading the tape, while hard errors are caused by permanent damage to the tape.

Several desirable features available in cassette recorders are tape alarms, which sense *both* the end of the tape and the beginning of the tape; automatic power shutoff with cassette removal; automatic stop with tape breakage; character-by-character reading and backspacing for editing convenience; front loading of cassette; and clearly visible front-mounted operator controls and lights such as WRITE, STOP, LOCK, ADVANCE, READ, BLOCK, REWIND, READY, HALT, etc.

A checklist for cassette recorders is shown in Figure 3-14.

Line Printers

OVERVIEW

The selection of a hard-copy device is determined by the minicomputer system requirements. The presently available printers are of two types: impact and nonimpact. A system where large amounts of printing must be done, and where two or more copies of the printed material are required, should use a heavy-duty, medium- or high-speed impact printer. If multiple copies are not required and the user can live without highly legible stylized characters, a significant cost saving can be achieved using a nonimpact printer. If expected print loads are medium to low, the system designer can select his printer from a wide variety of relatively low-cost, either line or character printers. The line printer prints an entire line at a time, while the character or serial printer prints a character at a time. Most low-speed devices are unbuffered* character printers, and the majority of them belong to the previously described group of RO teleprinters, operating between 10 and 120 cps. Here again, the desirable print quality determines the type of printer to be used. Almost all minicomputer manufacturers offer at least one line printer and one serial printer as part of their peripheral line of off-the-shelf devices, including interface control hardware and software device drivers (see Chapter 4).

TECHNICAL CHARACTERISTICS

Most medium-speed impact printers with a print rate of 200 to 600 lines/min (lpm) are using either a chain or drum for printing. Chain printers are generally faster than drum printers but also cost more because of their

---

* *Buffered* denotes a temporary storage of a line, in order to match the minicomputer I/O channel with the speed of the printer.

more complex control mechanisms. Chain printers also extend into the high-speed, over 1000-lpm, region. The truly high-speed impact printers are generally not used in minicomputer applications. Most minicomputer manufacturers include a drum printer in their peripheral line. The print mechanisms of both type of devices are shown in Figures 3-15 and 3-16.

Where multiple copies are not required, the electrostatic printer serves as an excellent device to print (and plot) up to speeds of 5000 lpm. Electrostatic printers generate characters by selectively charging paper in a small dot pattern or matrix, with individual electrodes (or nibs). In contrast to impact line printers, electrostatic printers require special electrically conductive paper and liquid or dry toners. The print mechanism of an electrostatic

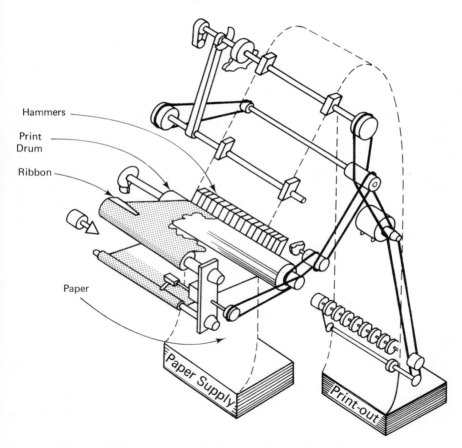

Figure 3-15 Basic print mechanism in a drum printer. Printing occurs when solenoid-activated hammers strike paper and inked ribbon against the raised characters on the rotating print drum

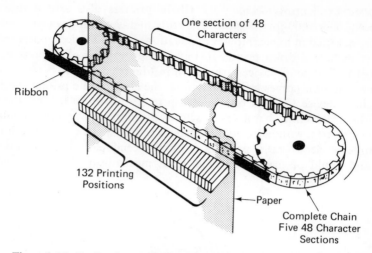

Figure 3-16   Basic print mechanism in a chain printer. A chain assembly contained by guides and sprockets moves horizontally across the print line

printer is shown in Figure 3-17. A major disadvantage of electrostatic line printers, in addition to not being able to produce simultaneous multiple copies, is the fact that the character font is usually formed by a 5×7 dot matrix, although in some printers 5×9, 7×9, 7×10, and 10×14 matrices are available. The larger matrices can, of course, produce legible upper- and lowercase characters but are still a far cry from the standard high-quality font, produced by all drum or chain impact printers.

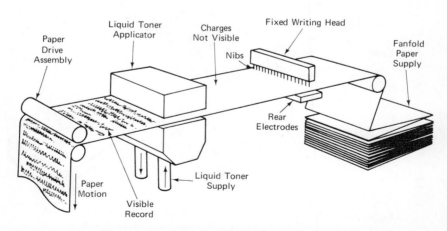

Figure 3-17   Electrostatic print-toner mechanism

Low-speed printers are usually asynchronous, printing one character at a time. A large number of the character printers are really teleprinters without the keyboard (RO). Several serial printers have, however, been specifically designed to perform as printers only. In the latter category, the most common types are impact printers using a wire matrix or cross point technique in which characters are printed in a 5×7 dot-matrix format (Figure 3-18); a rotating cylindrical drum with a protruding helix, which under the precise impact timing is hit by a narrow horizontal bar, also forming a dot-matrix character (Figure 3-19); and the type wheel with several repeated character sets, which operates in a fashion similar to both the IBM Selectric and a drum printer (Figure 3-20).

In addition to the previously discussed teleprinters, at least two non-impact printers are presently available which do not require any special-purpose paper: the ink "squirters." Of two types of ink jet printers presently on the market, one uses 40 stationary jet nozzles to print a line of 80 characters. The ink particles are electrically charged and deflected on the paper to form a dot-matrix character. The other type of ink jet printer uses a single nozzle that is positioned horizontally across the platen by a servo control system. This nozzle physically traverses the width of the page and is returned automatically to the left-hand margin by receipt of a carriage return signal. The ink is pumped into the nozzle assembly and squirted out of an orifice, two thousandths of an inch in diameter. The latter system can print up to 750 characters/sec. If shut down for some time, the ink jet printer may have a unique problem in terms of the ink clogging the nozzle(s). Both manufacturers, therefore, recommend that a special-purpose ink be used.

OPERATOR AND HUMAN ENGINEERING FACTORS

Most impact and nonimpact printers are available with either an 80- or 132-column print format. In some of the impact printers, particularly drum or chain type, the price differential is considerable between the two, and serious consideration should be given to the necessity for a 132-column printer.

Impact printers can make up to six copies simultaneously using special forms with interleaved carbon or pressure-sensitive paper. The quality of the last copy depends on the availability of operator-adjustable penetration controls on the printer, which allows for different settings, depending on paper thickness and number of copies.

Other desirable features are static eliminators, which prevent the paper from sticking; vertical formatting capability, which allows the printer to skip different numbers of lines on a form; and adjustable or dual tractors, which allow multiple size forms printing. For multiple copy printing, pin or sprocket feed is a must, and paper feed controlled by a *pull*-type mechanism is preferable

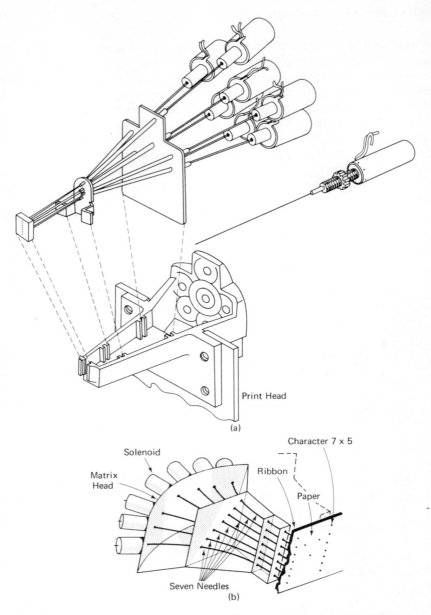

Print Head

(a)

Character 7 x 5

Solenoid

Matrix
Head

Ribbon

Paper

Seven Needles

(b)

Figure 3-18 Wire matrix type printer (Courtesy Centronics). In matrix type printers, characters are printed in a 7 × 5 dot matrix format by impact techniques that produce single or multipart copies. Seven wires individually driven by solenoids do the printing. The print head, with its wires and solenoids, moves along the print line at uniform velocity. Firing the solenoids at five successive intervals to form a 7 × 5 array generates the required character

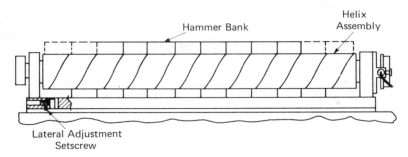

Figure 3-19 Helix, dot-matrix printer (Courtesy Potter, Inc.)

to the *push* type. The former type reduces the chances of paper jamming or becoming fouled and bunched up.

As a general rule, impact printers increase in weight, size, and noise level in proportion to the print rate. Some heavy-duty, high-speed impact printers are, however, built into a sound-absorbing enclosure. The noise level of impact printers can vary depending on the frequency of carriage returns and line feeds. The impact printer is often not only the noisiest component in a computer system but also the least reliable. A typical range of MTBF figures for impact printers is from 150 to 1000 hr compared to nonimpact printers, with an MTBF range from 3000 to 5000 hr or more.

The mean time to repair (MTTR) of an impact printer ranges between 1 and 2 hr depending on the ease of changing the ribbon and adjusting print hammers, as well as the accessibility of control electronics, power supply fuses, and the like. Some printers provide a diagnostic tool called a test generator card which allows the maintenance man to quickly diagnose the printer and determine whether the fault is in the printer or in the computer.

Flimsy mechanical design and excessive whiplashing of the print mechanism during the printing process are generally good indicators of potential

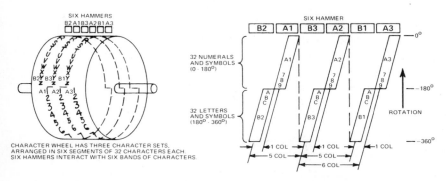

Figure 3-20 Printwheel type printer (Courtesy Printer Technology, Inc.)

mechanical problems early in the life of the printer. An important detail, although not related to preventative maintenance (PM), is the case of loading paper into the printer. Some designs make the paper loading a major project, requiring a highly trained expert to load the printer within a reasonable amount of time. Figure 3-21 includes a checklist of pertinent printer characteristics for the minicomputer system designer.

1. Operating characteristics	Speed (lpm)
	Font
	Record quality
	Multicopy
	Buffered
	Number of columns
	Vertical formatting
	Adjustable tractors
2. Reliability	MTBF (hr)
3. Maintainability	MTTR (hr)
	Modularity
	Accessibility to circuits, etc.
	Ease of loading paper
4. Environmental characteristics	Acoustical noise
	Electrical noise (from print hammer relays)
	Odor (from liquid toner)
5. Cost	Initial cost
	Operating cost (special paper, ink ribbon, toner, etc.)

Figure 3-21   Line printer selection checklist

Miscellaneous I/O Peripherals

OVERVIEW

A whole host of peripherals, traditionally belonging to the domain of large machine users, have won slow acceptance among minicomputer users, mostly because of recent cost reductions. Among these types of devices are graphic plotters and digitizers, optical character readers (OCR), and voice output devices. Most of these compromise either speed, accuracy, size, range, or some qualitative features in order to qualify as miniperipherals.

GRAPHIC PLOTTERS AND DIGITIZERS

Graphic plotters are generally of two types: the electrostatic and the pen-on-paper plotter. The former type is identical to the alphanumeric electrostatic printer and differs from it in terms of the addition of a graphics module, which allows the computer program to address each electrode or nib, individually. The plotting speed is a function of the paper movement and independent of the amount of information being plotted. The pen-on-paper-type plotter, must, however, draw each line or character at the time, and the plotting speed is a direct function of the amount of detail required in the plot.

Plotters are characterized by accuracy, repeatability, resolution, and plot speed. Plot accuracy is determined by how close a line, dot, or character can be placed to any given point on the paper on a repeatable basis; repeatability is a measure of the tolerance of the plotter in terms of producing several identical plots; while resolution is measured in terms of the number of resolvable lines or dots which can be plotted per inch. For electrostatic plotters, the resolution is determined by the number of electrodes, styli, or nibs per inch that are used as well as the longitudinal stepping increment of the paper feed mechanism. Plot speed is rated by the pen speed in inches per second and pen acceleration or deacceleration capabilities. Many plot manufacturers use "average" plot complexity to define the speed of the plotter. This term is, of course, meaningless since the term average plot complexity is undefined.

Low-cost pen plotters for minicomputer applications are either of the drum or flat-bed type (Figure 3-22). The most commonly used minicomputer plotters are of the drum type, where the vertical size of the plot is virtually unlimited (function of the length of the paper roll).

Most electrostatic plotters have a resolution of between 70 and 100 styli/in., while pen plotters have resolutions ranging from 40 to 200 points/in. (More expensive, nonminicomputer plotters have resolutions well beyond 1000 points/in.) Several minicomputer manufacturers provide an off-the-shelf interface between a plotter and the mini.

In summary, key plotter parameters are thus accuracy, repeatability, resolution, plot speed, size of plot (vertical and horizontal for flat-bed plotters), available minicomputer hardware interface, and plot subroutines.

While plotters are used to draw alphanumeric and graphic information on paper, where the complete plot is prestored in terms of plot instructions in the minicomputer memory, a digitizer translates operator-generated analog information into digital data, which is input directly and stored in the computer. The digitizer may consist of either a hand-held cursor which feeds x and y coordinates to the computer as it is moved across a chart or what is called a tablet.

A graph tablet is a device which senses the x and y positions of a pen or pencil when writing on the tablet and transmits the coordinate points to a computer. The coordinate points are sensed either through electromagnetic or capacitive pickup by x and y grid wires embedded in the tablet or by a pair of horizontal and vertical microphones which pick up the sound of a

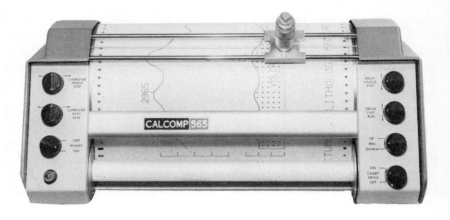

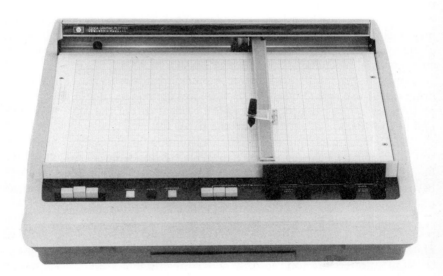

Figure 3-22 (a) Drum plotter (Courtesy California Computer Products, Inc.) and (b) Flat-bed plotter (Courtesy Hewlett-Packard)

periodic spark emitted from a *graf pen* and determine the pen position based on the time it takes the sound of the spark to travel from the pen to the respective microphones (Figure 3-23).

A digitizer is used in scientific applications to generate digital computer inputs from time chart recorders to analyze various types of data such as seismic, telemetry, and strain gauge readings; power line fluctuations, and as temperature, altitude, and humidity variations.

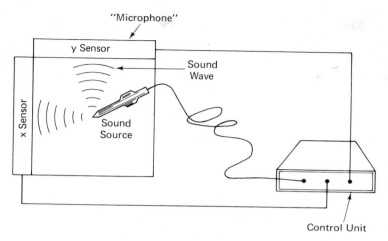

Figure 3-23 Digitizer, using a graf/pen* where the time traveled by the sound of the spark emitted from the pen is used to measure its position. (* graf/pen is a trademark of Science Accessories Corp. Used with permission)

Digitizers are also useful in medical applications to enter EKG, EEG, and X-ray information for subsequent computer analysis. In addition, these devices are often used to generate digitized computer control information for milling machines directly from drawings instead of having to specify contours from a teleprinter keyboard in terms of equations, vectors, and various parameters.

OPTICAL CHARACTER READERS

With the exception of a handful of very limited capability optical readers, OCR has still really not entered the miniperipheral market. A number of readers are presently available that read pencil marks, hand-printed numeric characters, and printer-generated numeric information. These devices bridge the gap between the most limited OCR devices and marked card readers. One unusual type of OCR device utilizes a coded strip underneath an alphanumeric character and can be termed a bar code reader. The latter device can read 60 typed characters/sec, which is equivalent to about 1 min of reading time for a typical double-spaced page. The typing must be made using a special type of IBM Selectric print ball, special paper, and carbon ribbon.

Most of the above devices can be connected to a minicomputer through a serial EIA (RS-232) interface.

VOICE OUTPUT

Voice output, also termed audio response units, as in the case of OCR equipment, has until the early 1970s generally been tied in with medium- or large-sized computers. Computer data outputs have been used to control the playback of a magnetic drum, tape, or photographic voice recording with the voice response unit. Based on computer commands, prerecorded words were "spoken" either individually or in phrases. Message assembly time was slow, and the messages were, of necessity, brief. Such systems are generally inflexible, slow, and expensive. The main advantage of these playback system is the high quality of the prerecorded voice.

One of the first truly low-cost audio response units was introduced by the Federal Screw Works Vocal Interface Equipment Group in the early 1970s. This device converts a string of digital phoneme commands into the corresponding audio signals. Phonemes are the basic components of speech. The English language contains some 2000 phonemes. The average word contains six phonemes, and the above audio response unit is limited to reproducing a subset of 50 phonemes out of the 2000. Each phoneme command uses 8 bits, where 6 of the 8 bits define the desired phoneme, and 2 bits are used to determine the inflection of the synthesized voice for each phoneme.

The voice output device is accessed using a touch-tone telephone by dialing the computer and subsequently accessing computer stored data which could, for instance, be customer credit, stock quotations, or inventory status information.

The vocabulary is typically between 20 and 2000 words but *can* be expanded up to 10,000 words. The only serious drawback of most low-cost voice synthesizers is the relatively poor quality of the voice output.

3.4 STORAGE DEVICES

Two basically different types of memories are available to the mini-computer system designer: static and dynamic. Static memories do not require mechanical motion to access data and are typically using either bipolar semiconductors or core. Static memories are also called add-on memories, since they compete with the internal memory sold by the mini-computer manufacturer. These memories are either mounted on plug-in cards, similar to the manufacturer-supplied main-frame memory units, or into a separate box which includes the memory boards, control circuits, power supply, and interface designed for the particular mini being matched. The cost advantages of using add-on memory must be weighted against possible voiding of the warranty given on the mini and the likely future software changes made on purpose by the manufacturer to discourage the add-on vendors.

Dynamic memories consist of drum, disk, and tape transports, which depend on mechanical motion to select or address information entered into or read out of these devices. This section will dwell on these types of devices.

Magnetic Tape Systems

Minicomputer tape systems fall into four categories:

1. IBM-compatible transports
2. Nonstandard tape transports
3. Cartridge recorders
4. Cassette tape recorders

IBM compatibility signifies that recorded information can be completely recovered when the tape is played back on a comparable IBM system and that, conversely, information recorded on an IBM tape system can be recovered when played back on an IBM-compatible tape transport. This capability will permit completely free interchangeability of tapes between transports regardless of who manufactured them. It should be noted, however, that IBM compatibility does not mean that the tape transport system itself can be plugged into IBM equipment. When the transport hardware is physically interchangeable it is called *IBM-plug-to-plug-compatible*.

Nonstandard tape transports, as the name implies, do not meet the IBM standards in terms of tape width, recording densities and formats, real capacity, etc., but generally provide favorable performance to price ratios compared with the IBM-compatible transports.

Cartridge recorders use specially designed tape containers which do not meet a standard but exceed the performance capabilities of cassette tape recorders.

Finally, cassette units, which often are designed to substitute for paper tape readers and punches, provide the data storage and handling capability at the low end of the scale. Owing to this fact, the cassette tape drives are discussed in Section 3.3.

IBM-COMPATIBLE RECORDERS

To qualify as an IBM-compatible transport, the recording must be either seven- or nine-track, meaning that seven or nine separate read/write heads simultaneously read or record digital data where the heads are positioned in a line, perpendicular to the length of the tape. The seven-track tape drive recording density must be either 200, 556, or 800 bpi in an NRZI* (non-return-to-zero) format, and the nine-track recording density either 800 or 1600 bpi, phase-encoded.†

The tape length is typically 2400 ft and the width, according to the IBM standard, is $\frac{1}{2}$ in. Additional requirements are in the area of track widths, center-to-center spacings, interrecord gaps, error-checking features, and special strips or markers to denote the beginning and end of tape.

IBM tape drives can read and write at tape speeds varying between 12.5 and 200 ips. A tape can be recorded at one speed and read at another. Tape velocity is, therefore, independent of other IBM compatibility requirements, and most IBM-compatible minicomputer tape transports read and write between 12.5 and 75 ips. The latter speed, based on an 800-bpi density, is equivalent to a 60K-byte/sec transfer rate.

A transport with a nine-track IBM type head and IBM-compatible read/write electronic will not, however, necessarily generate IBM-compatible tapes. It must be used with an appropriately designed controller which generates required gaps between blocks of messages and parity for error checking, provides timing and clock information, and formats the recorded data for the specific minicomputer. Many magnetic tape controllers can handle two or more transports, which, in turn, can be intermixed in terms of seven- and nine-track units. The data transfers between the controller and the minicomputer take place either under program control or automatically, via a concurrent DMA channel. DMA-type I/O operations are terminated with a controller-generated interrupt. Most minicomputers include magnetic tape controller instructions in their instruction set. Typical instructions include: TRANSFER REGISTER CONTENTS, TRANSFER BUFFER REGISTER CONTENTS, SENSE PARITY ERROR, SENSE BUFFER READY, SENSE END OF TAPE, SELECT TAPE DRIVE 3. The controller typically contains two or more full-word buffers for temporary word storage.

Most IBM-compatible transports use a single capstan drive to provide tape motion during read, write, and rewind operations. Tape speed is generally regulated by a velocity servo using some type of feedback from the capstan motor. Tape tension is controlled by supply and takeup reel motors in conjunction with mechanical tension arms or, as in some high-speed

---

* NRZI recording is based on the magnetization or flux reversal on the tape surface only on logical 1. A high rate of reversals therefore occurs when only 1s are written, while no reversals occur as long as the track contains a string of only 0s.

† Phase encoding records data as a series of bit cells. Each of these bit cells, regardless of whether they are 1s or 0s, contains a flux reversal. The direction of flux reversal determines whether the bit is a 1 or a 0.

transports, using a pair of vacuum columns. The mechanical tension arms are adequate for most low-speed applications but usually cannot respond fast enough without damaging the tape at read/write speeds exceeding 45 ips. The vacuum column tensions the tape by immersing it in a vacuum chamber to absorb the shock of fast starts and stops. The high acceleration during start-and-stop operations does not therefore reach the reel, which needs only accelerate fast enough to maintain a loop of tape in the vacuum column.

The major problems with any tape drives are tape skew and tape stretching. The former problem is of considerable concern in seven- or nine-track systems, where skew, unless electronically compensated for in the controller, may result in a tape being unreadable by a specific tape system. Tape stretching caused by nonconstant forces across the width of the tape will contribute to skew errors. The average skew on a good transport is less than 10% between the first and last bits of a character.

A system using an NRZI recording technique can tolerate a maximum skew of 40%. Skew is more tolerable in phase-encoded systems, since both clock and data can be placed on a single track.

A rare condition, but still encountered in a limited number of tape transports, is *spewing*. This refers to the tape spilling out because of a direction reversal at maximum speed, or some unusual sequence, or a combination of input commands. Tape spewing can often result in the destruction of sections of the tape as a result of wrinkling.

Figure 3-24 summarizes important parameters and tape characteristics to be considered by the minicomputer systems designer.

1. Technical characteristics	Density (bpi)
	Number of tracks
	Mode of encoding
	Maximum read/write rate (kHz)
	Read/write speed (ips)
	Rewind speed (ips)
	Interrecord gap (in.)
	Tension arms/vacuum column
	Reel diameter (in.)
2. Controller	Number of tape transports per controller
	Operating modes (under program control/DMA)
	Error detection
3. Software	Basic software package
	Diagnostic program
	Driver package with callable subroutines
4. Other	Controller and transport construction
	Mounting
	Operating power
	Operating temperature
	Manual controls

Figure 3-24 Summary and checklist for IBM-compatible tape units

NONSTANDARD, SEPARATELY MOUNTED REEL, TAPE TRANSPORTS

A number of systems exist which do not meet the IBM set standards. One of the most popular is the Digital Equipment DECtape system, which uses small (approximately 4 in. in diameter) reels with $\frac{3}{4}$-in.-wide tape. The tape is moved by direct drive of the reels, not using capstans or pinch rollers. Reading and writing is performed bidirectionally at the rate of 5000 16-bit words/sec, on two sets of tracks, where the second set of tracks is redundant and used to increase system reliability. To determine the exact position at which to record the information to be written or to locate data to be played back from the tape, four additional tracks are used, two redundant tracks for the block address and two for timing. Unlike the IBM-compatible tape systems, DECtape stores information at fixed positions on the tape rather than at unknown or variable positions. The stored information is in equal size blocks, where each block contains 256 data words (18-bit) and 10 control words. The structure of each block is symmetric, permitting search, read, and write in either direction. Block numbers and 16-bit checksums are recorded at both ends of a block.

The 16-bit checksum is based on a summation of all data words in the block generated in the controller. Upon reading or verifying a block, the checksum is recalculated and compared with the one originally recorded during writing. The redundant recording technique and uncomplicated transport mechanism, combined with efficient error checking features, make this device highly reliable.

The software control of the DECtape system is performed by means of five device registers in the PDP-11. These registers can be read or loaded using any PDP-11 instructions that refer to their address. The DECtape system is also available to other DEC minicomputers, such as the PDP-8.

The capacity of a single tape is approximately 148,000 16-bit words. This compares to 6 million words on an IBM-compatible 2400-ft tape, using 800-bpi density recording.

The above system has been developed in a slightly modified version by at least one independent peripheral manufacturer under the name of LINC Tape system. Similar to the DECtape, these systems use Mylar-"sandwiched" magnetic tape to preclude oxide contact with read/write heads, thus ensuring long head life and also eliminating possible damage being done to the magnetic recording surface. Also, as in the DECtape systems, the recording is redundant, the system using 10-channel or track heads. The LINC Tape type of systems may or may not be compatible with the DECtape system in terms of recording density or recording technique. Also, as in the case of IBM-compatible, nonminicomputer manufacturer-supplied magnetic tape systems, factors such as the instruction set for the tape controller, its instruction registers, which are given the memory address in core, where the beginning of data transfer will occur, the size of the data transfer, the data buffer, which reshuffles the data from one or more tracks into 8-bit bytes or 16-bit words, and the available software support from the independent magnetic tape manufacturer must be considered when evaluating the tape unit.

CARTRIDGE RECORDERS

The cartridge-type recorders combine the ease of handling and compactness of the cassette with the more reliable performance of the reel-mounted systems. In addition, many cartridge recorders, being originally designed for digital recording, provide a greater transfer rate and recording capacity than the lower-cost cassette units.

At least four different types of cartridge recorders exist, each one optimized for specific purposes. The 3M Cartridge has been designed for high transfer rates, with read and write at 90 ips and search at 180 ips. The tape is $\frac{1}{4}$ in. wide, and the recording density is 1600 bpi. A data transfer rate in the range of IBM-compatible drives is thus achieved. The 3M Cartridge is almost a complete recorder in itself, including in the cartridge everything except the motor, read/write head, and electronics. The usual capstan has been replaced by an internal belt-and-pulley rubber-like, tension-band reel drive (Figure 3-25).

At the other end of the performance scale, the Tri-Data cartridge system

Figure 3-25 Belt-driven Scotch brand data cartridge (Courtesy 3M Company)

called the Cartri-File, an endless-loop, $\frac{1}{4}$-in.-wide tape system, reads and writes at 7 ips and searches at 18 ips. The Cartri-File sacrifices performance for simplicity, ruggedness, and low error rates. A single continuous-loop cartridge stores between 75,000 and 180,000 16-bit words, depending on the number of words per record.

Other low-performance cartridge systems are the 0.15-in. coaxial cartridge and the heart-shaped cartridge made by Iomec/Digitronics and Cogar, respectively. The coaxial system uses a preloaded torsion spring coil between the two coaxial reels to keep the tape in tension (Figure 3-26). This type of

Figure 3-26   Schematic of coaxial cartridge (Courtesy Iomec Inc.)

cartridge is designed with easy loading in mind. The cartridge is loaded into the transport by "dropping" it into the recorder. The transfer rate of the Iomec cartridge system is approximately 400 bytes/sec.

The single-tape reel system has a transfer rate four times higher than the coaxial system. It is primarily designed to compete with the Philips-type cassette in terms of reliable recording. Because the tape is pulled all the way out of the cartridge, it can be driven by a single capstan that contacts only one side of the tape, leaving the other side, which is the recording surface, to be touched only by the tape read/write head. Because of the cartridge's simplicity, its price is comparatively low, and the error rate is less than 1 in 10^8. The transfer rate is roughly 1600 bytes/sec, which is equivalent to the transfer rate of cassette tape recorders such as the system made by Data General for the Nova.

The major problems with any devices which use new and improved technology but are not supported by the minicomputer manufacturer are the software operating system, software peripheral drivers, and peripheral system diagnostics. The best cartridge, or any other magnetic tape system, for that matter, is useless unless this software has been developed and operates correctly (see Chapter 4).

Disk and Drum Memories

FUNDAMENTAL DIFFERENCES

A disk or drum addition to a minicomputer will drastically increase the system throughput and performance. A disk or drum overcomes the sequential access limitation of magnetic tape and reduces total access time from seconds to milliseconds. Disks and drums differ basically in terms of read/write head arrangement, recording efficiency, storage per unit of volume, and ruggedness in the form of physical construction.

A drum is built in the shape of a cylinder with read/write heads arranged axially along the perimeter of the drum. Commonly, because of space limitations, the heads are staggered. The path length for each circumferential line that travels beneath the respective head, called a track, is the same, which permits maximum and equal recording density on all tracks (Figure 3-27). Drums can generally be built to stand a harsher environment than disks and are therefore often used in military applications. A limited number of drum memories are also available for commercial minicomputer system applications.

The disk-type memories are by far more popular than drums. The basic disk drive consists of either a single disk or a stack of disks rotating as a unit.

Figure 3-27 A drum with one head per track (Courtesy Datum, Inc.)

Data are stored and retrieved by the use of magnetic pickup heads positioned above the disk surfaces. The system may contain a single head which moves across the top of a single disk or two heads which move both on top and bottom surfaces. With stacked disks, heads are mounted on a comb-like structure, reading or writing simultaneously on all surfaces (Figure 3-28).

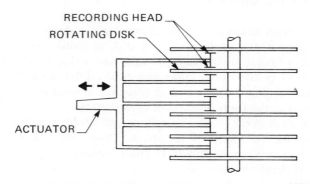

Figure 3-28   Disk pack with direct access to all surfaces (Courtesy IBM Corporation)

The head assembly is moved to the desired track position when a data transfer is desired. The time required to move the head or heads is called positioning time. Some types of devices, called fixed head disks, have a head permanently positioned above each track, as in a drum. The positioning time for fixed head disks and drums is obviously zero.

BASIC PARAMETERS

Whether the disk uses fixed or moving heads, rotational delay is encountered unless the desired data or recording position is directly under the read. The maximum rotational delay or access time is equal to the reciprocal of the disk rotational speed, measured in revolutions per minute (rpm). The average access time, defined as the time required to make an infinite number of seeks on the disk divided by the number of seeks or accesses, is equal to half the reciprocal of the disk rotational speed. The average access time is also called the latency time. Some manufacturers define the sum of positioning and latency time as "access time." The true access time is quite often a function of the organization of the data on the disk by the programmer. Depending on the type of data to be recorded, the programmer can arrange it in a manner which reduces the average rotational delay to less than the period of half a revolution.

For minicomputer applications requiring minimum access time, the fixed head disk is the obvious solution. The major disadvantage of the fixed head disk, in addition to its relatively high cost, is that it cannot be removed from the disk drive.

Two of the most commonly used types of removable disks are the disk-pack and the disk cartridge. Both types of systems were initially introduced by IBM and more recently adopted by the minicomputer industry. A large number of these minicomputer disk systems, although IBM style, are not necessarily IBM-compatible, such as the seven- and nine-track magnetic tape units.

The disk-pack consists of a stack of disks separated by central spacers. These disk-packs are stored in dustproof containers and are directly inserted onto the spindle of a disk drive. The container is always removed after the insertion and used again when the disk-pack is removed from the drive for storage. The cartridge, which contains a single disk, is inserted into a disk drive, and the read/write heads are automatically inserted through openings in the cartridge.

The recording area on both fixed and moving head disk systems is organized into tracks, which consist of circular rings of recorded data. Each group of tracks in a disk-pack is called a cylinder. Each cylinder is located a fixed distance from the center of the disk. Read/write heads can access only a single cylinder at a time. Most disk-pack systems are specified in terms of access time and number of cylinders.

A more general disk specification which applies to both disk-pack and cartridge-based systems as well as fixed head and/or fixed disk systems includes, in addition to access time, the capacity and transfer rate to and from the minicomputer.

No well-defined parameters exist presently for defining disk capacity. Disk capacity can be computed by multiplying the number of tracks and, in disk-pack systems, the number of cylinders, with the number of bits per track (bpt). The latter number is, of course, found by multiplying the recording density in bits per inch with the length of each track. This number does not, however, tell the whole story. Most disk systems divide the tracks into a number of sectors; some disks use 4 sectors (90° sectoring) and others use 8, 16, or more (45° and 22.5° sectoring). Each sector usually contains a single message block, which, similar to magnetic tape recording, contains a pre- and postamble plus some error-checking bits or characters. Therefore the net capacity is always less than the unformatted, full-track capacity.

The transfer rate is a function of recording density, rotational speed, and the number of tracks accessed in parallel by the electronics. Most specifications quote transfer rates in megabits per second (Mb/s). This must be converted into bytes per second or words per second in order to be able to assess the effect of one or more disks on the loading of the computer and the total system processing speed and throughput. Some disk systems provide limited buffering in the disk controller for proper match of data rates between the disk drive(s) and the minicomputer.

THE CONTROLLER, ERROR RATES, AND SOFTWARE

Most disk controllers contain, in addition to the buffer, several, if not all, of the following features:

- Data address (disk, cylinder, track, sector)
- Sector formatting
- Serial to parallel conversion
- Word count
- Error detection (cyclic redundancy check and parity) and correction
- Read/write control
- Control of two or more drives
- Fast track switching
- Real-time look-ahead

The disk address register is loaded with a number that selects the desired disk unit (if more than one disk drive is used in the system, specific track and sector). In many systems, this register is incremented automatically after each sector has been transferred.

The sector formatter performs a variety of functions and may differ drastically from controller to controller even if the disk drives controlled are identical. The formatter determines the amount of data that can be stored on a disk by defining the number and size of the sectors, the format of the data and error-checking information within each sector, and whether the sector address numbering is staggered or sequential (see Figure 3-29). A staggered organization allows for a certain amount of computation time between single sector data transfers. This compute time is equivalent to the time required by the read/write head to access the proceeding sector. In a sequential organization, the access time is approximately equivalent to a complete disk revolution.

Equal computer page and sector size may be of advantage in systems using a paged minicomputer. In most single-disk, moving head systems, the data are recorded serially and must be converted into the 8-, 12-, or 16-bit parallel words by the controller in order to transfer over the DMA channel.

Cyclic redundancy check (CRC) error detection is typically performed on a block basis, the blocks being randomly addressable. A block is usually equivalent to a sector. Error "correction" typically consists of one or more rereadings of a sector where an error was detected from a parity or CRC.

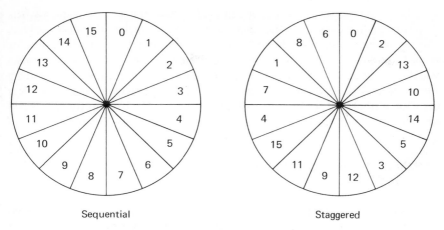

Sequential   Staggered

Figure 3-29 Sequential and staggered sector organization on a disk

About 96% of errors are corrected within three tries. Errors which cannot be "corrected" are termed *nonrecoverable*.

Fast track switching time permits *spiral* read and write. Data may be written in block format, perhaps up to the size of maximum core memory. When the last address on a track or surface has been used, the controller will automatically advance to the next track or the first track of a new disk surface. Many disk specifications include the track-to-track switching time.

Real-time look-ahead permits the minicomputer to continuously monitor the current position of the disk and minimize latency. Systems including this feature use a look-ahead register, which always points to the sector address currently passing under read/write heads. This register also contains the track number and disk drive number.

The disk drive and disk controller are of quite limited value without adequate software. Most disk manufacturers provide a controller and interface for at least one minicomputer, and many of these disk system manufacturers provide some type of disk operating system. The most comprehensive disk software package is, however, usually provided by the minicomputer manufacturer himself, with the purchase of his disk hardware. (For more on disk operating systems and disk software, see Chapter 4.)

RELIABILITY AND MAINTAINABILITY

Error rate, reliability, and maintainability information is seldom called out by the manufacturer, unless the disk or drum is ruggedized. The typical mean time to repair (MTTR) for moving head disks is 2 hr and for fixed head disks $\frac{1}{2}$ hr. MTBF numbers vary widely from disk to disk and are often not even available to the manufacturer.

The most common failures encountered in disk systems are head crashes. A head crash means that the head accidentally touches the disk surface, causing damage to the oxide and making it unusable for further reading or recording. Many disk systems provide a limited number of spare tracks which can be used to replace the damaged tracks. Each time the operating system (see Disk Operating Systems in Chapter 4) detects a nonrecoverable error on a track, this track is "replaced" by one of the backup tracks. When all spare tracks (usually 3–6) have been used up, the disk must be recoated in order to be of further use.

PERFORMANCE CHARACTERISTICS OF VARIOUS BASIC TYPES OF SYSTEMS

Disk and drum systems can be divided into two categories, IBM- and non-IBM-like devices. Minicomputer-interfaced drum memories are generally unique in their design and do not resemble any standard IBM devices. In addition, most head-per-track, fixed disk systems belong to the non-IBM-like device category. The majority of minicomputer disk systems are, however, in the IBM-like category. The latter type of systems can, in turn, be subdivided into several groups:

- Flexible, floppy disks (IBM 3741 Diskette)
- Top- or front-loading disk cartridges
- Disk-packs

The floppy disk was introduced by IBM with their 3330 disk file system. The floppy disk is used by the controller. The original IBM-designed floppy disk stores approximately 80,000 bytes with a per-track transfer rate of 4150 bytes/sec. The IBM disk rotates at 90 rpm. The floppy disk is housed in a plastic cartridge which resembles the cardboard jackets that 45-rpm audio records are sold in. The cartridge is slid into the disk drive, and the disk is rotated inside the cartridge. The read/write head is brought inside the cartridge and moved from track to track by a lead screw, driven by an incremental stepper motor (Figure 3-30). The access time is therefore very slow—more than 1 sec to move the head from track 1 to track 32. Several floppy disk memories are presently available, each successive system with both faster access capability and increased storage capacity.

The earlier versions of the floppy disk perform with error rates of typically 1 bit in 10^{10}, a significant improvement over cassette and cartridge tapes. Some more recently announced floppy disks exceed this number. To achieve better performance capabilities, the head contact with the disk has been eliminated, reducing media wear. One such system, called the Iodisc, manufactured by Iomec Inc., uses a rugged cartridge which contains the

Top View

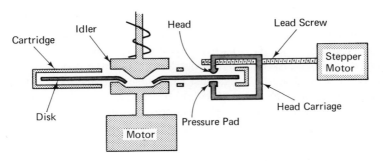

Figure 3-30 The Memorex 650 flexible disc (Courtesy Memorex)

flexible disk. The Iomec disk has a 250,000-character storage capacity, and the average access time has been reduced to 60 msec using higher-bit-density recording, higher rotational speed (1800 rpm versus 90 rpm for the IBM version), and voice-coil-controlled* head positioning. The Iodisc is

* A voice coil consists of a coil of wire inside a permanent magnet. As the coil moves in and out of the magnet, the recording head moves in and out of the disk cartridge the same way a loudspeaker voice coil moves back and forth to generate sound.

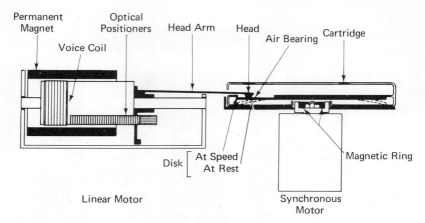

Figure 3-31   Iomec version of IBM floppy disk (Courtesy Iomec, Inc.)

shown in Figure 3-31. Its transfer rate is 150,000 bytes/sec, which exceeds by far that of tape cartridges and many IBM-compatible tape systems.

A unique variation on the floppy disk theme is provided by Diskette.* This system is based on a cartridge containing an evenly tensioned sheet of computer-quality tape in a rigid plastic frame. Unlike the IBM-like floppy disk systems, the Diskette is stationary, while the read/write head is rotated at 400 rpm. The transfer rate is roughly 13,000 bytes/sec, and the capacity of the Diskette cartridge is 124,000 bytes.

The next performance level is represented by the IBM 2315- and 5440-like disk systems. The 2315, used by IBM for the IBM-1800 and 360/44, consists of a single-disk cartridge, front-loaded into the disk drive. Several 2315-like systems use the single-disk cartridge with a fixed single disk mounted underneath the cartridge to double the capacity. Savings in design are achieved by both disks using the same drive shaft and motor. The 2315-like cartridge systems meet with heavy competition from the newer, IBM 5440-like top-loading single-disk cartridge. The 5440 is used by IBM in System/3 and contains more than twice the storage capacity of the 2315. Several top loaders are also available with a second, fixed disk. These cartridge systems store between approximately 1 and 5 million bytes/disk, with transfer rates ranging from 64,000 to more than 200,000 bytes/sec.

Disk-pack systems offer larger storage capacity, faster transfer rates, and, in general, faster access than the disk cartridge memories. Almost without exception, the disk-pack systems are IBM-like, starting at 7.25-million byte capacity such as the disk-pack made for the IBM 2311. The IBM 2314 type

---

* The Diskette is manufactured by the Innovex Corporation, Bedford, Mass. It should not be confused with the IBM 3741 Diskette or floppy disk.

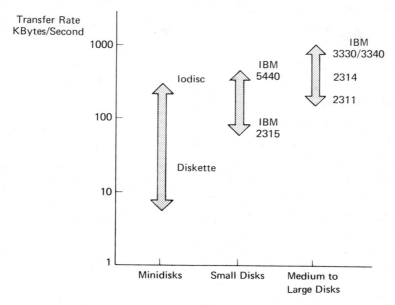

Figure 3-32   Transfer rates in kilobytes for various minicomputer disk systems

of disk-packs provide even higher storage capacity (29.2 million bytes/disk-pack), while the maximum removable disk-pack capacity is presently available with the IBM 3330-like disk. Because of the relatively high cost of the latter device, it is rather seldom used in minicomputer applications. The range of transfer rates and capacities for floppy disks, cartridges, and disk-packs are shown in Figures 3-32 and 3-33, respectively.

The critical factors to be considered in disk selection are too numerous to list on a single page. The application generally dictates the type of disk to be used. Other key factors are cost per bit per second, the availability of DOS software, a minicomputer interface, and system reliability.

3.5 MINICOMPUTER DATA COMMUNICATION EQUIPMENT

The preceding sections have included descriptions of various minicomputer terminals, I/O equipment, and auxiliary storage devices. Most minicomputer systems contain at least one of these units. Based on the particular system requirements, one or more of the peripherals may have to be remoted from the minicomputer. These peripherals may have to be placed in an adjacent room, on a separate floor in the same building, in a location

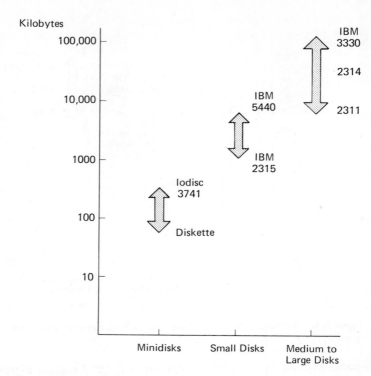

Figure 3-33 Storage capacities in kilobytes of various minicomputer disk cassettes, cartridges, and packs

several hundred feet away, or, perhaps, in another city, state, or even country. Also, the remoted equipment does not necessarily have to be any of the above-described type of peripherals; it could be either a second computer or some type of digital or analog control or sensor. The critical elements in a minicomputer data communications system are therefore the type of remote equipment to be used as well as the distance from the mini-computer the data must be transmitted, the anticipated volume, the traffic pattern, the minimum tolerable error rate, and the reliability of the data link. Each of these factors determines the hardware and software elements required in the system.

Applications, Remote Equipment, and Data Rates

A large number of data communication systems are used for interactive purposes, to retrieve or ask for information from a data base, enter trans-action-oriented data into the remote minicomputer, or enter and output batch data.

In interactive or transaction-oriented applications, the data are entered and received in a *conversational mode*. This means that the operator inputs or requests information from the minicomputer, the data are transmitted to the operator, upon which he, based on the new information output by the computer, makes another input to the computer, etc. The CPU processing time is brief compared to operator response time. The human operator is thus the speed-limiting factor in an interactive terminal. A trained typist can type between 75 and 100 words/min (average word length of five characters plus space). The most commonly used teleprinter equipment is therefore designed to operate at limited bit rates based on input speeds varying from 110 to 300 bps (10 to 30 cps, respectively). Some interactive terminals operate at higher data rates in a buffered mode, where the operator keys in a message which is later transmitted to the minicomputer (Section 3.2).

In batch data entry, a large quantity of data is gradually accumulated on cassette tape, punched cards, or some other machine-readable medium and later sent to the minicomputer. The accumulated data may represent hours or days of local business operations, while the total batch will take minutes to transmit.

In batch data output, the minicomputer may transmit information which is printed out by a line printer at a relatively high data rate. Unbuffered batch input and batch output to and from a miniperipheral is typically performed at 120 cps. Buffered I/O from, for instance, a floppy disk or cassette tape via a CRT terminal can be transmitted at up to 1200 cps (9600 bps).

Transmission Media, Speeds, Methods, and Modes

The common minicomputer data transmission media consist of either serial or parallel hard-wired data links or telephone lines. The most simple method of connecting a terminal to a mini is using a bit-serial 20-mA current loop. This connection can be several hundred feet. The EIA RS-232C bit-serial, hard-wired, point-to-point connection is limited to a maximum of 100 ft. A faster transmission rate can be achieved using either a character or word-wide parallel line. The length of this line is determined by the characteristics of either off-the-shelf or specially designed line drivers. For example, Data General offers a multiprocessor communications adapter (MCA) which makes it possible to connect up to 15 Nova minicomputers of any type into a multiprocessor system. The MCA permits data transfers at 250,000 words/sec up to 75 ft and 150,000 words/sec up to 150 ft.

However, the cost of a parallel, high-speed, intermediate-distance, hardwired connection is usually prohibitive. A 1000 ft-long line can, when installed, easily exceed the cost of the minicomputer, including a fair sized

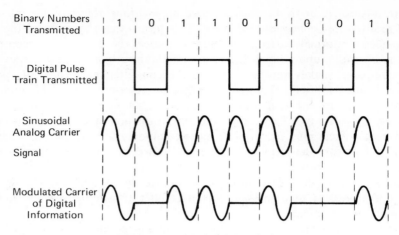

Figure 3-34   Modulation technique

core memory. A more economical approach is to use the bit-serial EIA RS-232C connection to the mini with a so-called base-band modem. When data are transmitted over a long-distance line or the telephone network, it is sent using some form of carrier signal. Perturbations to this carrier or constant "tone" signal are caused by "modulating" the carrier. When these perturbations are changed back into computer-readable binary pulses, this function is called *demodulation*. The word *modem* is a contraction of modulator and demodulator. This principle is illustrated in Figure 3-34. The original digital pulse-train frequency is called the base-band frequency. A base-band modem is therefore not really a modem in the strictest sense of the definition. Base-band or hard-wired modems operate on dedicated solid-conductor, twisted-pair, or coaxial lines and can perform well over distances of several miles. Operating at speeds up to 1 million bps, they are particularly useful for in-plant, on-campus, or military-base installations which use remote terminals and minicomputers.

The public telephone network is the most commonly used transmission medium. It is designed for ordinary voice transmission and makes use of communication channels having bandwidths of approximately 3000 Hz. Dial-up lines are generally limited to line speeds of 3600 to 4800 bps. Higher data rates can be achieved when a telephone line is leased from the telephone company. Modems are presently available which permit transmission rates up to 19,200 bps over leased lines.

The communications path from one point to another, such as from a terminal to a minicomputer, is often denoted a *channel*. This should not be confused with the I/O channel in a minicomputer. A single telephone line is also called a *voice-grade channel*. Channels operating faster than 9600 or

19,200 bps are called wide-band channels. Wide-band channels corresponding to the transmission capabilities of 60 or 240 voice-grade channels are available from Bell System Telephone companies. Wide-band channels operating up to 50,000 bps are called *group-band*. The so called supergroup-band channels, also available from the telephone companies or common carriers, offer transmission rates up to 230,400 bps.

The various data transmission speeds available to the prospective user today are usually separated into three ranges:

Low speed:	0–300 bps	usually used for tele-printers
Medium speed:	600–4800 bps	used for minicomputer to printer or display-type terminals
High speed:	Above 9600 bps	used for computer-to-computer communications

The dividing lines between the various speed ranges are perhaps artificial ones. The lower one may have become an industry-wide notation standard because of the speed ranges of Bell Telephone's Series 100 and Series 200 modems, while the higher one separates the leased line transmission capability from that of the dial-up line. Dial-up lines may presently be used with transmission rates of up to 4800 bps, while lines used for high-speed transmission must be leased.

The speed ranges and data transmission rates are quite often also called *baud* or *baud rates* as well as *bit* or *bit rates*. These units of measurement are often used in an intertwined manner. *Baud* is a word denoting 1 bit of the 5 bits/character sent in the Baudot Code (a five-level code used internationally). *Bit* is a word used as binary digit in the literal sense. Bits include not only those bits sent as parts of a character but also those sent as control information.

In actual usage, baud is also used for denoting the number of times the signaling voltage on the line changes. For those lines with two-stage signaling, such as two voltage levels, or +20-mA and −20-mA currents, *baud rate* has been used to specify bits per second. The terms baud and baud rate with their variety of meanings will not be used further in this book. The reader is cautioned to be wary of those who use baud or baud rate as a measurement of speed, especially in referring to any of the newer modulation techniques.

Since data signals between the minicomputer and the interactive terminal or remote peripherals are time-dependent (i.e., the bits are transmitted at precise time intervals), some means must be provided to ensure synchronization between the transmitting and receiving ends. The most common data transmission methods are *asynchronous* or *start/stop synchronization* and *synchronous transmission*.

Based on the first method, extra signals are transmitted with each character of data to identify the beginning and the end of the character. The data bits within each character are transmitted in a strict time sequence, but characters are transmitted asynchronously. This method allows data transmission from sources with highly irregular data input rates, such as a teleprinter. The probability of cumulative errors in synchronization are minimized in a start/stop transmission method. The disadvantage of this method is that it increases the required line capacity, because of the extra start and stop bits that need to be transmitted along with the data bits.

In the synchronous serial transmission method, a specific character, string of characters, or clock signal is transmitted to the receiving terminal, which interprets the character or characters and adjusts its synchronizing circuitry to conform with the transmitted bit rate. The message is therefore transmitted in block format with one or more synchronizing characters at the beginning and at the end of the block. The advantage of this method is that it permits higher data transmission rates than the start/stop method. The disadvantage is the increase in circuit complexity required to maintain synchronization. Furthermore, one bit time added to or missing from the data bit stream can cause the entire message to be faulty.

As noted above, data transmission channels are usually referred to as low, medium, or high speed. There is, however, another recognized and widely used breakpoint in the range of data transmission speeds. If low-speed data are sent well below the capacity of the channel in bits per second, the equipment can well afford to use the high-overhead, asynchronous method of transmission. The 3-kHz voice-band channels can easily handle 1200-bps asynchronous transmission. However, above this rate, regardless of what modulation technique is used, the channel capacity is strained. Speed ranges exceeding 2000 bps therefore use the more efficient synchronous transmission method. Hence, disregarding medium speed, low and high speed are also often separated in the literature and conversation by the breakpoint at which the data will be transmitted asynchronously or synchronously. The implications of asynchronous versus synchronous transmission on the minicomputer is discussed in Multiplexing, Multiplexers, and the Minicomputer.

There are three basic transmission modes: simplex, half-duplex (HDX), and full duplex (FDX). A simplex line can carry data only in one direction. This mode is usually used with parallel data transmission using Bell System 400 Series data sets. Voice response systems where data or inquiries are transmitted to the computer from a special input keyboard may be simplex in terms of digital transmission; the computer response is an audio message. Some monitoring systems may also use a simplex mode of transmission; the minicomputer functions as a data collection terminal, not taking any direct action regardless of the type of incoming data. Simplex service is, however, no longer available from the common carriers and will therefore not be discussed further in this book.

A half-duplex transmission system is one that is capable of transmission in both directions but that transmits data in only one direction at a given time. This is the most commonly used mode in minicomputer systems, mostly because of cost factors. Dial-up lines, supplied by the common carriers, generally use two-wire circuits. Since two-wire links in most cases limit the data transmission to a half-duplex mode, these are obviously the least expensive available communications channels.

A full-duplex transmission is one capable of simultaneous data transmission in both directions. Most modems can operate either in the HDX or FDX mode, but FDX transmission over a two-wire dial-up line requires the use of two parallel dial-up lines. However, most leased lines are four-wire links and can therefore operate in a FDX mode. Four-wire circuits are also used to connect minicomputers with remote half-duplex terminals, when frequent changes in transmission direction and consequent turnaround delays cannot be tolerated.

Modems, Data Sets, and Acoustic Couplers
TYPES OF MODEMS

As previously mentioned, the 100 and 200 series modems are used to differentiate between low- and medium-speed data transmission, respectively. There are four major types of modems called *data sets* furnished by the common carriers; namely, the 100, 200, 300, and 400 series.*

The 100 series is the most common type of data set that can be attached to voice-grade lines. The 100 series is limited to a maximum data rate of 300 bps. Comparable and compatible replacements which can be either leased or purchased are provided by a host of independent manufacturers. The 100 series data sets are used for asynchronous transmission.

The 200 series data sets, considered medium speed, are used both in asynchronous transmission up to 1800 bps over leased lines and up to 1200 bps over dial-up lines, and synchronous transmission up to 7200 bps over leased lines and 3600 bps over dial-up lines.

The 300 series data sets are used with high-speed or wide-band transmission up to 460.8K-bps synchronous service.

The 400 series is a parallel tone data set which enables tones to be received or transmitted in parallel. The touch-tone phone may be used as a remote

---

* Other types of data sets such as the 600 series used for facsimile transmission and the 800 series automatic calling data auxiliary sets are omitted since they are not used in minicomputer applications.

Figure 3-35   ITT's portable Asciscope CRT terminal with a built-in
coupler (Courtesy ITT Data Equip. and Systems Div.)

terminal, generating tones which are compatible to these data sets which
transmit and receive up to 75 characters/sec. The 402C and 402D data sets
transmit bit-parallel, using frequency division multiplexing at 75 characters
per sec. The 402A and B operate at 20 cps.

Data sets from the common carriers can only be leased, while independent
makers will either sell or lease their units. If a non-telephone-company
modem is used on a dial-up line, the user must use a telephone-company-
installed protective device called a data access arrangement (DAA) for which
the phone company charges a few dollars a month. This device is not required on leased lines, where the user can lease a data set or use a modem
made ·by an independent manufacturer, directly coupled to the line.

If the user wants immediate access to the dial-up line, he can use an
acoustic coupler. This device permits the interface of terminals to the
telephone line using a telephone handset. The majority of available couplers
operate at bit rates up to 300 bps, although one or two couplers can transmit
and receive at 1200 bps. The trend is presently to provide couplers as an
integral part of both portable teleprinters and CRT terminals (Figure 3-35).

ERROR CONTROL AND DATA EFFICIENCY

The dial-up line is generally the weakest link in a minicomputer system
where error rates of 1 bit/10^5 are quite usual. Furthermore, the higher the

transmission rate is over voice-grade lines, the greater the probability of errors. One of the most important factors in minicomputer systems using data communication facilities is data efficiency. Data efficiency is equivalent to the net data throughput, or the useful number of bits transmitted per second. Net data throughput is a function of the size of each block being transmitted, error probability, error control, and line turnaround time on dial-up lines.

Transmission errors on phone lines result from lightning; relay switching noise; electrical machinery; rain, which may cause moisture to accumulate in telephone cables; and even wind, which may cause microwave transmitter antennas temporarily to get out of alignment. Errors usually occur in a burst mode.

The most primitive method of error correction is based on redundant transmission, or a repeat transmission of each message, where the receiving end compares the two messages. This comparison may be performed by the operator as well as the minicomputer. If a mismatch is found, retransmission is requested.

Teleprinter transmission is often based on *echoplexing*, where a character transmitted from a keyboard terminal to a minicomputer is recognized and retransmitted to the keyboard terminal, where it is subsequently printed (Figure 3-36). Echoplex transmission is usually used only in interactive applications involving a human operator and asynchronous transmission.

In synchronous transmission, a terminal usually contains a buffer in

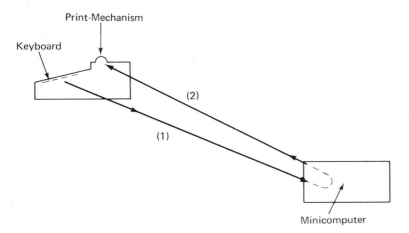

Figure 3-36 In "Echoplex" transmission, a key at the keyboard is depressed, and the desired character is transmitted to the minicomputer (step 1) and echoed back to the printing device in the teleprinter terminal (step 2).

which each character or word includes a parity bit. Data transmission is performed in character blocks, where each block, in addition to a parity bit per byte or word, also include longitudinal parity or what is called longitudinal redundancy checking (LRC). The LRC check consists of a final character transmitted at the end of a message to check message parity. The transmitted LRC character is compared in the receiving minicomputer with a computed parity check character. If the computed character matches with the transmitted LRC character, a positive acknowledgment (ACK) is sent back to the terminal. This acknowledgment will also initiate the transfer of the next block of data. If a mismatch exists, a negative acknowledgment (NAK) is returned to the transmitter, which initiates a retransmission of the same block. This ACK-NAK procedure, often called *automatic request for repeat* (ARQ), is commonly used with methods other than the LRC method.

Cyclic redundancy checking (CRC) used with synchronous communications is more efficient for higher-speed transmission than the VRC/LRC* combination because parity is not required with each character. The CRC is typically a two-character sequence that is transmitted at the end of each block in the same manner as the LRC character.

The net data throughput, therefore, depends on the number of times retransmission of each block is required, as well as on the overhead imposed by the various parity- or error-checking characters. Additional delay is also imposed by half-duplex line turnaround time. When a two-wire transmitter is turned off, a transient (noise pulse) is generated which is reflected back to the transmitter for up to the round-trip time delay of the circuit. To protect the demodulator from recovering the transient noise as data, a clamp circuit causes the demodulator to be squelched against (turned off) all signals for a short period, typically 150 ± 25 msec. It is generally impractical to attempt to optimize the turnaround time on a dial-up line because of the mix of facilities and large variations in propagation delay.

The net data throughput is best illustrated by the fact that a 1000-bit block at 4800 bps will take about 200 msec to transmit, while the turn around delay is approximately 300 msec. The net throughput is therefore only approximately 2000 bps. With the typical error rate of 1 in 10^5, statistically every tenth message will require retransmission. The transmission and turnaround periods are shown in Figure 3-37.

Assuming a single error in every tenth block, the net throughput is even less—approximately 10,000 bits in 5.5 sec or 1800 bps. The data efficiency in this example is therefore only 37.5%. Increased modem speed usually also increases the inherent error rate. The present state-of-the-art 19,200-bps

---

* VRC (vertical redundancy checking) provides an even or odd parity bit to each character; LRC (longitudinal redundancy checking) provides an extra character for each block, where each bit is either an even or odd parity bit for the corresponding bit column in the block.

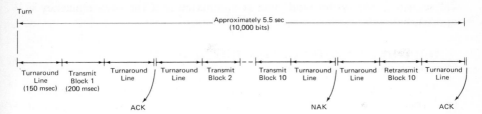

Figure 3-37 ACK-NAK transmission of 10 blocks with retransmission of 1 block

modem operates with a 10^{-3} error rate (one error per 1000 bits). At 14,400 bps, this modem* achieves an error rate of 10^{-5}. The data efficiency typically increases initially with increased block length and net data throughput, up to a typical block size of 10,000 bits and 3600 bps. Further increase in block size will result in decreased throughput (Figure 3-38).

The superiority of four-wire leased-line FDX operation is best illustrated using the same example: The transmission of 10,000 characters, assuming a 10^{-5} error rate and using a 4800-bps modem, is reduced to approximately

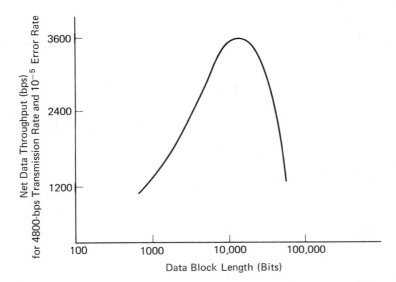

Figure 3-38 Net data throughout in bps versus data block length in bits (HDX transmission) (From "Data Communications Systems: Basics of Network Design" by Dixon R. Doll, McGraw-Hill *Electronics Deskbook Communications Systems,* McGraw-Hill Book Company, New York, 1972.) Copyright by McGraw-Hill Inc. 1972; all rights reserved.

* Honeywell Vodat Data Modem.

2.2 sec since line turnaround time is eliminated and the data efficiency is approximately 95%.

MODEM EQUALIZATION AND OTHER FEATURES

The line characteristics for randomly routed calls vary significantly in terms of electrical parameters. This factor is important in that it affects the performance characteristics and, with it, error rates for modems

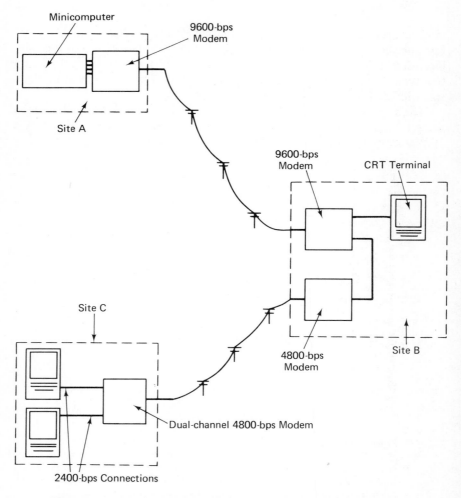

Figure 3-39   Multiport modems are used to drop off channels to various local terminals at sites B and C from the mini at site A.

which do not compensate for these inconsistencies of the transmission medium. To compensate for variable line conditions, most high-speed modems provide an equalization capability. In lower-speed modems, equalization is fixed and nonadjustable; higher-speed modems provide a manual equalization capability; the truly high-performance modems feature automatic equalization. The automatic equalization time may add to the turnaround time in systems using dial-up lines. Short block messages requiring frequent turnaround may severely penalize the system in terms of line efficiency, even to the point where the user may be better off using a lower-speed modem which does not require automatic equalization. For a significant savings in cost, he can thus achieve the identical throughput.

In addition to modem equalization, a second technique is commonly used to improve the performance characteristics of a channel. This is commonly referred to as line conditioning. Line conditioning is a process by which the phone company maintains the quality of private or leased lines at a guaranteed level. Three levels of equalization are presently available from the phone company, where each level improves the quality of the leased line by increasing the effective bandwidth. The highest level of line conditioning is approximately six times as expensive as the lowest level of conditioning.

Most of the high-speed modems include built-in diagnostic features, such as self-test and remote test. Self-test will allow the user to determine whether the modem is operating properly, while remote testing, such as *loopback*, permits checkout of the remote line.

Several high-speed modems offer a *multiporting* capability, which allows

1. Technical characteristics	Transmission speed
	Required type of line conditioning
	Equalizer: fixed, manual, automatic, HDX
	and FDX capability
	Turnaround times; receive-to-transmit and
	transmit-to-receive
	Error-rate performance
	Can be operated at several bit rates
	Multiporting
	Data plus voice option
2. Maintenance	Built-in diagnostic capability
	Self-test and loopback
3. Reliability and other features	MTBF
	For couplers only:
	Rejection of background noise
	Portability
	Compatibility with all telephone handsets
	Compatibility with common carrier data sets

Figure 3-40 Checklist for modems and acoustic couplers

a user to save a lot of line charges by using a single device such as a 9600-bps modem to handle two or four data channels (Figure 3-39). The multi-ported modem typically concentrates a limited number of high-speed channels, while the so-called multiplexers concentrate a large number of low-speed channels (see the following section).

The modem selection must be made in the context of the total system, including the terminal, dial-up or leased line, and the minicomputer with its interface. Some factors that influence the selection are transmission mode, data rates, allowable error rates, and diagnostic features. Some of the more important modem selection criteria are summarized in a checklist in Figure 3-40.

Multiplexing, Multiplexers, and the Minicomputer

As recalled from the discussion of minicomputer I/O, the data to and from the mini may be either under program control, typically one word at the time, or through a high-speed DMA channel. Bit-serial telecommunication is usually performed using the former type of I/O facility, because of the relatively slow transfer rates. Note that the typical teleprinter transfer rate of 110 bps is equivalent to 5 16-bit words/sec and that even what is defined as high speed in telecommunications, such as the 9600-bps rate, is still equivalent to only 600 16-bit words/sec. This is obviously very slow compared to both the typical DMA transfer rates of between 500,000 and 1 million words/sec, as well as the program-controlled transfer rates, which often exceed 50,000 words/sec. To match the low input rates from local and remote, medium- and low-speed peripherals, most minicomputers provide an internal multiplexing channel, which, in some minis, can handle up to 256 peripherals, time-sharing the CPU. In applications requiring several low-speed remote terminals, even the use of a single multiplex channel port may prove to be inefficient. Some minicomputers therefore provide an asynchronous data communications multiplexer, which can control the transmission of a large number of low-speed, asynchronous lines (Figure 3-41).

The use of the asynchronous data communications multiplexer saves hardware cost in the minicomputer when the crossover point between the cost of several single-line controllers and the multiplexer is exceeded. This varies from minicomputer to minicomputer, depending on the number of lines the multiplexer can control, the particular machine architecture, etc.

Multiplexing is also used externally to the minicomputer to save line costs. By means of multiplexing, one high-speed link can carry the same amount of traffic that several low-speed ones could handle without it. The cost trade-offs in this case are between the cost of additional modems and the multiplexers and the cost of additional lines. Other factors that enter into the trade-off consideration are the geography of the network and the time and frequency of the respective line use.

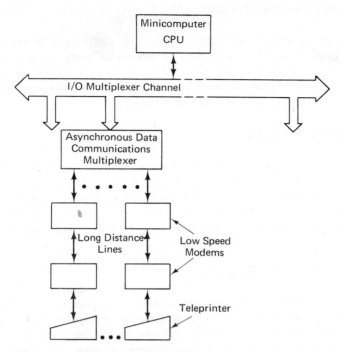

Figure 3-41 Minicomputer-asynchronous communications multiplexer, remote terminal network

The selection of a multiplexer is thus based on the following factors:

- Mixed- or single-terminal bit rate
- Dial-up or leased lines
- Channel capacity
- Method of multiplexing
- Type of system
- Special features

MIXED- OR SINGLE-TERMINAL BIT RATE

In contrast to most of the internal minicomputer asynchronous data communications multiplexers, which limit the bit rates of terminals or lines connected to them to a single bit rate, several of the *external* multiplexers permit the *mixing* of terminal rates. Many of these multiplexers mix data rates, such as 110 bps for Model 33 Teletypes, 134.5 bps for IBM Selectric-like terminals, and 150 bps for Model 37 Teletypes.

DIAL-UP OR LEASED LINES

Dial-up or leased line requirements are, as previously mentioned, a function of required throughput. Some multiplexers include a built-in modem which may perform poorly over nonconditioned dial-up lines. If high speed is mandatory, the user should consider the use of separate modems and multiplexers to maximize his net throughput.

CHANNEL CAPACITY

The channel capacity is a function of the maximum bit rate that the multiplexor is capable of operating at. The multiplexer bit rate operating capability varies between a maximum of 2400 and 9600 bps, depending on make and manufacturer. A 9600-bps capability will typically allow the use of a maximum of 58 terminals based on a mix of 110-, 134.5- and 150-bps terminals.

METHOD OF MULTIPLEXING

The two most widely used methods of multiplexing are time division multiplexing (TDM) and frequency division multiplexing (FDM). TDM can be visualized as a system of several sources and their receivers connected to corresponding contacts of synchronous rotating distributors at two channel terminals. Each terminal is allocated a time slot which is recognized and sorted out at the remote TDM receiver. Consequently, in a TDM system, each character is converted from an asynchronous to a synchronous state as several parallel low-speed channels are merged into a single high-speed serial data stream. For transmission over telephone lines, the high-speed serial data is modulated/demodulated at the respective multiplexer terminal.

The high-speed data may be either bit or character interleaved. Bit interleaving requires data formatting into blocks with the addition of internal *framing* information to ensure that channel identity will be maintained at the receiver. Character interleaving requires the transmission of a periodic sync character. Synchronization is therefore maintained between each terminal scan cycle.

The bit-interleaved multiplexer stores a maximum of only 1 low-speed channel bit at the input and 1 bit at the output multiplexer terminal. The channel propagation delay is consequently held to a minimum. However, loss of synchronization may result in the loss of several characters. The loss of synchronization in the character-interleaved system will result in the loss of only a single character from each terminal. The main disadvantage of the bit-interleaved method lies in the fact that only one bit rate can be used.

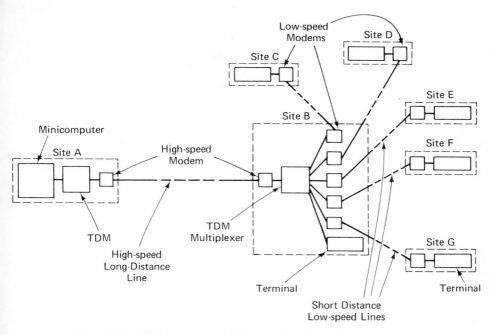

Figure 3-42 Minicomputer-terminal network, using TDM multiplexers

In the FDM technique, the frame reference is the bandwidth of the communication channel itself. This is divided into a number of independent data channels separated by guard bands. TDM is therefore more efficient than the FDM since a considerable amount of bandwidth is wasted in FDM in order to separate the low-speed channels.

If a large number of terminals are required, FDM is more costly than TDM and should therefore be avoided unless the system configuration dictates the use of it. The cost crossover point is approximately at eight channels.

Since FDM is based on a simultaneous transmission of several low-speed channels, no frame synchronization is required. Furthermore, FDM can be used in a multipoint system.

Shown in Figure 3-42, the minicomputer at site A is connected to remote site B over a high-speed line operating at data rates of 4800 or 9600 bps. At the remote site, the multiplexed lines are distributed to other remote sites in the vicinity of site B. These sites, C, D, E, F, and G, including site B, may be within the same city or state, on the East Coast, while site A is on the West Coast.

In networks where *clustering* is less pronounced, the alternative to TDM

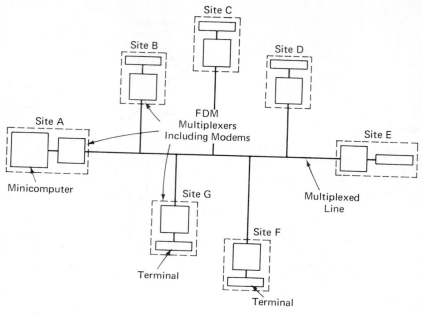

Figure 3-43 Minicomputer-terminal network, using FDM multiplexers

may be an FDM-based system. In this case, distances between the minis and their respective terminals are of the same magnitude. Since in FDM each line has a continuous appearance within the multiplexed channel, high-speed modems, as indicated in the TDM configuration, are not used. Modems, in a FDM system, are, however, still used between the minicomputer and the multiplexer and between each remote multiplexer and the respective terminal. These modems are thus of the low-speed type. In fact, some FDM equipment includes the low-speed modems in the multiplexers for the respective channels. A typical FDM-based system is shown in Figure 3-43. The main advantages of FDM over TDM are its insensitivity to the mixing of codes, the possible mixing of asynchronous and synchronous transmission, and the reduced number of modems required in a system. The *multidrop* capability is, however, not unique to FDM but is also available, in a limited sense, in TDM-based systems.

TDM-based multidropping is achieved through *line splitting*. A high-speed channel can be split into a smaller line capacity channel, as shown in Figure 3-44. Here a 4800-bps line is split into a 2400-bps line and again, a second time, into a 1200-bps line. At each split, a smaller multiplexer and lower-speed modems are used to distribute the line.

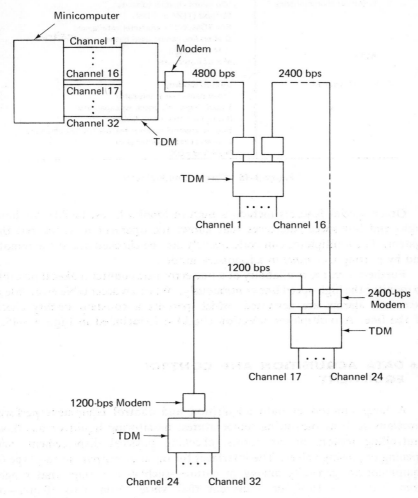

Figure 3-44 Minicomputer-remote terminal network, using TDM and line splitting

SPECIAL FEATURES

As previously indicated, modems are required between FDM terminals, since each low-speed signal is modulated at its specific *carrier* frequency. However, some TDM systems also include a modem with the multiplexer unit. This is generally a disadvantage, since the user does not have the option of using an available modem, or of leasing a modem from the telephone company.

1. Technical characteristics	Maximum channel capacity
	Method (TDM or FDM)
	For TDM; bit or character interleaved
	Dial-up line can be used between multiplexer terminals
	Mix of input rates
2. Special features	Built-in modem
	Front panel status indicator
	Visual diagnostic checking capability
	Built-in loopback test facility
	Built-in channel lockout feature for test checking
	Line error rate counter alarm
	HDX and FDX

Figure 3-45   Checklist multiplexers

Other special features include a built-in loopback test facility for both high- and low-speed interfaces that allows the operator to check out the system. The multiplexer can consequently also be checked out at the remote end by putting a channel in a loopback mode.

Furthermore, the availability of a line error rate counter makes it possible to monitor the high-speed line continuously. When an acceptable error rate is exceeded, alarms are activated, which permits a constant quality check of the line. A multiplexer selection checklist is included in Figure 3-45.

3.6 DATA ACQUISITION AND CONTROL EQUIPMENT

A large amount of data acquisition and control equipment perform functions such as measuring temperatures, monitoring liquid or gas flow, controlling motors or generators, checking physical displacement, and opening or closing valves. The interfaces for input or outputs to this type of equipment are generally analog in nature—such as a voltage that ranges from $+10$ to -10 V, or a current that varies from 0 to 10 mA—or digital in terms of a relay, where the relay contact closed represents a 1 and the contact open represents a 0.

Analog-to-digital (A-D) converters are therefore used to input the analog information to the minicomputer, and, similarly, digital-to-analog (D-A) converters are used to convert the digital output from the mini-computer into an analog voltage or current. A special form of D-A and A-D converters used in angle control of motors and rotating shafts is called synchros. Synchro-to-digital (S-D) and digital-to-synchro (D-S) converters, unlike A-D and D-A converters, are not available as off-the-shelf products from commercial minicomputer manufacturers. However, since this type of interface is commonly used in navigational and aircraft control systems, several airborne "minicomputers" provide S-Ds and D-Ss as standard "off-the-shelf" hardware.

Several minicomputer manufacturers offer as standard equipment relay registers, which can be used to provide an output voltage of perhaps 100 V, or a current of $\frac{1}{2}$ A. A typical application of this type of device is to provide a large number of voltages, under program control, from an external power supply.

Characteristics of A-D and D-A Converters

A-D converters are found at all interfaces between sensors of physical quantities and minicomputer equipment. In spite of this, little or no standardization exists, and, worse yet, the diversity in nomenclature and error definition makes it very difficult to make any reasonable comparisons between various pieces of equipment. Many users therefore approach the problem of A-D equipment selection by limiting themselves to converters provided by the minicomputer manufacturer. The key parameters to be considered are the number of inputs, resolution, accuracy, number of samples per second per input channel (or conversion time in microseconds), and the analog input voltage range.

Minicomputers, such as the Nova, provide converters which are either unmultiplexed or multiplexed. The unmultiplexed converter consists of a single analog channel which is typically supplied with either $+5$- or $+10$-V input ranges and a resolution of either 8, 10, 12, or 14 bits.* The conversion time is typically 10 to 20 μsec for 10 bits and up to 100 μsec for 14 bits. Conversion rates in the 1-to-5-μsec range with converters providing more than a 14-bit accuracy generally represent state-of-the-art performance and, if required in a system, must be interfaced by the user himself. The cost breakpoint for A-D converters occurs at a 12-bit accuracy. The price will usually increase drastically above this accuracy.

Multiplexed A-D converters can handle a large number of analog input channels (32 channels for the Nova and the PDP-11). The conversion time for multiplexed A-D converters is slightly longer than for unmultiplexed converters.

The A-D converter is usually a D-A converter with suitable feedback. The parameters used for A-D converters also apply to D-A converters. Both A-D and D-A converters exhibit drift over a period of time and must therefore be recalibrated. A common recalibration interval is 6 months.

---

* Resolution refers to the minimum voltage step that can be converted. A 10-bit resolution means that for a 10-V input range, 1 part in 2^{10} ($= 1024$), or a minimum of approximately 0.01 V can be resolved. This is approximately 0.1 % of full scale or a 0.1 % accuracy.

Characteristics of Contact Closure Devices

Contact closure devices are often made available as complete modules which provide a general-purpose relay-buffered data link between special external devices and the minicomputer.

In the relay-buffered input configuration, input relay contacts are activated by voltages from the user's equipment through an input relay coil. An energized input relay coil closes a contact that is gated into a 12- or 16-bit register, which, in turn, can be accessed by the computer program.

The relay output module permits isolated parallel transfer of a 12- or 16-bit word from a register in the mini via relay contacts to the user's equipment. The relay contacts typically remain closed until the register is cleared or reset.

Important parameters in this case are contact ratings (resistive and maximum voltage), operating and release time (typically 1 msec), and I/O drive requirements. Output drive usually relates to the electronic ratings of the output circuit in the minicomputer. Similarly, input drive relates to the maximum voltage and current ratings of the receiving electronics in the minicomputer input interface.

Semi-custom-made Interface Equipment

Most minicomputers include in their product line various types of interface cards that can be used to tailor special nonstandard devices used in applications involving on-line production testing, lab design work, instrumentation measurements for computer analysis, etc. Typically, these interface modules include storage registers and control and interrupt logic, plus

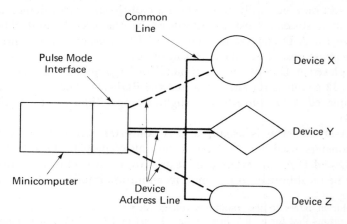

Figure 3-46 Pulse mode operation, showing common line and device address lines to X, Y, and Z

various control lines which can be used under program control using assembly language (see Chapter 4). Ofter these modules provide space for mounting whatever extra circuitry is required to handle the idiosyncracies of the particular external device.

Several minicomputer manufacturers provide the user with a large selection of these types of building blocks. Cards are available that permit combined I/O operations, pulse mode operation, and direct memory access operations. Combined I/O operation interface cards allow the user, for instance, to interface a nonstandard printer to the mini, where data are transferred through an output register to the printer, while printer status information is read back into an input register. In the pulse mode of operation, data lines may be shared by several devices, and data can appear at the output of the interface module for a certain period only through the use of various encoded lines. The desired device can be alerted to information appearing on the common line, which is uniquely addressed to it (Figure 3-46). Interface modules permitting DMA operations can handle, for example, inputs from nonstandard A-D converters or outputs to telemetry command links at high data rates.

REFERENCES

BURNETTE, K. T., "Evaluating the Man-Display Interface," *The Electronic Engineer*, July 1972, 64–67.

CUSHMAN, R. H., "Digital Cassettes . . . Growing Like Wonderful Weeds," *EDN/ EEE*, February 1, 1972, 28–35.

DAVIS, S., "Selection Criteria for A-D and D-A Converters," *Computer Design*, September 1972, 67–79.

———, "Digital Cassette and Cartridges Today," *Computer Design*, January 1973, 59–71.

DOVE, R. K., "Grow Your Own Minicomputer Systems," *Computer Decisions*, December 1972, 26–31.

FEIDELMAN, L. A., "The Low Cost OCR," *Modern Data*, February 1971, 32–33.

FORSBERG, R. W., "Printout Devices—The Computer's Eyes and Ears," *EDN*, December 1, 1972, 20–27.

GRAY, P. J., "Optical Readers and OCR," *Modern Data*, January 1971, 66–82.

GREENBLATT, S., "360/370—Compatible Peripherals, Part I—Tape, Disk and Main Memory," *Modern Data*, August 1972, 46–56.

HIMMELFARB, M., "Digital Tape Recorders, A State-of-the-Art Survey," *Digital Design*, October 1972, 16–29.

HOLLAND, E. (ed.), "Minicomputer I/O and Peripherals," *IEEE Computer Group News*, July/August 1970, 10–14.

KAMMAN, A. B., "How to Pick CRT Terminals," *Data Processing Magazine*, April 1971, 41–45.

KARP, H. R., *Deskbook, Data Communications Systems*, Vol. 1, No. 1, McGraw-Hill Book Company, New York, 1972.

KAYE, D. N., "Focus on Disc and Drum Memories," *Electronic Design 10*, May 11, 1972, C16–C24.

KRAFT, R., and T. HORNSBY, "360/370—Compatible Peripherals, Part II—Data Communications Terminals," *Modern Data*, September 1972, 38–46.

LYMAN, J., "The Digital Cassette Recorder—An Adopted Whiz Kid," *Electronic Products Magazine*, October 16, 1972, 56–61.

MURPHY, J. A., "Punched Card Equipment," *Modern Data*, January 1972, 52–56.

MURPHY, W. J., "Mag Tape Systems, Part 1," *Modern Data*, July 1971, 32–46.

———, "Magnetic Tape Systems, Part II—IBM Compatible Transports," *Modern Data*, August 1971, 48–57.

N.A., "Input-Output Devices—Part III How to Evaluate Hard-Copy Trade Offs," *The Data Communications User*, August 1972, 17–19.

OTTERSON, W. W., "The New Cassette Standard," *Datamation*, September 1972, 54–55.

PETERS, J., "Need a Hard-Copy Peripheral?," *Electronic Design*, September 18, 1972, 54–60.

RILEY, W. B., "The Technology Gap Starts to Close for Computer Peripherals," *Electronics*, July 31, 1972, 59–74.

ROSENBAUM, P. L., "Minicomputer Add-On Memory," *Modern Data*, February 1972, 43–44.

SAVIERS, G., "The Minicomputer and the Engineer—Part 5 (Peripherals Expand Your Mini's Capabilities)," *Electronic Design*, June 10, 1971, 72–76.

STIEFEL, M. L., "Digital Plotter Terminals and Systems," *Modern Data*, September 1971, 48–57.

———, and J. A. MURPHY, "Teleprinters," *Modern Data*, May 1971, 66–76.

TALBOT, J. E., "The Human Side of Data Input," *Data Processing Magazine*, April 1971, 28–35.

WEITZMAN, C., "Performance Evaluation of Interactive Alphanumeric Displays," *Document TM-4278*, System Development Corporation, Santa Monica, Calif., January 1970.

4

MINICOMPUTER SOFTWARE AND PROGRAMMING

4.1 FUNDAMENTAL PROCEDURES AND BUILDING BLOCKS

In the preceding chapters minicomputers and miniperipherals have been discussed in terms of functional design and performance characteristics. To understand the total system from an operational point of view, some of the procedural, computer-loading, and programming steps must be explained. Basic software terminology, as well as hardware-related items such as minicomputer front panel switches and peripheral device control, may seem confusing to the uninitiated. A short hands-on learning period will usually overcome this initial confrontation problem. To the first-time user, the loading procedure in itself may seem more complex than it really is, unless he understands the significance of each step. When the appropriate software is loaded into the computer, the hardware will become transparent to the programmer, and he can interact with the system from a keyboard terminal without concerning himself with switches, buttons, lights, or other hardware-related controls.

The Loading Procedure

As explained in Chapter 2, all minicomputer instructions are stored in memory in binary encoded form. In principle, it is possible to manually load a program or sequence of instructions into memory from the front panel, setting each bit in a word and loading one word at a time. However, from a practical standpoint, this method is extremely tedious. Even a short subroutine of some 15 to 20 instructions will take several minutes, including error checks to assure that the proper bit settings have been made for each word. The initial program loading is therefore performed in two steps.

The first 15 to 20 instructions are keyed in manually from the front panel. This short instruction sequence will subsequently instruct the computer to read in the remainder of the loading routine, typically stored on paper tape. The short, manually loaded subroutine is usually called a *bootstrap loader*. To speed up the initial loading process, the bootstrap loader is also available as a wired-in option, consisting of a hardware ROM, which contains the bootstrapping instructions. This feature allows the user to load the bootstrap loader simply by flicking a switch or pushing a button on the front panel. Both the bootstrap and paper tape loaders are in purely binary form. The latter is therefore also called the *binary loader*.*

When a ROM is available in the mini, the user is thus spared from having to perform the following sequence of operations:

1. Load the initial address of bootstrap program into the address register using the front panel switches. The contents of this address register can usually be examined from the front panel.
2. Use the switches to key in the first bootstrap instruction into the address location specified in step 1.
3. Push the deposit switch. (The first address location and instruction of the bootstrap loader can now be verified in octal or hexadecimal notation, as indicated by the front panel lights on the mini.)
4. Deposit the next instruction in the bootstrap loader subroutine repeating steps 2 and 3. (The next address location does not, have to be inserted manually, since the contents of the address register are automatically incremented by 1.†)
5. When the end of the list of bootstrap instructions is reached, the bootstrap instructions are executed and the binary loader can be loaded from the paper tape reader. The initial address location of the binary loader program must, however, first be specified by setting the front panel switches to appropriate positions.

Several minicomputer manufacturers provide the user with a combination binary load/dump program. The dump program allows the user to prepare a paper tape containing the binary contents of memory. This tape can later also be used by the binary loader. The binary loader tape is usually divided into equal-sized blocks. Each block contains a checksum character. The checksum character is usually a logical binary sum of the characters or words

---

* The binary loader loads one complete module or program into the computer and makes it ready to run.

† In the Data General Nova this is accomplished only when a *deposit next* switch is pressed.

in the block. The calculated checksum is compared with the checksum on the paper tape. If a discrepancy is detected, the binary loader will halt. The user must now return the tape to the previous start-of-block position to reread the block in which the error occurred. If more than one or two errors are encountered during the loading of the binary tape, an error exists in the binary loader program.

The binary loader is usually loaded via a teletype or a high-speed paper tape reader. A typical minicomputer binary loader includes the following error-checking features:

- Parity checking of each byte
- Use of one or more checksum characters in each block on the tape

The main task of the binary loader is to load various programs into the minicomputer memory. Since most minicomputers contain a limited amount of memory, the loader is used quite frequently during software development. The same memory space is therefore used both for creating applications software and, later, prior to execution, for storing the applications program or programs as well as data.

From Source to Object Tape

As previously indicated, loading of binary computer instructions from the front panel, one word at a time, is a slow and error-prone process and therefore is performed only for the relatively short bootstrap loader. However, the writing of programs in binary code is an even more tedious, if not hopeless, task. Minicomputer manufacturers therefore provide the programmer with mnemonics, which typically consist of a limited number of letters that signify a specific operation or location in memory. These mnemonics are considerably easier to work with than various bit patterns or binary codes. An example of a mnemonic is given in The Instruction Repertoire in Chapter 2 to demonstrate a typical loading instruction, in this case "load accumulator A with the contents of memory location E" or LDA. These mnemonics, also called *symbols* or *symbolic codes*, mean different things for different minis. The programmer can assemble or write his program using a Teletype by typing in symbolic code, one *source statement* at a time, in *source language*. The assembler program is loaded into memory using the binary loader. The assembler, once stored, will translate the symbolic instructions, also one statement at a time, into binary machine code, called *object code*. After being stored, object code is executed by the computer, also one statement at a time.

Each source statement usually consists of some of these four items of information:

1. Label (optional)
2. Operation code
3. Operand or variable field
4. Comment field (optional)

The label or name is used when needed as a reference by other statements. The label may define a location in the program, a name of a common storage element, a data storage area, or a constant. Each label is unique within the program; two or more statements may not have the same symbolic label.

The operation code or operation field contains the instruction OP code, such as ADD, STORE, LDA, and JMP, or actual data. OP codes are discussed extensively in Chapter 2.

The operand or variable field may contain an expression consisting of a character, an integer,* a number, a special symbol,† or any of these, combined with arithmetic operators such as + for addition or / for division. The meaning and format of the operand or variable field depends on the type of operation code used in the source statement. Often, minicomputer assemblers require the symbol used in the operand field to be a symbol that is defined elsewhere in the program, either as a label in the label field or as a name in the operand field. Exceptions to this are quite common, however; and several assemblers permit the programmer to designate a register as well as an address without defining the register elsewhere in the program.

An example of a typical source program is shown in Figure 4-1. The assembler maintains a location counter which it uses to assign consecutive memory addresses to the object code of source statements. As statements are read by the assembler, a *symbol table* is generated. This table contains every symbol in the source program and the current value of the location counter when the symbol is encountered by the assembler in its process of translating the source program. The symbol table for the source program listed in Figure 4-1 is shown in Figure 4-2.

To facilitate the writing of the source program, a standard coding form is often used. This form consists of 80 columns, where the label, operation, and operand fields as well as comments area are each assigned a predetermined number of columns (Figure 4-3). When the statements are typed on the Teletype, the same general format is adhered to.

---

* An integer is a string of numerals, specifying a nonfractional value.

† Symbols may be a numeric, predefined value or instruction mnemonic, telling the assembler to perform a specific operation. (Purely operational symbols are often called *pseudo-OPS*.)

Name or Label	OP Code or Operation	Operand	Comment
	ORG	X'100'	SET THE LOCATION COUNTER
BEGIN	LHI	2,TOP	TOP OF DATA TABLE
	LHI	3,2	HALFWORD INCREMENT
	LHI	4,BOTTOM	BOTTOM OF DATA TABLE
	LHI	10,15	SEARCH VALUE OF 15
LOOK	CLH	10,0(2)	COMPARE
	BE	FINI	BRANCH ON EQUAL TO FINI
	BXLE	2,LOOK	NOT FOUND GO LOOK FURTHER
FINI	LPSW	WAIT	STOP THE PROGRAM
WAIT	DC	X'8000',A(BEGIN)	
TOP	DS	1000	
BOTTOM	DS	2	
	END	BEGIN	

Figure 4-1 Typical source program containing 13 source statements (Courtesy Interdata, *Model 70 User's Manual*, p. 11–17). Note that one of the two numbers in some of the operand statements represents a register address, while the other number represents a value.)

Once the source program is entered, it can be translated by the assembler into an *object program* for execution on the computer. However, before assembly can be performed, the assembler program must be loaded into the computer memory. The minimum equipment required for assembler use is usually a minicomputer with 4K memory and an ASR Teletype. Where memory is at premium, an *absolute assembler* is generally used. The memory address calculated by this assembler for every source program address field is always fixed at the same memory address and cannot be altered without reassembling the source program.

Similarly, the binary loader, used for the absolute assembler, can also be absolute. Programs loaded by the absolute loader will execute only in one area of memory.

Symbol	Value of Location Counter (in hexadecimal)
BEGIN	0100
BOTTOM	050C
FINI	011C
LOOK	0110
TOP	0124
WAIT	0120

Figure 4-2 Symbol table for the source program shown in Figure 4-1 (Courtesy Interdata)

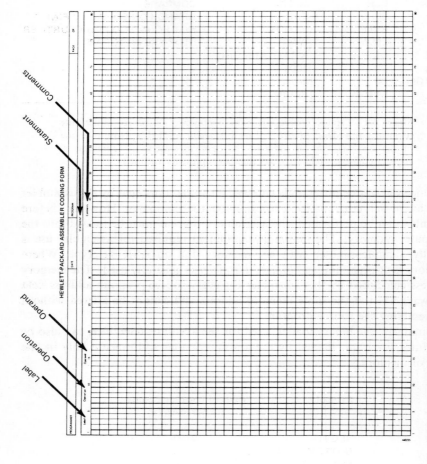

Figure 4-3 Sample coding form from *A Pocket Guide to Hewlett-Packard Computers*, p. 2–2. The actual size of this form is $11 \times 13\frac{1}{2}$ inches. (Courtesy Hewlett-Packard Corp.)

Greater flexibility can be achieved using a *linking loader*. The linking loader,* also called a relocatable loader, requires slightly more memory space than the absolute loader but can load a program in any area of memory and modify the addresses into absolute addresses as it loads. Thus, when a program previously loaded at a specific starting address is moved to a different starting address in memory, the linking loader will automatically relocate all data referenced by the individual program instructions, thereby remapping the program in memory.

Even when only 4K of memory is used in a system to store the software, the program is relatively large and therefore divided into several subroutines or modules. It is quite common for a program module to require access to other modules in the system. The linking loader will identify the *external references* in each subroutine or module and load the correct memory address. When all modules have been loaded, the relocatable loader will list all undefined names or labels as errors. However, to be able to use the linking loader, memory address calculations must be partially processed by a relocatable assembler. The relocatable assembler generally assumes a starting location of zero. All instructions and data areas are assembled relative to this zero base. When the program is loaded, the relocatable operands are adjusted to correspond with the actual locations assigned by the linking loaders.

Before the source program can be assembled into a relocatable or absolute object program, it may have to be edited. Editing is performed using a source program editor. This text editor gives the user the capability of modifying the source program easily when making a minor change so that all the paper tapes do not have to be regenerated from scratch.

The editor is loaded into memory using the binary loader. Once the editor is loaded, source programs can be loaded directly into computer memory from a Teletype, one statement at a time, adding identifying line numbers to each statement. Source programs formatted on paper tape can be loaded using the binary loader. The editor usually operates in as little as 4K of memory.

The edit commands allow the programmer to insert, delete, or print lines of text, search for specified character strings, and list (output on the Teletype or printer) various lines based on certain conditions. Some edit programs, such as the Varian 73 EDIT, have two modes of operation: command and text mode. In the command mode, the source program can be edited on-line from the Teletype keyboard; while in the Text Mode, characters typed or read-in are stored in a text buffer for subsequent manipulation and output. The Interdata 70 editor, called TIDE, creates a text buffer for up to 2000 characters.

---

* The linking loader, in contrast to the binary loader, takes one *or more* modules and loads them into the computer, making it ready to run.

```
12607 024115 DECFO:LDA    1,DAC     ;FØRMATTED ØUTPUT
12610 125112       SSP    1,1       ;EXPØNENT <'O|?
12611 134401       NEG    1,3,SKP   ; YES, GET ABS VALUE
12612 176401       SUB    3,3,SKP   ; NØ
12613 126400       SUB    1,1
12614 102400       SUB    0,0
12615 044123       STA    1,DBC     ;ACTUAL # ØF CHAR TØ ØUTPUT
12616 040121       STA    0,DB+2
12617 054562       STA    3,DZAP    ;NUMBER LEADING ZERØ'S AFTER PØINT
12620 040562       STA    0,FCBT    ;CLEAR FØRMAT CØMMAND CØUNT
12621 040562       STA    0,SFBA    ;CLEAR STARTING FØRMAT BYTE ADDRESS
12622 040562       STA    0,EFBA    ;CLEAR ENDING FØRMAT BYTE ADDRESS
12623 040562       STA    0,ECNT
12624 040562       STA    0,FCBP
12625 040562       STA    0,FCAP
12626 040562       STA    0,PFLG
12627 040562       STA    0,DCFOF
12630 040562       STA    0,DPBA
12631 006754 DECØA:JSR    0.DCCR    ;GET FØRMAT BYTE
12632 000424       JMP    DECOC     ;END ØF FØRMAT STRING
CHECK FØR START ØF STRING,CØMMAS,DEC PT.
12633 020550 DECØB:LDA    0,SFBA    ;START BYTE ADD
12634 151014       SKZ    2,2       ;END ØF FØRMAT STRING ?
12635 000404       JMP    .+4       ; NØ, LEGAL CHAR
12636 101015       SNZ    0,0       ;WAS THERE FØRMAT INFØ ?
12637 004326       JSR    ERRSY     ; NØ, FØRMAT ERRØR
12640 000416       JMP    DECOC     ; YES, END ØF FØRMAT STRING
12641 101015       SNZ    0,0       ;BEGIN ØF FORMAT ?
12642 044541       STA    1,SFBA    ; YES, STØRE ADDRESS
12643 020350       LDA    0,0256
12644 142414       SEO    2,0       ;IS IT A "." ?
12645 000404       JMP    .+4       ; NØ
12646 044544       STA    1,DPBA    ; YES, STØRE ADDRESS
12647 102520       SUBZL  0,0       ;  AND SET PERIØD FLAG
12650 040540       STA    0,PFLG
12651 020361       LDA    0,0254
12652 142415       SNE    2,0       ;IS IT A "," ?
12653 010527       ISZ    FCBT      ; YES, INC "," CØUNT
12654 010120       ISZ    DB+1      ;INC FØRMAT PØINTER
12655 000754       JMP    DECOA     ;GET ANØTHER FØRMAT CHARACTER

12656 014120 DECØC:DSZ    DB+1      ;GET #'CHAR BEFORE & AFTER PØINT
12657 044122       STA    1,DB+3    ;STØRE END +1
12660 024523       LDA    1,SFBA    ;GET START FORMAT ADDRESS
12661 006131       JSR    0.ACBY    ;GET FIRST FORMAT BYTE
12662 034120       LDA    3,DB+1    ;GET END ØF FORMAT
12663 054521       STA    3,EFBA    ;STØRE AS END
12664 020526       LDA    0,DPBA    ;GET "." ADDRESS
12665 101014       SKZ    0,0       ;IS THERE A "." ?
12666 000404       JMP    .+4
12667 161400       INC    3,0
12670 040522       STA    0,DPBA
12671 000403       JMP    .+3
12672 116400       SUB    0,3
```

Figure 4-4 Typical assembly listing (written for the Data General Nova)

The programmer has until now performed the following tasks:

1. Loaded the bootstrap loader
2. Loaded the binary loader
3. Loaded the edit program
4. Created and edited the source program in assembly language
5. Punched out the formatted source program paper tape (or cards)
6. Loaded the assembler

He is now ready for the assembly procedure. Depending on the system hardware configuration, the assembly is made in two or three passes. In the first pass, the assembler creates a symbol table from the labels used in the source statements (Figure 4-2). It also checks for error conditions and generates diagnostic messages, if necessary. These messages are printed together with the corresponding symbols and location counter values as *error flags*. An error flag may signify a format error, a multiply-defined symbol, use of

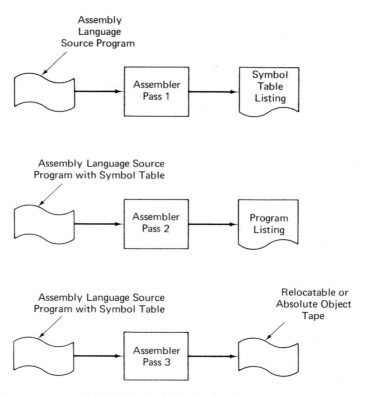

Figure 4-5 Three-pass assembly

invalid operation mnemonic, or an undefined symbol. The printed output of the table is called a *symbol table listing*.

On the second pass, the assembly listing is printed and the object tape is punched. A section of a typical listing is shown in Figure 4-4. The listing contains the source statements and the object code or data generated from each statement. The object program and the source program are listed side by side. The first two columns contain the object program in octal notation, while the third and fourth columns contain the operation and operand, respectively, followed by a comment.

A three-pass assembly must be used when the hardware I/O device configuration does not permit printing and punching at the same time. The three-pass assembly creates the symbol table in pass 1, prints the listing in pass 2, and punches the object tape in pass 3. Each step is shown in Figure 4-5.

Program Testing and Correction

In almost all cases, the object program from the first assembly contains errors in both logic and statement structure. Most minicomputer manufacturers therefore provide at least one set of routines to aid the programmer in checking out his program. These routines are included in debug programs, which allow the programmer to control program execution in discrete steps via commands entered at the Teletype. The feature which permits the programmer to do this is called a *breakpoint*. A breakpoint is an instruction address at which the programmer would like to stop execution and examine the current state of his routine. The breakpoint is entered by the programmer beforehand, during debugging. The operational registers and memory locations may usually be examined and modified from the Teletype after a breakpoint has been reached. The number of available breakpoints provided by a debugger is often an indication of the size and versatility of a debug program. Some limited-size debuggers provide only a single breakpoint to the programmer, whereas others provide four or eight breakpoints.

In addition to being able to change the contents of registers and memory addresses using breakpoints, the programmer may (1) transfer into or out of selected blocks of memory by inserting *traps* in the object code, (2) search for specific conditions, and (3) alter binary program instructions and data. He can also change the contents of selected memory words containing instruction through *patching* by which he immediately alters the object code. When patching memory, the programmer should also correct the source code to reflect the changes. Failure to do so will result in errors if assembly is later performed based on the nonupdated source program. A typical patch and source program update is shown in a program excerpt in Figure 4-6.

As an added feature, data can be *dumped* or transferred from memory

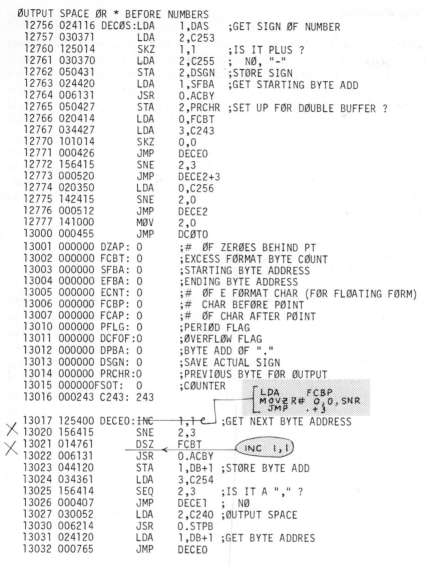

```
ØUTPUT SPACE ØR * BEFORE NUMBERS
12756 024116 DECØS:LDA   1,DAS    ;GET SIGN ØF NUMBER
12757 030371       LDA   2,C253
12760 125014       SKZ   1,1      ;IS IT PLUS ?
12761 030370       LDA   2,C255   ;  NØ, "-"
12762 050431       STA   2,DSGN   ;STØRE SIGN
12763 024420       LDA   1,SFBA   ;GET STARTING BYTE ADD
12764 006131       JSR   0.ACBY
12765 050427       STA   2,PRCHR  ;SET UP FØR DØUBLE BUFFER ?
12766 020414       LDA   0,FCBT
12767 034427       LDA   3,C243
12770 101014       SKZ   0,0
12771 000426       JMP   DECEO
12772 156415       SNE   2,3
12773 000520       JMP   DECE2+3
12774 020350       LDA   0,C256
12775 142415       SNE   2,0
12776 000512       JMP   DECE2
12777 141000       MØV   2,0
13000 000455       JMP   DCØTO
13001 000000 DZAP: 0          ;# ØF ZERØES BEHIND PT
13002 000000 FCBT: 0          ;EXCESS FØRMAT BYTE CØUNT
13003 000000 SFBA: 0          ;STARTING BYTE ADDRESS
13004 000000 EFBA: 0          ;ENDING BYTE ADDRESS
13005 000000 ECNT: 0          ;# ØF E FØRMAT CHAR (FØR FLØATING FØRM)
13006 000000 FCBP: 0          ;# CHAR BEFØRE PØINT
13007 000000 FCAP: 0          ;# ØF CHAR AFTER PØINT
13010 000000 PFLG: 0          ;PERIØD FLAG
13011 000000 DCFOF:0          ;ØVERFLØW FLAG
13012 000000 DPBA: 0          ;BYTE ADD ØF "."
13013 000000 DSGN: 0          ;SAVE ACTUAL SIGN
13014 000000 PRCHR:0          ;PREVIØUS BYTE FØR ØUTPUT
13015 000000 FSOT: 0          ;CØUNTER
13016 000243 C243: 243
                                           LDA    FCBP
                                           MOVZR# 0,0,SNR
                                           JMP    .+3
13017 125400 DECEO:INC   1,1      ;GET NEXT BYTE ADDRESS
13020 156415       SNE   2,3
13021 014761       DSZ   FCBT        INC 1,1
13022 006131       JSR   0.ACBY
13023 044120       STA   1,DB+1   ;STØRE BYTE ADD
13024 034361       LDA   3,C254
13025 156414       SEQ   2,3      ;IS IT A "," ?
13026 000407       JMP   DECE1    ;  NØ
13027 030052       LDA   2,C240   ;ØUTPUT SPACE
13030 006214       JSR   0.STPB
13031 024120       LDA   1,DB+1   ;GET BYTE ADDRES
13032 000765       JMP   DECEO
```

Figure 4-6 Example of patching of source program

to paper tape or hard copy in octal or hexadecimal format, depending on the particular notation used in the minicomputer.

The debugging routine is normally loaded into the minicomputer following the user's relocatable programs and before the library subroutines. Library subroutines are discussed in the next section.

Utility Routines

Most minicomputers provide a library of commonly used subroutines called utility routines. These modules are usually divided into various categories, such as mathematic, arithmetic, exponential, I/O service, and conversion routines. The mathematic, arithmetic, and exponential subroutines include fixed- and floating-point multiply and divide, fixed- and floating-point operations in absolute values, sine, cosine, tangent and arctangent, logarithm, and square root. I/O service routines, in addition to input and output, perform memory allocation for buffering; print various messages on printers, teletypes, or CRTs; and load and complement a floating-point quantity. Finally, conversion routines exist which convert fixed single-precision integer decimal to binary, EBCDIC to Hollerith, as well as EBCDIC to ASCII.

4.2 ASSEMBLERS, COMPILERS, INTERPRETERS, AND HIGHER-LEVEL LANGUAGES

The process of developing assembly-level programs is based on writing statements containing labels, instruction mnemonics such as OP codes or operators, and operands or variables. The assembly language follows the structure of the machine language very closely. In the assembly process, each statement written in symbolic form is translated into its equivalent binary form, consisting of instruction code and memory location. There is thus a one-to-one correspondence between the assembly language statement and the machine language instruction.* There are several advantages and disadvantages of this inherent feature.

Pros and Cons of Assembly Language

Since the assembly language is closely related to machine architecture, the programmer can take advantage of various hardware features such as arithmetic and logic instructions and addressing modes unique to the particular mini. In small stand-alone systems which do not have an auxiliary type of storage, such as a magnetic tape or disk unit, and where the economics of the systems dictates the use of a minimum amount of internal memory,

---

* This is not altogether true; assembly language *macros* are quite common in most assembly languages. An assembly language macro consists of a single statement expanded into several machine instructions. The macro is the assembly equivalent of the execution subroutine. It is defined once and can then be included within the program by a special OP code call which embeds the translated macro within the object code assembly output.

the programmer is forced to economize on the number of instructions in his program. Only assembly language permits such optimization of program size.

Assembly language programming allows the programmer to tailor the program to his unique requirements. For instance, if execution time is of greater importance than the use of a minimal number of memory locations to solve a problem, the program can be designed to perform the particular task at high speed, sacrificing memory space. However, owing to the previously mentioned close relationship between assembly language statements and machine language instructions, the user, once his program is written in the assembly language of a particular mini, cannot run the program on a different minicomputer unless the other machine emulates the instruction set of the original minicomputer. Many of the new minicomputers emulate older machines designed by the same manufacturer, such as the Varian 73, which emulates the earlier Varian 620, and the Hewlett-Packard 2100A, which emulates the HP-2115. A few minis, such as the Prime 200, can emulate the Honeywell DDP-516. (Some minicomputers can emulate larger machines designed by other manufacturers. The Digital Scientific Meta 4 emulates both the IBM 1130 and 1800 machines and the Control Data 160A.)

In addition to being machine-dependent, although vastly superior to pure machine language coding, assembly language programs are time-consuming, are difficult to write, and require intimate knowledge of the hardware. Considerable effort by the programmer is therefore required to learn the particular minicomputer assembly instructions. Also, since all problems must be broken into simple steps, much repetition and, with it, unnecessary effort must be exerted by the programmer. Because of the complexity of a particular programming task, there is a direct impact on the number of errors introduced and, thus also, on the length of the debugging cycle. Many of the above-mentioned problems of assembly language programming are circumvented using a higher-level language. The programming task is thereby simplified to the point where the programmer can perform his task nearly independently of the peculiarities of the minicomputer being used.

Compilers and Interpreters

Universal programming languages, originally designed for second- and third- generation small-, medium-, and large-scale computers, are applications-oriented and include, to a great extent, words and phrases used in English. Of these programming languages, FORTRAN and ALGOL are designed for scientific users, RPG and COBOL for business systems, and

BASIC for instructional time sharing or general problem solving. Once a source program is written in a high-level language, a special program called a *compiler* converts the program to binary object code, which is consequently run on the mini. The compile process or *compilation* follows essentially the same line as assemblers, in assembling the source code into machine-readable object code. BASIC differs from FORTRAN, ALGOL, and RPG in that it is designed specifically for *interpretation* instead of compilation.

An interpreter, unlike a compiler, translates the instructions of the source program and also executes them immediately. In addition, when more than one execution of a statement is required, the interpreter will repeat the translation, together with the execution, as many times as required. The interpretation process is therefore inherently slower. In a program written in BASIC, this is acceptable, since the program is generally developed

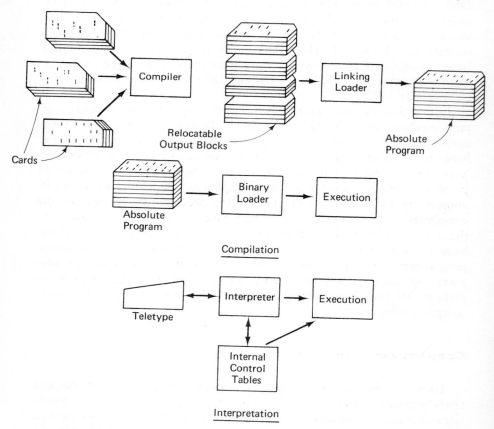

Figure 4-7 Basic differences between compilation and interpretation procedures

in an interactive environment where the programmer types in from a Tele-type one statement at a time, which, may be immediately transláted and executed. Programs can thus be developed in a relatively short time, and the user can obtain solutions to his problem(s) while on-line to the com-puter. The difference between compilation and interpretation is shown in Figure 4-7.

Higher-Level Languages and the Application

FORTRAN AND ALGOL

The most widely used standard language in science and engineering is FORTRAN, which is an abbreviation of formula translation. Several versions of FORTRAN exist, the most commonly used being FORTRAN IV. FORTRAN is a problem-oriented language expressing algebraic computations in a notation familiar to anyone without previous programming knowledge or experience.

A FORTRAN program consists of a series of statements divided into physical sections called *lines* that must be coded to a precise grammatical format. FORTRAN statements fall into two broad classes: *executable* and *nonexecutable.* Executable statements specify program action; nonexecutable statements describe the use of the program, the characteristics of the operands, editing information, statement functions, or data arrangement. A standard FORTRAN coding form, which includes 80 columns, is usually used for program coding.

FORTRAN allows the programmer to construct loops or repetitions and conditional jumps to other statements, subroutines, or arithmetic formulas. FORTRAN IV, provided for the DEC PDP-11 and the Data General Nova, permits random I/O access for disk-based data files, provides mixed mode arithmetic* support, and allows the use of generalized expressions as array subscripts. In addition, the PDP-11 FORTRAN provides error diagnostics with an *error traceback* feature which specifies where any error occurred with all the linkages back to the main program.

Generally, FORTRAN does not provide various logical relationships† in its instruction set. Many complex expressions must be broken down into independent FORTRAN statements. Applications requiring programs where the basic language elements such as variables, constants, expressions, and

---

* Mixed mode arithmetic refers to combining both integers and real data types (numeric data) in single arithmetic expressions.

† The term logical relationships refers to Boolean logical operators such as AND, OR, and NOR.

FORTRAN	ALGOL
IF(A+5−B) 100, 200, 200 100 C=A GOTO 300 200 C=B 300 CONTINUE	IF A+5<B Then C←A Else C←B

Figure 4-8   FORTRAN versus ALGOL (from "Programming: The Key to Your Mini's Success," by Robert Green, *Electronic Design*, 10, May 13, 1971, pp. 76–82)

procedures are integrated into highly complex structures, to be easily understood in terms of the implied logic, should be written in ALGOL.

ALGOL (short for algorithmic language) makes programs almost self-documenting by having variable names in the program describe the information. ALGOL permits statements to be formatted in a manner which makes it easy to grasp the logic of a program for programmers that did not write it. It is easier to convert the ALGOL description of a method into FORTRAN than it is to decipher the logic behind a FORTRAN program and convert it into ALGOL. A program written in ALGOL is usually also more compact than a program written in FORTRAN (Figure 4-8).

RPG

The RPG (report program generator) language is, as its name implies, designed for processing data for the output of reports. Typically, RPG software is divided into *two parts;* the first part *specifies* the form that the data to be processed will take and how the data in the defined forms will be processed, and the second part *consists* of the actual data to be processed.

The Varian RPG IV compiler is loaded into the computer from a card reader. The card deck used for compilation consists of the binary loader, the RPG compiler (in two parts), the data defining statements, the desired forms structuring (format of printed reports), and the procedure for processing the data going into the forms. The Varian compiler produces both a listing and an object deck in a single pass. The compiled object deck is loaded into memory using a binary loader, RPG IV loader, and RPG IV runtime support program, together with data cards.

Figure 4-9 shows a flow chart for the production of a calendar, Figure 4-10 contains the source listing for this program, and Figure 4-11 shows the printed output of the 1975 calendar.

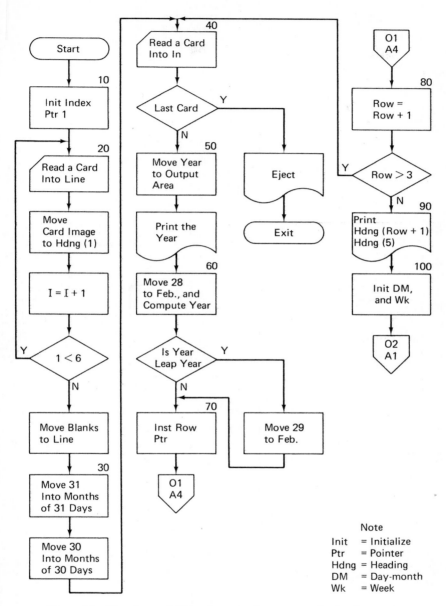

Figure 4-9 Flowchart of Gregorian calendar program for Varian RPG IV (Courtesy Varian Data Machines). The actual algorithm for the computation of the Gregorian calendar is also included in a book authored by Fred Gruenberger and George Jaffrey, *Problems for Computer Solution*, John Wiley & Sons, Inc., New York, 1973

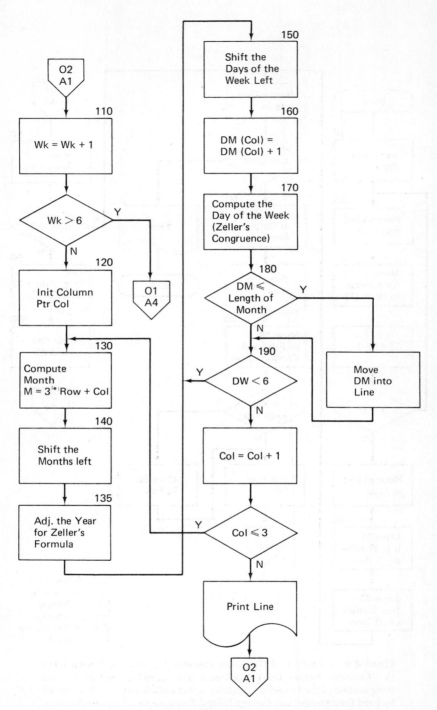

Figure 4-9 (continued)

```
*
*
RECORD LINE
        YOUT       (35,38),B
        COL1       ( 1,71),B
        COL2       (26,71),B
        COL3       (51,71),B
        COL4       (54,71),B
        D          (70,71,0),B,Z
RECORD IN
        YIN        (1,4)
        YEAR       (1,4,0)
        C          (1,2,0)
        B          (3,4,0)
        M          (5,6,0)
        DW         (7,9,0)
        SD         (10,12,0)
        SP         (10,13,1)
        SQ         (14,15,0)
TABLE   HD         (5)
        HDNG       (1,72)
TABLE   T          (12)
        LM         (1,2,0)
        DM         (3,4,0)
*
                   PROCEDURE
*
                   MOVE 1,I
10                 READ CARD LINE
                   MOVE COL1,HDNG(I)
                   COMPUTE I=I+1
        (I<6)      GO TO 10
                   MOVE ' ',COL1
                   "    31,LM(1),LM(3),LM(5),LM(7),LM(8),LM(10),LM(12)
                   "    30,LM(4),LM(6),LM(9),LM(11)
20                 READ CARD IN
        (#LC)      PRINT SC1
        (#")       CALL EXIT
                   MOVE YIN,YOUT
                   PRINT SC1,LINE
                   COMPUTE SP=B/4
                   "       SQ=C/4
                   MOVE 28,LM(2)
        ((B=4*SD) AND ((B><0) OR (C=4*SQ))) MOVE 29,LM(2)
                   COMPUTE ROW=-1
30                 "       ROW=ROW+1
        (ROW>3) GO TO 20
                   COMPUTE ROW1=ROW+1
                   MOVE HDNG(ROW1),COL1
                   PRINT SA3,LINE
                   MOVE HDNG(5),COL1
                   PRINT LINE
                   MOVE 0,DM(1),DM(2),DM(3),WK
40                 COMPUTE WK=WK+1
        (WK>6)     GO TO 30
                   MOVE 1,COL
50                 COMPUTE M=(3*ROW)+COL
                   MOVE COL2,COL1
        (M=1)      COMPUTE YEAR=YEAR-1
        (M=3)      "       YEAR=YEAR+1
60                 MOVE COL4,COL3
                   COMPUTE DM(COL)=DM(COL)+1
                   "       N=M-2
        (N<1)      "       N=N+12
                   "       SP=2.6*N-0.2+DM(COL)+B-2*C+105
                   "       SP=SD+B/4
                   "       DW=SD+C/4
                   "       SP=DW/7
                   "       DW=DW-7*SD
                   "       SQ=LM(M)-DM(COL)+1
        (SQ>0) MOVE DM(COL),D
        (DW<6) GO TO 60
                   COMPUTE COL=COL+1
        (COL<=3)GO TO 50
                   PRINT LINE
                   GO TO 40
                   END
```

Figure 4-10 Gregorian calendar program Varian Data Machines, RPG IV

```
                    CALENDAR FOR WHAT YEAR
                          1975

JANUARY                              JULY
            1    2    3    4                      1    2    3    4    5
 5   6   7  8    9   10   11          6    7   8  9   10   11   12
12  13  14 15   16   17   18         13   14  15 16   17   18   19
19  20  21 22   23   24   25         20   21  22 23   24   25   26
26  27  28 29   30   31              27   28  29 30   31

FEBRUARY                             AUGUST
                          1                                 1    2
 2   3   4   5    6   7    8          3    4   5    6    7   8    9
 9  10  11  12   13  14   15         10   11  12   13   14  15   16
16  17  18  19   20  21   22         17   18  19   20   21  22   23
23  24  25  26   27  28              24   25  26   27   28  29   30
                                     31

MARCH                                SEPTEMBER
                          1                   1    2    3    4    5    6
 2   3   4   5    6   7    8          7    8   9   10   11   12   13
 9  10  11  12   13  14   15         14   15  16   17   18   19   20
16  17  18  19   20  21   22         21   22  23   24   25   26   27
23  24  25  26   27  28   29         28   29  30
30  31

APRIL                                OCTOBER
            1    2    3    4    5                   1    2    3    4
 6   7   8  9   10   11   12          5    6   7    8    9   10   11
13  14  15 16   17   18   19         12   13  14   15   16   17   18
20  21  22 23   24   25   26         19   20  21   22   23   24   25
27  28  29 30                        26   27  28   29   30   31

MAY                                  NOVEMBER
            1    2    3                               1
 4   5   6  7    8    9   10          2    3   4    5    6    7    8
11  12  13 14   15   16   17          9   10  11   12   13   14   15
18  19  20 21   22   23   24         16   17  18   19   20   21   22
25  26  27 28   29   30   31         23   24  25   26   27   28   29
                                     30

JUNE                                 DECEMBER
 1   2   3   4    5   6    7                   1    2    3    4    5    6
 8   9  10  11   12  13   14          7    8   9   10   11   12   13
15  16  17  18   19  20   21         14   15  16   17   18   19   20
22  23  24  25   26  27   28         21   22  23   24   25   26   27
29  30                               28   29  30   31
```

Figure 4-11   Calendar output from Varian RPG IV program

BASIC

BASIC (beginner's all-purpose symbolic instruction code) is the easiest to learn of all the most common minicomputer languages. Furthermore, being interpretive, BASIC is a self-contained system handling complete editing, translation, and execution of programs. It is used for scientific, business, and educational applications. Some minicomputer manufacturers supply several versions of BASIC. Varian provides BASIC as well as advanced BASIC. The advanced version includes Boolean logical operators such as AND, OR, and NOT; special functions; and powerful matrix manipulators not available in the conventional BASIC statements.

The Data General version permits execution of certain statements in a *desk calculator* or *keyboard* mode for testing and debugging programs as well as performing simple computations or evaluating complex formulas without the necessity of writing a program. In addition, as data are entered at the Teletype, it is immediately examined for format and logical errors and the appropriate error messages are printed out. The time-sharing BASIC can support up to 16 keyboard terminals, while the single-user BASIC can support only a single teleprinter.

BASIC is also available from various independent sources, such as Educational Data Systems, which provides BASIC for the Data General Nova. This version of BASIC is somewhat more powerful in terms of language operators than the standard Data General BASIC packages.

Characteristics and Hardware Requirements of Various Minicomputer Languages

Assembly language programming makes it possible to minimize program execution time as well as required storage space by taking maximum advantage of the unique machine instructions provided by the minicomputer or microprogram designer. Also, the one-to-one relationship between source program statements and object program instructions simplifies the assembly language program checkout. On the negative side, machine language is machine-dependent and usually more difficult to use than higher-level languages. Unlike most high-level languages, assembly language is not self-documenting and is therefore highly dependent on the completeness and clarity of comments included in the source program statements.

Of all minicomputer languages, FORTRAN is most widely used for complex arithmetic operations. ALGOL provides the most powerful structure permitting the output to be formatted and allows for bit manipulation and easy manipulation of character string data, together with the use of multiprecision arithmetic and nesting of one structure inside another structure.

BASIC is the quickest program to learn and can be used in a stand-alone configuration where the user can write his program in a conversational mode, editing the program as he writes it.

RPG, the fourth higher-level language, is used less frequently with minicomputers. RPG is of value in business and other applications requiring forms processing or the preparation of statistical data and tabular reports, such as inventory records, sales analysis, and personnel summaries.

All the above-discussed languages can be run in a stand-alone hardware configuration with a minimum of an ASR Teletype except for RPG, which usually requires a card reader/punch and a high-speed printer. Assembly or compilation is, of course, an extremely tedious process on a system which

Hardware / Software	CPU 4 K Memory Teletype	CPU 8 K Memory Teletype	CPU 12 K Memory Teletype	CPU 16 K Memory Teletype Disk	CPU 16 K Memory Teletype Disk Additiona Peripherals
Assembler					
RPG					
Basic					
Fortran					
Algol					
Extended Basic					

Figure 4-12 Internal memory requirements for various commonly used minicomputer languages. RPG requires card readers, a card punch, and a line printer usually.

does not include high-speed I/O equipment, such as a paper tape reader/ perforator, card reader/punch, or cassette tape drive. Most assemblers fit into 4K words of memory, while programs such as BASIC or FORTRAN require a minimum of 8K words. However, this minimal memory size will generally severely restrict the user in terms of his application program size. Also, more than 8K of memory provides faster compilations. A comparison of minimum memory requirements for various languages is shown in Figure 4-12. BASIC differs from the other high-level languages in that it is inter-pretive and can thus run as a stand-alone program, while most of the other programs must usually be run under a system executive. COBOL has not been discussed, since a COBOL compiler is too large to fit into most mini-computers. The features of the system executive are discussed in the following section.

4.3 OPERATING SYSTEMS

Software can be divided into three major classes:

1. Software that *performs* a specific task, such as solving a par-ticular equation, controlling a machine tool, tracking a missile,

or monitoring an oil refinery process. This type of software is called *applications software.*

2. Software that *aids* the programmer in writing the applications software. This includes assembly language and higher-level language compilers and interpreters, editors, debuggers, etc.

3. Software that *controls* the operation of the minicomputer system. This software is called the *executive program, monitor, supervisor, system software,* or *operating system.* Either the assembler or compiler may be under the control of the operating system, and, once the applications software has been developed and debugged, it too can be run under the control of the operating system.

Basic Functions Performed by the Minicomputer Operating System

When programming in assembly language, the user must prepare, load, and execute his programs in several steps. As previously described, the various loaders must first be loaded into memory in order to load the assembler. Again, when the object program is created, editing and debugging must be performed step by step, loading and reloading the various software modules. (The complete process is summarized in Figure 4-13). Not until the applications program is free from errors can it be loaded into memory to perform its assigned task.

In applications which require the punching of cards or printing forms on a line printer, the user must also load applicable I/O subroutines, while simultaneously making sure that the desired data are read into and out of the correct memory location. And, of course, each of these steps must be performed sequentially, requiring a large amount of continuous operator interaction with the hardware.

Programming in an interpretive language such as BASIC will save the user from most of this "nonproductive" work since programming is performed directly from the Teletype keyboard. However, applications requiring the use of more powerful, higher-level languages, such as FORTRAN or ALGOL, put the burden back again on the operator. Instead of assembling, he must compile his source programs. In other respects, most of the required steps indicated in Figure 4-12 are identical. For this reason, a large number of systems are operated with an executive.

The executive schedules, loads, and executes assembly or higher-level language programs with a minimal amount of user interaction. Most minicomputer executives perform task scheduling, storage allocation, and memory management; control of I/O operations and peripherals; error

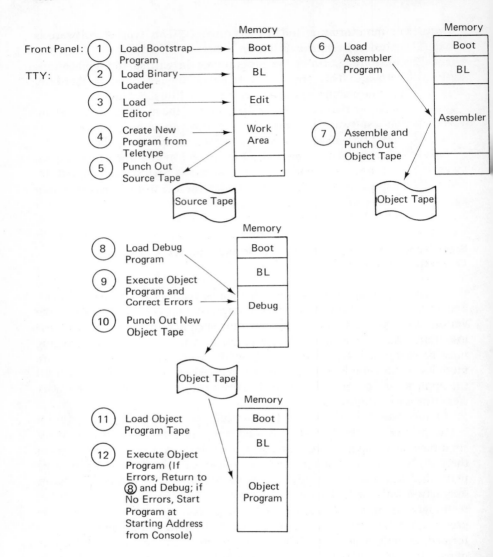

Figure 4-13 Steps 1–12 summarize the development of operational software

monitoring and processing; as well as handling of communications between the hardware/software system and the operator. Consequently, the various hardware and software elements become transparent to the programmer, who now interacts with the system only through the Teletype or CRT terminal.

Minicomputer operating systems are usually either stand-alone or disk-based. The stand-alone version is, in most cases, batch- or real-time-oriented, while many of the disk-based systems are either batch-, real-time-, or time-sharing-oriented.

Stand-alone Operating Systems

The stand-alone batch-oriented operating systems provide features such as operator system control, job control of all system activities, compilation, editing, debugging, and program loading, including linking of various subroutines with the main applications program. Steps 1–16 in Figure 4-14 summarize the software development procedure using this type of executive. Commonly, the minimum memory requirement for the above stand-alone system is 12K words.

The advantage of using the batch-oriented stand-alone system lies mainly in the fact that once the executive is in memory—all further interaction with the system can be performed from a Teletype instead of having to work with the minicomputer front panel switches. In other respects, the advantages appear to be minimal, comparing the number of steps to be followed as indicated in Figures 4-13 and 4-14.

The second type of stand-alone operating system, the real-time monitor, often a minimal time-sharing system, allows the user to develop applications software concurrent with the system operating in a real-time environment. *Real-time* in this context pertains to the actual time during which a physical process transpires. This process may consist of the reading or writing of a block of data while simultaneously performing some other unrelated tasks, such as monitoring several devices at the same time or communicating with a number of remote terminals. These real-time tasks receive the highest priority in the system and are therefore said to be operating in a *foreground* mode. The real-time executive prevents the programmer during his program development activity from interfering with programs that operate in the foreground mode. The executive, in this case, provides *partitioning* between the foreground tasks and the software development activity which, because of its low priority, is said to operate in a *background* mode.

A task, as defined by Data General for the Nova/Supernova Real-Time Operating System (RTOS), consists of a "logically complete program segment, operating at a specified priority level, whose execution may proceed in an interleaved fashion with, and independent of, other tasks." Data General's RTOS provides four *task states*. The task may be (1) *executing* with control of the CPU, (2) *pending* or ready for execution, (3) *suspended* or awaiting the completion of another task being executed, or (4) *dormant*. A task is dormant only when it has not yet been entered in the system or when it has

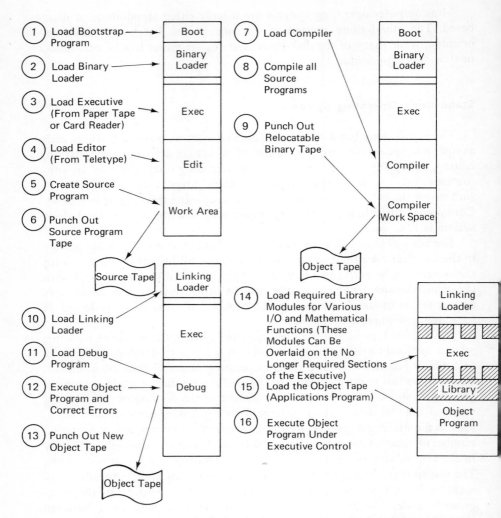

Figure 4-14 Steps 1–16 summarize the development of operational software, using an operating system (executive)

already been executed. The communication between the operating system and user tasks is implemented through *meta instructions* or machine language subroutine calls.

A key feature of all real-time systems is their ability to handle several concurrent tasks based on assigned priorities of the tasks. When two or more tasks are active at the same priority level, the current one will remain running unless a higher-priority task interrupts it. A real-time clock is used to schedule predetermined *time slices* during which each equal priority task must be performed. The Nova family of computers can be set under program control to one of four different clock frequencies for the RTOS clock time. The DEC Real-Time Executive (RSX-11C) for the PDP-11 provides a software Task Watch Dog Timer.* This timer is set at the start of each task to the maximum duration a task may run, at a particular level before being suspended. The time limit can be arbitrarily selected by the programmer to different values for each priority interrupt level.

A stand-alone real-time system is useful, for instance, in a development laboratory where large amounts of data are recorded and analyzed and new data are taken based on the results of the analyses. A real-time system will provide increased utilization of the computer by allowing nonlaboratory-related processing to be performed in a background mode. This processing may include the running of accounting and payroll packages or developing programs for new experiments.

Such a system, using the various levels of interrupt together with the watchdog timer, operates typically in the following fashion:

1. Emergency control programs which monitor alarm conditions and system limits are assigned the highest priority (level 0).
2. Experimental data collection is assigned the second highest priority (level 1)
3. Data reduction and analysis programs are assigned the third highest priority (level 2)
4. Automatic periodic print-outs of data values are assigned the fourth highest priority (level 3)
5. Diagnostic programs for the machine are assigned the fifth highest priority (level 4)
6. Background mode operation running non-real-time programs and compiling or assembling source programs are assigned the lowest priority (level 5)

Programs run in levels 0–4 are interrupt-initiated with the watchdog timer suspending each task at a predetermined point in time. The sequence of tasks in terms of foreground/background operation on the various priority levels based on the above example is shown in Figure 4-15.

The minimum memory requirement for running the DEC Real-Time Executive is 12K words. Obviously, the larger the number and size of the programs, the more memory is required. In spite of the relatively low cost of internal memory compared to a disk, the crossover point is reached relatively

---

* PDP-11/20 Processor Handbook, Digital Equipment Corporation, Waltham, Mass. 1971, p. 176.

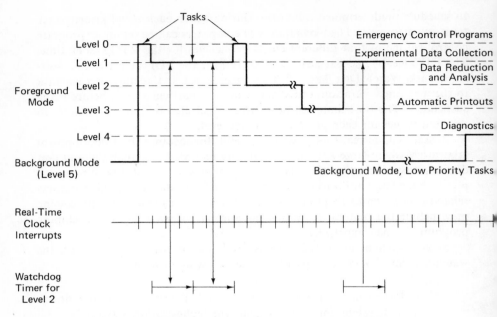

Figure 4-15 Tasks related to priority levels and the watchdog timer

quickly. For this reason more than any other, a large number of mini-computer operating systems are presently based on one or more disks.

Disk Operating Systems

While in stand-alone applications, a trade-off generally exists between using and not using an executive; a disk-based system almost exclusively requires the use of an operating system. The question is therefore no longer whether or not to use a monitor, but what type of monitor will best serve the purpose. The three most commonly available disk operating systems for minicomputers are batch-processing-, real-time-, and time-sharing-oriented systems.

BATCH-ORIENTED DISK OPERATING SYSTEMS

The two main functions of a disk operating system are to simplify software development and facilitate system operation. Loading various program modules from paper tape or cards usually takes seconds or, perhaps, minutes. Under the control of a disk operating system, the same program, or set of programs, can be "swapped" or read from disk into main memory in milli-seconds. The use of a disk operating system also removes the restriction of program size, allowing a large part of the operating system software to remain on disk, while the program segments required to operate the user system and perform the required applications tasks are swapped in and out of main memory.

The important features are (1) the ability to bring programs into main memory from the disk and vice versa and (2) performing applicable file-handling jobs.

Part of the operating system is permanently stored in main memory, consisting of a program which can load from the disk into main memory desired application programs and parts of the executive program, which executes all commands and updates lists of files stored on the disk.

Commands to the disk operating system can originate from user programs or from a disk resident program, which can be brought into main memory upon demand. These commands may instruct the program to (1) transfer the contents of a file to another file, (2) print a file, (3) punch out a file on paper tape or cards, (4) create or delete a file, or (5) load a file to main memory from disk. Commands can also be used to bring loaders, editors, assemblers, compilers, or debuggers from disk to main memory.

The file organization, access, and protection features are important for the understanding and evaluation of various batch-oriented disk operating systems. The key elements when evaluating disk file characteristics are

- File directory
- File structure
- Data blocking size
- File length
- File access method
- File protection
- File types
- File names

The file system on secondary storage, such as disk, drum, or tape, uses three types of file structures: indexed, sequential, or linked. Each of these methods is illustrated in Figure 4-16.

The indexed files provide maximum flexibility. All block addresses in a file are stored sequentially in a master index file, which, in turn, can be stored either on disk or in the main memory. When stored on disk, two accesses are required for reading or writing of each block—one to access the index file and one for the block of data itself. The index file can also be stored in main memory, thereby eliminating one of the two required disk seeks.

Sequential or contiguously organized files are composed of a number of

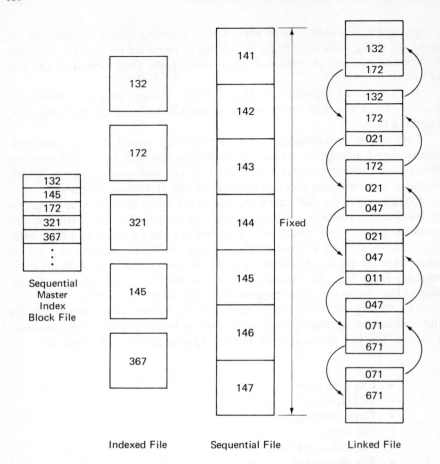

Sequential
Master
Index
Block File

Indexed File   Sequential File   Linked File

Figure 4-16 Comparison of three commonly used-file structures in a disk operating system. Note that linked-file access can occur in both the forward and reversed directions.

disk blocks* which constitute an unbroken series of disk block addresses. The length of the file is always fixed. The blocks within a file, typically consisting of 256 or 512 words, may be accessed randomly using a single-disk seek (see Disk and Drum Memories in Chapter 3). Sequential files can be created only if sufficient numbers of free neighboring disk blocks are available.

---

* A file is a physical collection of data which resides on a storage device and is usually referenced through its name. A file consists of one or more blocks. A block is a group of adjacent words of a specified size. A block is also the smallest addressable sector. The length of a segment on a disk or drum is usually one block.

Linked files can grow serially and may or may not have a logical limit on their size, depending on the design of the particular disk operating system. The blocks in the file may be distributed throughout the storage device. Each block contains a *pointer* or address to the next block in the field. Linked blocks are, however, sequential in terms of program access. The system can access only the preceding or succeeding block in the file. To access the tenth block after the first block, the system would have to read the eight intervening blocks.

The selection of the file structure will thus determine the length of the file (sequential files always have a fixed length) and the file access (indirect for indexed files and relative for linked files). The data block size may be variable for linked files while fixed for sequential files. Hewlett-Packard allows the user to determine the data block size when he creates the file for the HP-2100A.

Some disk operating systems provide file protection by degrees or levels. This may consist of READ protect, WRITE protect, or DELETE protect; the user is restricted from performing one or all of the above operations on or with the disk.

The file types may consist of any combination or relocatable, executable, source, ASCII-type, absolute, or binary programs.

Disk operating system capability is closely related to the flexibility and availability of special features in the file handler. Slow access methods, rigid structural requirements, and lack of file protection will put an undue burden on the entire system, needlessly handicapping the programmer.

A key feature, closely related to file organization, is the file address or *disk file directory*. The directory resides on disk, and each time a file is added, altered, or deleted, the directory is immediately updated by the operating system. The directory contains at least two entries for each unique file on the disk. These are the *file name*, which consists of a number of characters, anywhere from 5 to 16, depending on the particular computer system, and the *file address* of the first block of a file.

Some operating systems divide the disk into *partitions*, where each partition may include one or more files. In such systems, each partition may include its own directory, which not only includes the name and location of each file within the partition but also the length and address of the last operation for each of the files in the partition (Figure 4-17). The partition is an important concept in real-time disk operation systems and will be discussed in more detail in the next section.

In addition to the directory, most if not all disk operating systems use a disk-resident *disk map dictionary*. This dictionary is in single-bit format, where each single bit corresponds to a block on the disk. A bit setting of 1 indicates that the corresponding block is used, while a 0 indicates that it is unused.

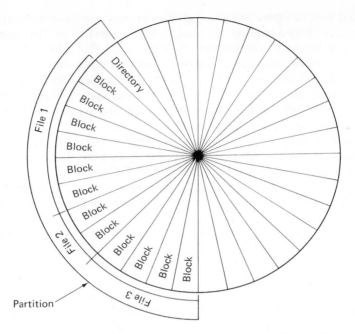

Figure 4-17 The smallest unit of data stored on a disk is a block of record. Blocks are assembled into sequential, random, or contiguous files, which in turn may be contained within a partition.

REAL-TIME DISK OPERATING SYSTEMS

Real-time disk operating systems combine the advantages of real-time processing with the availability of relatively fast access bulk storage, generally based on a disk or drum. The key features of a real-time disk operating system are (1) the efficiency of memory management, (2) the system response time and throughput, (3) the effectiveness of I/O control, and (4) the methods used to keep the total system operating with minimal down time.

Memory management is a function of executive design, job scheduling, task partitioning, and memory economizing features such as program overlay and roll in/roll out capabilities. In real-time operationing systems, the main memory is typically divided into the following areas, or partitions:

1. Resident executive program, including scheduler, interrupt processor, disk and Teletype handler, and operator command decoder

2. System tables describing partitions in the system and where they are, a description of all system peripherals, and the status of all system tasks and task queues
3. I/O control module containing various required I/O handlers
4. Common pool of blocks shared between tasks, permitting inter-task communication
5. Task execution areas for foreground and background tasks

The various memory allocations or assignments are shown in Figure 4-18.

In some systems, the task execution area, reserved for foreground tasks, is divided into two segments or sections: resident and nonresident. The resident area is used for storage of programs which must respond more rapidly than a rotating memory transfer permits. These programs are, of course, loaded into main memory at the time the system is initialized. (See System Initialization.) The nonresident programs are rolled in and out of disk into the main memory under control of the resident portion of the real-time operating system executive.

In several systems, the nonresident programs can be loaded into the main memory area usually reserved for background programs. When this occurs, the background program is automatically interrupted and saved by storing it

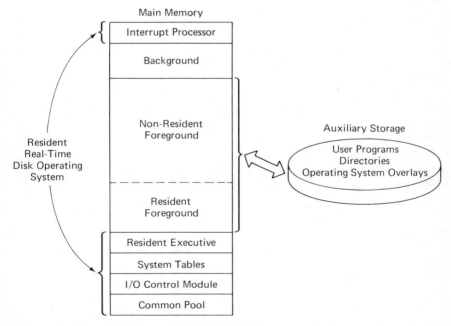

Figure 4-18 Main memory and auxiliary storage allocation for real-time disk operating systems

on disk. The latter function is performed either manually through operator intervention or automatically by the operating system. Once the foreground task is completed, the background program is returned to main memory and the execution continued from the point where the interrupt occurred.

The minimum amount of total main memory required by disk operating systems running solely in a foreground mode varies from 8K to 16K words, while the minimum amount of main memory which will permit a full-scale operation varies between 12K and 20K depending on which minicomputer is used.

The name of the game is therefore to utilize the storage space available in main memory at maximum efficiency. Since the available main memory is obviously not sufficient to hold all the necessary programs at one time, a program read-in scheme is usually used to bring in from disk storage the minimum portion of a program's code required to perform a given task. The programmer must therefore segment his program into one or more parts which fit into fixed-size main storage areas. The program segments are called *user overlays*. Overlays are used not only for applications programs but also for operating system software. Parts of an executive required for a specific task can be rolled into main memory, executed, and rolled out on disk again. The entire operation is performed under control of the resident part of the executive.

Overlays are thus very helpful in conserving memory space, but this saving is achieved at the price of longer program execution time. Frequent use of overlays should therefore be made only in applications where time is not a critical factor. However, most real-time systems are, of course, time-critical.

A program already existing on disk can usually be expanded through the addition of new sections. (This may be a problem when contiguous files are used.) Data General calls the addition of new sections to an existing program *program chaining*. To use chaining, a program must be written in serially executable segments. Each segment will thus call the next segment. Chaining, together with the use of overlay techniques, will consequently permit the programmer to write individual programs which are considerably larger than the maximum available main memory space. However, in writing the program, the programmer must keep track of the various program segments and overlays.

This limitation is presently partly overcome by the use of *virtual memory*. Virtual memory as presently implemented in minicomputers is, however, limited to remapping the program in main memory alone. For every memory reference by the programmer, an address translation takes place in hardware by the use of a high-speed look-up table. This permits the programmer to treat memory as a block of contiguous locations while the actual corresponding physical locations may be scattered throughout the main-frame memory. The only penalty paid by the user is in terms of overhead on the time required for a memory reference. The net effect is approximately 25% overhead in terms of memory speed (a delay from 330 to 430 nsec for the Varian 73 operating under Vortex II, its real-time disk operating system).

The large-scale computer manufacturers carry the virtual memory concept beyond the main-frame memory. In the IBM 370 virtual memory scheme, the virtual memory can be greater than the main memory, where the secondary storage appears as an extension of the main memory through the use of segmentation and hardware-controlled paging. However, with this scheme, the system will again spend much of its time transferring program segments between disk and main memory. If the segments are too small, the time the program has to spend waiting for the required segments to be read in from disk may be excessive. On the other hand, if the segments are too large, a single program may use up a large part of the available background and foreground program area in the main memory.

The system response time is equally as dependent on the flexibility of task handling as it is on memory management. The number of ways available for scheduling tasks is often used as a measure of real-time operating system capability. The most common ways can be divided into four groups:

1. *Hardware interrupts* based on one or more interrupt levels in the machine
2. *Operator requests* based on operator commands from the Teletype
3. *Program requests* from other tasks executing in memory
4. *Time scheduling* based on actual time (time of day), elapsed time (time delay), synchronized to a predetermined unit of time (hour, minute, second), offset from a predetermined unit of time, or periodic (after each program cycle)

The various task-scheduling methods are summarized in Figure 4-19. Task scheduling based on external interrupts uniquely distinguishes the disk-oriented real-time operating system from the batch-oriented operating system. The assignment of task priority is usually dependent on the application. *Input/output-bound* tasks should be assigned the highest available priority regardless of their relative importance. Truly I/O-bound tasks generally have to wait for I/O enough of the time to allow *compute-bound* tasks ample time to execute. The non-I/O-bound tasks can therefore be assigned lower priority.

Input-output data transfer and control is provided by peripheral device driver I/O routines, which, in turn, are selected by the resident real-time disk operating system I/O control module (Figure 4-18). Provisions are usually made for adding new device drivers as the system grows. Several

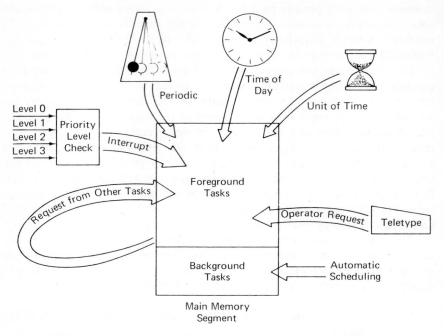

Figure 4-19   Common ways of task scheduling in a real-time disk operating system

systems provide a queuing facility in order to achieve maximum and continuous overlap of the slow I/O-bound tasks with the high-speed, compute-
bound tasks. The I/O-requesting tasks are thus placed in a queue, waiting
for previous I/O task completion. While in the queue, these tasks may
temporarily suspend themselves, thereby increasing the usable CPU time.

Data transferred in and out of disk files to various peripherals is double-
buffered, first in a block size main memory operating system buffer and
second in a small-device-handler buffer. The latter buffer varies in size
depending on the speed of the device. Card reader buffers typically store
80 characters, paper tape punch buffers, 40 bytes, and line printer buffers,
132 or 160 bytes.

Simultaneous peripheral operation on-line (SPOOL) permits the buffering
of low-speed peripheral messages on disk instead of having to use precious
main memory space. Spooling works as follows: Assume that a 2000-char-
acter message is output to a 10-character/sec teletype. The Teletype device
handler buffer stores only 64 characters. It will, therefore, take 6.4 sec for
this buffer to be emptied. If main memory were to be used to store the remaining 1936 characters, approximately 1000 words of main memory
(assuming the machine uses a 16-bit word) would be tied up for over 3 min

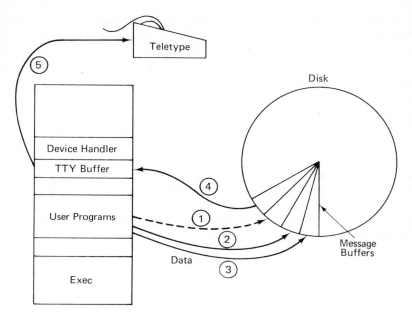

Figure 4-20 Messages from various user programs are buffered on disk (steps 1, 2, and 3). Message files are transferred in one block or Teletype buffer size at a time to main memory (step 4). The Teletype buffer is emptied, and data transmitted to the Teletype one character at a time (step 5)

while the device handler buffer is filled up and emptied. Spooling permits Teletype messages to be stored on disk, thereby freeing main memory storage partitions for other tasks. Spooling also frees the user from having to optimize his message requests for maximum system throughput. The message flow using spooling is shown in Figure 4-20.

As many users of newly installed minicomputer systems have quickly discovered, one of the most serious problems with operating systems is reliability. The question of operational reliability becomes even more important when the system must operate in a real-time environment, which by its very nature requires maximum system availability.

As a minimum, the system must guarantee that programmers developing software in the background mode do not interfere or destroy operating applications software running in the foreground mode. Some systems may run programs which are of a sensitive nature (such as payroll). It is therefore imperative that the operating system provide a method whereby protection is given to particular files against accidental or unauthorized access. The type of protection made available in some systems is in the form of a software *key*, which provides restricted access to particular files.

In the case of hardware failure, such as in the line printer, the system will grind to a halt unless programs are written in a device-independent manner. This device independence will permit the operator, upon detection of the failure, immediately to reassign alternative devices for backup, such as the Teletype, until the line printer has been repaired. In the likely incident of an operator Teletype console failing, some systems allow for a quick switch to a device which may be used as a backup, such as a CRT terminal. Systems which include a CRT terminal must be designed to prohibit the CRT terminal user from gaining unauthorized access to priviledged operator commands when the system is operated in the normal mode from the Tele-type console. Some systems, such as the DEC RSX-11D, require the console operator, when he switches to the CRT terminal during an emergency, to enter a system password, which, in turn, allows him to access the privileged operator commands. This password is assigned during system generation (see System Initialization).

Time-Sharing Systems

Time-sharing systems differ from real-time operating systems in that the former may run different jobs, from user to user, while in the latter case there are programs running in the CPU which control remote terminals and, at the same time, permit local processing in background mode. The time-sharing user generally enters program statements, creating his own application programs, which he later runs, while the real-time user enters data for processing by application programs, previously loaded into the system, usually in an off-line mode. Furthermore, real-time system users have access to the system on a priority basis, while time-sharing users typically share the use of the system on a round-robin basis where each user is given an equal time slice.

The minicomputer-based time-sharing systems differ mainly from the larger time-sharing systems in terms of computing capability and memory capacity. Minicomputer time-sharing systems are either stand-alone systems with relatively short programs, 8 or 12K words of memory and 4 or 8 low-speed Teletype-like terminals, or disk-based systems, which can support perhaps 16 or more simultaneous terminal users. All the presently available minicomputer time-sharing systems provide interpretive languages such as BASIC, extended BASIC, BASIC-PLUS, or FOCAL.*

---

* FOCAL-8 stands for formula calculator, an interpretive BASIC-like language developed for the DEC PDP-8 family computers.

System Initialization

The system design process, discussed in Chapter 5, will yield a system configuration which meets the data processing requirements of the particular user. The operating system requires the user to define the various hardware elements and how memory is going to be utilized. This tailoring function is called system generation (SYSGEN).

A bootstrap system is usually available to the user which contains the basic elements essential to perform SYSGEN. SYSGEN is performed in an interactive manner from the console teletype, defining main memory size; real-time clock frequency (if more than one is available); number of disk

```
SYSGEN
SYSGEN REV 2.ØØ
VALID ANSWERS ARE IN PARENTHESIS RESPOND ACCORDINGLY
DUAL PROCESSOR ENVIRONMENT? ("Ø =NO "1"=YES) 1
MAPPED SYSTEM? ("Ø"=NO "1"=YES) Ø
CORE STORAGE (IN THOUSANDS OF WORDS) 28
ENTER NUMBER OF STACKS (1-5) 4
ENTER NUMBER OF EXTRA BUFFERS REQUIRED (Ø-N) 6
MAXIMUM NUMBER OF SUB-DIRECTORIES/SUB-PARTITIONS
ACCESSIBLE AT ONE TIME (Ø-32) 3
ENTER NUMBER OF CONTROLLERS FOR FIXED HEAD DISKS(Ø-2)  1
DEVICE PRIMARY("Ø") OR SECONDARY("1")? Ø
ENTER NUMBER OF DISK PACK CONTROLLERS(Ø-2) 2
ENTER NUMBER OF DEVICES FOR CONTROLLER #1(1-4)  2
ENTER NUMBER OF DEVICES FOR CONTROLLER #2(1-4)  4
ENTER MASTER DEVICE DPØ
ENTER NUMBER OF CONTROLLERS FOR MTA(Ø-2) 1
DEVICE PRIMARY("Ø") OR SECONDARY("1")? Ø
ENTER NUMBER OF DEVICES FOR CONTROLLER #1(1-8)  1
ENTER NUMBER OF CONTROLLERS FOR CTA(Ø-2) 1
DEVICE PRIMARY("Ø") OR SECONDARY("1")? Ø
ENTER NUMBER OF DEVICES FOR CONTROLLER #1(1-8)  3
AUTO RESTART ON POWER FAIL?("Ø"=NO "1"=YES) 1
OPERATOR MESSAGES ? ("Ø"=NO "1"=YES) 1
RTC?("Ø"=NO "1"=YES) 1
ENTER RTC FREQ (1=1ØHZ,2=1ØØHZ,3=1ØØØHZ) 1
ENTER NUMBER OF PTR(Ø-2) 1
ENTER NUMBER OF PTP(Ø-2) Ø
ENTER NUMBER OF LPT(Ø-2) 1
ENTER COLUMN SIZE FOR DEVICE  #1(8Ø OR 132) 132
ENTER NUMBER OF CDR(Ø-2) 1
ENTER NUMBER OF PLT(Ø-2) Ø
QTY ? ("Ø"=NO "1"=YES) Ø
SECOND TTY?("Ø"=NO "1"=YES) 1
R
```

Figure 4-21 System generation for Data General Nova (from "Introduction to the Real-time Disk Operating System," Data General Corporation Document Number 093-000083-00; Courtesy Data General Corporation, Southboro, Mass. 01772)

units available to the system, number of sectors, tracks, and heads per disk; the amount of space for system tables, reentrant libraries, I/O device drivers, size, number, and type of task partition areas; etc. Figure 4-21 includes a sample of SYSGEN for the Data General Nova Real-Time Disk Operating System.

Operating System Checklist

Operating systems are considerably more complex to evaluate, in terms of using a fixed set of performance parameters or features, than minicomputers or minipheripherals. System reliability for hardware can be measured in terms of quantitative values such as MTBF. Operating system reliability is, however, qualitative in nature. Some operating systems may "bomb out" with the slightest error or omission in data inputs as a result of mispunched cards or misread paper tape. Others may have problems with features such as file deletion or updating of directories. The list of items shown in Figure 4-22 is therefore by no means inclusive and may not even

```
Minimum memory requirement for O.S.
Maximum number of nonresident tasks in main memory
Dynamic repartitioning of memory
Number of ways of scheduling tasks
Roll in/roll out of background programs with automatic restart
Message spooling
Number of disk file structures
Levels of file protect
Queued I/O
Use of overlays for user tasks
Virtual memory feature
Number and type of fail-soft features
Reliability features
Directory feature (number of characters used for reference)
```

Figure 4-22 Checklist for Operating Systems (Fail-soft refers to a gradual degradation of system operation in contrast to a catastrophic failure where total system operation is halted.)

apply for some operating systems and should consequently be used only as a starting point for evaluation of various operating systems.

4.4 SOFTWARE DEVELOPMENT AND ITS ECONOMICS

The previous sections have touched upon two of the three major software elements in minicomputer systems: applications program development tools and system software required to develop and run applications programs.

User Approach / Software	Purchase, Lease, or Use Manufacturer-Supplied Software	Modify Existing Software	Develop New Software
Software tools (assembly and higher-level languages, etc.)	Almost always	Rarely	Rarely
System software (disk operating systems, real-time executives, etc.)	Usually	Occasionally	Rarely
Applications software	Rarely	Occasionally	Usually

Figure 4-23   User buy-or-build approach for software

The third equally important software element is the applications package itself.

The software tools, consisting mainly of programming language assemblers and compilers, editors, debuggers, etc., are rarely developed or even modified by the user. This is also true for system software. Operating systems are perhaps modified or extended, but few users undertake the extensive task of building their own software operating system. The reverse, however, is true for applications software. In the majority of cases, the user must tailor his applications software to the particular task at hand. He is less frequently in a position where he can buy a ready-made software package which meets all his unique requirements. This situation is summarized in the table in Figure 4-23. The above approaches have, up until now, generally been dictated by economic reasons.

Depending on the application, it may be more economical to develop the applications software in-house from scratch rather than buying someone else's software package and redesigning it. The fast-growing minicomputer market may, however, eventually change this as more systems are being developed. The user has the additional options of buying the entire system off the shelf or subcontracting the software development to a software specialist. Before a decision is made, it is important that the user be aware of all possibilities, thereby being able to perform the appropriate trade-offs.

Off-The-Shelf Software

The availability of software application packages for minicomputers is not nearly so abundant as for larger machines such as the IBM 360/370,

Univac 1100, or CDC and Honeywell 6000 Series families of computers. Minicomputer software packages can be categorized according to whether they facilitate using the computer for applied tasks or perform internal computer system functions. COMTEX-II (communications-oriented multiple terminal executive), provided by DEC for the PDP-11, is an example of the former type of software. It can be debated whether this software package is an operating system or an applications package. COMTEX-II does, however, facilitate the use of the PDP-11 for communications processing. Examples of the second category of software packages are payroll and accounting packages; numerically controlled machine tool control software; laboratory data analysis software, such as DECs PHA (pulse height analysis), GASPAN (gamma spectral analysis), and SCOLDS (spark chamber on-line data system); and clinical and hospital packages such as DEC's CLINICAL LAB-12 and RAD-8 (radio-therapy planning system).

These and other off-the-shelf software packages are available from several sources:

1. Minicomputer manufacturer (Digital Equipment Corporation, Data General Corporation, Hewlett-Packard, etc.)
2. Miniperipheral manufacturer (Tektronix: Plot routines, Calcomp: Graphic software routines, etc.)
3. Independent hardware/software houses (Decision, Inc., Educational Data Systems, System Development Corporation, etc.)
4. Minicomputer system houses (Basic Four, Datapoint Corporation, Sanders, etc.)
5. Minicomputer system users (Allis-Chalmers, Cincinnati Milacron, North American Rockwell, etc.)

How does the potential user determine what software is available for his particular application? The most straightforward approach is to find out from the minicomputer manufacturers. Most manufacturers provide information on programs written for their machines either by themselves or by their customers. Programs written by users of DEC minicomputers are often submitted by the user to the DECUS Library (Digital Equipment Corporation User's Society). These programs are immediately available to PDP-8 and PDP-11 users. Minicomputer manufacturers that provide system houses with hardware on an OEM (original equipment manufacturer) basis are in the position to point the user to the right subset of system houses.

The user can also consult with periodic publications such as *Datamation, Computer Decisions,* and *ICP Quarterly.* Furthermore, a wealth of information on available software is provided by data processing information services such as Auerbach and Datapro Corporation.

Evaluation and selection of off-the-shelf software packages are generally performed using the same approach taken for hardware. The selection considerations are as follows:

- *Functional capability or capabilities* encompassing functions or tasks performed by the program and the system on which it runs
- *Vendor Support* in terms of software installation, personnel training on how to use package, and software maintenance assistance
- *Vendor reputability and stability*, corporate size, geographic location, and number of installed software packages
- *Documentation* such as package overview, file layout descriptions, operations manuals, as well as the general quality of documentation

The functional capability may be extremely difficult to assess unless the potential user has full access to the software package and is sufficiently experienced in terms of software. Obviously the best way to evaluate the package is to run the program.

The importance of vendor support usually depends on the background and resources of the prospective buyer. An organization with limited programming and analytic capability requires extensive vendor support while the experienced data processing professional is less dependent on it.

The reputability of the software vendor is usually a good indication of what to expect of the deliverable product. The relative simplicity of producing software makes it possible for an individual to write a software package in his spare time and market it. The support and documentation may therefore be minimal or nonexistent. This does not, however, mean that software company size alone guarantees the product to be of high quality. In many of the large software firms, the design and programming is a relatively limited area of activity. Furthermore, in the large software houses, minicomputer programming is fairly low on the list of software package development.

The line between independent hardware/software and minicomputer system houses is quite blurred. Several of the large, so-called software companies are gradually entering the turn-key* system business, while many of the turn-key system houses, which build "intelligent terminals," medical systems, text editing systems, etc., are marketing their own applications

---

* A system which, upon delivery, is immediately ready to start performing its intended task, once the electric power is turned on from a switch or key, is termed a *turn-key system*.

software packages. Moreover, nonsoftware companies are selling or leasing programs which they originally developed for in-house processing.

In-House Programming Considerations

The first consideration faced by the in-house applications software development manager is whether he should use an operating system or not. Very small systems, based on 4K words of main memory or less, usually cannot support an executive. However, except in the very smallest of applications, the use of a system executive greatly simplifies the applications programming and improves system performance.

The next question is, Should the program be written in assembly language or a higher-level language? Assembly programming, as already pointed out, economizes on main memory and provides maximum throughput. Here again, limited memory size will usually make assembly programming a more attractive alternative compared to higher-level language programming.

The high cost of writing applications software often outweighs cost savings in hardware. One-of-a-kind applications with possibilities of expansion and change are certainly more cost-effectively programmed in a higher-level language. Again, the particular higher-level language selected is a function of the particular application or, perhaps, the training and background of the in-house staff. ALGOL programmers prefer to program in ALGOL, while programmers versed in FORTRAN generally prefer to stay with it.

There are also several alternatives available in terms of program production. The program can be written and checked out using the deliverable hardware end items full time or developed using the background mode of real-time disk operating system. If written in a higher-level language, the user should make sure that the particular real-time operating system permits compilation in the background mode. The compiler must, of course, be a FORTRAN compiler if the higher-level language to be used is FORTRAN.

The concept of the *overhead facility* may be a viable alternative if the user system will be operating in an environment which does not require peripherals such as a paper tape reader, line printer, or disk. Software development time is considerably shortened using a disk-based system, which may be leased for the time required to build and check out applications software—or it may be a permanent production facility, when a large number of different types of small systems are built on a production-line basis.

The use of *cross-assemblers* or *cross-compilers* provides an alternative to the concept of the overhead facility. Cross-assemblers are assemblers that run on large computers to assemble programs and produce machine code for a minicomputer. They may be offered by the minicomputer manufacturer or by an independent source. Several cross-assemblers are presently available for the more popular minicomputers.*

Cross-compilers allow the programmer to develop his applications software using a higher-level language and, again, perform the compilation on a large machine. The large machine will thus produce machine code for the particular minicomputer to be used.

At the other end of the spectrum is the sophisticated software developer who wants to tailor his system for a specific application and market it as a product. This user is well advised to consider microprogramming techniques to optimize the system from a cost-performance point of view. Several of the user microprogrammable minicomputers provide micro-assemblers for microprogram development. This effort is probably best left to the expert programmer, who is also well acquainted with the intricacies of the minicomputer hardware design.

Without going into the details of purchasing, software development, and system installation, the schedule shown in Figure 4-24 is characteristic of the various steps or tasks required, starting with system design to final installation and delivery.

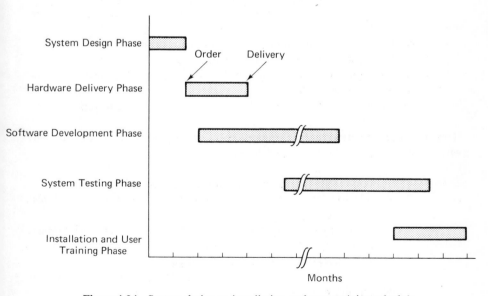

Figure 4-24 System design to installation and user training schedule

---

* An example of this is a cross-assembler for the Data General Nova minicomputers developed by Comtek Research, Inc. This package operates under IBM DOS/360 or OS/360 or DEC TOPS-10 (Total Operating System).

System design typically requires from 1 to 2 months. Once the system design is completed, purchase orders can be given to manufacturers on the various hardware elements. Hardware delivery schedules depend on how much of the system is off-the-shelf and the extent of special-purpose hardware design, such as nonstandard interfaces. The software development phase, which can be started independently of hardware delivery, is a function of job size, complexity, and number and experience levels of available personnel. The software development period is often equally divided between design, coding, checkout, and testing from event to system level. Installation and training are, of course, also functions of system size and complexity.

Software Development Tasks

To make a meaningful trade-off among purchase, subcontracting, or in-house applications software development, some thoughts should be given to the relative magnitude of the various tasks that must be performed if the programming is undertaken by the user himself.

The logical sequence followed is typically based on

1. System definition describing what the system will do. The general system definition phase is explored in greater length in Section 5.2
2. Identification and listing of required programs
3. Description of required data base
4. Examination of time schedules and programming effort in terms of manpower
5. Examination of available resources (people and equipment)

The next level of software development detail is a rough estimate of time and effort required to implement the following tasks:

1. System design with system-level flow charts
2. Translation of system design into detailed program modules, system tables, and I/O buffers
3. Translation of module-level flow charts into assembly or higher-level language instructions (coding)
4. Module checkout and program testing
5. Concurrent documentation effort starting during the system design phase (phase 1)
6. Program and user integration

It is quite common in the software industry to "guesstimate" main memory requirements and, based on the number of words of storage, to use a dollar-per-instruction cost figure (typically ranging from $5 to $20) to come up with a price for the software package. It is also quite common for this method to yield a dollar value which later, after the system has been implemented, is proved to be off by a factor ranging from 2 to 10.

Depending on the background and experience of the user (or rather lack of it), the subcontractor approach may turn out to be a more sound one than going it alone, particularly if the minicomputer system is fairly complex. Here again the user is well advised to consider factors such as the reputability of the subcontractor and his past track record in terms of performing similar tasks, the monitoring of progress after award of the contract to the subcontractor through frequent design reviews and milestone checks, and, finally, the prescribed acceptance tests to be performed prior to final approval and signoff.

The third attempt, buying the entire system off-the-shelf, merits a separate discussion, which is included in Chapter 6.

REFERENCES

Cowles, C. C., "Software Package Overview," *Modern Data*, October 1971, 50–53.

Green, R., "The Minicomputer and the Engineer—Part 3, Programming: The Key to Your Mini's Success," *Electronic Design 10*, May 13, 1971, 76–82.

Hooper, R. L., "The Minicomputer, a Programming Challenge," *Proceedings, Fall Joint Computer Conference*, 1968, 649–654.

Katzan, H., Jr., "Advanced Programming," Van Nostrand Reinhold Company, New York, 1970.

Mateosian, R., "Minicomputer Cassette Software," *Digital Design*, January 1973, 26–30.

"Microprogramming Handbook," 2nd ed., Microdata Corporation, Santa Ana, Calif., April 14, 1972, copyright 1971.

"Programming Languages," *Document 082X-00570-AMR*, Digital Equipment Corporation, Maynard, Mass., May 1970, Copyright 1970.

Sayers, A. P., "Operating Systems Survey," Auerbach Publishers, Inc., Princeton, N.J., 1971.

"Software Handbook," *Document DP-120-12/71-5*, Varian Data Machines, Irvine, Calif., November 1971.

Spencer, H. W., H. P. Shepardson, and L. McGowan, "Small Computer Software," *IEEE Computer Group News*, July/August 1970, 15–20.

Vachon, B., and W. Weiske, Jr., "The Minicomputer and the Engineer—Part 4, Interfacing: A Balancing Act of Hardware and Software," *Electronic Design II*, May 27, 1971, 58–64.

5

MINICOMPUTER SYSTEMS OVERVIEW

5.1 SYSTEM CATEGORIES, OPERATING CHARACTERISTICS, AND IMPLEMENTATION ALTERNATIVES

The Minimal Configuration

The minimal minicomputer system configuration usually applies within the areas of data collection, dedicated process control, peripheral control, and communications line control. In its minimal form the system typically consists of a 4K mini, an ASR 33 Teletype, and a simple I/O channel interface to an analog-to-digital converter with multichannel input capability, perhaps a second Teletype or a CRT, photomultiplier detectors, oscilloscope displays, or some other analog type of laboratory instrument. Such a stand-alone system does not operate under the control of an executive. The basic elements of a typical data acquisition system are shown in Figure 5-1. The important computer parameters in this type of system are input/output rates, word length and structure, memory bandwidth and cycle time, computer reliability, and the availability of mathematical language, as well as utility software.

The data acquisition from a large number of analog and digital sources may strain the program-control-handling capability in terms of timing. In this case it is important to analyze the potential worst case data input rate to make sure that the computer will not be tied up 100% of its time in I/O activities without being able to perform any other processing.

Some data collection systems may have to operate unattended for long periods of time, which requires features such as power-fail-safe and automatic restart. In this case, it is also important to make a trade-off between

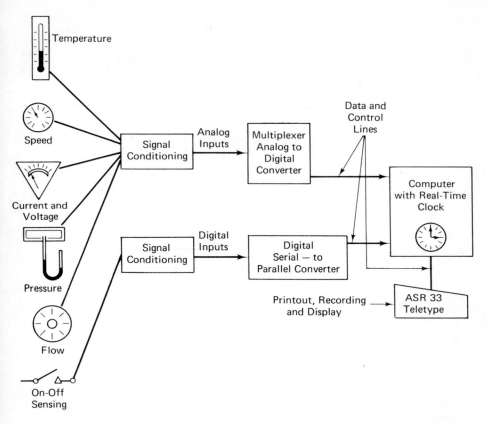

Figure 5-1   Data acquisition system

performance capability and general system reliability. A minicomputer using a relatively large-diameter core with resulting longer cycle time may be attractive because of its higher noise insensitivity.

The typical data acquisition system accepts information in analog form from various transducers. The analog data are thus converted into digital form for processing. The minimum number of bits per word is an important consideration. Most A-D converters require at least 10 significant digits. This rules out the 8-bit machines, where speed is important, and double-word processing is therefore wasteful in terms of timing.

In process control applications, the minicomputer provides signals which manipulate processes. Feedback from sensors may be analyzed in real time to adapt the characteristics of control signals to the external environment according to some predetermined limits.

The process control system is therefore highly adaptive and analogous to the classical closed-loop system. Most process control applications require

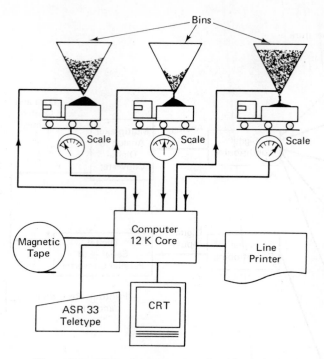

Figure 5-2   Minimal process control configuration

a flexible I/O equipment capability which will permit efficient interaction between the minicomputer and the devices being controlled.

The typical process control system, because of its closed-loop characteristics, is significantly more complex than the acquisition system. Depending on the application, the I/O requirements may be more sophisticated and demanding in terms of varying data rates. Also, since components in process control systems have a well-defined hierarchial structure, a more complex multilevel interrupt capability may be required. The nature of peripheral equipment for process control environments varies greatly, and, quite often, custom development may be necessary. Owing to this fact, a thorough system analysis is generally economically justified. A typical process control configuration is shown in Figure 5-2.

In this system, the computer controls the loading of trucks for concrete and gravel distribution. Each truck carries a different load and mix of raw materials, and the loading process is such that a truck may occasionally become overloaded and must therefore dump more of its load before new weighing. The computer controls several scales as well as the loading machinery. When a predetermined amount has been loaded, the computer will automatically turn off the supply and record the weight on the scale. From this it will subtract the weight of the truck, record the type of material loaded, and print out customer billings.

The computer must therefore do a fair amount of calculations, control its peripherals as well as analyze the data from the scales, and take appropriate action depending on factors such as mix of materials ordered, previous loads if several materials are loaded from separate bins, and the amount of material still available in the respective bins. The computer must also signal the various trucks when a scale is available, which scale it should proceed to, and when the operation is completed. The interface must therefore convert the analog signals from the scale into digital format, and the computer must be capable of receiving and transmitting signals over a considerable distance in case it is remote from the scales. The designer will have to consider trade-offs between various data transmission methods, which often depend on the capabilities of the selected computer, or, more likely, select the computer based on his optimum system design solution.

Minicomputers are frequently used to control input and output devices which service large computers. The overhead for simple data manipulation tasks, control sequences, assembly procedures, and error checking is thus removed from the expensive large machine to the relatively inexpensive mini. The most commonly used I/O control environment for the mini is in the data communications area. There the minicomputer can serve either as a remote peripheral concentrator, a preprocessor and message switcher (front-end communications controller), or a batch terminal controller. Emphasis in this type of environment should be put on input/output rates, conflict situations between lines and/or peripherals, minimum and maximum response times, computer cycle time, interrupt processing time, and communications code and control signals. A vast market for replacing the expensive hard-wired inflexible transmission control units provided by IBM for its 360 line had materialized in the late 1960s and early 1970s. This replacement market has, however, been threatened by IBM through the introduction of the IBM 3704 and 3705. Computers such as Honeywell DDP-516, Data General Nova, and Digital Equipment PDP-11 can replace the earlier IBM 2701, 2702, and 2703 with variable degrees of success. A host of manufacturers developed special-purpose minicomputers strictly for this replacement. The problem with many of these systems has been in the software area, where lack of appropriate software has forced the user to create his own. An example of large main-frame manufacturers developing their own minicomputer specifically for this purpose is Honeywell. Honeywell is using their Datanet 305 or 355 to provide the data communications preprocessing for their large 6000 series of machines.

The minimal configuration for a data communications preprocessor is shown in Figure 5-3. The essential features in such a system are the conversion

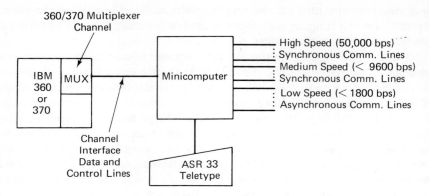

Figure 5-3   Data communication system

of bit streams into characters and vice versa, data buffering, line handling, code conversion, and terminal control instructions. What enhances the efficiency of this type of processor are line scanning and message handling, line command and status control, binary synchronous error checking, list processing and queue manipulation, byte manipulation, and a stack mechanism and recursive procedure entry. A read-only memory is of value for various macros related to instruction and control, data communications functions, extended arithmetic, message mode transmission, user-defined functions, boot load, and multiplex block I/O.

The Stand-Alone Configuration for Business Applications and Scientific Problem Solving

The stand-alone configuration ranges anywhere from a CPU with 8K memory, a Teletype, a low-speed printer, a CRT, and a cassette tape to a CPU with 16K or 32K memory and all the peripherals of a small- or medium-sized computing system, such as line printers, card reader/punches, magnetic tape drive(s), CRTs, and possible communications device interfaces. Such a stand-alone system may in some cases use operating system software.

In selecting a stand-alone system, the ability of the minicomputer manufacturer to deliver and support all the system components should be carefully evaluated. The desirability of a higher-speed printer or card reader that can be delivered by a minicomputer manufacturer should be seriously weighed against the availability of a lower-performance peripheral but with an existing hardware interface, software driver, and software diagnostics (albeit at a higher cost than if the same hardware were purchased from the original manufacturer).

Whether the system is going to be used in a business environment or for scientific problem solving, the system designer should consider the *total* system: software, hardware, special interfaces, etc. A large number of minicomputer manufacturers can provide complete systems off-the-shelf for such applications as research, simulation modeling, and medical and business processing. In autonomous problem solving, the instruction set available to the user will determine the limits of the system's computational capabilities. The data manipulation and testing instructions, arithmetic operations including Boolean algebra, address modification, and conditional and unconditional branching are of prime importance here. If additional software is required and must be developed, such features as debug and edit packages are useful. One very useful hardware feature is an efficient arithmetic unit with short add and multiply times, floating-point multiply and divide, and a large number of double-precision operations.

Figure 5-4 shows a medium-sized, business-oriented system. The system is large enough (12K memory) to run BASIC and employs peripherals such as character and line printers, a CRT, several cassette tapes, and a low-speed data communications interface. The system is singularly based on a bit-serial EIA, RS-232C interface where the cassette tapes, the CRT, and the line printer all run at 1200 bps while the communications and the keyboard/ hard-copy device interfaces are constrained to 300 bps. This approach— although limiting the expandability to higher-speed devices—enables the user to replace his peripherals with other newer ones when they become available. He may want to replace his unbuffered, Teletype-like CRT with a

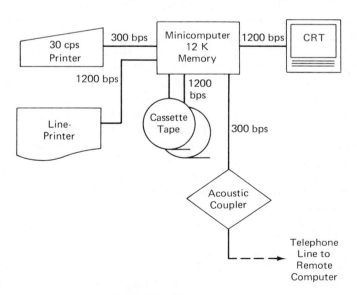

Figure 5-4 Medium-sized stand-alone system

buffered, split screen device as well as replacing the cassette tape with a more reliable unit when such a device is available on the market.

The user can gather data, format and transmit the data to a larger central computer for further processing, or use the minisystems on a stand-alone basis for bookkeeping and accounting applications as well as for sorting data retrieval, selection, and update. The computer must therefore have byte manipulation and extensive interrupt handling capability in addition to a core-resident compiler (such as BASIC in this case).

The General-Purpose, Medium-Sized, Real-Time System

Computers used in process control, data acquisition, and time-sharing applications operate in real time. A control program, designed for efficient real-time operation, handles such functions as interrupts, input/output data, and memory allocation. Real-time monitors that handle a number of programs are called foreground/background monitors. In a data acquisition system the foreground program possesses the highest priority, and the background program typically handles batch jobs, data analysis, and reduction. A real-time executive monitor contains debugging and diagnostic routines used for program error and fault detection. Real-time monitors are necessities in minicomputer time-sharing systems. Equally important in time-sharing systems is the requirement for one or more high-level conversational languages such as BASIC or FORTRAN to operate under the monitor.

Most, if not all, present general-purpose minicomputer time-sharing systems are based on a disk operating system. This system responds to commands from the programs as well as from the user's terminal. Some disk operating systems (DOS) include a batch capability allowing for command inputs through a card reader. This feature allows the user to submit jobs to be run while he is not present. The typical minicomputer DOS is composed of a disk and core-resident modules which form the monitor and basic programming modules. The DOS monitor handles I/O transfers, requests for programs, and other supervisory tasks. The basic programming support modules are the editors, assemblers, linking loaders, and debuggers necessary for creating new programs. Most minicomputer DOSs support FORTRAN or ALGOL. The typical monitor attempts to make I/O transfers flexible and device-independent where I/O devices are identified by mnemonics or numbers. The above system software and languages are discussed in greater detail in Chapter 4.

A typical minicomputer time-sharing system is based on either a fixed head or a moving head disk (the latter having typically 2.5 million bytes of storage, I/O devices such as a card reader/punch or a paper tape reader/ punch, a line printer, and a number of terminals (local or remote). This

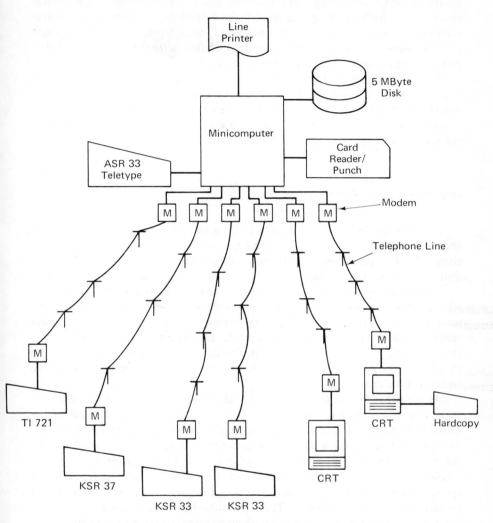

Figure 5-5   Minicomputer time-sharing system

terminal could consist of either CRTs with hard-copy devices or character printers such as KSR 33s. Such a configuration is shown in Figure 5-5.

The central processing minicomputer permits a mixture of low- and high-speed devices to be serviced. The system storage and swapping areas are capable of making large transfers very quickly to maintain a satisfactory response time. Additional file storage capacity is available in terms of available DMA channels, and additional disks can be added to the system since the controller can handle several fixed head disks. Important features such as hardware multiply speed, number of index registers, system response time, and the number of communications channels have been considered in order to maximize system throughput capability.

No basic rules exist for selecting the best computer for data acquisition, time sharing, process control, etc. Each application with its unique requirements dictates the parameter weights in system selection and design. The machine requirements are more a function of the complexity and size of the job than the type of job to be performed.

Implementation Alternatives

For the single-system end user it is generally less costly to limit the choice of system components to a single vendor who can supply both the computer, the peripheral controllers, peripherals, and as much of the required software as possible.

The advantage of this approach is that he gets a fully debugged system as well as software which is regularly updated with new versions, where the manufacturer foots the bill for this relatively large and costly effort. Unless some or all of the peripherals are made by the computer manufacturer, the user will have to pay for the manufacturer's markup, which may be significant. This may, in turn, be offset by the support from a single source when trouble develops.

At the other end of the spectrum is the OEM who may want to tailor his system to meet specific requirements and can afford to build some of the missing elements himself since he is counting on being able to amortize this development cost over a significant number of units. He may want to buy the CPU from the main-frame manufacturer, the compatible core from a specialized memory manufacturer, and the cassette tape drive from a specialized cassette manufacturer and go as far as packaging the drive and building the interface himself. The same may be true for other peripherals. He has the option of buying the disk from a system house which also provides its own disk controller and computer interface board with a tailor-made DOS, which may be either more efficient or less costly than the comparable DOS from the main-frame manufacturer. The less off-the-shelf the system is, the more it will cost in terms of integration for both software and hardware, which, in turn, means higher cost and longer development time. The only reason for all the extra cost and effort is, of course, the fact that no off-the-shelf system can meet the design requirements for the system.

Some of the higher-level trade-offs will be discussed in Section 5-2.

5.2 SYSTEM DEFINITION PHASE: HOW TO GENERATE PERFORMANCE REQUIREMENTS

System Definition

All the previously discussed applications fall into one or more of the following three categories:

- Data manipulation
- Computational processing
- Control processing

Systems in the first category receive, manipulate, and output data. The data may arrive in terms of digital character strings or analog signals converted into digital form. Furthermore, systems in this category require a computer, where prime qualities are high speed, flexible I/O, and good byte-handling capability. Typical examples of data manipulation systems are found in areas of business data processing, data communication, text editing, data acquisition and conversion, as well as code and level conversion. Data manipulation generally requires little or no feedback and is usually performed in real time.

Computational processing encompasses equation solving, data reduction, simulation, signal processing, and computer graphics. Most scientific applications fall into this category and therefore require a computer with powerful arithmetic capability and a large number of addressing options. Computational processing systems do not necessarily have to operate in real time or provide a large amount of feedback to the outside world.

Finally, control processing, as its name implies, refers to direct digital control, computer-aided design testing, sensing, and action taking, as well as tool scheduling, monitoring and control, automated quality assurance and assembly, instrument calibration, and inspection and testing, in addition to total manufacturing control.

Control processing, by its nature, functions in a classical feedback environment where information fed into the computer is analyzed in real time and appropriate control signals are generated based on external conditions. Control processing systems therefore operate in a closed-loop environment. These systems require an interrupt-driven processor with flexible interface.

Needless to say, a large number of applications overlap, requiring both data manipulation and computational processing, or any other combination of the above-mentioned three fundamental capabilities. A typical example of category overlap is the time-sharing system, which generally receives and transmits the data in a character format over telephone lines and also offers a computational processing capability. Several processing environments require remoting of the computer, which, in addition, is time-shared. The examples of multiple functions are obviously too numerous to be listed here.

From the previous discussion, it is clear that most systems can be defined qualitatively from both an applications and a performance point of view. The two approaches to system definition are complementary and will support the system definition phase in terms of what general system characteristics to look for *once the application has been defined and analyzed.* It should be emphasized that not until the system category and applications area has been defined can the system designer proceed with the generation of performance requirements. It has been said that if a problem cannot be solved with a slide rule, the computer will be of no help. This may be true in a computational processing environment, but it does not apply to data manipulation. Thus the implication is that the system designer must not only understand the problem but also be able to realistically relate it to a computerized solution. Since this definition process is iterative, we are really talking about a *matching* process, where a system definition must be generated in the framework of a potential (and, later on, optimized) computer-based solution.

No simple formula exists for the generation of performance requirements. The size and complexity is generally proportional to the magnitude of the problem. In areas where a minicomputer will replace an older, more expensive or less reliable system but remain compatible with the system interface boundaries, the performance requirements are quite straightforward. A typical example of this is in the peripheral control area. IBM 2701, 2702, or 2703 Transmission Control Units or Data Adapters used to interface communication lines to IBM System/360/370 computers are relatively expensive and, being hard-wired, are difficult to adapt to a changing telecommunications environment. The programmable preprocessor or minicomputer presents the ideal solution to this problem. However, the mini must meet several well-defined requirements, such as having a compatible interface to the IBM 370 multiplexer channel and IBM-compatible software and providing a binary synchronous protocol for telecommunications. (This feature is explained in more detail in Section 6.2.)

At the other end of the performance requirements' spectrum is the data conversion, process control, or data acquisition system, which may require nonexisting interfaces to special-purpose control lines and nonstandard peripherals. The gross configuration and sizing, as well as various throughputs, may be a function of the external noncomputer system environment, which sometimes is ill-defined for the simple reason that it is part of a larger system which at the time has not yet reached the final design definition phase.

From the previous discussion, it is clear, however, that once the problem is defined, basic steps can, in most cases, be followed in generating performance requirements in spite of the wide range of applications and levels of system complexity. The system designer can determine the gross configuration, the type of I/O required, the desirable internal computer architecture, the range of performance capabilities for required peripherals, the

System Category	Application	System Feedback	High I/O Rate	Sophisticated Addressing Capability	Powerful Arithmetic Capability	Powerful Byte Manipulation Capability	Several Levels of Interrups	Flexible Analog Interfaces	Large Variety of Communications Interfaces	Large Number of Peripheral Controllers	Large and Powerful Instruction Set	Large Amount of Software and Higher-Level Language Compilers
Data manipulation	Data acquisition	Limited →	X									
	Local and remote business batch processing		X	X		X				X		X
	Tele-communications		X	X		X			X			
Computational processing	Time sharing	Moderate →	X	X	X	X	X		X			X
	Time sharing Scientific problem solving		X	X	X	X	X		X		X	X
	Simulation			X	X			X		X	X	X
Control processing	Peripheral control	Extensive →	X	X			X	X		X		
	Manufacturing control						X	X				
	Process control		X	X			X	X				

Figure 5-6 System capabilities related to categories and applications areas

size and speed requirements for internal memory, the type and magnitude of applications software, and the specific reliability and maintainability requirements imposed by the operational environment. General relationships and target features for the three system categories and various application areas are cross-referenced in Figure 5-6.

From Performance Requirements to System Specifications

In most cases performance requirements must be related to definitions or standards that can later be equated to available computer system and component specifications.

In a time-sharing environment, the number of users must be defined, as well as the type and size of problems each user will attempt to solve, the amount of time the user is willing to accept as waiting on response time, and the requirement for user hard copy (or copies). Similarly, in a telecommunications environment, performance requirements must clearly state the number and type of communications lines used, the codes used, the maximum allowable error rates, the total response time for each line, the computers being interfaced and the software operating systems being interfaced to, etc.

Based on the available performance requirements, realistic system specifications can be generated. The system specifications may, for instance, describe the allowable range of desired machines in terms of word size (12–16 bits); memory cycle time (less than 1.0 μsec); instruction set (decimal or floating-point instructions); double-precision arithmetic functions; storage-to-storage, storage-to-register, and register-to-register instructions; minimum number of general-purpose hardware registers, etc. Similarly, at this point, required peripherals can be defined such as type of mass storage, I/O equipment, and nonstandard interfaces.

Well-defined performance requirements should enable the system designer to generate system configuration requirements which can be met by at least two alternative sets of vendor-supplied hardware/software configurations. Figure 5-7 shows a typical example of a remote batch processing facility system configuration.

5.3 DEVELOPMENT OF THE FUNCTIONAL CONFIGURATION: SYSTEM-LEVEL TRADE-OFFS AND COMPARISONS

System specifications may be impossible to meet with standard off-the-shelf equipment or with any minicomputer. There may also be several alternative solutions in terms of functional configurations.

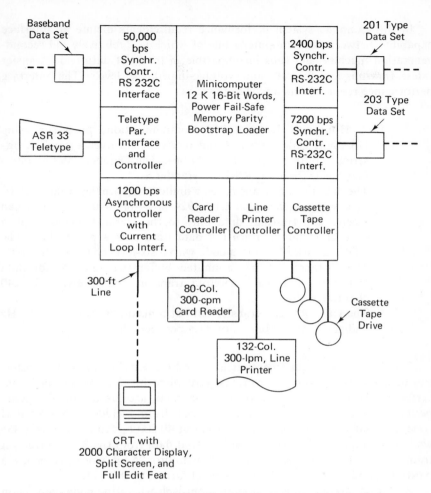

Figure 5-7 Basic configuration diagram for remote batch and data concentration

For a more realistic understanding of the trade-off process, several examples in various system areas are discussed in the following subsections.

Hardware Versus Software Conversion

It may sometimes be necessary to communicate with a device which is incompatible in terms of interface and data format, such as code. An example of this is the requirement for a data communications link, from a new third- or fourth-generation computer to an existing, older system.

In this example, system performance requirements dictate an interface capability between two computers, one of which is a relatively old second-generation machine and thus incompatible in terms of data code, transfer rates, transmission format, and voltage-impedance levels. The interface performance requirements are as follows:

1. A Honeywell Datanet 355 Communications processor using USASCII code transmits and receives data over a parallel, bit-serial full-duplex line at 40,800 bps. The Datanet 355 line interface meets the EIA, RS-232C standards.
2. The data must be transmitted a limited distance (less than 1000 ft) to a second-generation CDC 924, a 24-bit machine which can receive and transmit data only to the Datanet 355 through a parallel 25-bit interface (24 data lines plus a parity line). The CDC 924 uses Fielddata code with a six-level character format.
3. The Datanet 355 has a limited buffer size reserved for data transmission. It can therefore transmit and receive only 240 characters/block.
4. The CDC 924 can transfer data at a maximum rate of 62.5 kHz and generates 50 blocks of data per second.

Based on these requirements it is clear that satisfactory data transfers can be achieved by several means. A hard-wired bit-multiplexer code converter can be designed which, on the one hand, accepts the parallel data, performs an error check, converts the data from Fielddata to USASCII code, and outputs it in a bit-serial format at 40,800 bps to the Datanet 355 while it simultaneously receives the bit-serial data from the 355, converts it from USASCII to Fielddata, assembles it into 24-bit words, appends a parity bit, and outputs the data in parallel format to the CDC 924.

A second alternative is a software approach where the code conversion is performed by software in a minicomputer. Critical problems inherent in the latter approach are questions of the parallel data path between the minicomputer and the CDC 924 and the processing speed of the mini to perform the required conversions, error checks, etc, and still meet the system data transfer requirements.

In either case the nonrecurring development cost, be it software for the minicomputer or hardware design of the special-purpose converter, must be amortized over a single unit. The minicomputer solution is definitely more attractive in terms of spares and maintenance since it is an off-the-shelf item. Its attractiveness also lies in the fact that if the system is expanded, the same type and model minicomputer can possibly be used without having to stock additional spare parts.

A shortcut evidently exists in terms of the minicomputer approach. This involves the use of a 24-bit machine which also includes an additional twenty-fifth parity-bit in the I/O interface controller. Let us, however, assume that several low-cost 16-bit minis are already used elsewhere in the system. (Also, the 24-bit machine may approach the hard-wired controller in cost.) Let us, furthermore, assume that a standard, 1.2-μsec cycle-time minicomputer is used for the code conversion and interface control.

The maximum transfer rate from the CDC 924 according to system specifications (item 4) is 62.5 kHz. This is equivalent to a word transfer time of 16 μsec. Since the block size is 240 characters (item 3) and since each 24-bit word contains 4 characters, the total output time from the CDC 924 to the minicomputer is (240/4) (16 μsec) = 960 μsec.

The conversion time in the minicomputer depends on the instruction set and instruction times. Based on a four-step approach of data input to a register, parity check, USASCII conversion, and move of each byte into core, the total instruction execution time is 200 μsec/24-bit word, or a total of approximately 12 msec for a block.

The conversion from a six- to an eight-level code requires the addition of two *blank* bits to each 6-bit character. A 60-word Fielddata block is therefore equivalent to 240 8-bit bytes of data in USASCII code. The transmission of 240 bytes at 40,800 bps will therefore require

$$\frac{40,000 \text{ bps}}{240 \times 8 \text{ bits}} \approx 5 \text{ msec}$$

Assuming the CDC 924 must wait until the transmission to the Datanet 355 is completed from the minicomputer, the total data transfer of 60 blocks will take 0.960 msec + 12 msec + 5 msec $\approx$ 18 msec.

Since the buffer size in the CDC 924 is unknown, it must be assumed that each block can be stored in the CDC 924 for a maximum of 20 msec (item 4; 50 blocks/sec). Although the computed process is marginal, it appears as if the minicomputer can meet this requirement.

In terms of interfacing the 16-bit minicomputer to the 24-bit CDC 924, several possibilities exist. Two 16-bit parallel interface boards can be used where each one inputs and outputs 12 bits to the CDC 924. The 12 bits in each 16-bit parallel I/O register either can be emptied under program control in an interleaved fashion or a special switch can be added to the interface, allowing for automatic, alternate register switching to the minicomputer DMA channel. A third alternative would be to use one modified interface control circuit board for input to and a second one for output from the CDC 924. The controllers would have to be modified to handle 25-bit I/O with parity check. A block diagram of the controller interface is shown in Figure 5-8. The detail in the various levels of trade-off has been included in order to illustrate the total systems approach which must be taken in order to fully

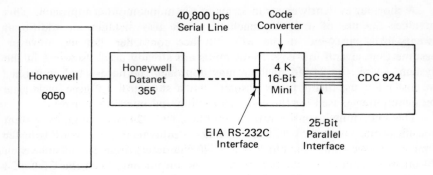

Figure 5-8 Minicomputer code converter, buffer and parallel-to-serial line interface

explore all options. Although true in this case, the minicomputer may not always offer the most optimal and cost-effective solution.

Minicomputer Versus Multiplexer

Based on previous system definitions, the following application falls into the data manipulation category. The performance requirements are as follows:

1. Three sites are to be connected over communications lines to a large central computer facility in San Francisco, which is using a Xerox Sigma 9 computer.
2. Site A in Los Angeles is presently equipped with a minicomputer with a 2400-bps telecommunications controller.
3. Site B, also in Los Angeles, will include two 1500–2000-character CRTs with a minimum data transfer rate of 1200 bps bit-serially. Site B will, in addition, include a line printer with a 1200-bps bit-serial interface and a card reader also with a 1200-bps bit-serial interface.
4. Site C in San Diego will contain various keyboard terminals operating at 110, 150, and 300 bps with an aggregate data rate of 2400 bps.
5. The load between A, B, C, and the Sigma 9 will be "heavy," and leased lines should therefore be considered.

Several possible solutions exist to this system design problem. The most "secure" from a reliability point of view is to connect site A over one line to the Sigma 9, and to connect each CRT, the line printer, and the card

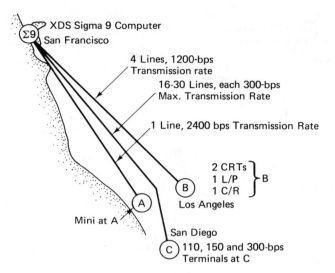

Figure 5-9 Each terminal at A, B, and C, with its independent line to the Sigma 9, using 103, 202, and 201 data sets.

reader, each using its own data link to the Sigma 9. Each device at site C can also be directly connected to the Sigma 9 over a dial-up or leased line. Depending on the number of keyboard terminals being used at C, some 16 to 30 lines would be required for communications links, each one with a length of 400 to 500 miles. The system configuration is indicated in Figure 5-9.

A more cost-effective solution saving on the highest cost item—line cost— would be to install a centralized multiplexing facility at A or B and to use a single high-speed line for the longest distance to the Sigma 9. However, an even more efficient solution is to add a second set of multiplexers at D and C, thus concentrating all low-speed lines into a single high-speed line. The second and third solutions are shown in Figures 5-10 and 5-11, respectively. Both the multiplexer and the separate line solutions will, of course, require the peripheral control function to be provided by the Sigma 9. The Sigma 9 may, however, already have a heavy data processing load. If this is the case, a possible solution would be to add a colocated preprocessor or minicomputer. We shall then have remote and local hard-wired concentrators as well as a minicomputer in the system.

A fourth solution may therefore prove to be even more beneficial. If a minicomputer is required in the system, it may be advantageous to remote it at B, and let it handle both the control and concentrating (multiplexing) function. Since site B already includes a keyboard input terminal (CRT) and a card reader, the mini can be quickly loaded and troubleshooted

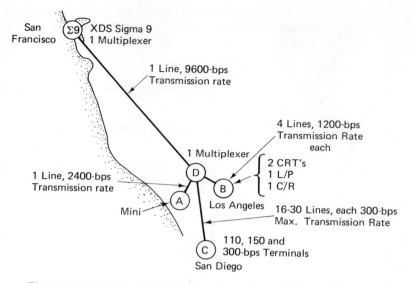

Figure 5-10   A multiplexer located at D, where D is close to A or B. The multiplexer at D uses a single high-speed line to the main computer at San Francisco

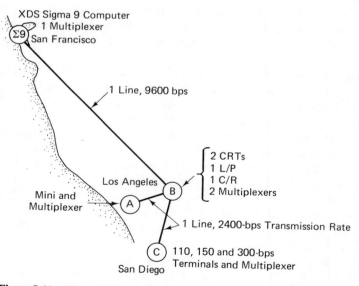

Figure 5-11   The multiplexer previously at D (see Figure 5-10) is now located at B. An additional multiplexer/demultiplexer is located at C, concentrating all low-speed lines into a single 2400-bps line

without the cost of additional peripherals. This approach has the additional advantages of the flexibility of a programmable processor, in case future changes are expected in terms of additional terminals, or higher data rates. In addition, since terminals at C are character-oriented, no control is required at C.

However, owing to the nature of operation, and since the keyboard terminals are unbuffered, the data rates over long distance lines from C to B

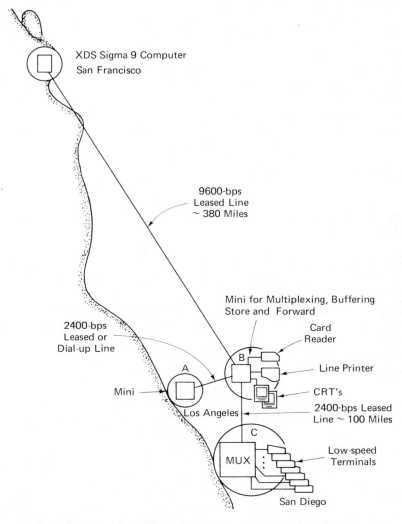

Figure 5-12 Minicomputer/concentrator for remote batching and multiplexing

are low, and consequently line costs are significant. It is therefore advantageous to multiplex these terminals over a single long-distance line to B, which will result in more efficient line usage. The fourth alternative based on a minicomputer based on software multiplexing is shown in Figure 5-12. The line cost between A and B being in the same city is obviously less than the cost of a long-distance line from A to the Sigma 9 in San Francisco. The multiplexing/demultiplexing function at B for the remote terminals transmitting and receiving data at C is best performed at the Sigma 9 site in San Francisco. There is no reason the character bit streams from C have to be disassembled as well as reassembled at B for final disassembly again in the Sigma 9.

The minicomputer I/O on one side therefore consists of two 2400-bps synchronous line controllers and four 1200-bps asynchronous controllers which are all multiplexed over a 9600-bps synchronous line to the Sigma 9, which performs the demultiplexing either internally or externally in a preprocessor. It should be clear that the latter approach differs significantly from the case where the remote peripheral control functions, in addition to the multiplexing function, have to be performed by the Sigma 9 preprocessor as shown in Figures 5-10 and 5-11.

Process Control Approach Versus Data Communications Approach

Both previous examples have dealt with trade-offs between minicomputers and controllers in two different areas: data conversion and communications processing. This example illustrates common trade-offs in data acquisition approaches, which impacts on basic computer system design decisions. The end result may be a process-control-type system or a data-communications-oriented system.

The system has been outlined in The Minimal Configuration. The performance requirements for the system are as follows:

1. The system controls scales for truck loading, keeps inventory of plant materials, stores customer order data, generates invoices, and performs various accounting functions related to customer account monitoring and billing.

2. Data are inserted through a keyboard terminal into a permanent file (magnetic tape) as well as into a semipermanent file (core memory). The permanent file contains a minimum of 50 blocks of data based on daily transactions. Each block consists of 200 alphanumeric characters. The semipermanent file holds 8 blocks of 200 characters each.

3. A hard-copy printer provides 300 characters of print-out. The printer will be located close to the scales.

4. Function 2 is performed either locally, adjacent to the scales, or remotely, 450 ft from the scales. The distance between the scales is 50 ft.

5. Each scale is connected to an adjacent control console. There are eight consoles of which only four are active at a time.

6. The number of binary signals from analog-to-digital converters, switches, and comparators is 80/console. All 160 lines must be sensed twice each second, per console. Eight return signals (binary) for console control have to be transmitted by the computer to each of the four active consoles, each half second.

7. The customer files are stored remotely in a large data processing center which provides a telecommunications capability if required.

There are several similarities between this and the previous examples: Data are gathered locally from several sources, and the information is preprocessed and thereafter transmitted to a remote computing center for further processing. As in the previous example, it would be possible to perform all the data processing at the remote large computing facility. This center would, however, also have to perform the real-time process control function. There again, a large bandwidth data path would be required for the long-distance connection to the remote facility. The hazard of this approach lies in the fact that in case of line failure the local operation would immediately grind to a halt. However, if sufficient local "intelligence" were to be provided in the vicinity of the control consoles, the real-time data transfer between the central data processing center and the process control site would no longer be necessary. Records could be partially processed and recorded on magnetic tape at the control facility and later mailed to the central data processing facility for further batch processing. The savings from not having to resort to telecommunications are significant in this application.

It is clear from the performance requirements that relatively limited processing is required by the small remote computer. A cursory analysis indicates that no more than approximately 1K 16-bit storage is required for the semipermanent file. An inexpensive cassette storage is probably adequate for the permanent storage. The data processing and control functions can be performed using no more than 8K or 12K or memory. The major hardware investment is therefore in the interface between the control consoles and the minicomputers. The cost of cabling alone between the minicomputer and the consoles will vary considerably, depending on the design approach.

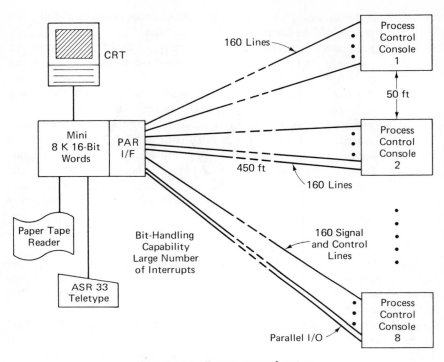

Figure 5-13 Process control system

Three alternatives are shown in Figures 5-13, 5-14, and 5-15. Figure 5-13 shows a process-control-based solution, where each of the consoles are individually connected to the minicomputer. Each cable contains 80 control lines and the computer is process-control-oriented, with adequate interrupt and bit-handling capability. Some 5000 ft of cable would be required to connect the consoles to the minicomputer. Based on $10/ft, the cabling alone would run to $50,000.

The second alternative, shown in Figure 5-14, eliminates the large number of cables using multiplexers at both ends. These multiplexers are probably special-purpose designs, and the savings based on this approach may be questionable.

Figure 5-15 takes advantage of the availability of relatively low-cost minicomputer Teletype interface controllers. Each console switch output register is addressed through a simple hardware decoding scheme built into the console. The various registers in each console are subsequently connected to an 800-ft daisy chain, which starts at the furthermost console position and connects, at the other end, to the minicomputer. The bit-serial line also includes some address and control lines whereby each console can

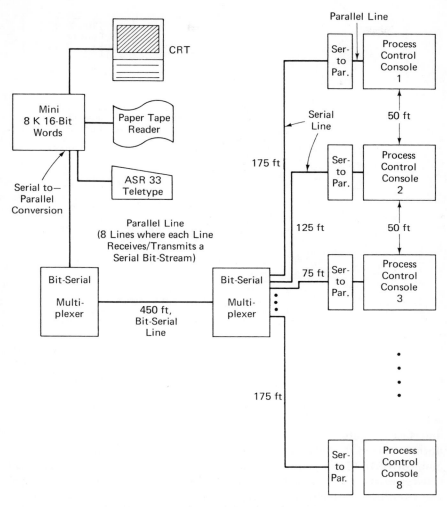

Figure 5-14 Data communications/concentrator system

be sequentially addressed. The resulting system is consequently data-communications-oriented in terms of hardware. (The programming is essentially the same in all three cases.)

The end result of the various trade-offs is a well-defined system block diagram, with basic definitions of data flow as well as functional subunit definitions. Additional performance parameters, such as data rates, accuracies, processing functions, data formats, and number and types of peripherals, complete the performance specifications for the total system. Subsystem specifications, which are of equal importance, include system

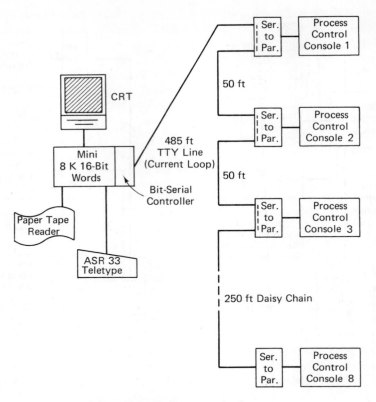

Figure 5-15   Data communications system

interface requirements as well as software program specifications. The former category contains, where and if applicable, specifications on the number of I/O lines, data rates, and interface procedures, and, if external, devices exist which are to be incorporated into or connected to the system, the required status and control lines, control codes, and device addresses.

The software specifications for the system include processing functions, data rates and characteristics, definitions of general subroutines, and process definitions, number and size of files, as well as I/O data content and formats.

5.4 THE SYSTEM EVALUATION AND SELECTION PROCESS

Criteria for System Evaluation

The system designer can proceed with the system evaluation and selection process once the system has been defined and the optimal functional configuration, as previously discussed, has been developed. However, to perform a meaningful system evaluation in terms of optimum hardware, software, maintenance support, etc., criteria for system selection must be established. The evaluation criteria are dictated by the system application, whether the system is developed by the OEM user or the end user, the level of system complexity, the technical know-how of the system integrator and/or user, the quantity of identical or similar configurations to be developed, the operational environment and geographical location(s), and, finally, the envisioned or planned future change or growth of the system.

The evaluation criteria universally fall into three categories: technical, support, and financial. Technical criteria are used as the basis for evaluating computer architecture, required I/O devices, peripherals and auxiliary storage, ease of programming, quantity and quality of supporting software, and potential growth and expansion capability and modularity. Support criteria are used to evaluate reliability of equipment, level of hardware and software maintenance, quality of documentation, extent of vendor or manufacturer cooperation, and warranty. The financial criteria are used to measure prices, discount terms, price-performance ratios, the level of system assembly and field maintenance required, the financial stability of the hardware manufacturer, and, in the case of the OEM user, potential future competition as well as future marketing cooperation and support by the manufacturer.

The majority of these criteria can be defined in relatively simple and practical terms. However, a few of these criteria may be difficult to apply, mostly because of lack of readily available information, forcing the designer to second-guess the manufacturer, thereby introducing a degree of subjectivity into the system evaluation process. Except for the self-explanatory criteria, each one is defined as follows:

Computer *architecture* is a measure of functional design for optimal software implementation. The CPU, memory, and I/O structure provide the foundation or building blocks, and the support software, the systems software, and the applications software make up the "mortar" that holds the system together and makes it work. All these elements are discussed in detail in Chapters 2 and 4.

Input/output devices, *peripherals*, and *auxiliary storage devices* are measured in terms of throughput, versatility, flexibility, and capability as they relate to the specific application. The quantitative and qualitative measures are discussed in Chapter 3.

The *ease of programming* is generally difficult to determine quantitatively. It depends on the application, the past experience of the programmer(s), and the skill level of the programmer(s). It can also be measured in terms of learning time to program the machine, debugging time, and suitability of assembly language for application programming.

The *support software* encompasses software made available by the manufacturer and the user's groups, free of charge or at a certain cost (see Off-the-Shelf Software in Chapter 4). There is also a time element involved; some minicomputer manufacturers depending on the popularity of their product may substantially expand the support software library for their mini in the predictable future.

Minicomputer system *growth* is linked to the architectural structure, which may or may not permit growth of memory size and speed as well as the addition of more instructions. *Expansion* is related to possible increase in circuit modules within a chassis or to the capability of adding expansion chassis to the mini. *Modularity* is a function of system expandability in terms of substituting different speed memories and peripherals within the framework of the existing system architecture.

Hardware *reliability* is measured in terms of mean time between failures (MTBF), which is equivalent to the average number of hours of elapsed time between failures. MTBF is a term generally associated with militarized hardware, which, with few exceptions, is designed to meet certain statistical criteria for total system availability.* Commercial equipment manufacturers generally do not provide information on MTBF. In spite of the obvious difficulty in obtaining this information, some ground rules can be applied by the system designer for gross estimates of hardware reliability (see Chapter 7).

Hardware maintenance is considered in terms of the manufacturer's reputation for service (data can be obtained from previous customers), the number of installations (which is particularly important to the OEM user, assuring him of continuity and permanence), the number of manufacturer service centers (again, importance to end user), the monthly production capacity (important to the large-scale OEM user), manufacturer provided documentation, and the design of hardware to permit easy diagnostics and service. The last feature relates to mean time to repair (MTTR), which is a measure of maintainability used by military computer users. As in the case of MTBF, MTTR is generally not defined for commercial equipment.

Software maintenance factors are generally more difficult to pinpoint. They refer to estimates of initial release failures, the history of adequate updates, and the response to reported software malfunctions.

Vendor or manufacturer cooperation criteria are based on responsiveness to complaints and willingness to work on nonstandard problems. The former

---

* Availability $= \dfrac{\text{MTBF}}{\text{MTBF} + \text{MTTR}}$

where MTTR is defined as mean time to repair; 100% availability is, of course, 1; MTTR is the average number of hours between a failure and the time that the system is up and running.

factor is, of course, difficult to determine before the hardware purchase. Some manufacturers may be highly responsive during the prepurchase phase but seriously deficient, after receiving the purchase orders, in meeting promised delivery schedules and providing backup support during the initial system installation and system debugging phase. In general, however, the initial hardware manufacturer response to the first call is a good indication of potential future cooperation.

The type of *warranty* is generally a function of whether or not the equipment is purchased under an OEM agreement. Typical warranty periods are 60 to 90 days. Some manufacturers may provide a warranty extending beyond 90 days, and in some cases the warranty is negotiable. The warranty extension is particularly important to the OEM user who may purchase a large amount of computers and peripherals which may not be delivered to the potential end user until after a significant period of time. In this case it is desirable to have the warranty extend to the end user.

The *cost* comparison is meaningful only in terms of total life-cycle cost, which includes hardware and software cost, development cost, installation cost, and system maintenance cost. The total system economics is discussed in Section 5.5. In terms of hardware cost alone, the hardware prices are easily obtained from the manufacturer. Regardless of whether the purchaser is an OEM user or an end user, the discount schedules are equally easy to obtain. The *price-performance ratio* is discussed in detail in the Cost Relationships portion of Sec. 5.5.

The criteria for *system assembly* relate to the potential and willingness of the vendor to perform complete system assembly and checkout. This is an area which generally differentiates the minicomputer manufacturer and the large computer manufacturer. One of the main reasons the minicomputer manufacturer is capable of offering his equipment at a low price is the low overhead he sustains in terms of total system assembly, integration, and field support. This does not, of course, imply that minicomputer manufacturers offer no support. On the contrary, the present trend is to provide complete, integrated hardware/software systems including computers, peripherals, auxiliary storage, communications interface, software drivers, operating system software, higher-level languages, and, in some instances, even applications software. This should still not be interpreted as being equivalent to the support from the large system houses such as IBM, Univac, Control Data Corporation, or Honeywell.

Field maintenance is generally a function of the extent of the system being provided by a single vendor. A mix of computers and peripherals from several vendors complicates the problem of field maintenance. The maintenance function is also a function of the size and geographical coverage of the hardware supplier. Smaller hardware manufacturers obviously cannot afford to provide the same extensive nationwide coverage as the few large ones. The field maintenance function can, however, also be performed by special service companies such as Sorbus and Raytheon (discussed in more detail in Chapter 7).

The OEM user who plans to develop a total turn-key system is well advised to consider the *potential competitive position of the hardware manufacturer*, who, later on, if the OEM user is successful with his product, may start competing for the same marker. Several minicomputer manufacturers presently offer turn-key systems; among them are Hewlett-Packard and Digital Equipment Corporation. These companies, as well as many others, also cater to the OEM market.

On the other hand, the hardware manufacturer can also offer valuable *marketing support* to the OEM. This is particularly true for the large minicomputer manufacturers with nation- or worldwide marketing organizations.

The above-defined criteria are, in many instances, still relatively generalized. Each subject must be subdivided into detailed classification areas. An example of this is the criteria for peripheral evaluation. Performance requirements in most cases dictate the mandatory base-line characteristics. In the case of an alphanumeric character printer, the requirement may be for a print speed of a minimum of 15 characters/sec with a 132-character/line capacity. The evaluation criteria must, in this case, reflect the relative merits of impact versus nonimpact printing; the ease of loading paper; optional 30-, 60-, and 120-cps printing capability; internal current-loop, RS-232, or parallel interface, keyboard design; print quality and general legibility; and availability of sprocket feed. All these characteristics do, of course, again relate to the particular application; in an office environment, a quiet, 15-cps impact printer which generates multiple copies and provides a highly legible font is more desirable than a 120-cps lightweight, portable terminal which prints only uppercase characters formed by a 5 × 7 dot matrix, which locks the user into a single character set.

Criteria based on limited detail in each of the previously discussed areas may well be an indication of a poorly defined system with nebulous performance requirements. Lack of system definition and precise performance requirements will in most cases bring disaster in terms of system selection and implementation. A poor understanding of the relative importance of various criteria as well as the relative importance of capabilities and characteristics within each area may likewise result in disaster.

The Flow Chart

The flow chart is a helpful tool in terms of clarifying the relative importance of system parameters and selection criteria. It will also enable the designer to fully comprehend the effect of higher-level decisions on detailed system capabilities. It also provides an indication of the interrelationships among the three categories of evaluation criteria. As an example, computer hardware is priced on the basis of configurations that provide identical service. This service is in part predicated upon the reliability of the equipment and the level of manufacturer service available. The equipment reliability and maintainability are again functions of hardware design and so on. If two minicomputers have about the same execution times for equivalent programs, the computer which requires fewer cycles can use lower-speed memory. This feature, in general, will make it more reliable. A more reliable system means lower maintenance cost and, as a result, a lower life-cycle cost. The interrelated areas are thus related to technical, support, and financial factors.

The flow chart, as its name implies, is nothing more than a decision tree where, at each point or level, a yes or no decision is made. An example of a flow chart is shown in Figure 5-16. In this example the flow chart serves a dual purpose: It rapidly eliminates a large number of devices which do not meet the high-level criteria (in this case multiple copies and upper- and lower-case alphanumerics). It may also force the system designer to take exception to or modify the performance requirements, which, for all practical purposes, could not be met if speed were considered the most important criterium and a minimum print speed of 30 cps was required. The flow chart process is mentally pursued by the majority of minicomputer system designers, although in a haphazard way, outside the framework of a formal, well-organized, and structured approach.

The flow chart is probably of greatest value in establishing the quantative importance levels among the various parameters within each selection area. If no performance specifications exist for the selection of a CRT display, the designer must analyze the total problem and decide which subset of the following features are of prime importance, such as number of displayable characters, maximum editing features, method of character transfer, background/foreground field display capability, or remote tab. As previously mentioned, the more well defined the system is, the easier is the designer's task. In a text-editing environment, for instance, editing, block transfer, and protected field are of prime importance; in an accounting and business environment, limited graphics capability, a numeric keyboard pad, and remote tabbing are all highly desirable features.

Based on the various degrees of importance, weighting factors can be assigned to each group of characteristics.

Weighting Factors and Scoring Techniques

Weighting factors are related to the relative importance levels of the various characteristics or system parameters. They are also intimately related to the particular application. A meaningful assignment of weights

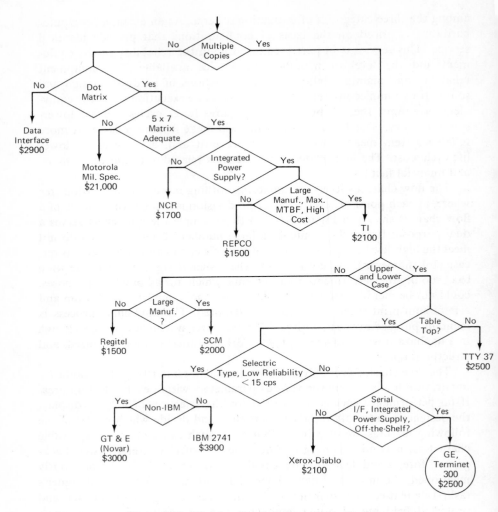

Figure 5-16 Decision flowchart for printer selection

must obviously reflect a thorough understanding of the system and the trade-offs that have been made in generating the system specifications. Detailed information in the latter area may not necessarily always be available, which is particularly true for military procurements where system specifications have already been generated before the request for proposal (RFP). The flow chart process may in this case be helpful as a tool in assigning weights.

In an example of this process* for the selection of a computer for a data

---

* Robin T. Ollivier, "A Technique for Selecting Small Computers," *Datamation* **16**, January 1970, 141–145.

acquisition system, a scale of 10 is used for weights, where word size receives a maximum weight of 10 and physical size a minimum weight of 1. It is almost impossible to keep the weight assignments objective. Two independent designers may assign grossly different values to these weights. The importance of this procedure lies in the fact that an organized approach is followed, and even if two independent designers were to assign weights with 20% variation in tolerances, the result would nevertheless be close enough to guarantee an optimized design. A basic understanding of the system parameters and their relationship to the application (Figure 5-6) is, of course, mandatory.

The scoring should be based on the range of characteristics, such as, in the case of word size, 4 for a 16-bit word size, 2 for a 12-bit word size, and 0 for an 8-bit word size. Zero to 4 is, of course, not the only or "best" range. The scoring could go from 0 to 100, 0 to 10, etc, where ideal characteristics receive a maximum score (100, 10, 4) and very poor characteristics receive a 0. The important and necessary requirement, in this case, is consistency. Varying the base will be equivalent to assigning weights to the analysis.

A simple rule to follow when assigning weights is to list all criteria, starting with the least important and adding the most important at the top. If the list contains 27 criteria, the range of weights could follow a scale from 1 to 27 (or whatever the number of criteria amounts to). An alternative approach is to list the n number of major criteria and assign percentage weight to each category. Such a list is shown in Figure 5-17. This list is based on 10 major system criteria.

Basic machine features or characteristics have been used in the previous example. It may be more advantageous to score features such as efficiency

Criteria	Weight (%)
1. Performance (hardware, software)	20
2. System life	3
3. Availability of applications software and documentation	2
4. Cost (nonrecurring, recurring, life-cycle)	15
5. Corporate stature of vendor	15
6. Risk and status of hardware product	13
7. Availability (function of reliability and maintainability	12
8. Equipment weight and form factors	15
9. Compatibility with other systems and subsystems	2
10. Future growth and flexibility	3
	100%

Figure 5-17   Percentage weight of various system criteria

of memory utilization by comparing the memory required for equivalent operating or system modules. For example, if BASIC will be used, the size of memory required for the BASIC compiler in the various machines considered should be compared. The operating and system software made available by the minicomputer manufacturers should be compared in terms of time required to assemble or compile and debug various programs, since the time and associated expense in converting programs to executable machine code may vary significantly between manufacturers. The latter types of characteristics tend in general to be more qualitative than quantitative in nature. For this reason, most system designers prefer to compare instruction set size and arithmetic capability as well as number of addressing features, registers, and interrupt levels.

Software elements are, because of their very nature, more difficult to define than hardware characteristics. For this reason alone, the computer is probably the most difficult element to evaluate in almost any system.

The same weight assignment-scoring technique can be applied to manufacturer support and financial criteria, as defined in Criteria for System Evaluation. An example of the application of this methodology is shown in Figure 5-18. The intent is to select a graphic display which is controlled by a minicomputer.

The weighted sum of the display system characteristics have been arrived at by multiplying each weight factor by numbers from 0 to 5, which were determined from the appraisal criteria. In this case 5 is considered excellent (top of the scale) and 1 is considered marginal, poor, or inadequate. A 0 is assigned to items where no information can be obtained from the vendor. The weight assignments are based on the 100% weight scale (Figure 5-17). The maximum score for any one product is obviously 500 (100% × 5).

The ratings for the display systems (Figure 5-18) range from 119 to 411 on a maximum scale of 500. Model 8 from manufacturer R is obviously far superior, in terms of its rating, to the closest competitor, G company with its model 4 (333 points).

This example is given only to illustrate the general method and is also applicable to complete minicomputer systems.

The small-system designer, who is constrained by financial factors as well as time, may not want to, or be able to, afford the thorough analysis previously described. An alternative method is available to him, which is a compromise between the extensive weighting analysis and flipping a coin (= sound engineering judgment).

This approach is based on a simple scoring method where plus (+) is equivalent to good, excellent, or superior, 0 is equivalent to fair or adequate, and minus (−) is equivalent to poor or deficient.

An example of this type of evaluation is shown in Figure 5-19. Four

Manufacturer		A	B	C	G	H	I	L	R	U
Display model		1	2	3	4	5	6	7	8	9
Selection criteria	% Weight									
Performance Quality (viewing area, resolution, linearity, legibility, brightness, contrast ratio)	8	32	24	40	32	16	24	40	40	8
Quantity of data (alphanumeric and vectors)	8	24	8	40	24	32	8	40	40	8
Interactive capability	4	16	16	16	16	16	16	12	20	4
Life Logistics (parts commonality)	1	3	3	3	3	3	3	3	3	3
Consumables (wear-out parts)	2	6	6	6	6	6	6	6	8	8
Operational software and documentation	2	8	6	0	2	6	10	2	10	0
Cost Nonrecurring	2	8	10	8	8	6	8	8	6	0
Recurring	5	15	10	5	15	15	10	25	15	0
Life-cycle cost	8	16	24	16	24	8	24	8	24	0
Corporate stature	15	45	60	75	75	75	75	15	75	75
Risk/status (level of development, customer acceptance)	13	39	39	13	26	39	65	13	65	13
Availability Reliability	8	24	40	0	24	24	32	16	40	0
Maintainability	4	8	20	0	12	12	16	8	20	0
Equipment characteristics Weight Volume Power Noise Electromagnetic interference	15	45	15	30	45	45	15	15	30	0
Compatibility with interfaced equipment	2	6	4	6	6	6	4	4	6	0
Future growth and flexibility	3	9	9	9	15	9	6	6	9	0
Total	100%	304	294	267	333	318	310	221	411	119

Figure 5-18   Graphic display evaluation

minicomputer systems have been analyzed for a OEM business application. Insufficient information was available on reliability (new product), software maintenance (new product), lack of understanding of certain hardware features, and negotiable warranty.

The summary table in Figure 5-19 indicates that minicomputer systems

Criteria	Computer			
	A	B	C	D
Technical				
Architecture	+	0	0	—
Supporting software	+	+	+	0
Ease of programming	+	+	0	—
Hardware and peripherals	+	+	0	0
Growth and expansion	+	+	0	0
Support				
Equipment reliability	0	0	+	0
Hardware maintenance	0	0	0	0
Software maintenance	0	+	0	—
Quality of documentation	—	+	0	—
Cooperation	—	+	0	0
Warranty				
Financial				
Ability to fill orders	+	+	0	—
Prices and discounts	+	+	—	—
System assembly and maintenance	+	+	—	—
Potential competition by hardware manufacturers	—	+	+	+
Marketing cooperation	0	+	0	—

Legend: + = Good, excellent, or superior
             0 = Fair or adequate
             — = Poor or deficient

Figure 5-19   Evaluation summary: four minicomputer systems

C and D are clearly inferior to A and B in almost all respects. System A is superior to B in technical areas, while B is more attractive in financial and support areas. Since both are sufficiently close in the technical area (A has superior architecture), B is the best choice.

5.5 SYSTEM ECONOMICS AND ACQUISITION

Cost Elements

The cost elements for system hardware typically encompass the following elements:

1. *Computer:* CPU and memory, power monitoring and automatic restart, hardware multiply and divide, floating-point hardware, automatic program load, expansion chassis, DMA ports, DMC,

multipurpose interfaces with extra I/O registers, real-time
clock, additional interrupts, memory parity and automatic
memory protect. (Some or all of these items may be covered by a
single computer price quote.)

2. *Keyboard and CRT Display Terminals: Communications Equipment:* Communications controllers, modem controllers, bit-serial
   multiplexer channels.

3. *Digital Input/Output Channels: Peripherals:* Paper tape readers/
   punches, card readers/punches, line printers, plotters, fixed head
   disks, moving head disk pack and cartridge drives, magnetic tape
   drives, cassette and cartridge drives, digital-to-analog and
   digital-to-synchro equipment.

4. *Cabinets.*

5. *Cables.*

6. *Software:* Text editor, relocatable assembler, linking loader,
   debug aids, diagnostics, macro-assembler, FORTRAN IV,
   BASIC, ALGOL, disk operating system, tape operating system,
   real-time operating system, RPG, emulators.

Some or all of the software may be free with the purchase of a computer,
or use of some or all of it may require the user to sign a license agreement
where he can use it only on a single processor.

The user is well advised to carefully consider the implications of not
using standard interface controllers from the manufacturer (the reason for
not doing it may be a system performance requirement which forces the
user to consider nonstandard hardware). Peripheral device controllers are
generally the least understood components of a computer system, and the
user may wind up paying more for the peripheral controller than he pays for
either the peripherals or the computer. Computers with very complicated
I/O architecture may also force a cost increase on nonstandard peripheral
controllers.

The most predominant cost element is, without any doubt, the nonstandard software which the user must develop himself. The programming
expenses are a function of the computer instruction set, the power of
available software tools, and the number of instructions required to write
the program. Programming costs on a per-instruction basis, including
debugging and documentation, have been quoted anywhere between $5 and
$50. Here again, the cost is highly dependent on the application and the
experience level of the particular programmer.

Cost Relationships

Hardware or software costs by themselves are meaningless. A comparative analysis requires that cost elements are related to each other or

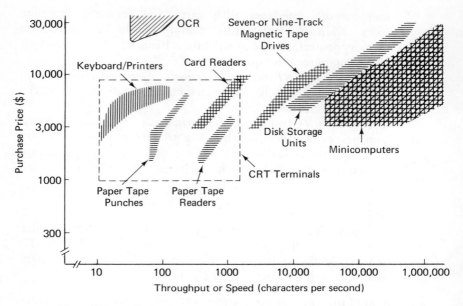

Figure 5-20   Price/performance comparisons, minicomputers, peripherals, and storage (early to mid-1970s)

measured in common terms. This may be hardware cost in terms of effective throughput, price/performance, or life-cycle cost.

Hardware cost based on relative throughput is, again, a relatively useless yardstick mostly because of the rapidly declining cost of hardware. Its value lies mostly in the face that various types of devices can be compared in terms of equivalent throughput for a given price at a specific time.

Price/performance in terms of throughput (normalized to characters per second; see also Figure 1-8) versus purchase price is summarized in Figure 5-20 for various minicomputers and minicomputer peripherals. This chart clearly illustrates that paper tape devices are more cost-effective for low-speed I/O but that card reader/punch equipment is superior for higher I/O rates. It also points out that, at the time the chart was constructed, OCR equipment, as an input medium, was not cost competitive with card readers or paper tape readers at equivalent speed.

A more comprehensive method for computing price/performance ratios for minicomputers has been proposed by James L. Butler.* He suggests the use of three equations for establishing the total system price/performance

---

* J. L. Butler, "Comparative Criteria for Minicomputers," *Instrumentation Technology* **17**, October 1970, 67–82.

ratio P, where P is the average between hardware and software price/performance (P_h and P_s, respectively). P_h is defined as follows:

$$P_h = \frac{\text{Basic system cost (\$)}}{\{0.1M[1 - [(W - F/2W]\} + (20/T)(A_h + L_h + I_h) + 100N + 50R\}}$$

where M = total number of bytes of internal storage

F = number of bits in the address field of single-word instructions

W = word length in bits

R = number of general-purpose registers

T = memory read/write cycle time

N = options included, such as real-time clock, memory protect, ports to memory, and power-fail-safe

A_h = measure of arithmetic capability (0 = none; 25 = hardware add and complement; 50 = hardware add and subtract; 75 = hardware add, subtract, multiply, and divide; 100 = hardware fixed- and floating-point arithmetic)

L_h = logic capability varying from 0, which is equivalent to no logic capability, to 100, which includes AND, OR, EXCLUSIVE OR, test and conditional branch, bit test, and manipulation as well as arithmetic rational test instructions

I_h = I/O capability, where 0 is equivalent to no I/O processors and 100 is equivalent to multiple I/O processors, DMA, DMC, and programmed I/O

P_s is defined by the following equation:

$$P_s = \frac{\text{Basic system cost (\$)}}{500(D + B + L) + 1000A + 2000C + 50S}$$

where D = 0 for no off-line diagnostic routines

D = 1 for off-line diagnostic routines

B = 0 for no debugging routines

B = 1 for debugging routines

L = 0 for no loader routines

L = 1 for loader routines

A = number of assemblers

C = number of compilers

S = power of on-line operating system

range = 0 to 100

At the time these equations were applied (1970) some typical calculated minicomputer price/performance ratios were

Data General Nova: $P = 2.14$

DEC PDP-8/I: $P = 1.28$

IBM 1800: $P = 4.64$

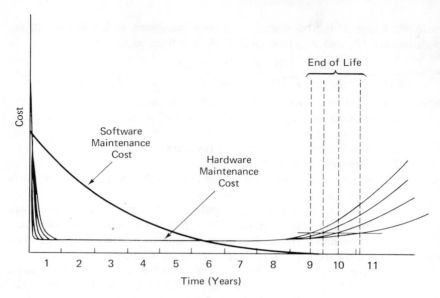

Figure 5-21 Typical software/hardware maintenance cost curves

The IBM 1800 was included to show the difference in price/performance ratios between minis and older, small computers.

The rapid improvement in technology has made the relative scoring used for A_h, L_h, and I_h obsolete. The general approach is, however, still valid and can be used as a supplementary tool for minicomputer evaluation on a cost relationship basis.

Life-cycle cost is a term initially used for military systems but can be applied universally to almost any type of system. This cost includes initial hardware, off-the-shelf software, special-purpose hardware design and development, software design and development, system integration, test and installation, operator training, documentation, and lifetime maintenance, including spare parts.

System lifetime is determined by when the system maintenance cost exceeds the cost of replacing the system with a new, more cost-effective system. The maintenance cost can be divided into hardware and software maintenance. The software maintenance typically follows a curve with a negative slope, whereas the hardware maintenance curve is shaped in the fashion of a bath tub. Initially, the hardware maintenance costs are high because of remaining bugs in the system. The flat part of the curve is related to replacement of parts worn through normal wear and tear, and, finally, the steep increase is contributed to overall system wear reaching its end of life (see Figure 5-21). More detail on system installation and maintenance is given in Chapter 7.

Life-cycle cost calculations are further complicated by line cost if the minicomputer system is used in a data communications environment. In this case, considerations must be given to modem rental, dial-up or leased line costs, potential future cost increase, etc.

Following the cost analysis, a hardware purchase will be made, based either on acquiring a maximum amount of hardware/software capability for the dollar amount budgeted for the system, procuring the lowest-cost system that meets the minimum performance requirements, or purchasing a system which provides the maximum performance per dollar ratio.

The Purchase Order

The purchase order should include all deliverable items such as the computer, peripherals, interfaces, nonstandard cabling, and all software provided at no charge. It should also list the specific delivery dates, where the equipment should be shipped (location), and whether the shipment should be made using air freight or surface transportation. Other important details are the invoicing terms (net 30 days, 2% 10 days, etc.) as well as the amount of quantity discount provided by the manufacturer.

If an OEM agreement is made prior to purchase, the buyer should consider the penalties imposed on him if he, at a later date, decides to break the OEM agreement. Some manufacturers offer two types of agreements. The first type is based on a flat discount such as 20% regardless of how many units (computers, memories, disk drives, etc.) are procured within a specific time period (1, 2, or 3 years). The second type is predicated upon the buyer acquiring a certain percentage of units in the OEM agreement to be delivered within predetermined time intervals.

In either case, the OEM user must carefully analyze his position in terms of a long-range sales projection. Depending on the option he chooses, a change midstream can turn out to be quite costly in terms of discount rebates to the manufacturer. The manufacturer is, of course, protecting himself against the customer who would sign an OEM agreement for a large number of computers which are never intended to be purchased, so that he can for a limited time take advantage of the low-to-high discount differential between a small and a large number of machines.

The buyer should also, at this time, clarify in the purchase order or in a separate agreement the availability of an overhead facility for predelivery training as well as other, manufacturer-provided training courses.

REFERENCES

BHUSHAN, A. K., "Guidelines for Minicomputer Selection," *Computer Design*, April 1971, 43–48.

BROCATO, L. J., "Getting the Best Computer System for Your Money," *Computer Decisions*, April 1972, 12–16.

CADY, R. C., "Get the Mini You Really Need," *Electronic Design 10*, May 11, 1972, C28–C34.

CORSIGLIA, J., "Matching Computers to the Job—First Step Towards Selection," *Data Processing Magazine*, December 1970, 23–27.

EGGERS, C. W., "The Minicomputer and the Engineer—Part 6, A Mini-Based System Takes Careful Planning," *Electronic Design 13*, June 24, 1971, 56–60.

HILLEGASS, J. R., "The Minicomputer—Getting it All Together," *Computer Decisions*, October 1972, 34–39.

KAYE, D. N., "For Buyers of Computing Equipment: More Power at Less Cost," *Electronic Design 23*, November 11, 1971, C8–C13.

KILGORE, G. L., "Selecting a Mini," *Automation*, May 1970, 102–106.

MEAD, R. V., *Real-Time Business Systems*, Holt, Rinehart and Winston, Inc., New York, 1964.

MILSTEAD, F. C., and G. L. NEELY, "The Minicomputer and the Engineer—Part 2, Get the Facts Behind Mini Specs," *Electronic Design 9*, April 29, 1971, C20–C27.

SELIGMAN, L., "Buying a Minicomputer? Ask These Questions First," *EDN*, May 1, 1972, 20–25.

SHARPE, W. F., *The Economics of Computers*, Columbia University Press, New York, 1969.

6

MINICOMPUTER SYSTEMS
APPLICATIONS

The previous chapters have dealt with most of the elements available to the system designer and the tools used to evaluate them. A brief overview has also been given of various system categories. Several basic types of systems are now described in greater detail in terms of what they can and cannot do for the user, how they work, the type of hardware and software they are based on, and the industries that use them. These categories are as follows:

1. Word processing and text-editing systems
2. Intelligent and remote batch terminals
3. Data gathering, events recording, monitoring, and data entry systems
4. Concentrators, message-switching controllers, and communications preprocessors
5. Process and numerical control systems
6. Computational and time-sharing systems

In spite of the fact that a large amount of overlap exists (many word processing systems are based on time sharing, and several process control systems use so-called intelligent terminals), it is believed that the six categories are different enough to merit separate discussion.

6.1 WORD PROCESSING AND TEXT EDITING

Word processing was originally conceived as a method of providing assistance to the typist. Word processing systems consist typically of IBM-Selectric-type typewriters coupled to storage devices using paper tape, magnetic cards, or magnetic tape. The typist types a letter, form, or document, using a conventional typewriter. During the typing process, the typed message is simultaneously recorded. The operator can later obtain a copy of the typed letter simply by rewinding the magnetic tape or reinserting the paper tape or magnetic card into the reader and replaying it. The typewriter will thus automatically provide a copy of the prestored message. In several systems, it is also possible for the typist to edit the letter or document by overstriking previously typed characters, words, or sentences. Some systems permit text to be divided into blocks and assembled at will during the editing process. The small non-computer-based word processors are, however relatively slow and limited in flexibility and capability. The word processing power is therefore greatly enhanced using minicomputers, which can quickly recall information and perform both text management and transcription tasks. Text management allows the user to store thousands of preformatted paragraphs and phrases which can later be recalled by the typist or text editor during the text composition process. Document transcription allows an unlimited number of revisions and updates based on random access to a large amount of pretyped letters or documents.

How do Minicomputer Word Processors Differ from Other Types of Word Processors?

Word processing systems can be divided into the following basic categories:

1. Automatic word processing typewriters using paper tape, magnetic cards, or cassette or cartridge tape
2. Minicomputer-based word processing and formatting systems
3. Time-sharing systems where the computer is either a local or remote mini or a larger machine

Each of the systems in the first category suffers from a host of disadvantages. When large amounts of data must be stored, paper tape is a bulky and awkward-to-handle storage medium. Data punched on paper tape can obviously not be changed and therefore requires recopying when corrections have to be made. Magnetic tape is more flexible in that errors can be overwritten. Magnetic tape, however, is also more expensive than paper tape. Use of two cassette or cartridge tapes, called *stations* in text-editing systems, greatly enhances the system capability. A single station device is basically used for form letters or short correspondance. A two-station device permits storage of standard words or phrases on one tape, which at appropriate times can be inserted or "merged" into the composed text. In spite of this, magnetic cassettes or cartridges become difficult to work with when extensive editing is required. Retyping is generally a necessity when editing changes exceed 15% of the total text.

In addition to magnetic and paper tape, some word processing systems use magnetic cards. One magnetic card generally holds one page, roughly equivalent to 2500 words of text. Two-station systems permit the storage of the original text on one card, while the second card is used to make corrections, additions, or deletions to the text. Since the cards can be individually altered, recopying is not required as with paper tape. However, where large amounts of text must be stored, the high cost of each card makes this word processing technique the most expensive of the three.

Offices using more than a handful of typists or secretaries may greatly reduce their operating cost using computerized word processing. Minicomputer-based systems allow several operators to simultaneously use the same paragraphs or documents for text editing, in contrast to card- or tape-based systems, where usually only one copy of a card or cassette tape is available with the individual text. The process itself is also speeded up by using a disk-based system which has faster access time to strings of text than a cassette tape system. A minicomputer-based system with an IBM-2315-like dual disk can typically store up to 5 million characters or bytes, which is equivalent to more than 3000 pages of indexed text.

Most minicomputer systems permit up to 16 terminals to be connected on-line using either teleprinters or CRT terminals. The typist can compose the letter from the CRT terminal and use the internal memory of the CRT terminal for editing storage. Once he or she is satisfied with the text, it can be stored on disk for subsequent print-out using a high-speed line printer.

A further advantage of the minicomputer text-editing system over automatic word processing typewriters is its capability of performing functions such as automatic hyphenation, insertion of date, page and section numbering heading and footing inscription, insertion of variables within any paragraphs, and table-of-contents preparation. In addition to letter writing and document preparation, the computer can run other programs simultaneously, such as accounts receivable, budgets, and payroll.

The cost of a word processing system may be reduced if a minicomputer is available and already used for other purposes and can be upgraded or expanded to perform this additional task.

The third alternative to word processing is the outside time-sharing system. Several companies currently offer time-shared word processing capabilities on an hourly basis. Additional charges are typically made for the amount of storage used, high-speed printer utilization, and telephone connect time. The last feature may turn out to be prohibitive, depending on how far the user is located from the time-sharing center. The only hardware the user needs is a keyboard terminal, a modem, or an acoustic coupler plus a telephone line. The user of a time-sharing facility will, however, have to consider the problem of error control resulting from long-distance data transmission.

A system marketed by Wang Laboratories, Inc. emulates the operation of the IBM 2741 Selectric terminal, transmitting at 134.5 bps to a remotely located processor. A parity bit is transmitted with each character, and the computer asks for retransmission in the event a parity error is detected.

The use of an outside time-sharing service may turn out to be less costly than adding hardware, such as a disk, internal memory, transmission control equipment, and a high-speed line printer, to the in-house time-sharing system. An expanded in-house facility may also require additional personnel to monitor the print-out quality of the high-speed printer and maintain the word processing software. Furthermore, the present user schedule of the in-house time-sharing system may make it impractical for the future word processing user to access the machine during remaining available hours.

How Do the Minicomputer-Based Word Processing Systems Work?

The overwhelming number of off-the-shelf word processing systems are presently based on CRT terminals for editing and input to the computer. The output is either in the form of magnetic or paper tape or hard-copy print-out. Several systems are designed for the newspaper or publishing business where the paper or magnetic tape output is used for later input to a photo composition machine (photocomp).

At the low end of the scale, limited-size minicomputer systems are used in various office environments, such as in law offices, shipping companies, and insurance firms, while at the high end dedicated systems for text editing are sold to various newspaper, magazine, and book publishers.

LCS Corporation (Springfield, Mass.) provides a system based on a DEC PDP-8/e with one or more Selectric terminals, an auxiliary disk storage device, and a Mohawk Data Sciences MDS 4330 230-lpm line printer (Figure 6-1). Based on a cost-performance study performed by Robert A. Mendel of the law firm of Kamberg, Berman, and Mendel, Inc.,* the LCS two-terminal computer-based word processing system saves some 20% in cost compared to the cost of using three IBM manufactured automatic word processing typewriters. When operating the system in a text management mode, the letter writer, when composing his letter, may select from a list of standard phrases or paragraphs which he can mix with material he is writing or dictating. The dictated material is typed in, while at the same time the paragraph numbers of the desired standard material are inserted. The

---

* R. A. Mendel, "Minicomputer Word Processing: A Two-Year Case History," *Infosystems*, August 1972, 35–37.

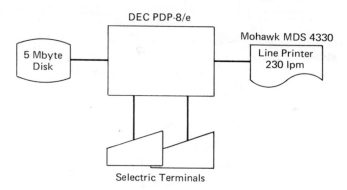

Figure 6-1 LCS Corporation word processing system

computer text management software will now automatically insert the standard material as requested and the complete text will be printed out by the line printer.

The transcription program permits the secretary to type out a rough draft on plain paper, quickly backspacing and overtyping any errors. The computer program will store the entire text, assigning numbers to each paragraph.

During the final editing process, the writer can request any of the paragraphs to be retrieved from the computer in order to make corrections. Finally, when satisfied with the format and content of the text, the user can request a hard-copy print-out from the line printer.

In contrast to text management processing, transcription processing is performed on-line in real-time. This is usually also true for word processing and text-editing systems used by newspapers for classified ad and news entry. These types of text-editing systems permit all proofing to be accomplished prior to typesetting.

In a typical classified ad system, an ad taker accepts ads submitted by telephone conversation or on ad forms completed by advertisers or ad salesmen. The ad taker uses a CRT terminal on which he calls up a form from the minicomputer auxiliary storage device. Depending on the available hardware features of the terminal, the operator can perform all necessary editing on the terminal, such as keying in, changing, inserting, or deleting characters. When the operator is satisfied with the form and content of the ad displayed on the CRT, he can transmit it to the computer by depressing the send or transmit key. The data are then copied from the CRT terminal's buffer to the minicomputer.

Once the entire message has been received by the computer, software in the computer will perform line justification, hyphenation, and ad costing before the reformatted ad is transmitted back to the ad taker for review.

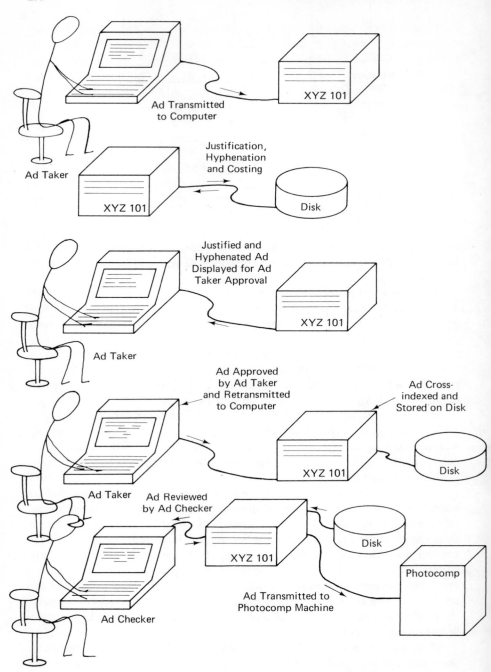

Figure 6-2 Word processing and text editing for classified ad system

Line justification is performed by measuring the width of the specified newspaper typeset and comparing this measurement against the line width of the entered text. If a word must be broken, it is presented to the hyphenation routine for determination of hyphen points. The justification program selects the hyphen point which permits the most suitable interword spacing.

The hyphenation routine generally operates as a subroutine to the justification routine. Hyphenation is accomplished through word look-up in a 40,000- to 50,000-word dictionary residing on disk. A typical 200-word ad will require some three to four accesses to the disk for hyphenation look-up.

Upon justification, the ad costing program will count the number of justified lines and compute the cost of the ad. Provisions are usually made for the number of times the ad will appear as well as minimum charge conventions.

The ad, once it has been retransmitted in its justified and hyphenated form back to the CRT display, can now be remodified by the operator or ad taker. If changes are made, the ad can be rejustified and recosted by depressing the CRT terminal transmit key.

When the appearance and content of the ad is acceptable, it is retransmitted to the computer, where it is cross-indexed within its classification and stored on disk.

In a separate process, each ad stored on disk is reviewed by an ad checker before newspaper printing.

The sequence of events from the initial reception of a phone call from the advertising customer to final message transfer to the photocomp machine is shown in Figure 6-2.

Hardware Selection Criteria for In-House Text-Editing System Design

Each system component must be evaluated in terms of requirements peculiar to the user's operating environment. A text-editing application based on the previously described classified ad system requires a large number of CRT terminals, a minicomputer line printer, and disk and perhaps some optional equipment such as magnetic tape drives and optical character readers.

The CRT terminal is the key element in the system, permitting locally buffered data entry and editing. It is generally desirable to be able to display at least 500 characters and perform various editing functions such as character, word, and line insert and delete. Most ad taking systems are combined with news-text entry, requiring a maximum amount of space for CRT character display. The upper limit for low-cost CRT terminals is presently approximately 2000 characters.

Most text-editing systems benefit from terminals with built-in foreground

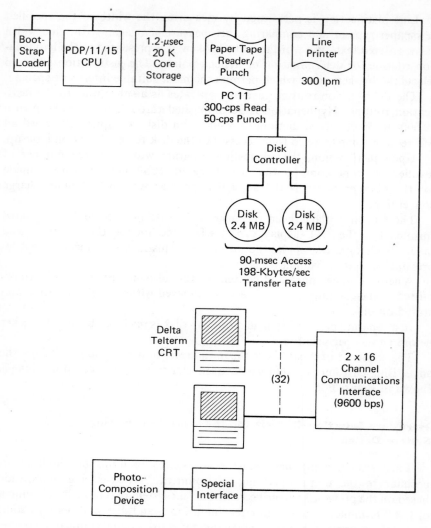

Figure 6-3 Text-editing system based on digital equipment

and background capability, remote cursor positioning, and upper- and lowercase character display capability (7 × 9 dot matrix).

For more information on CRT evaluation criteria, see Interactive Alphanumeric Display Terminals in Chapter 3. For fast block data transfer between the CRT terminal and the computer, high-speed bit-serial or parallel transmission is a desirable feature.

The most economical way of interconnecting CRT terminals is to use

EIA RS-232C interfaces with serial transmission. The highest bit-serial data rate for CRT terminals is generally 9600 bps.

A block diagram of such a system is shown in Figure 6-3. Note that the photocomposition unit either can be directly interfaced through a custom-designed interface or paper tape can be punched out by the text-editing system for later off-line photocomp loading through a paper tape reader. The particular system is based on a DEC PDP-11.

Critical Performance Parameters for Text-Editing Systems

System performance is heavily influenced by the system's software architecture and hardware characteristics. In the previously described hardware selection process, trade-offs must be made between performance characteristics and cost factors. It should be kept in mind, however, that some of hardware selection criteria are fixed, such as the availability of upper- and lowercase characters on the CRT display. Other parameters must be traded off against software and hardware cost.

Text-editing systems used in real-time environments are generally designed or evaluated in terms of system response time. In the case of the classified ad system, response time is measured from the time the operator is finished with keying in data on the CRT terminal and depresses the transmit key, being satisfied with the appearance of the screen and the return message being displayed in its entirety on the CRT.

The total response time can be subdivided into several time segments:

1. Queue time
2. Transfer time to the computer
3. Processing time on the computer
4. Transfer of processed message to the CRT

The queue time is a function of the assigned priority to a CRT terminal and the number and length of programs waiting in line to be processed. The queue length also depends on the number of terminals having simultaneous access to the CPU. The computer will respond to the *request-to-transmit* message from the console operator with a *ready* message when other terminals are no longer being processed or waiting to be processed. When this occurs, the computer initiates the data transfer from the CRT console with a *computer-ready* signal.

The timing sequence is shown in Figure 6-4.

The transfer time to the computer is a function of the terminal-to-computer interface. For a 9600-bps bit-serial interface, the transfer time, is a function of the number of characters transmitted. Average ad length is

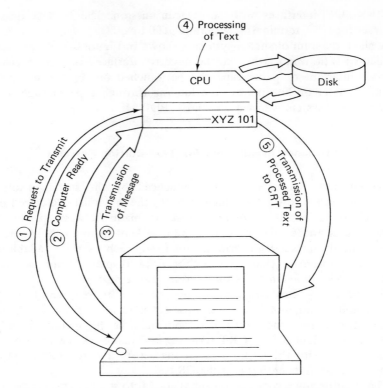

Figure 6-4 Time segments from request to transmit to receipt of processed text

typically 200 characters, which, in this case, requires approximately 0.2 sec to transmit. Faster transmission rates can be achieved with a parallel interface. Regardless of the distance from the CRT terminal to the computer, this type of interface is always more expensive from a hardware standpoint.

Once received by the computer, the text will be justified and hyphenated and the ad will be costed. In the course of processing, several accesses will be made to disk memory for programs not located in main memory, as well as for hyphenation dictionary look-up and storage index retrievals.

Because of the relatively long disk access time (approximately 90 msec—Figure 6-3) compared to instruction execution time (several hundred computer instructions can be executed each millisecond), the processing time is largely a function of the number of disk accesses which must be accomplished in the processing of the CRT terminal's input.

At an average of 90 msec/access, approximately 900 msec will be required for 10 disk accesses. Although some processing is accomplished simultaneously with disk transfers, most of the processing will be delayed. An additional 200 msec will permit 30,000 to 50,000 instructions to be executed in addition to perhaps another 100,000 instructions executed during the disk transfers. The total processing time is, therefore, about 1.1 sec. This time can obviously be reduced using a disk with shorter access time. A fixed head disk would reduce the total processing time to perhaps one-third, or 400 msec. The user would, however, have to make the trade-off between higher potential throughput and more limited storage available on a comparably priced fixed head disk.

The transmission of the processed data back to the CRT terminal will approximately equal the time of the initial transmission from the CRT to the computer, or for a 200-character message, 0.2 sec. With only a single terminal operating, the queue length is 0, and the total response time, based on the above example, is $0.2 + 1.1 + 0.2 = 1.5$ sec. However, as the number of terminals in the system are increased, a certain wait time will be imposed on the operator. This wait time should obviously be kept to a minimum.

Assuming that it takes 2 min to key-in and edit a typical ad and that the system is based on 32 CRT terminals, the average operator waiting time in seconds is determined in the following manner:

$$W = L\left(\frac{3600}{M}\right)$$

where M = number of transactions processed per hour
L = average number of messages in the system
W = average operator wait and service time

The average number of messages in the system may be computed based on either an exponential or constant service time. In an ad taking system, the time to service successive messages does not vary exponentially.

The average number of messages in the system can therefore be determined from the following equation:

$$L = \frac{\rho(2 - \rho)}{2(1 - \rho)}$$

where ρ = ratio of average number of messages per hour being processed, divided by the maximum throughput rate of the system, assuming infinite input queue length.

(The above two equations are given in *Real-Time Data Processing Systems* by Saul Stimler, McGraw-Hill Book Company, New York, 1969, pp. 94 and 96.)

The average wait and service time is thus computed as follows:

$$\rho = \frac{(30 \text{ messages/hr})(32 \text{ terminals})}{(3600 \text{ sec/hr})/(1.5 \text{ sec/transaction})} = 0.4$$

$$L = \frac{\rho(2 - \rho)}{2(1 - \rho)} = \frac{0.4(2 - 0.4)}{2(1 - 0.4)} = 0.533$$

$$M = (30 \text{ messages/hr})(32 \text{ terminals}) = 960 \text{ terminal messages/hr}$$

and

$$W = L\left(\frac{3600}{M}\right) = 0.533\left(\frac{3600}{960}\right) = 2 \text{ sec}$$

The average wait time is thus $2 - 1.5 = 0.5$ sec, which is transparent to the user.

6.2 INTELLIGENT AND REMOTE BATCH TERMINALS

Intelligent or "smart" terminals are defined in several ways depending on who the manufacturer is and what the inherent capabilities are of the particular product. Commonly, intelligent terminals are described as systems that contain a stored program control unit or a minicomputer. An intelligent terminal is generally designed to fit into an office as an integral part, with the computer built into a "standard" office-type desk. The system can be used either in a stand-alone configuration or as a remote terminal which can be programmed to share some of the processing load with a central computer.

Remote batch terminals may or may not contain a computer. They are generally less flexible than intelligent terminals. However, while many intelligent terminals can perform in a remote batch processing mode, remote batch terminals often cannot be used in a stand-alone configuration to perform even limited processing tasks.

What Are the Hardware/Software Elements of an Intelligent Terminal?

The *power* of an intelligent terminal is closely linked to its architecture, processor capability, available software packages, programming language capabilities, memory storage capacity, peripherals, and communications capability. Most intelligent terminals fall into two categories: systems using minicomputers specifically developed by the intelligent terminal manufacturer and systems using off-the-shelf minis such as the Data General Nova, Microdata 1600, and Digital Equipment Corporation PDP-8.

Terminals in the former category are designed by both the large computer manufacturers such as NCR, Burroughs, and Control Data Corporation and intelligent terminal "specialists" such as Four Phase Systems and Datapoint

Corporation. Systems in the latter category are built by so-called *buy-and-tie* manufacturers, where the main *value added* consists of total system integration of computer, peripherals, communication equipment, and applications software.

Many of the available intelligent terminals, not designed around a general-purpose minicomputer, are relatively slow in terms of memory access time, are restricted in terms of internal memory growth capability, and can be used only for limited off-line functions such as listing, data transcription, and key-punching. Several terminals are built around CRT displays designed to operate either in a stand-alone or multistation environment (Datapoint 2200, Four Phase System IV/70, Incoterm SPD 10/20, Raytheon PTS 100, Sanders Can Do, etc.).

Peripherals available consist of card readers, serial character and line printers, cassette units and industry-compatible tape drives, fixed and moving head disks, and paper tape readers. Although the type and range of peripherals may vary from terminal to terminal, intelligent terminal houses generally provide the same type of peripherals with their systems as do minicomputer main-frame manufacturers. In some cases, intelligent terminal manufacturers select what they consider to be the most cost-effective and optimum-performance peripherals. Many times, these peripherals are not identical to those provided by the particular minicomputer manufacturer whose minicomputer is used in the terminal. The intelligent terminal manufacturer may therefore have to design his own peripheral interface and software driver.

The user of the particular intelligent terminal may thus not be able to run software available directly from the minicomputer manufacturer in his terminal. In the long run, this may turn out to be a disadvantage, particularly since most large minicomputer manufacturers continually update and expand their software.

Many intelligent terminals can be programmed in either assembly language or in at least one high-level language. This language may be interpretive such as BASIC (BASIC/Four), DATABUS (Datapoint 2200), or RPG (Clary DataComp and Qantel).

The reason for the rapid growth of the intelligent terminal industry can be attributed to its total systems approach, providing all the hardware and software as an integrated package. The intelligent terminal performs a particular task or solves a specific user problem without the user having to worry about technical factors relating to either software or computer hardware.

The majority of minicomputer manufacturers also provide both peripherals and applications software, but total system responsibility, in most cases, must still be borne by the end user. This way the manufacturer avoids competing with his OEM customer, the intelligent terminal manufacturer, who not only provides applications programs and installs the system but also trains the user and maintains both hardware and software, thereby taking full system responsibility.

Selecting the Off-the-Shelf Smart Terminal

The selection of the optimum off-the-shelf intelligent terminal depends largely on user requirements and estimated savings that can be achieved by replacing the presently used system. The functions most commonly performed by intelligent terminals are forms completion, bookkeeping, accounting, inventory control, credit checking, on-demand report preparation, and editing and creating and maintaining large data files at remote locations. The typical smart terminal is, therefore, used by the small business or manufacturing firm, the department or subdivision of a larger corporation, or local, state, and federal governments.

To the uninitiated user, technical terms such as throughput, access time, memory cycle time, and interrupt structure are relatively meaningless. The nontechnical business manager will evaluate a new system based on factors such as ease of data input, level of required operator training, cost of system installation, and maintenance and operation, including hardware and software lease cost and salaries of operating personnel. The system user is concerned with how long it takes to prepare an invoice, how much time must be spent on sorting source documents such as shipping vouchers, how long it takes to find and correct a record, how safe the records are in terms of being restricted to authorized persons, and how long it takes to answer a

---

- Current inventory listed with present wholesale and retail value.

- Retrieval can be made of data on last activity or quantity on hand.

- Listing of items equal to or below reorder level.

- Balancing entry can be made to ledger for cost of sales and inventory account.

- Items automatically subtraced from inventory upon shipment, added to inventory when received from supplier, or returned by customer.

- Inventory data base can be queried on various item costs, inventory value, lead time, quantity discount, committed status, or on-order value.

- Reports can be requested on stock status register, transaction journal, back orders, turnover report, and purchase authorization list.

Figure 6-5 Inventory control capabilities checklist

customer's inquiry on back orders, invoices, credit limits, etc. These questions are obviously applications-oriented and therefore difficult to assign quantitative numbers to for trade-off analysis purposes. Consequently, the most straightforward approach is to list the required capabilities in addition to the hardware equipment configuration. An example of such a checklist for inventory control is shown in Figure 6-5. An inventory file structure usually contains at least the following information:

- Item number
- Item description
- Balance on hand
- Quantity on order
- Quantity back-ordered
- Quantity committed
- Balance available
- Selling price
- Cost price
- Reorder point
- Lead time
- Date and amount of last shipment or receipt

Since a large number of intelligent terminals are designed to operate in an office environment with a secretary or typist at the keyboard, the human side of data input is of considerable importance. In the office environment, the emphasis on speed and throughput lessens, while accuracy looms significant. High personnel turnover and part-time help may mean that relatively inexperienced people often operate the terminals. The intelligent terminal must therefore contain software programs which monitor the operator's inputs, guiding him or her through the various input sequences and keeping the operator informed of the current status. In effect, the terminal must act like an elementary teaching machine; once the operator chooses the type of transaction, he merely responds to technical instructions.

Data input accuracy is also closely tied to operator fatigue. Important considerations for intelligent terminal equipment evaluation are therefore features incorporated into the design which enhance operator convenience for using the system. A list of specific considerations which affect operator comfort and convenience is shown in Figure 6-6.

What to Look for in Remote Batch Terminals

Remote batch provides a cost-effective solution to users that require sophisticated data processing capabilities but cannot afford a large computer facility. Remote batch terminals are presently available that cover a large

- Relative placement of keyboard, controls, and display, including the angle of the keyboard with respect to the operator (controls display panel and work surfaces grouped at roughly the same level minimizes head movement).

- Comfortable seating for correct posture; ample knee and leg room.

- Size, color, and typography of CRT characters, and hard copy designed for maximum legibility.

- Display shielded to minimize reflections.

- Availability of movable keyboard, storage space for personal belongings and modesty panels.

- Quiet system operation (no noisy cooling fans in the computer or CRT, "click-click" sounds from CRT keyboard, or excessive noise from the printer, when it is running).

- System designed to operate in normal office environment without requiring additional air-conditioning of facilities.

Figure 6-6 Human engineering considerations for intelligent terminal selection

spectrum of data processing capabilities. At the low end, hard-wired terminals are available which do little more than read in cards or data stored on magnetic tape, and transmit it over a phone line to a central computer. Once the computer has processed the data, the result is transmitted back to the remote batch terminal, which either records it on magnetic tape or prints it out using a medium-speed line printer. This type of terminal is generally rather unsophisticated in that its hard-wired logic is limited to code compression, error checking, and request-for-retransmission tasks. Intelligent terminals used for remote batching are more flexible, containing a minicomputer which performs a significant amount of processing, thereby reducing the data transmission load.

Most of the large computer manufacturers offer their own remote batch terminal. IBM, for instance, provides a number of remote batch terminals for their 360/370 family of computers, the 2780 Data Transmission Terminal being the most widely used. The IBM 2780 permits data transfer of up to 4800 bps. It typically contains a 240-lpm line printer and a 400-cpm card reader. The IBM 2780 remote batch terminal data communications protocol is based on IBM's binary synchronous communications (BSC) technique. BSC is a series of generalized procedures which permit transmission of coded data such as EBCDIC and USASCII. BSC procedures provide a number of

Basic elements
   Synchronization procedure
   Text message block formats
   Negative and alternating affirmative acknowledge replies
   Error detection and correction procedures
   Enquiry function
   Timeouts
   End-of-text (EOT) signal

Selective elements
   Transmission code
   Transmission initiatization modes: contention, centralized
      and supervised modes

Special-purpose elements
   Transparent text
   Heading
   Circuit assurance mode of operation
   Disconnect signal
   Wait-before-transmit reply

Performance improvement elements
   Blocking of data
   Intermediate blocking
   Conversational mode feature
   Fast selection feature
   Noncentralized mode

Figure 6-7 Summary of IBM Binary Synchronous (BSC) Features

ground rules for the synchronous transmission of binary coded data, incorporating a set of basic control characters. (The main features are summarized in Figure 6-7.)

Control Data Corporation's earlier remote batch terminal, the CDC 200 User Terminal (200 U.T.), a 1000-character capacity CRT terminal, also contains a 333-cpm card reader and a 300-lpm line printer. Control Data's 730 series intelligent batch terminals, which replace the 200 U.T., include a 16-bit 4K word 1.1-μsec-core minicomputer, a 300-cpm card reader, a 300-lpm line printer, a control console, and an operator keyboard. Neither the IBM 2780 nor the CDC 200 U.T. can operate in a stand-alone mode.

A host of IBM 2780 and CDC 200 U.T. replacement terminals are presently available from independent manufacturers. Several of these terminals provide the same capabilities as the IBM 2780 or the CDC 200 U.T. in addition to a host of other features, all at reduced cost. These terminals are usually based on a minicomputer programmed to provide IBM BSC conventions, thereby maintaining compatibility with a large number of existing operating systems and terminals. This feature eliminates the need for costly reprogramming and special interfacing equipment at the central site. By loading different software into the terminal computer, it can emulate an IBM 2780, a CDC 200 U.T., a Burroughs TC 500, or a Univac DCT-2000 or 1004. Unlike the higher-cost terminal it replaces, such as the IBM 2780, which is oriented to card reading and punching, the intelligent remote batch terminal can store on tape the data transmitted from the IBM 360/370. The data can later be printed, using the high-speed line printer at the terminal. Unlike the IBM 2780, many of the smart remote batch terminals can be interfaced to an almost unlimited range of miniperipherals.

In addition to independent terminal manufacturers, some of the mini-computer houses also provide IBM 2780 remote batch terminal replacements. An example of this is the DEC PDP-11 baesd DECcomm 11D26, which consists of a PDP-11/20 with 8K words of memory, a console Teletype, a 300-cpm card reader, and a 300-lpm printer. The PDP-11 can obviously be used for other tasks in addition to performing remote batch.

At a more complex level, a remote batch terminal can be used to temporarily store data accumulated from several local input devices. The inputs from various keyboard terminals may be stored on disk in the terminal. When all work is finished at the remote site, the information stored on the disk is transmitted at high speed to a central computer for batch processing.

Before the user can proceed with the selection of an appropriate remote batch terminal, he must analyze system requirements, providing answers to the following questions:

1. What type of batch processing is required, and whose computer will provide him with processing capability at lowest cost? This question may already be answered if the user had access to an in-house computing facility.
2. What kind of operating system and data communications software requirements will be placed on the remote batch terminal in order for it to be able to communicate with the central facility (such as BSC for IBM 360/370 series of computers)?
3. What types of data communications controllers are available or will be required at the central computer facility (IBM 2701, 2702, 2703, 3704, 3705 for IBM 360/370 series of computers)?
4. What is the total amount of data that must be transmitted to and from the remote batch terminal?
5. How much of the communications load can be reduced by performing preprocessing or data reduction locally?

Not until answers are available to these questions can the system designer consider the next level of system trade-offs, which usually consist of various cost-effectiveness analyses.

The cost effectiveness of a remote batch facility is determined by the following factors:

- Average daily volume of input and/or output of data
- Required terminal equipment to handle the volume
- Required transmission facility to handle the net volume

As a first approximation, data compression, error checking, and communications protocol can be ignored.

Based on a hypothetical case where, each day, on the average, 100,000 cards are transmitted from a remote batch terminal to a central computer and 500 pages are printed by the terminal, the total transmission time for the cards, using a 4800-bps line rate, is approximately 4 hr. (See Figure 1-8; 2 boxes of cards = 2000 cards. Hence, for 4800 bps, 13 boxes can be transmitted per hour, and since 100,000 cards are approximately equivalent to 50 boxes, it will take $\frac{50}{13}$ hr $\approx$ 4 hr to transmit all cards.) For a transmission rate of 4800 bps, 260 pages can be printed in 1 hr (again based on Figure 1-8, it will take roughly 2 hr to print 500 pages).

One of the major trade-offs is between the use of leased or dial-up lines. A leased line will permit full-duplex transmission, whereby the total information in both directions can be transmitted in 4 hr. A dial-up line can be operated only in a half-duplex mode, thereby requiring 6 hr to transmit the total information to and from the remote batch terminal. In this example, assuming the cost for the call is 90 cents for the first 3 min and 40 cents for each additional minute, a dial-up connection would far exceed the cost of a leased line. The line cost in dollars per month can therefore be computed as follows:

Remote batch terminal	$1200
Two 4800-bps modems	300
Cost of leased line	2000
Transmission control unit at central computing facility	500
Cost of batch processing at central computer facility	1000
	$5000

The above system elements are shown in Figure 6-8. Since 500 pages of print-out contains approximately the same number of characters as 50,000 cards, the cost per card is

$$\frac{\$5000}{150,000 \text{ cards}} = 3.3 \text{ cents/card}$$

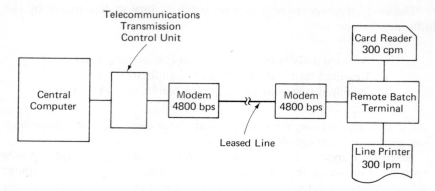

Figure 6-8 Elements affecting total remote batch processing cost

Increasing the data rate from 4800 bps to 9600 bps will reduce the transmission time, which in turn may require either higher-speed devices in the remote batch terminal or the use of disk or magnetic tape for data buffering. A doubling of the transmission rate will also increase modem cost and error rates in the system. Increased error rates will, of course, require a larger amount of message retransmission, decreasing the effective or net data throughput.*

Developing Your Intelligent Terminal In-House

It is not uncommon for users to develop their own intelligent terminal. A valid reason may be the fact that no off-the-shelf systems are available which meet the unique requirements of the user. The user may want to develop a proprietary in-house system which gives him a competitive edge in his line of business. Furthermore, having a special-purpose system which has been tailored to a specific application, he may want to market it as a product. Several other factors may contribute to the user deciding to develop the terminal himself, such as sizable OEM discounts available from a minicomputer manufacturer, the availability in-house of a highly trained group of programmers and system designers, or, perhaps, the availability of in-house hardware, which is presently not being utilized.

Once a decision has been made for a go-ahead, the user should seriously consider following at least these basic guide lines (assuming that all technical

---

* Several useful equations for computing achievable throughput are given in an article written by Berglund Associates, Inc., "A Throughput Approach to Batch Transmission," Communications Clinic, *Modern Data*, January 1972, 22–23.

requirements can be satisfied):

- Select a single vendor for the minicomputer and peripherals.
- Make sure that this vendor is qualified to provide local maintenance on his equipment (to be discussed further in Chapter 7).
- Take advantage of all the vendor-supplied software development tools.
- Write applications programs in a higher-level language. (The cost of additional memory for a single system is considerably less than the cost of labor for programming and program checkout.)
- If nonstandard peripherals have to be used, stay with the industry standard bit-serial EIA RS-232C interface to minimize cost.

6.3 DATA ENTRY, AUTOMATIC TESTING, AND DATA ACQUISITION SYSTEMS

Stand-alone data entry, information handling, and automatic testing systems all have at least one thing in common: They provide an efficient, automated approach to data entry or acquisition at various levels of sophistication. Data entry systems differ from word processing systems primarily in terms of function; data entry systems replace older, less efficient methods such as keypunching with direct keyboard to magnetic tape or disk input. Partially under computer control, word processing systems provide editing and reformatting capabilities of source data. The former systems accept programs, text, or data in the format in which they are keyed into the system, while the latter recomposes input messages before "permanent" storage in the system.

Automatic testing and data acquisition systems are used to analyze data acquired during test runs and generally do not provide feedback to the system being tested. In test systems where feedback is applied, it is generally on a less complex level than in systems primarily designed for process control (see Section 6.5).

Data Entry Systems

Data entry systems where the minicomputer performs control are of two types: keyboard input and optical reading systems. The keyboard input type of systems replace older, more cumbersome data entry devices, while optical reading systems perform previously nonautomated tasks.

Keyboard data entry systems are available either in stand-alone or multistation configurations. Stand-alone systems are often based on a minicomputer with cassette or IBM-compatible seven- or nine-track tape unit. Several systems include a limited-capacity CRT display for verification of input data.

Data preparation, such as filling out a keypunch coding sheet, keypunching, and verifying of keypunched cards, may be performed directly on the data entry device. Since data are recorded magnetically, key errors can be corrected immediately. Later the tape can also be read into an intermediate buffer for display on the CRT, and various records stored on tape can be found quickly and erased if so desired.

Using magnetic tape, the user is no longer limited to 80 or 96 character records and can, in fact, input records that range from 160 to 300 characters. Magnetic tape storage also allows for higher input speeds when the data are read into the computer. Furthermore, overall system reliability is enhanced by using magnetic tape drives instead of more failure-prone card readers.

Multistation systems usually employ a shared processor with intermediate bulk storage such as a fixed or movable head disk. A large number of keyboards, anywhere from 8 to 64, are time-shared by a minicomputer which stores, formats, edits, and processes the data. Under control from a supervisory console, the disk contents are periodically batch-transferred to IBM-compatible magnetic tape.

In these systems, it is quite common for the key stations to provide limited local display of the current mode, such as WRITE, READ, VERIFY, STATUS, and error conditions.

A block diagram of a typical computer-controlled keyboard data entry system is shown in Figure 6-9.

Optical data entry systems are the latest addition to the rapidly growing number of data entry systems. The most common applications area is various types of retail operations. These types of data entry systems are also called point-of-sale (POS) systems. The main purpose of POS systems is to replace cash registers, providing for more automated and faster sales transaction data collection, inventory control, and report generation. POS systems can control all checkout data input and interpret the raw data to report buying patterns, throughput, and cash receipts by the month, week, and day or in real time. Some systems also prepare store orders and transmit them to the warehouse.

One such system, called APOSS (manufactured by Zellweger in Switzerland), uses a laser-based optical unit that reads code marks printed on the merchandise. The code is deciphered and interpreted by the minicomputer, which retrieves the price information and sends it to the checkstand POS unit for display and tabulation. A manual override is also available for unreadable or unmarked items.

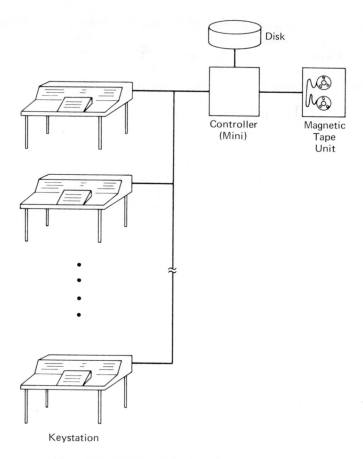

Figure 6-9   Disk-based, keyboard data entry system

Automatic Testing and Data Acquisition Systems

Automated testing using a minicomputer is commonly used by both component subsystem and system manufacturers, mainly in the electronics industry. Manufacturers of electronic components such as capacitors, resistors, diodes, and transistors use minicomputer-oriented testing to improve both product quality and reliability. Computer manufacturers use similar systems to check out computer circuit boards, assemblies, and even the entire computer. Avionics, missile, and satellite systems are often checked out using automated test facilities, and the same approach has also been applied to commercial products, such as radios, television sets, and automobiles.

Automatic testing, as applied in the electronics industry, may differ in terms of desired results depending on the particular test phase. The first test phase usually consists of evaluating the various components—such as large-scale integrated circuits or operational amplifiers—to determine their particular performance characteristics before the commitment is made to use them.

The second phase is based on incoming inspection of the selected components during the manufacturing process. Intermediate steps may take place, such as testing of circuit boards and subassemblies. The latter are often of the go/no go type to separate various items into "good" and "bad" categories, where the bad ones can later be fixed without holding up the production line. The manufacturing test phase is completed with a final inspection test, again of the go/no go type. If the total system fails to pass final inspection, it may be tested to localize the area in the system which caused the system not to pass the go/no go test.

The final inspection test phase may be proceeded by an *acceptance test*

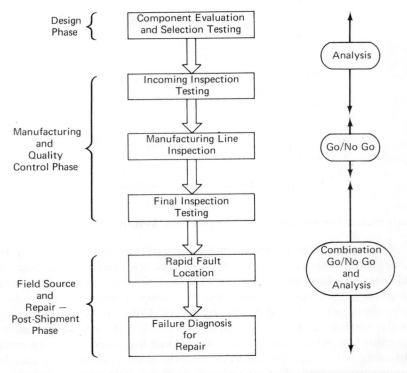

Figure 6-10   Test phases for electronic systems, using automatic mini-computer-based test equipment

by the customer. Acceptance testing, usually in the go/no go test category, is, with few exceptions, performed by the end user or various agencies on government-procured subsystems or systems.

When the system fails during operation in the field, the same type of automatic test equipment used to diagnose problems during the manufacturing process may also be used by the field service group to pinpoint the cause of failure and for rapid repair of the equipment. The various test phases are shown in Figure 6-10.

The Test System and the Minicomputer

The following items are the major elements in an automatic test system:

- Device being tested
- Stimulus (input)
- Test-conditioning equipment
- Measuring device
- Test control unit
- Device for analysis and reduction of test data
- Unit for display of test results (output)

The device being tested may be an analog or digital circuit, gyro, pressure sensor, fusing subsystem, cable harness, accelerometer, electrical or electronic component, controller, minicomputer, or a complex avionics system. The stimulus used may be dc voltage or current, voltage pulse or waveform, or digital data. The stimulus may be generated by an oscillator, pulse generator, power supply or external computer.

Test-conditioning equipment is used to simulate various test environments such as noise on electric input lines, temperature extremes, vibration, shock, electromagnetic radiation, or interference.

The measuring device will record critical parameter variations in the device being tested when stimuli are applied during various test conditions.

Stimulus sources, test-conditioning equipment, and measuring devices should be programmable, i.e., controllable by signals from a minicomputer. The latter provides the required test system control and analyzes the test data received from the measuring devices.

Measurement results and test conditions may be output from the minicomputer, displaying the information on a CRT or providing hard copy using a line printer or plotter. A block diagram of a typical automatic test system is shown in Figure 6-11. This system is designed to test a small avionics computer, applying a large number of stimuli for several load conditions and test environments.

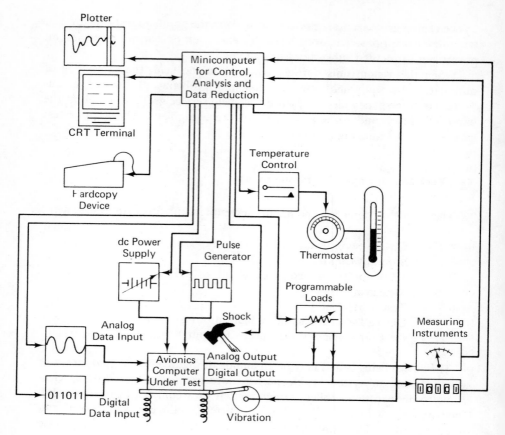

Figure 6-11   Automatic test system to test Avionics computer

The computer is tested for supply voltage and timing margins, applying both digital and analog input signals. The avionics computer system operating noise is monitored at critical points internally in the machine (power supply lines, memory lines, signal I/O lines, etc.) for various external conditions induced under control of the minicomputer. The unit under test is submitted to vibrations, shock, and extreme temperatures, while at the same time its output signals are measured and analyzed by the same minicomputer. Finally, loads on the output line are varied to simulate various worst case conditions which the unit must meet according to test specifications.

The test data maybe analyzed either simultaneously during the test data acquisition phase, providing an interactive capability between the operator and the test system, or later, as a batch operation.

The CRT terminal serves as an interactive I/O device, while the batch-processed test results may be output, using a plotter or hard-copy device.

The three primary functions performed by the test system minicomputer are total test system control and sequencing, data acquisition, and data processing. Typical system requirements are therefore the capability of monitoring and controlling a large number of dissimilar devices as well as sampling and storing information from a substantial number of test points.

In addition, the computerized test system must usually provide the capability of being rapidly converted to perform tests on a wide range of equipment. However, minicomputers alone cannot efficiently control a large number of devices at reasonable cost, since most minis do not have sufficient numbers of output channels. In fact, adding a large number of output channels to a mini often outweighs the cost of all other system components because a large number of devices in automatic test systems require control signals in forms other than the normal binary computer output.

Several minicomputer manufacturers therefore provide special functional modules that plug, into their standard computer chassis (or expansion chassis). These modules consist of various programmable arithmetic elements, stimulus sources, measurement devices, and control circuits for I/O. An example is the Hewlett Packard Model 6936A/6937A Multiprogrammer System, which allows a single 16-bit computer output channel to control up to 240 individually addressable 12-bit output subchannels. Each of these subchannels can provide outputs in the form of resistance, dc voltage, contact closures, or logic levels. Both Modcomp, Texas Instruments (TI 960A) and Westinghouse (2500) provide a large number of modules for various automated measurement systems. A communications register unit in the TI 960A enables the computer to interface through as many as 512 lines, expandable externally to a capacity of 8192 lines.

Test System Software

Each 1000 words of debugged software written in assembly language may take between one and two man-months to produce. A large number of test systems requiring more than 4K words of software are therefore written in a higher-level language. This may be either in BASIC or FORTRAN or a language specifically developed for automatic test systems.

The latter may be either problem- or test-oriented languages. Problem-oriented test languages such as POL (problem-oriented language) are applications oriented, using terms related to the device being tested, while test-oriented languages such as TOOL (test-oriented operator language) and ATLAS (abbreviated test language for avionics systems) are test-equipment-oriented, relating to test instruments used in the test system. The language and program size relationships are summarized in Figure 6-12.

It is not uncommon to use both a test-equipment- and problem-oriented

Test system operating program size	System changes	Language used	Test set-language relationship
Less than 4000 words	Infrequent	Assembly	Dedicated to specific application
	Frequent	Higher-level	Dedicated to specific application
More than 4000 words	Infrequent or frequent	Higher-level Problem-oriented	Dedicated to specific applications
		Higher-level Test-equipment-oriented	Universal use or change of operating constants or test sequences

Figure 6-12   Software language relationships to test system

language in an automatic test system. The test-equipment-related language is initially used by the programmer to change constants, test sequences, etc., before a test run. Subsequently, during testing, the operator will use the problem-oriented language to control the test set for a specific test. The programmer will thus load his program using a paper tape or card reader, while the operator may interact with the system using a Teletype or CRT console.

Off-the-Shelf Systems

Several systems are presently available to perform various forms of testing, such as the Lorlin Industries Impact 100 based on a DEC PDP-11 and designed for discrete semiconductor testing and Avco Systems Division Avmots based on a Clary 404 minicomputer and designed for computer testing.* Texas Instruments has designed a system called ATS (for automatic test system) 960 which is based on a TI 960A minicomputer. This system can be used to test both electronic components and equipment assemblies. The ATS-960 uses a high-level language which is an adaptation of ATLAS. The test program is written in two sections, a preamble section which contains reference information and a procedure section where each statement corresponds to a specific step in the execution of a test.

_____

* G. Roberts. "New Approach to Automated Testing," *Electronic Design News*, February 1, 1971, 12–13.

After the program is written in source language, it can be stored on mag-netic tape for later compilation into machine language code when read into main memory. The program may again be decompiled into source language for debugging and editing.

In addition to the ATLAS compiler-decompiler, ATS-960 contains soft-ware routines to control various instruments, taking the place of hardware controllers, and an applications-link processor for interactive conversation between itself and the operator.

The above-mentioned software is supervised by the 960A process-automation monitor (PAM), which includes a test-control executive that directs the editor, compiler-decompiler, test-instrument drivers, applications-link processor, and various other software modules. To keep track of various tasks, PAM also includes a multilevel priority scheme. PAM can be used in a stand-alone configuration or with a disk. The disk version of the operating system is called PAM/D, where D stands for *disk*.*

6.4 DATA COMMUNICATIONS PROCESSORS

The minicomputer is used to perform a variety of data communications tasks, some of which have been discussed in the previous chapter. Although communications processing systems usually do contain minicomputers, the special-purpose front-end hardware and, in particular, the dedicated data communications software often set these minicomputers apart from general-purpose minis. Data communication applications may be divided into at least three major areas: data concentration, message-switching control, and front-end processing.

Data Concentrators

The terms *concentrator* and *multiplexer* (see Multiplexing, Multiplexers, and the Minicomputer in Chapter 3) are often used interchangeably. There is, however, a significant difference between the two; concentrators are defined as those communications devices that provide one additional capa-bility beyond those normally attributed to time division multiplexers (see Multiplexing, Multiplexers, and the Minicomputer in Chapter 3), namely, optimization of line-loading efficiency. A time division multiplexer divides a higher-speed data stream into a number of lower-speed channels, each of which is assigned to a particular terminal. A concentrator basically performs the same subdividing task but has the added capability of varying the

---

* Wilbur L. Allain, "Integrated Instrument Setup Tests Intricate Assemblies," *Electronics*, October 9, 1972, 104–109.

channel assignments based on terminal usage. In a time division multiplexer, the total data rate of all the terminals connected to the multiplexer must amount to slightly less than the high-speed transmission capacity. However, the total data rates of all the terminals connected to a concentrator can be greater than the high-speed transmission capacity. The concentrator, being based on a minicomputer, can store incoming messages for later transmission when the on-going line is free. The line is therefore utilized more efficiently than with a multiplexer, where a low-speed line, when idle, still takes up signal space on the high-speed line. Concentrators also differ from multiplexers in that they can store blocks of many characters or, in some cases, complete messages in a local buffer before transmitting the messages to the computer.

In addition to intermediate data buffering, concentrators often change the data format and sometimes its content before forwarding it. Some concentrators can handle simultaneous traffic from different types of terminals operating with different codes and at different speeds. Furthermore, the central computer may use a code different from any of the terminals, in which case the concentrator often performs the code conversion.

One of the main benefits of a concentrator is its capability to perform error checking as well as adding checking codes to each block transmitted to the host computer. The concentrator, when detecting an error, can request retransmission without involving the host computer. Error checking can, of course, be implemented either in hardware or software or a combination of both.

Message-Switching Controllers

Message switching provides an alternative to circuit switching. In the circuit-switching approach, terminals contend for connection to individual subchannels in a time division multiplexed data stream. One contention mode is similar to that of a telephone company *rotary*, which connects individual subchannels on a first-come-first-served basis. In this case, the first available subchannel is "seized" as a terminal requires service. In the most elementary circuit-switching system, the subchannel remains assigned to the serviced terminal until either the computer or terminal end of the communication link determines that no more data are to be sent. The subchannel is immediately released for other users when the previous user "hangs up." When all lines are busy, a terminal requesting a line will therefore have to wait until one of the lines is released. Additional terminals are thereby easily prevented from entering a fully loaded system. However, once on line, the message block is transmitted directly without any intermediate buffering to the computer.

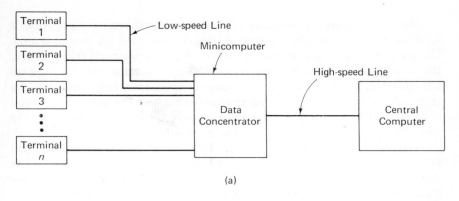

(a)

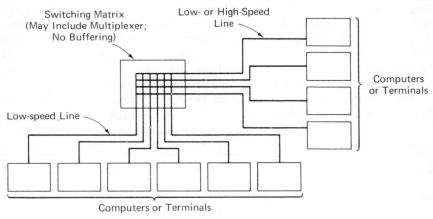

(b)

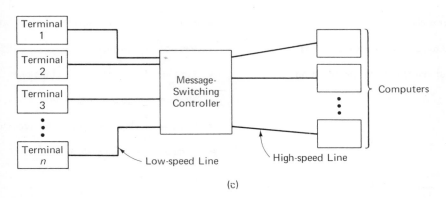

(c)

Figure 6-13 System based on (a) a data concentrator, (b) a circuit switch, and (c) a message switch

Message-switching controllers allow for transmission of data from a terminal to the computer without having to wait for an available line. During conditions when all lines to the central computer are fully utilized, the message-switching controller, in a fashion identical to that of the data concentrator, assembles and stores blocks of messages transmitted from the terminal. When a high-speed transmission line between the message-switching controller and the computer becomes available, the data buffered in the controller will be transmitted to its final destination.

The message-switching controller, similar to the data concentrator, also provides error control, code translation, and fault isolation capability. The message-switching controller does, however, differ from the data concentrator in one major respect: The data concentrator, as its name implies, concentrates messages from several sources such as Teletypes and CRT terminals for transmission to a single destination, usually a central computer, while the message-switching controller concentrates messages from several sources and forwards them to one or more destinations, which may be computers or other terminals. Block diagrams of data concentrator, circuit-switching, and message-switching systems are shown in Figure 6-13.

Since there is no one-to-one correspondence between data source and link, the message-switching processor must be prepared to store messages

Data concentrator	Message-switching controller
• Character-to-message assembly/disassembly	• Message assembly/disassembly
• Control of multiple communication channels	• Message type and destination analysis
• Message buffering	• Message routing
• Transmission speed conversion	• Polling and addressing terminals
• Error checking and control	• Error detection and control
• Automatic answering and dialing	• Message reformatting
• Automatic terminal identification	• Time and data identification of messages
	• Message management in storage
	• Message stacking and sequenced transmission
	• Code and speed conversion
	• Line control

Figure 6-14 Comparison of tasks for data concentrators and message-switching controllers

from any one terminal or computer. The message form is therefore more complex in a switching system than in a data concentrator system. The former types of systems therefore differ from the latter in that they employ auxiliary storage, such as disk or magnetic tape, in addition to main memory.

Major functions performed by data concentrators and message-switching controllers are listed in Figure 6-14 for reference. At least one off-the-shelf

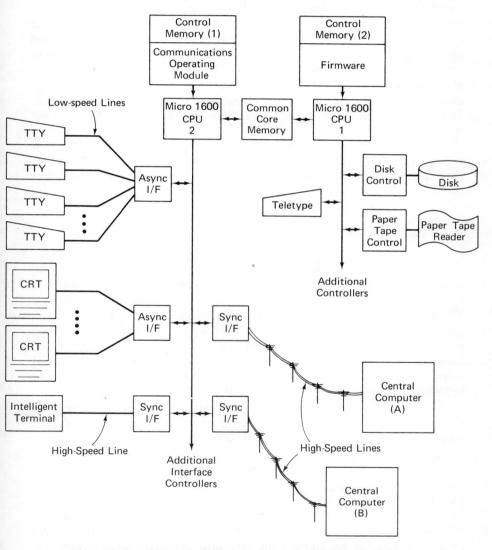

Figure 6-15 Functional diagram of Microdata 1600/60 serving as a message-switching controller

system which performs all these tasks is available from Microdata Corporation. This system is based on a dual-processor concept incorporating two independent Micro 1600 CPU elements with separate microprogram control memories and a common main core memory shared by the two processors. The first CPU is intended primarily for central message processing and for control of system peripheral devices but may also handle communications lines. The second CPU, under control of firmware, controls up to 256 synchronous and/or asynchronous lines. Tables containing communication line control information for the individual lines are stored in the common memory along with character translation tables. These tables provide independent control of each line with respect to line speed, character and message formats, external control codes, and other terminal characteristics. Data and control information to and from the various communication channels are transferred between both CPUs via the common core memory.

A functional block diagram of the Microdata 1600/60 system, where it serves as a message-switching controller between a large number of various type of terminals and two central computers (A and B), is shown in Figure 6-15.

Front-End Processors

The concept of the programmable front-end processor is discussed in some detail in Cost Elements in Chapter 5. The programmable front-end minicomputer was originally introduced as a more cost-effective and flexible alternative to the main-frame manufacturer-supplied hard-wired transmission control units. These minicomputer-based front-end processors are in reality nothing more than standard, off-the-shelf minis with appropriate hardware interface to the host computer I/O channel. In addition, special software packages are offered to provide interface to the host computer and to handle network, message, and line control.

Line control or terminal interface programs provide control character recognition, error checking, and format control for remote terminals and local peripherals. Serial-to-parallel conversion of bits to bytes and vice versa is generally performed by inexpensive hardware interfaces.

The network and message control program usually performs polling tasks, terminal addressing, and automatic dialing and answering. When incoming characters are received, the message control program inserts and deletes transmission control characters and translates data from processing code to transmission code or vice versa. Finally, the network control program assembles incoming characters into message blocks, which are transmitted to the host processor.

The software interface program in the front-end processor must interface the access method in the host computer. The purpose of the access method is to continuously interrogate the concentrated data stream from the front-end processor to determine the source and address of the individual messages from various terminals received by the front-end processor.

IBM provides a number of access methods for the System 360/370 to enable the user to construct telecommunications service and control programs that meet the installation's line, terminal, and network requirements. The following access methods are used with non-IBM minicomputer-based, front-end processors:

1. The sequential access method for magnetic tape reading and writing. The interface program mates the front-end processor to the host machine by emulating a magnetic tape unit.

2. The graphic access method (GAM) for access to IBM's Model 2848 CRT display control unit, which services several IBM 2260 CRT displays. In this case, the interface program emulates the IBM 2848. An example of this is the Digital Equipment Corporation Comtex-11* Emulator Terminal Application Programs (ETAP). The ETAP responds exactly as the S/360 control unit that it is emulating.

3. The basic telecommunications access method (BTAM) is a tool providing I/O macro instructions and control program functions that can be used in constructing a telecomminications application program. BTAM software modules are used according to what terminals are interfaced to the system. Typically, where a large number of low-speed terminals are interfaced to the front-end processor, the BTAM program in the host computer handles the multiple lines as if they were a single high-speed (BSC) line.

4. The queued telecommunications access method (QTAM) is a more powerful access method than BTAM, providing a high-level message control language.

5. The telecommunications access method (TCAM) extends the functions of QTAM, including expanded system control, message control and editing capabilities, system recovery and serviceability features, and installation and debugging aids.

6. The virtual telecommunications access method (VTAM) is used exclusively with IBM 370 series stored program communications controllers in IBM S/370 virtual systems.

---

* Comtex stands for *communications-oriented multiple terminal executive*.

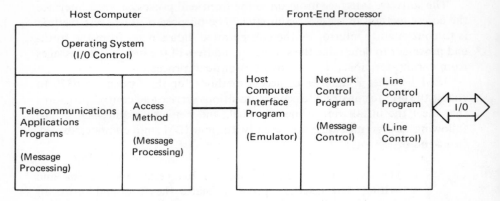

Figure 6-16   Interrelationship among various telecommunication program modules

Any of the above access methods are, of course, interfaced to the particular operating system.

Finally, the host computer-resident applications programs, generally user-written, perform the actual message processing. The interrelationship among the various program modules are shown in Figure 6-16.

Most of the presently available front-end processors are designed to emulate hard-wired or programmable, main-frame manufacturer-supplied communications control units. These front-end processors function with the IBM 360/370 computer systems through the previously listed access methods.

A second, less common type of front-end processor system not only replaces the expansive main-frame computer manufacturer's communications control units but also existing access methods. An example of this is the PHI Computer Services, Inc. 3700 Telecommunications Processing System.* The IBM 360-resident access method, replacing BTAM, QTAM, or TCAM, called communications access method (CAM), transfers message control from the host computer to the front-end communications processor. The emulator program stored in the front-end processor is therefore not needed by this system.

Communications Processor Throughput and Memory Size

The selection of a communications processor for applications such as front-end processing must take into consideration factors additional to those

---

* The PHI 3700 is based on a DEC PDP-11.

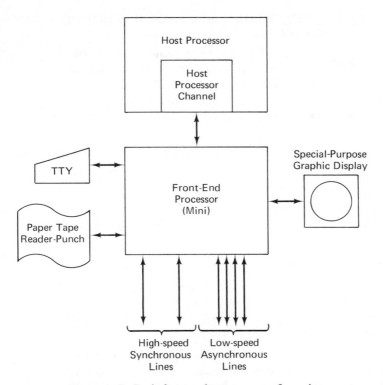

Figure 6-17   Basic front-end processor configuration

listed in Section 5.4, namely, present and future requirements for local and remote terminals, local peripherals, special devices, and access method to be used in the host processor. The average and peak data communication and local peripheral support processing loads will determine the present and expected future internal memory size as well as the type of interface required to support the data transfer load between the front end and the host computer. Each of the elements affecting front-end processor utilization is shown in Figure 6-17.

The size or compute capacity for a specific application may be determined using the following formula:

$$T = \sum_{i=1}^{n} U_i$$

where T is equivalent to percentage CPU utilization and the U_is are application load elements to be serviced by the front-end processor.

Based on Figure 6-17, the following five U_i components are specified as an example of the type of elements comprising the general formula:

$U_1 = \%$ CPU utilization as a result of transferring data between mini and host

$U_2 = \%$ CPU utilization as a result of terminal processing (including interrupt servicing, character searches, data translations, buffer transfers, commands)

$U_3 = \%$ CPU utilization as a result of special-purpose graphics display processing (CRT refreshed from front-end processor memory)

$U_4 = \%$ CPU utilization as a result of paper tape device processing

$U_5 = \%$ CPU utilization as a result of interactive console Teletype processing

Each of the load elements is derived for the case where the host processor is an IBM 360/370. Hence, owing to data transfer, mini to 360,

$$U_1 = \alpha \left(\frac{n}{b}\right) \frac{B}{10^4}$$

where $n =$ processor overhead (cycles per word)

$b =$ bytes in a word ($b = 2$ in a 16-bit mini)

$\alpha =$ microseconds per cycle ($= 1$ in a 1-μsec cycle time mini)

$B =$ bytes transferred per second

This equation is valid only for blocks equal to or larger than 1000 bytes. For blocks less than 1000 bytes, channel setup time must be included. The size of the word being transferred must equal the channel register bit width. Also, the channel register-to-front-end processor byte/word packing and unpacking must be handled by interface hardware. In those cases where the minicomputer character is different from the channel register and where packing and unpacking is handled by software,

$$U_1 = \left[\alpha \left(\frac{n}{b}\right) + P\right] \frac{B}{10^4}$$

where $P =$ microsecond per byte utilized for packing/unpacking in the mini.

Owing to remote terminal processing,

$$U_2 = \frac{1}{10} \sum_{j=1}^{k} \frac{t_j}{b_j} (L_j B_j) \gamma_j$$

where for a given communications lines type, j,

$t =$ milliseconds per character for mini to process a character

$b =$ number of bits per character

$L =$ number of lines at a given line rate B

$k =$ number of different line types

$\gamma =$ line utilization factor ($\gamma = 1$ for 100% utilization)

Owing to graphic display processing,

$$U_3 = \frac{1}{10^4}\,(S)(n)(r)(\alpha)$$

where S = core buffer size in number of words
n = processor overhead (cycles per word)
r = display refresh rate in frames per second
α = microseconds per cycle

The above formula for U_3 applies only when the CRT is refreshed from the mini. In those instances when the CRT has its own refresh buffer, the time consumed is utilized only for block transfers and $U_3 = U_1$.

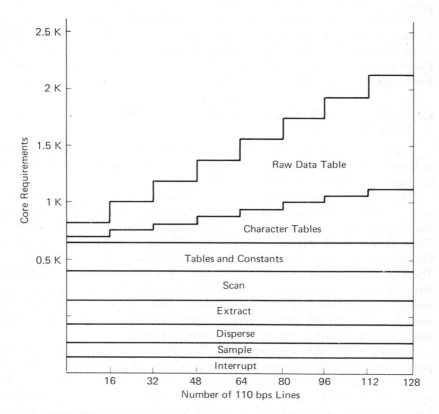

Figure 6-18 Core requirements as a function of the number of lines for Honeywell DDP-516 PMLC (Courtesy Honeywell Information Systems)

Since the paper tape reader/punch and Teletype are operated only during system initialization or loading, U_4 and U_5 may be ignored.

Summarizing, for the preceding example,

$$T = \alpha \left(\frac{n}{b}\right) \frac{B}{10^4} + \frac{1}{10} \sum_{j=1}^{k} \frac{t_j}{b_j} (L_j B_j) \gamma_j + \frac{1}{10^4} (S)(n)(r)(\alpha)$$

In the same example (Figure 6-17), the memory size requirement is dictated by the storage needed for display processing and control, interface, message and line control programs for data transfers to the 360, buffering for Teletype and paper tape reader/punch, and communications handling of the various lines.

A guide for core requirements as a function of the number of lines is shown in Figure 6-18. The table is given by Honeywell and relates to their programmed multiline controller (PMLC) for the Honeywell DDP-516.

The above equations are approximate and should be used only to obtain a rough estimate of throughput. For a more comprehensive analysis, the reader is referred to "Description of the Remote Data Concentrator," *Data Communications Capabilities*, Honeywell Computer Control Division, Framingham, Mass., January 23, 1969.

6.5 MANUFACTURING PLANT AND PROCESS CONTROL

Industrial minicomputer systems differ from previously discussed systems in three major areas: complex I/O, the use of nonstandard peripherals, and the harsher environments they must withstand.

The "typical" manufacturing plant or process control environment contains recorders, indicators, transmitters, valves, conveyor belts, measurement equipment, control panels, and other electromechanical devices. These devices are monitored and controlled by the mini, where the interface linkage usually must convert analog signals to digital pulses and vice versa. Therefore the emphasis is not on the speed of a single input or output line but on the number and types of I/O methods available and the ease of controlling the various I/O lines by software. Low or intermediate transfer rates coupled with the use of a large number of control lines has also made the manufacturer adapt various multiplexing schemes.

Second, industrial operations rely heavily on special-purpose display panels which provide the man-machine interface and permit the production worker or system monitor to interact and supervise system operations. The emphasis in control systems is therefore on special-purpose, often one-of-a-kind keyboards, switch panels, numerical readouts, and system flow charts with built-in computer-controlled visual and audible alarm indicators. The trend in the mid-1970s has been to replace some of the large, inflexible wall-type displays with minicomputer-controlled graphic CRT display consoles.

Third, the industrial environment is usually poorly controlled in terms of dust, contaminants, humidity, and fluctuations in temperature. Furthermore, the close proximity of electrical machinery contributes to electrical noise, such as radiation and power line transients. This, more than anything else, has put special demands on ruggedness and highly reliable design to minimize problems associated with catastrophic failures.

Minicomputers used in various aspects of manufacturing and plant control perform tasks such as machine tool, transfer line and production control, tool scheduling and monitoring, automated production, instrument testing and calibration, and total integrated production management and computer-aided manufacturing (CAM).

The process control system operates often in different environments from a parts-producing manufacturing plant, such as monitoring of oil fields, petrochemical plants, petroleum refineries, chemical plants, cement production facilities, electric power utility networks, and metal production facilities, to name a few.

The following sections will provide a discussion of how minicomputers are applied to some of these areas, how the systems work, and the way they differ functionally.

Minicomputers in Manufacturing

The minicomputer is presently used in machine tool control, tool scheduling and monitoring, transfer line monitoring, and management control.

Traditionally, machinery of metal parts has been performed either manually or using a hard-wired controller located next to the controlled machine. The hard-wired controller is fed a prepunched tape which contains the part dimensions and instructions for the controller. The controller typically provides signals to a servomotor, which in turn controls the work-table upon which the metal part to be cut is placed. A conventional numerical control (NC) system is shown in Figure 6-19. The disadvantages of conventional NC systems are the following: Tape corrections must be provided for each program change, a separate tape reader is required for each machine tool, and the hardware controller is relatively inflexible in terms of operational changes.

With minicomputers driving the machine tool directly from a program stored in main memory, between two and four machine tools may be

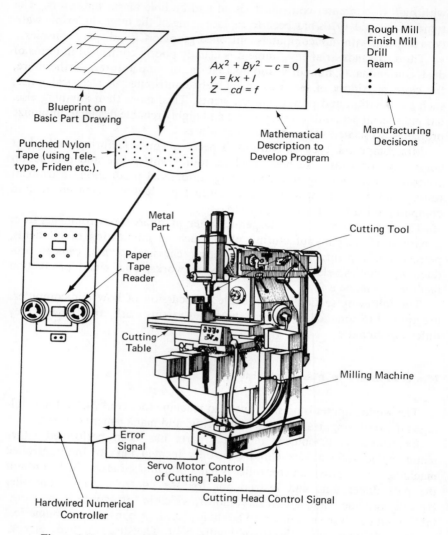

Figure 6-19 Conventional numerical control process from blueprint to punched tape, and final finished metal part

controlled per mini. Changes in parts programs can be made by the man at the machine, rather than having to go back to a central computer or off-line to produce the tape. The on-line editing feature can save a lot of time, especially in debugging the program to produce a part.

Several off-the-shelf computer numerical control (CNC) systems are presently available, among them Data General's Contour 1, General Auto-mation's Adapt-A-Path, and GE's Mark Century 8500.

Data General's Contour 1 system, shown in Figure 6-20, can simul-taneously control two different machine tools doing two different jobs. The basic system includes a Nova 1220 computer with 8K words of memory, a paper tape reader, and a console. A group of 15 pushbuttons allows the system operator to control a number of functions from the control console, such as automatic, semiautomatic, and manual mode of operation; *master reset* for zero coordinate establishment; *feed hold* for system interruption; and SEARCH, DELETE, INSERT, and PUNCH for editing.

It has been established that the use of the minicomputer in numerical control becomes more cost-effective than conventional NC systems when more than three machines are controlled per mini.*

In most machine shops, delivery dates are frequently changed, and as completion work is shipped, the schedules of work for various tools and

Figure 6-20 Data General's Contour 1 CNC system (Courtesy Data General Corporation, Southboro, Mass.)

---

* David G. Josza, "Numerical Control Systems Need User Input," *Electronic Products Magazine*, February 19, 1973, 43–49.

groups also change constantly. Through the use of computerized shop scheduling and inventory control, the cost-effectiveness of CNC equipment can be increased while at the same time minimizing schedule change problems.

Basically, production data are gathered on the shop floor by the machine tool operators and transmitted to a central computing facility where the entire shop production-load reports are stored for all facilities. These data are processed by the central computer, and reports are returned on a daily basis to supervisors who are responsible for assuring that all reported work time is accounted for.

Computerized shop scheduling and production maintenance control are, of course, not process-control-type operations but serve as examples of the additional advantages gained through total manufacturing automation or CAM.

Another manufacturing and plant control application for minicomputers is the monitoring and control of a transfer or production line. A typical computer-controlled transfer line consists of many machining stations connected to a minicomputer. As the line operates, the mini continuously compares the status of the various machining stations with a programmed table of conditions stored in the mini. If the proper conditions are met, the mini activates solenoid valves and other control devices to accomplish the next step in the production process. If improper conditions are detected, steps are immediately taken to determine the cause of the fault and, if necessary, the faulty tool or conveyor belt is repaired.

The computerized monitoring scheme also enables the user to obtain regular reports of failures, which later can be used to call for the correct type of maintenance or repair as well as for keeping account of the total number of operations performed by each tool to signal optimum points in time to perform preventative maintenance.

Plant and Process Control

In the automated factory or process control environment, the minicomputer is typically in charge of one or more parts of an operation. In many applications, one set of minicomputers performs a host of control subfunctions. These minicomputers are, in turn, connected to a central facility containing a mini or, perhaps, a larger computer which controls the entire system.

A typical example of this is the automated warehouse, where various minicomputers may be used for the control and dispatch of trucks, coordination of loading and unloading operations, control of conveyor belts and sorting devices, etc. All these minicomputer subsystems may, in turn, be connected to a central minicomputer which handles purchase orders, sales accounting, accounts payable and receivable, payroll, inventory control, and other bookkeeping and management control functions.

In contrast to the previously described computerized machine tool control application, which may be considered an operation that is performed in discrete steps, the material handling, process control function or auto-mated manufacturing system is a continuous operation, often performed in a closed-loop environment. By this it is implied that each control step or function is closely related to the step or function preceding it. A critical breakdown anywhere in the system may result in total system failure unless a redundant path exists or the system design allows for adequate backup capabilities.

The majority of the present-day minicomputers are, however, data proc-essing computers, not control computers. The major distinctions between the two are as follows:

1. In most control environments, raw processing speed is not of major importance. Instead, control computers stress reliability rather than speed. Slower cycle times, as a rule, permit the designer to increase his internal signal-to-noise ratio in the memory area. Less stringent requirements on logic speed allow the designer to use circuits with higher noise thresholds.

2. In a manufacturing environment, and particularly in the early stages of computer control implementation, machines will be connected and disconnected; a new variable is added to be sensed or controlled; a variable is found redundant and is re-moved, and the total number of I/O lines between the mini and the machines is increased. These continuous physical changes require the computer I/O structure to be flexible and simple to use, easy to change around, and easy to expand. The designer (or user) should be able to plug in or remove I/O modules without having to make internal wiring changes in the computer. He should also be able to plug I/O modules into whatever I/O slots are available without being constrained by predetermined physical restrictions on where certain devices are to connect to the mini, and he should be able to directly address, in the software, the respective I/O lines without having to use an accumulator or I/O buffer.

3. Several minicomputers allow for both byte and word addressing. However, the typical process control environment is *not* character- or byte-oriented, where most of the I/O occurs with other com-puters, disks, magnetic tapes, line printers, Teletypes, etc. but,

rather related to the particular I/O of the machine it will interface. This interface may be a single line or a 10-, 12-, or 14-bit
analog-to-digital converter. The I/O lines should therefore be
directly addressable, preferably by means of a single instruction
to the bit or "single wire" level or to some multiple group of bits.

Plant and process control systems controlled by a mini are of two types:
material changing and material handling systems. The material changing
system refers to a process wherein the raw material input to the system is
changed or modified in the process. Typical examples of this are the aluminum
pot line control system where the input is the raw material alumina and the
end product is aluminum, the injection molding process where the input
material is plastic and the output is a finished part, or the oil cracking plant
where the input is "raw" petroleum and the outputs are various cracked oil
products.

In contrast to the material changing system, the material handling system
performs a mechanization function of material handling. Examples of the
latter are the automated railroad yard, where the minicomputer performs
automatic car routing, car retarder operation, and generation of data on
cars handled in the yard; the automated warehouse, where pallets are moved
into or removed from storage under computer control; and the freight
terminal, where packages are sorted, stored, and distributed, also under
computer control.

In the material changing process, the minicomputer typically solves a set
of equations characterizing the change in state of the raw material to a
finished end product. The input to the mini is therefore quite often an analog
signal. The mechanization control systems differ from the previous types of
systems in that the computer does not generally have to solve a set of differential equations, but rather sense the condition of various lines and take action
based on the signal levels on the respective lines. Typical examples of the
latter are

- Check if a contact is closed or open.
- Check if a photocell is dark or light.
- Check if a switch has been broken.
- Check if a function key has been depressed.
- Check if a piece of material has arrived at a certain point.
- Check if a motor has actually started.
- Check if a machine is ready to operate.
- Turn a relay off (on).
- Start a motor.
- Shut off an operation.
- Start or shut off a pulse.

The primary task of the mini in a mechanization system is therefore to perform a large number of table look-ups, timing control functions, and algorithms for flow control.

The following example is used to illustrate the use of minicomputers for mechanization control in a freight terminal system. Continental Parcel is a freight forwarder with its own trucking network. The main task of Continental Parcel's freight terminal is to accept a large number of packages, parcels, sacks, boxes, and containers; sort the various items according to their respective destination and shipping mode (surface or air); and schedule the loading and shipment based on whether the items are to be shipped by truck, rail, or air freight. Similarly, items arriving by air or through some other mode of transportation must also be sorted and forwarded by truck or van to local receivers.

In addition to the control and distributor function, the freight terminal handles all accounting and billing functions associated with the freight forwarding process.

The major functions performed in the terminal are thus vehicle unloading and loading, vehicle dispatching, sorting of all incoming and outgoing parcels and packages, as well as internal routing of all items in addition to general data processing. Parcels or packages are either forwarded individually or shipped in containers.

Continental Parcel's freight terminal is therefore divided into four subsystems: vehicle control, mechanization control, container routing, and support processing systems.

The vehicle control system controls vehicle movement into, within, and out of the terminal. This subsystem also controls entry into and exit out of the terminal, schedules the unloading and loading of vans or trucks at the docks, monitors the movement of yard tractors used to move vans between parking stalls and docks, and schedules the departure of both loaded and empty vehicles.

The mechanization control system controls various parcel-sorting machines in the terminal and performs time-sharing conveyor control and monitoring. The mechanization control system is using several mechanization processing computers for sorter and time-share conveyor control. All these computers are identical and can readily substitute for one another.

The container routing system governs the routing and travel of independent containers which transport packages or parcels on a towline system from one location to another within the terminal. Two basic functions are performed: container routing control through reading of destination code on each container by an optical scanner and switching of the respective container to its destination, and monitoring an inventory of empty in-house shipping containers.

Finally, the support processing system handles statistical accumulation and analysis for each application system, reports ma·functions to maintenance operations, and performs the necessary accounts receivable invoicing and other bookkeeping functions.

Figure 6-21 shows a block diagram of the basic system elements. When entering the freight terminal, each vehicle is identified and automatically directed to a preassigned parking stall. The driver then reports to a vehicle control office and gets his trip ticket completed. The inbound van is subsequently directed to the appropriate loading dock for unloading. During the unloading operation, the dock and van numbers are entered into the computer system by a dock technician using a special-purpose keyboard terminal.

The parcels, sacks, or packages are loaded onto a conveyor belt, which moves them to an induction station. Each bag or parcel automatically stops

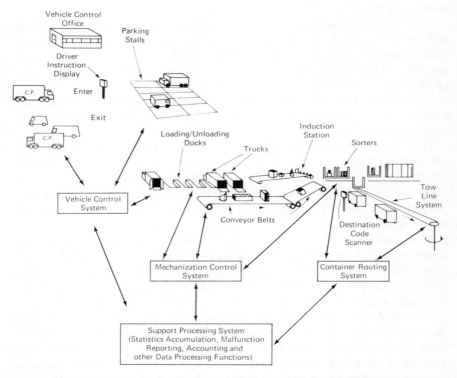

Figure 6-21 Block diagram, continental parcel freight terminal process control system

at one of the several induction lines when it interrupts a photoelectric sensor beam. An operator then reads the parcel destination code or address and enters it into a keyboard. This action starts a sort cycle for that particular item, which then automatically dumps onto an empty tilt tray for transport to its proper discharge chute.

Once sorted, the packages and sacks are loaded into trucks or vans and shipped to their destinations. The loading process and vehicle control is handled by the vehicle control system. A block diagram of the parcel-sorting subsystem is shown in Figure 6-22.

The container routing controller governs the routing and travel of independent containers, which transport a large number of packages that are to be shipped point to point and that therefore do not require individual sorting. These containers are transported within the terminal using a tow-line system. These containers are moved in a manner similar to freight cars in a railroad yard, through various loops and bypasses to outbound dock spurs for van loading.

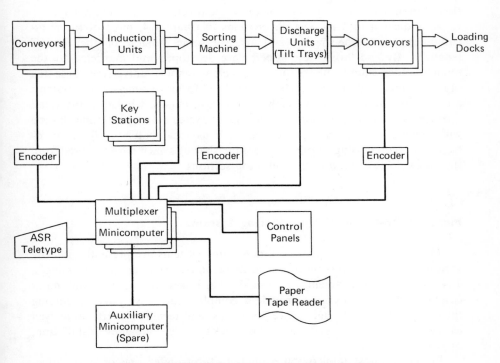

Figure 6-22 Block diagram, parcel-sorting subsystem

6.6 COMPUTATIONAL AND TIME-SHARING SYSTEMS

Scientific applications requiring solutions to large complex mathematical equations have traditionally been the domain of the large machine. These large *number crunchers* have been accessed either in a batch or time-sharing mode. The minicomputer was originally introduced as a tool for the scientist or mathematician to solve some of the less complex problems in a dedicated environment. However, since the introduction of the mini in the mid-1960s its processing power has been growing to the point where it competes favorably with several larger machines in terms of scientific processing capability. The minicomputer has also developed to the point where it competes with the large time-sharing systems for the low end of the market. While standard time sharing retains its advantage principally where many users must share a single large data base, the flexibility and low cost of the time-shared mini have brought it into many more diverse applications today.

As indicated in Time-Sharing Systems in Chapter 4, most of the minicomputer-based time-sharing systems use some version of the BASIC language. By and large these systems are developed and marketed by the minicomputer manufacturers for users such as schools, universities, research organizations, and libraries. More specialized forms of time-sharing systems are built by OEMs for users such as hospitals, clinics, wholesale and retail operations, hotels, and motels. The latter systems combine time-sharing with other types of data processing such as local batch or foreground-background processing. Both types of time-sharing systems are explored from the user's point of view in the following sections.

More on Off-the-Shelf Time-Sharing Systems

The majority of off-the-shelf time-sharing systems are presently used by various educational institutions such as secondary schools, junior colleges, and university departments. Hewlett-Packard was among the first minicomputer manufacturers to provide a complete turn-key system, including the computer, disk-storage device, terminals, and terminal interfaces as well as all the necessary software. This package also includes installation, service, and training.

Presently, most minicomputer manufacturers offer one or more time-sharing systems. Hewlett-Packard's systems are called the HP-2000 series,

Data General's go under the name of the Seminar Series, and Microdata calls them Educational Systems. One of the smallest versions is Seminar 3, which includes a Data General Nova 1220 with 16K words of core and five Teletype terminals. At the other end of the scale, the HP-2000F may include a system processor with 32K words of core, a communications processor with 8K words of core, a fixed head drum, and a 23.5 megabyte disk file with up to eight disk pack facilities, a nine-track magnetic tape unit, a high-speed paper tape reader, an on-line line printer, and up to 32 ASCII-type terminals operating at rates ranging from 10 to 240 cps (Figure 6-23).

The latter system supports three levels of libraries:

1. Public library programs are available to any user but can be modified only by the system master or system operator.
2. Group libraries are available for up to 100 user codes and are administered by a group master, such as a class instructor in the educational environment. Each user has a user code or password which is changeable and which can be a nonprinting character. The user must type this password in order to access the system.
3. Private libraries are available to the various users and are accessible only by the respective user's unique ID code and password.

Several time-sharing systems permit operation of the system in non-time-shared modes. The HP-2000F can be operated in a batch mode where programs written in FORTRAN, ALGOL, or assembly language may be loaded and run in a batched environment. The system can also be configured to run in a background/foreground environment.

The key elements to be considered in selecting a minicomputer time-sharing system are as follows:

1. Maximum number of terminals that can simultaneously access the CPU
2. The maximum size of the user program that is swapped from disk to main memory
3. Number and type of multispeed terminals that can be connected to the system (including remote terminals using modems)
4. System status reporting such as statistical data on cumulative connect time for each user, last date accessed, location and length of all programs and data files, and which user, if any, is logged onto each port
5. Amount of operator invervention required, if any
6. Cost per hour per terminal

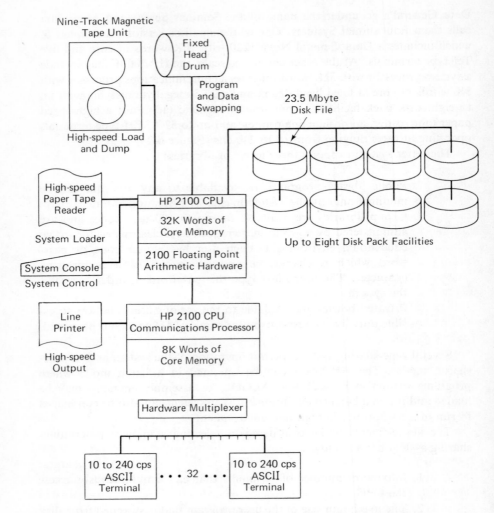

Figure 6-23 Hewlett-Packard HP-2000F time-sharing system hardware block diagram (disk file mass storage configuration) (Courtesy Hewlett-Packard Corp.)

OEM Systems for Hotels and Motels

One of the largest markets for minicomputers and miniperipherals is the OEM customer who buys the components from one or more manufacturers and builds them into his own product line or simply transships them with other component assemblies, also supplying his own marketing distribution or programming expertise. The OEM's product line usually caters to special-purpose system users such as wholesale distributors, hotel or motel chains, hospitals, clinics, convalescent homes, and department stores.

The dilemma the OEM is usually faced with is how to make his product flexible enough to meet the demands of each individual user within a group while at the same time not making it too general-purpose, thereby precluding the amortization of system development costs over a sufficiently large customer base. From the viewpoint of the end user, selecting an OEM-designed system which is inflexible or too costly to tailor to his particular requirements leaves him no other alternative but to alter the mode of operation to be able to .use a particular system or build a system in-house from scratch. The former approach is generally unacceptable to most end users, while the latter may be an even more difficult decision to make for the inexperienced.

In spite of these obvious difficulties, a very large number of OEM-developed systems are presently on the market. Several of the more successful products incorporate features such as on-line data entry, data communications, time sharing, and batch processing capabilities. Characteristically, these systems are often designed for foolproof operation by relatively unskilled people, where data are entered into the minicomputer either from a CRT terminal or a special-purpose data entry device. The controlling computer is programmed to make life simple for the operator by using code words for data base inquiry, using file update based on actual customer or account names and inventory items, and leading the operator through functional sequences step by step.

An example of such a system, where one of its major functions is time sharing, is Comtel, developed by Metric Systems Corporation. Comtel was designed to provide computer-controlled management for hotels and motels. The primary purpose of the system is to improve hotel check-in/check-out procedures, reducing guest delay; to eliminate the problem of lost charges; to simplify room reservations; to reduce clerical expenses for payroll, accounting, posting, and billing; to increase inventory control and control of guest credit; to provide automatic credit verification at point of sale in the hotel coffee shop, lounge, gift shop, etc.; and to increase cash control.

During the initial system design, it became apparent that three distinct processing activities would be required:

1. Servicing of remote on-line terminals sending point-of-sale charges to the system in real time
2. Communication with central facility in real time, providing data processing capability for such functions as check-in, check-out, reservation posting, and employee earnings posting
3. Batch processing of payroll and various reporting programs

Two approaches to satisfy the above processing activities were considered initially:

1. On-line processing during peak business hours and batch processing during the slack hours
2. Concurrent processing of all three activities

The disadvantage of the first approach is that on-line processing would be disabled during batch processing. This would create problems when transactions would occur such as late check-ins and charges from guests or customers in all-night lounges. Further, personnel requirements would have to be expanded, since an employee capable of processing payroll and other batch programs would be required in the early hours of the morning. Many hotels employ part-time or temporary personnel and experience a high turnover rate at that shift. The problem would also be compounded by training requirements for the latter type of personnel. In addition, the management information reports produced by the system would not be available at the times they would be most useful. Today's inventory-control problem would not become apparent until tomorrow.

The second approach solves the above problems and provides more efficient overall utilization of the system. The Comtel system diagram shown in Figure 6-24 is based on a Data General Nova 1200, a 1.3-million-character Iomec disk storage unit, a Centronics VDT-01 Video Display Terminal (VDT), and up to 64 Metric RCT-01 Remote Cash Terminals. The printer is used to produce reports and documents such as payroll checks, income tax statements, various inventories, reservations, accounts receivable, and room status and guest history reports. The VDT or CRT terminal is used for communications between the CPU and the operator at the central site and for immediate visual display of information requested by the operator, such as room status, room availability, inventory status, and revenue status. Room reservations, payroll earnings, check-ins, check-outs, etc., are also input from the VDT. Finally, the RCT performs two basic functions: transmission of point-of-sale transactions from remote locations to the central computer and printing of guest receipts following transmission of transactions. The RCT allows transmission of cash charge, tab, and credit transactions to the computer for immediate updating of guest ledgers, accounts receivable files, inventory files, etc. Up to 64 bit-serial low-speed lines can be multiplexed from the Nova to the respective RCTs.

The software consists of an executive system and six major processing programs or applications modules. The three processing activities—I/O to and from RCTs, operator communications through the VDT, and batch processing at the central facility—logically dictated the design and priority

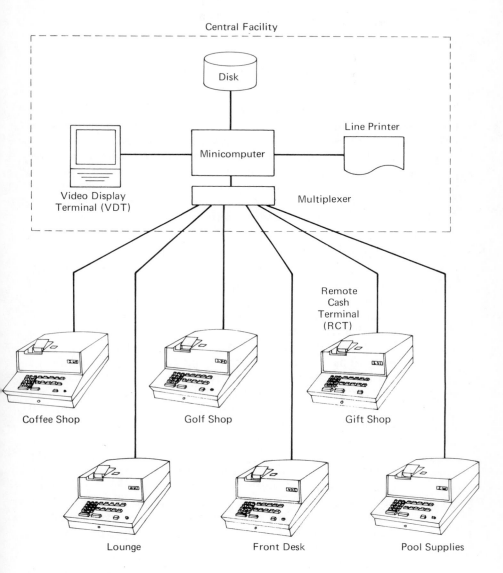

Figure 6-24 Comtel computer-controlled management system for hotels and motels (Courtesy Metric Systems Corporation)

scheme of the multiprogrammed system. The priority scheme is established on the following basis:

Top priority level: RCTs

Intermediate priority level: VDT

Lowest priority level: Batch Processing

The executive analyzes and services system interrupts, allocates processor time to the three competing activities on the above priority basis, performs I/O functions, and performs and controls memory overlays of processing program modules. A skeletal supervising module for each of the three processing activities resides in main memory, while "function" modules, that is, program overlay modules designed to perform one or more distinct functions, reside on the disk and are called into main memory when needed.

The six major applications modules perform the following functions:

1. *Guest Accounting System:* Guests are "checked into" the system at the central facility or "work station" by entering pertinent information such as room number, guest name and address, and room rate. From that moment until check-out, the great majority of all guest charges are automatically accumulated from point-of-sale cash terminals and posted to the guest ledger stored within the system. Posting of the daily room rent charge is an automatic function of the system. Point-of-sale cash terminals are normally located in the common charge points such as restaurants, lounges, coffee shops, and gift shops. These terminals transmit guest charges, as well as cash transactions, directly to the central computer. This allows instantaneous updating of the guest ledger. It also allows the system to provide an accounting of all cash terminals. Following transmission of the transaction, the system sends back to the terminal a printed receipt which indicates the name in which the room is registered. This feature provides protection against errors such as improper room number, since a name discrepancy would most likely be noted. At the time of check-out, the desk clerk merely types the room number and depresses the check-out button on the terminal. The detailed guest receipt is printed immediately, requiring only 5 to 10 sec for a typical stay of four nights with 40 charges. The guest, having previously been presented with receipts from the various remote cash terminals, will already anticipate the approximate amount, resulting in a faster check-out operation.

Another feature in the system allows reporting of room status: Upon check-out, a message is automatically transmitted to the housekeeping terminal, providing notice that the room has been vacated and should be made ready for the next guest. After the room has been prepared, a message is transmitted from the housekeeping terminal for updating of the room status. An occupancy and room status report can be printed on request at the central work station. This report indicates at a glance the rooms which are available and the status of the rooms.

2. *Room Reservation System:* Considerable problems in hotel operations are encountered in internal reservation control. Metric's system provides sufficient storage capacity to allow for up to 1 year's advance reservations. The reservation clerk can simply request a display of available rooms of a particular type on a particular date. This information is immediately displayed on the video display terminal. The clerk then selects a room and enters the date of the reservation, the name of the guest, and other pertinent information. This information is stored in the computer's disk storage files. Reservations may easily be changed or canceled at a later time. Information typically contained in the reservation file includes name and address, check-in date, number of nights, room rate, number of persons, amount of deposit, and special instructions. Reports and CRT display formats provided by the room reservation system include the reservation by date display, the arrival report, and the departure report.

3. *City Accounts Receivable System:* City accounts (charge accounts for nonguests) are processed in almost exactly the same manner as guest accounts. A special block of numbers is reserved for assignment as charge-account numbers. These numbers are used in place of room number when entering charges. Upon request, a ledger of these accounts will be produced. Also upon request, statements will be produced.

4. *Guest History System:* An additional feature of the system is accumulation of guest history information. The history file typically contains information related to preferred guests, frequent guests, undesirable guests, bad checks, and poor credit risks. The guest history file may also be used to accumulate statistics from guest opinion questionnaires. With the exception of guest opinion data, accumulation of guest history is largely an automatic function of the system. Upon check-out, if requested by the operator, certain information is automatically transferred from the guest ledger file to the history file. The

history file contains the following information:

- Guest name and address
- Name of company (optional entry)
- Guest opinion of room, service, food, etc. (optional entry)
- Auto tag number (optional entry)
- Guest codes (VIP, bad check, skipped, undesirable)
- For each visit: dates of stay, room number, number of persons, amount of bill by category

The guest history file may be used to produce

- Mailing list/labels of preferred guests prior to anniversary
- List of past VIP guests
- Guest opinion statistics
- Miscellaneous statistics: average stay, average bill, etc.
- Holiday greeting card lists/labels

5. *Employee Payroll System:* An employee file is maintained which contains all information necessary to calculate and produce a weekly or biweekly payroll. The only manual action necessary is keying in of the number of hours worked by each employee during the pay period and any miscellaneous income such as tips. The payroll program automatically calculates all deductions, updates the year-to-date earnings and deductions for each employee, produces payroll checks, a payroll register, and annual W-2 statements. Keying in of employee earnings may be intermixed with other functions performed at the work station, such as reservation posting and guest check-in. This prevents interruption of the guest accounting and reservation functions.

6. *Inventory Control System:* Inventory control provides dynamic control of any or all controllable, expendable items. Once stock levels and quantities on hand are established, the system monitors consumption and resupply and provides inventory status reports on request. Inventory consumption is recorded immediately upon receipt of transactions from point-of-sale terminals.

REFERENCES

ALLAIN, W. L., "Integrated Instrument Setup Tests Intricate Assemblies," *Electronics*, October 9, 1972, 104–109.

BAIRSTOW, J. N., "The Terminal that Thinks for Itself," *Computer Decisions*, January 1973, 10–13.

BOREN, J. T., "Picking a Process Control Computer," *Electronic Products Magazine*, March 15, 1971, 27–30, 59–62.

BYRNS, P. D., "Considerations in Designing a Computer Communications System," *Datamation*, October 1969, 47–49.

ENFIELD, M. C., "Front-End Communications Processor Utilization," *Document TM-4420*, System Development Corporation, Santa Monica, Calif., September 1969.

FORD, K. W., "About Communications Processors," *Infosystems*, February 1973, 46–47.

FRIEDMAN, G. H., "Small Business Systems Help Managers Control Large and Small Companies," *Computer Decisions*, September 1972, 12–14.

FRIEDMAN, J., "Minicomputer Time-Sharing: Filling the Cost Gap," *Data Processing Magazine's Data Dynamics*, July 1971, 26–30.

GILDENBERG, R. F., "Word Processing," *Modern Data*, January 1973, 56–64.

GOLDSTERN, P., "Can a Mini Solve Your Communications Problem?," *The Electronic Engineer*, August 1972, DC-5–DC-7.

HENDEL, R. A., "Minicomputer Word Processing: A Two-Year Case History," *Infosystems*, August 1972, 35–37.

JOSZA, D. G., "Numerical Control Systems Need User Input," *Electronic Products Magazine*, February 19, 1973, 43–49.

MASON, J. F., "Minicomputers Taking Over in Factories in Blue-Collar and White-Collar Jobs," *Electronic Design 15*, July 20, 1972, 28–32.

MCALEER, H. T., "A Look at Automatic Testing," *IEEE Spectrum*, May 1971, 63–78.

MOUNT, R. L., "Computers . . . Mainly Minis . . . Help Industry Push into the Second Industrial Revolution," *Infosystems*, October 1972, 38–46.

MURPHY, J. A., "Small Business/Accounting Computer Systems," *Modern Data*, March 1972, 42–49.

————"Programmable Communications Processors, Front End Selections," *Modern Data*, July 1972, 38–50.

NESTLE, E., "Using Small Computers in Data Communications Networks," *Communications News*, May 1971, 29–30.

PYES, R. N., "Selecting Terminals for Data Entry Role," *The Data Communications User*, August 1972, 29–34.

RANDALL, H. B., and E. L. RUDISILL, "Production Monitoring with a Small Computer," *Electronic Products Magazine*, March 1, 1971, 28–32.

SALZMAN, R. M., "An Outlook for the Terminal Industry in the United States," *Computer*, November/December 1971, 18–25.

SULLIVAN, J. K., "Small Business System Speeds Office-to-Warehouse Communications," *Computer Decisions*, September 1972, 20.

THEIS, D. J., "Communications Processors," *Datamation*, August 1972, 31–44.

TOWNSEND, M. J., "Communication Control by Computer—An Introduction," *Telecommunications*, May 1972, 33–38, 60–62.

WESSLER, J. J., "POS for the Supermarket," *Modern Data*, January 1973, 52–54.

7

MINICOMPUTER SYSTEM
USER PROBLEMS

The user is generally faced with a set of problems that is different from that of the system designer. The user is concerned with the reliability of the system, how to get the system installed, where to go for best possible maintenance within his budget, and, eventually, what to do when he has outgrown his system's capabilities.

Total system reliability and maintainability are related indirectly. Although a highly reliable system does not necessarily require a limited amount of maintenance, the reverse is generally true: The well-maintained system is usually more reliable.

Total system reliability is, to a great extent, dictated by the following features:

- Reliability of each critical hardware component in the system
- Reliability of all interfaces and communications lines in the system
- Reliability of operating system and applications software
- Provisions made for the system to cope with adverse environmental conditions
- Procedures instigated and design precautions taken to minimize the effects of operator and other human errors

System maintenance is to a large extent people-oriented, requiring that adequately trained personnel be available upon short notice when a failure occurs. System downtime depends not only on how long it takes for the maintenance man to arrive at the minicomputer site but also on the effectiveness of available system diagnostic tools and procedures. The user must therefore consider factors such as equipment warranty, level of diagnostics, quality of maintenance and repair manuals, required minimum spare parts provisioning, and the comprehensiveness and cost of the service contract.

Eventually after years or perhaps only months of usage, when the system load exceeds existing system capabilities, the time has arrived to either modify and expand the system or replace it with a larger one.

7.1 SYSTEM RELIABILITY, TYPES OF FAILURES, AND THE APPLICATION

System reliability, in contrast to hardware reliability, has been defined as "the prevention of system downtime" and "protection of the data base."* Hardware reliability is related to the (statistical) length of time the unit operates before it fails (see Minicomputer Reliability in Chapter 2). Failure in this case could mean a head crash in a disk unit, power supply failure in a cassette drive, or a broken print chain in a line printer.

However, although a particular piece of hardware in a system may have failed, it does not necessarily signify a total system failure. System downtime may be a result of one or more of the following factors:

- System-critical hardware failure
- Loss of system power
- Software failure
- Operator error
- System overloading because of poor system design, etc.

Acceptable maximum downtime is, as a rule, a function of the particular application. A minicomputer system used in a laboratory for test purposes may be unusable for hours or even days without causing serious problems. Failure in a minicomputer-based remote batch terminal may be tolerable if the terminal can be repaired within hours. However, a failure in a real-time system used for text editing, point-of-sale, or process control may be disastrous if the system is down for more than a few minutes. Without a backup capability, the user may incur serious cost penalties in terms of dissatisfied customers, stalled production lines, or faulty products.

How to Optimize System Reliability

The minicomputer system is composed of *task-critical* and *task-non-critical* elements. A failure in a task-oriented element will result in total

---

* Edward Yourdon, "Reliability of Real-Time Systems," *Modern Data*, January 1972, 36–42.

Unit	MTBF (hr)
Minicomputer (CPU, 8K words of memory, real-time clock, automatic power restart, automatic load feature)	5000-8000
Line printer (impact, 300 lpm)	400-800
Paper tape reader	2000
Paper tape punch	1000
Card reader	1000
Card punch	200
CRT terminal	3000-5000
Keyboard printer terminal (nonimpact)	3000-5000
Keyboard printer terminal (impact)	300-1600
Fixed head disk	3000-10,000
Moving head disk	1000-5000
Magnetic tape unit (industry-compatible seven or nine track)	1500-3000
Modem	10,000-20,000
Typical peripheral interface	20,000

Figure 7-1 Typical values of MTBF for minicomputers and peripherals

system failure, while a noncritical element will not seriously hamper system operation. A failed CPU in a single-computer, text-editing system will result in total system failure. However, a failure in a single CRT terminal in a multiterminal system will not necessarily bring the entire system down.

System reliability can therefore be enhanced in several ways:

1. Relaxation of design constraints, where possible, to allow for the use of equipments which exhibit inherently high reliability
2. Choice of the most reliable hardware items within a particular performance and price range

3. Use of redundancy while, at the same time, optimizing the cost effectiveness of the system

The reliability of a system can be greatly improved during the conceptual or initial design phase, when the required hardware performance limits and characteristics are defined. A minicomputer using a 1.2-μsec cycle-time core memory is generally more reliable than a mini using a 0.6-μsec core memory. Similarly, a thermal printer is generally more reliable than the equivalent impact printer. Moreover, a CRT terminal is generally preferable to a Selectric or a Teletype in terms of reliability.

Typical MTBFs, which can be expected of standard commercial equipment, are listed in Figure 7-1. It is conceivable that some pieces of hardware are either above or below these limits. To use these numbers, it is important to understand how they are determined.

The most common approach is to gather information based on the frequency of field service calls required to restore the failed piece of equipment to operating condition. The number of failures for each piece of equipment is recorded over a period of time, such as 3, 6, or 12 months. Assuming that the system has been operating 24 hr a day for a full year, or a total of 8760 hr, with a total of 10 failures in the card reader, the MTBF for the card reader is 876 hr ($= 8760$ hr/10 failures).

The most common method of computing MTBF, where λ is the failure rate, is based on the following equation:

$$\text{MTBF} = \frac{1}{\lambda}$$

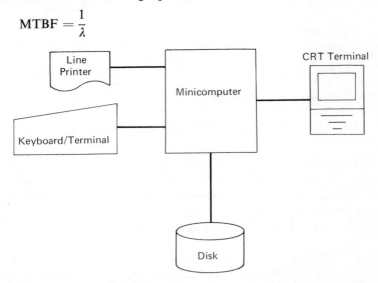

Figure 7-2 Minicomputer configuration used to compute hardware MTBF

This assumes that statistical information is available for over 100 units which have been in the field, operating 24 hr a day for over 1 year, or 10^6 hr.

Again, assuming that valid data on failure rates are available, system hardware MTBF for the configuration shown in Figure 7-2 is computed as follows:

Description	Failure Rate Per Million Hours (λ)	MTBF (hr)
Minicomputer	200	5000
CRT terminal	250	4000
Disk	400	2500
Hard-copy keyboard terminal	1000	1000
Line printer	2000	500
	2850	351*

* MTBF $= 1/\lambda = 10^6/(200 + 250 + 400 + 2000) = 351$ hr. (Note that the hard-copy keyboard terminal is backed up by the CRT terminal and is not a task-critical item therefore.)

Great caution should be exercised in using MTBF values. They can be greatly misleading based on equipment operating only 8 hr/day or based on an inconclusive, limited number of samples. This is usually quite obvious when the equipment is recently introduced and no failure records have yet been established.

Furthermore, the available MTBF is often based on minimum equipment duty cycles, as, for instance, in the case of printers, which may have the motor running 8 hr/day but only print a total of 1 hr during the same time period. Initial MTBF values, available on recently announced minis, can be equally misleading (in either direction). Hardware reliability for militarized equipment in terms of MTBF is often generated by a series of theoretical calculations based on various distribution curves, where the data used to generate these curves are obtained from accelerated subelement or component tests performed in an environment which simulates the extremes of the actual operating system environment. Such component tests are based on failures that are encountered during environmental conditions such as humidity, shock, extreme temperatures, and vibration. The reliability figure is usually only an indication of expected design reliability and must therefore be verified by accelerated system acceptance tests or by data obtained from actual field experience.

The following example illustrates the method for calculating theoretical reliability: For a minicomputer consisting of three parts—the CPU, the memory, and the power supply—the probability of successful operation is equal to the product of the probabilities of each unit operating properly,

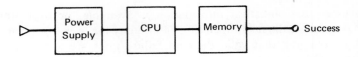

Figure 7-3   Reliability model for minicomputer

because failure of any of the three units to operate constitutes a failure for the entire computer. The failure rate for each unit is the sum of the failure rates for every part in the unit. This is a rather conservative calculation since there is some inherent redundancy built into most minis because of their general-purpose nature. The reliability figures calculated would be those if every circuit in the machine were required for successful operation. Generally not all the memory is being used, and some applications may not use all four accumulators available in the CPU. Thus, for an actual application the reliability should be higher than results based on theoretical calculations depending on the percentage of circuits used and whether or not programming is used to take advantage of the redundancy inherent in the machine. Hence,

$$P_S = P_{PS} P_{\text{CPU}} P_M$$

where $P = e^{-\lambda t}$

P_S = probability of success for total system
P_{PS} = probability of success for power supply
P_{CPU} = probability of success for CPU
P_M = probability of success for memory
λ = failure rate
t = time

Since $\lambda = 1/\text{MTBF}$,

$$P = e^{t/MTBF}$$

The reliability model is shown in Figure 7-3. Based on the model, Rolm Corporation has performed a reliability analysis for its Model 1601 militarized minicomputer for various environments and applications. A summary of these calculations is shown in Figure 7-4.

The computer has a basic MTBF of 11,250 hr for ground application in an ambient temperature of 25°C. At this same temperature the MTBF is about 9000 hr for shipboard applications and 2000 hr for airborne application. It drops to 650 hr for missile application because of the very large application factors (K factors*) specified by Mil Handbook 217A for a missile environment. These failure rates are for operating hours; generally there will be extensive periods of nonoperation in less severe environments so that the expected actual MTBFs should be greater than those given.

---

* The K-factor multiplier is due to the environment (shipboard, airborne, etc.).

Application	Failure rate (λ) (per million hr)	MTBF (hr)
25°C		
Airborne	482	2,080
Ground	89	11,250
Shipboard	110	9,100
Missile	1532	654
95°C		
Airborne	2312	433
Ground	491	2,040
Shipboard	871	1,050
Missile	7424	135

Figure 7-4 Rolm Model 1601 reliability based on a configuration consisting of power supply, CPU, and 4K memory (Courtesy Rolm Corporation, Cupertino, Calif.)

Calculations were also made of the MTBF for a 95° ambient condition. As might be expected, the MTBF is considerably lower because all the thermal stresses are quite high. Even so, the unit has a basic MTBF of greater than 2000 hr for ground operation at this temperature.

Given an operational profile, the actual MTBF of the equipment can be calculated from the following formula:

$$\lambda = \sum_{i=1}^{n} \lambda_i K_i$$

where λ = expected failure rate
λ_i = failure rate for the ith environmental condition
K_i = percentage of time the computer is in the ith environment

As an example, suppose that the computer is used in a supersonic aircraft. If it is located close to the skin in supersonic flight, it will be exposed to temperatures as high as 95°C. Suppose that the unit is operational for 100 hr of flight out of every 500 hr. Out of these 100 hr, 10 hr are assumed to be supersonic flight, while the rest are at temperatures or 25°C or less. Another 50 hr are assumed to be used for ground operational check-out at 25°C. The failure rate during nonoperation is assumed to be one-tenth of the operating failure rate. Hence,

$$\lambda = 2312(0.02) + 482(0.18) + 89(0.1) + 8.9(0.7)$$
$$= 46.24 + 86.8 + 8.9 + 6.23 = 148.17$$

Since MTBF = $1/\lambda$,

$$\text{MTBF} = \frac{1}{148.2} = 6760 \text{ hr}$$

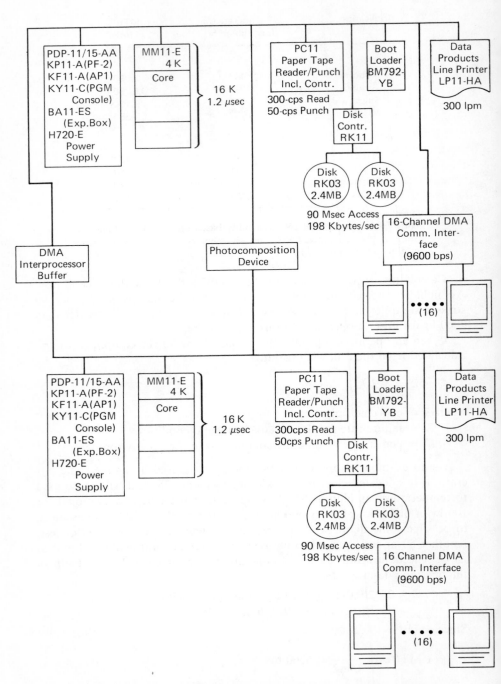

Figure 7-5 Dual text editing system based on digital equipment PDP-11/15

System reliability is not only a function of the quality of the hardware but also of the procedures followed in the installation process. Poor grounding procedures, inadequate shielding, improper termination of cables, and inadequate environmental control all contribute to high failure rates. Systems operating in a military or manufacturing plant environment usually require a power-fail-safe feature in the computer. It is quite common to experience short noise pulses on the line which are sufficient to disrupt system operation but are transparent to the user if operation is automatically restored. Similarly, it is preferable to run remose data terminals using current-loop instead of the more noise-sensitive EIA-voltage interface in electrically noisy environments. Furthermore, static electricity from carpeting in the office may occasionally destroy programs running on the mini when the operator touches the system hardware.

Lack of adequate and often straightforward system design and installation procedures may therefore offset the advantages of carefully chosen, highly reliable hardware units.

In addition to the use of highly reliable off-the-shelf hardware, the commercial system designer can further increase system reliability by adding redundant elements to it or by using either ruggedized or militarized equipment. The former approach is generally more attractive in commercial applications, since the cost of militarized hardware often exceeds the cost of equivalent commercial equipment by a factor ranging from approximately 3 to 10.

Again, using the example given in Critical Performance Parameters for Text-Editing Systems in Chapter 6, maximum system reliability is obtained by using two minicomputers and two disk units. The redundant mini can be switched into the system, either manually or automatically, once a failure in the first CPU has been detected. Such a redundant configuration is shown in Figure 7-5.

Protection against data base failures is achieved through the use of two disks. Through periodic copying of disk contents from the first to the second disk, the user stands less risk of losing critical information that cannot be reconstructed if destroyed.

The problem of data base failures is of less significance in intelligent batch terminals or problem-solving systems where, once the system has been repaired, the entire program can be reloaded and rerun.

Software Reliability

In contrast to hardware reliability measures which are directly related to statistical analysis of random failures of components with age and/or faulty processing methods, software, although it is a symbolic product not subject to physical failure once it has been debugged, is infinitely more complex to measure in terms of reliability. Errors in software may be attributed to the programmer, who may have failed to understand the problem attacked, conceived a faulty algorithm, written an incorrect program, overlooked special cases of input data, or conducted insufficient debugging tests. Also, errors in software could have been introduced in the keypunching process or because of bugs in the compiler. Furthermore, errors in the software could have been introduced by transient failures in the hardware.

It is not unusual for minicomputer disk operating systems to be extremely unforgiving. The slightest error or omission by the programmer will crash the system. A well-designed disk operating system (and there are a few) does all it promises in the manual and cannot be inadvertently crashed from the console by the system operator or programmer. However, the majority of DOSs exhibit various idiosyncrasies not obvious to the user without hands-on experience. There is no meaningful value that can be assigned to operating system reliability or MTBF. The user is therefore faced with an even more difficult task evaluating the impact of software reliability on total system reliability.

The difference in failure characteristics is illustrated in Figure 5-21, which shows the traditional "bathtub" curve for hardware errors with low initial MTBF, relatively constant MTBF after initial system check-out, and, finally, rapidly deteriorating error performance once the end of the system life cycle is reached. In contrast, software errors decrease less rapidly initially but seldom to a point where the system is fully debugged.* Increased system reliability in terms of its software elements is therefore related to the amount of time the software has been in use and the number of updates and amount of maintenance given the software by the vendor.

The user is consequently well advised in bypassing new, more sophisticated hardware systems that lack the capability of emulating their predecessors, which usually have an extensive, proved software library developed over a period of several years.

7.2 SYSTEM MAINTENANCE AND REPAIR

System maintenance falls into three categories: preventive maintenance (PM), remedial maintenance, and software maintenance. PM generally consists of periodic checkup, machine adjustments, and replacement of worn-out parts. Inadequate or infrequent PM will result in increased remedial maintenance. Software maintenance is an on-going process, usually undertaken by the hardware manufacturer, who periodically issues updates to the system software.

---

* Bernard Elspas, M. W. Green, and K. N. Levitt, "Software Reliability," *Computer*, January/February 1971, 21–27.

The user may opt for one of three alternatives to hardware maintenance and repair. The first alternative is to have maintenance performed by in-house personnel. Second, the user may choose to have maintenance provided by the equipment manufacturer on a yearly contract basis or as an on-call service. Third, regardless of whether he is the OEM or end user, he may elect third-party maintenance service from a specialized service company.

The answer to the question of who is best suited to perform maintenance is, in most cases, determined by the application and environment in which the system must operate. In a manufacturing and process control environment, where the computer serves as an integral part of the system, it is often preferable to have the maintenance available permanently, on location. Under these circumstances, it may be more cost-effective to have internal personnel capable of maintaining all elements of the system instead of having to rely on an outside maintenance crew from the manufacturer or a third-party service organization. On the other hand, if the minicomputer system is an intelligent terminal located in a business office, it may be more cost-effective to rely on thirdparty maintenance.

The pros and cons of various maintenance policies are discussed in the following sections.

In-House Maintenance

The user deciding to perform his own maintenance must carefully consider the following items:

- Extent of equipment warranty provided by manufacturer
- Available training courses given by manufacturer
- Level of spare parts provisioning
- Special test equipment
- Maintenance documentation
- Maintenance personnel

The warranty period from the manufacturer varies from 30 to 90 days, depending on the manufacturer. The warranty may provide on-site repair or be limited to the cost of parts and labor, where the faulty equipment must be shipped at owner's expense to the manufacturer's service center.

Most minicomputer and peripheral manufacturers provide a series of standard courses where, upon completion, the student will be able to perform preventive and corrective maintenance on the equipment. A course on the minicomputer typically covers the logic operation of the CPU, including manual functions, instruction set, memory, and I/O section. Most courses provide the student with hands-on opportunity for system familiarization and troubleshooting. A minimum of 2 weeks is generally required to give the student a basic knowledge of system maintenance, covering the computer and a limited set of peripherals. In cases where a considerable number of people must be trained, it may be more economical to have the course conducted at the user's facility rather than sending the students to the manufacturer's educational facility.

As a rule, the level of spare parts provisioning is a function of the particular application. The main purpose for having any spare parts available is, of course, to keep the entire system from becoming useless when one component fails.

A large number of spare parts must usually be available in process control environments where the tolerable mean time to repair seldom exceeds 15 to 30 min. A high level of spare parts is equally necessary for systems operating in a remote location where the access time to a manufacturer's parts depot is prohibitive, as in the case when the system is located on a ship. In the latter case, a minimum working configuration must be determined, and that configuration must be spared extensively.

The following example is used to illustrate the approach taken for spare parts provisioning for a stand-alone data processing system using the Data General Nova 1200. Based on the configuration shown in Figure 7-6, needed capabilities are CPU, memory, input, output, and either disk or tape. The minimum operable capacity is 16K (2–8K boards).

Input devices in the total system are the Teletype, CRT terminal, paper tape reader, cassette tape, and card reader. Because all the software is initially on paper tape, the tape reader must be spared.

Output devices available are the Teletype, cassette unit, CRT terminal, and line printer. Since a hard-copy output is required, the choice is between the Teletype and the line printer. This decision is facilitated by the fact that the paper tape reader is connected to the Teletype. Therefore, even though the Teletype is slow, it is the logical answer for backing up both input and output capabilities.

For time-sharing purposes, either the disk operating system or the cassette tape operating system will be required for backup. Since the system already includes two independent cassette tape units, no additional auxiliary memory devices have to be spared. In addition to the spare circuit boards and the ASR Teletype, a number of miscellaneous parts should also be included.

A list of spare parts therefore includes the following items:

    1   2071   CPU
    1   4075   I/O board
    1   4077   TTY interface
    1   4010A TTY with paper tape reader
    1   2063   miscellaneous spare parts for Nova 1200

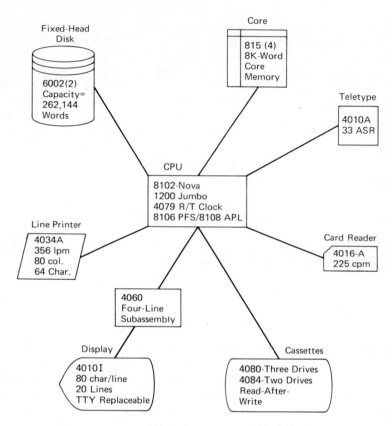

Figure 7-6 Stand-alone configuration used to illustrate spare parts provisioning analysis

In addition, it is recommended that the user performing his own maintenance be equipped with a maintenance tool kit containing items such as pliers, screwdrivers, wrenches, wire strippers, tweezers, a flux remover, test clips, a soldering iron, core solder, a multimeter, current probes, and an oscilloscope. In addition, maintenance documentation and diagnostic software tapes are required to determine causes of failures quickly.

Unlike larger computers, which often contain a large amount of diagnostic hardware, most minicomputers must rely solely on diagnostic software. Minicomputer software test programs are usually stored on paper tape and perform diagnostic checks on CPU instructions, memory address selection logic, memory sense amplifiers, and inhibit logic and system interrupts. Diagnostic tapes also check the operation of system peripherals such as the Teletype, paper tape reader and punch, magnetic tape and disk units.

The answer to the question of who should be performing the in-house maintenance depends on the user. A user with a large number of in-house systems may be able to keep a maintenance crew occupied on a full-time basis. In contrast, the user of a single system who, for various reasons, is forced to provide his own maintenance is faced with the choice of either hiring maintenance personnel and training them for other tasks or expanding the duties of existing personnel to encompass maintenance. In many instances, the best solution is to have the user-personnel also perform the maintenance. This solution may turn out to be the most cost-effective, since the system operator is usually well acquainted with the system, which therefore minimizes the training required.

Maintenance and the Hardware Manufacturer

All minicomputer manufacturers offer at least one of the following options for maintenance once the warranty has expired:

1. On-call service
2. Per-call service
3. Warranty extension or depot repair service

On-call service is based on preventive maintenance (PM) being performed on a scheduled basis. The user must, in this case, sign a 6- or 12-month contract with the manufacturer, where the service consists of regular PM, in addition to a manufacturer's service representative's being available for emergencies during the period of 9:00 A.M. through 5:00 P.M. Monday through Friday. This emergency coverage may be extended up to 24 consecutive hours of on-call coverage, Monday through Sunday. Some typical monthly maintenance charges for various system elements are shown in Figure 7-7. (The differentials in maintenance charges to some extent reflect the relative reliability of the various system elements.)

Because of the possible critical nature of an application, several manufacturers provide, in lieu of on-call coverage, an on-site resident engineer for a large and complex installation. Typically, this service consists of the resident engineer's being available at all times during a normal work week. In addition, in this case all necessary spare parts, materials, and test equipment are physically stationed at the user's site to minimize the possible downtime of the system.

The savings of using a resident engineer may be significant in cases where the installation to be serviced is located at a considerable distance from the nearest manufacturer field service office, since remotely located installations are usually subject to a monthly mileage premium charge in addition to the normal monthly service contract price.

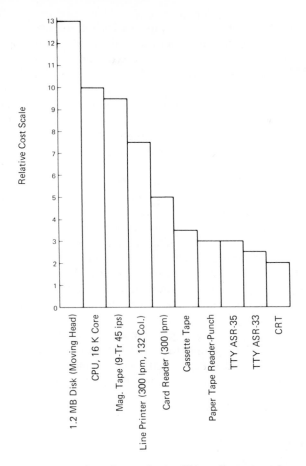

Figure 7-7 Comparative chart of monthly maintenance charges for various minicomputer system elements. Each device includes controller, where applicable, and computer interface

In contrast to on-call service, per-call or hourly service does not require a contract. Per-call service is based strictly on travel charges for the service representative, charges for the time he leaves the manufacturer's field service office to when he returns there, as well as the cost of parts and other materials used for repair.

Per-call coverage is usually relied on by users who have their own service capabilities or who are not critically tied to their equipment. Per-call service is often limited to hours between 9:00 A.M. and 5:00 P.M. Monday through Friday, and requests for per-call service receive second priority behind users with a service contract. In addition, several minicomputer and peripheral manufacturers also have a minimum charge per call.

Finally, depot repair or a warranty extension service contract permits the user to send the faulty equipment to a repair depot or the factory, respectively. Depot repair is generally provided on a noncontractual basis, where the user is charged on an hourly basis for labor. The warranty extension service contract allows for either repair at the user's installation where labor is charged at reduced rates or the user shipping the faulty equipment to the factory for repair. In the latter case, the user pays for parts and labor on a monthly payment schedule in addition to paying for freight and insurance to and from the plant. Per-call, depot repair, and warranty extension service excludes PM.

For systems based on peripherals and special interfaces not purchased from the minicomputer manufacturer, the problem of repair may be more complex than if all equipment is provided by a single vendor. In some instances, a failure in a peripheral may cause a secondary failure in the minicomputer or in the interface between the failed peripheral and the CPU. In this case, while under warranty the minicomputer manufacturer may refuse to repair the equipment at his expense. Also, for unauthorized changes made to the minicomputer or its interface, the user must bear all maintenance costs, regardless of the type of service contract between the minicomputer manufacturer and the user.

Although increased system performance may be achieved through selection of nonstandard peripherals, the user should be aware of potential unpredictable maintenance costs that may be incurred. For this reason, third-party maintenance may be more attractive than relying on manufacturer support.

Third-Party Maintenance Service

A handful of third-party service companies are presently available on both a national and an international basis. Third-party maintenance service is therefore often relied on by the OEM who wants to market a system consisting of minicomputer and peripherals, where the latter are made by a large number of manufacturers. Although several of the peripherals may be standard items also available from the minicomputer manufacturer, the OEM usually prefers to purchase these items directly from the original manufacturer in order to save on handling charges imposed by the middleman— the minicomputer manufacturer—who is forced to pass on these charges to the OEM.

Third-party service may or may not be more expensive than the maintenance contract from the minicomputer manufacturer. Some third-party service companies charge an initial development or *unit fee* of several thousand dollars to cover the expense of initial training of support personnel, such as

Manufacturer or Third-Pary Service Company Reporting	A	B	C	D	E
Reporting system	Good	Poor	Very good	Excellent	Excellent
Terms	Contract, $\frac{1}{2}$ year	Contract, 2 years	Contract $\frac{1}{2}$ year	Contract, 1 year	Exclusive contract 2 years
Training cost Unit fee ($)	None	None	$5000	None	$7500
Per-area fee ($)	None	None	$5000	None	$5000
Past service capability	A's equipment only	B's equipment only	Limited	Nearly all OEM system components	Nearly all OEM system components
Future service capability	A CPU only non-standard peripherals	Not known	All OEM components	All OEM components	All OEM components
Spares and parts stocking	Branch offices, district offices, regional offices		Customer sales	Local, central depot, manufacturer	3 levels; on-site, local offices, central depot
Size (number of employees)	1200 (48 sites in USA, 100 worldwide)		53 (20 sites)	2600 (world-wide)	1300
Number of installations maintained	N.A.		N.A.	N.A.	More than 6000
Typical monthly charges ($) PM and remedial maintenance					
Nova 1200 w/4 K	—		60.00	10.00	30.00
Potter LP3000	—		75.00	50.00	37.50
Centronics	75.00		40.00	30.00	28.00
Hazeltine 2000	35.00		25.00	12.00	12.00
Any cassette	—		50.00	30.00	35.00
Per call, hourly rates ($)	25.00		25.00	18.00	20.00
Response time (hr)	2		3 average	2 average	1.5 average
Installation service	A equipment only		Yes	Yes	Yes

Figure 7-8   Comparison of service companies (A and B are minicomputer manufacturers)

product specialists, regional specialists, and instructors, and the cost of general administration setup.

The product specialist is assigned to the OEM at the manufacturing level to assure proper coordination of field activities and communications concerning technical developments. The regional specialist will supply the technical support, while the instructor will assume responsibility for training the user. In addition, a per-area development fee may be charged the OEM to cover the cost of area training and parts setup for the end user. Furthermore, the third-party service company, similar to the minicomputer manufacturer, also charges a monthly maintenance fee for each item being serviced. In some (rare) cases, depending on where the end user is located, the third-party service company charges only for monthly maintenance on a 1- or 2-year contractual basis without the unit and per-area fees.

A typical OEM checklist, prepared for the evaluation of service companies, is shown in Figure 7-8.

The importance to the OEM of being currently aware of his system's performance and service activities, particularly in the initial stages of a program when the first units are installed and become operable, cannot be overestimated. An adequate reporting and documentation program must therefore be provided either by the OEM himself or by the service company.

Typically, an incident report or service report is generated as a basic document to provide a complete management information system (MIS) of reports reflecting each service representative's weekly activities, parts usage, inventory status, and incidents by each machine type, indicating service activity, the unit involved, and cause of malfunction. A typical service report is shown in Figure 7-9. An example of a monthly summary report is shown in Figure 7-10. In addition, MTBF reports should be published on a regular basis to keep the OEM continually informed of the service operation and the system's performance for required changes and continuous product improvements.

7.3 SYSTEM INSTALLATION

Once the system design is completed, the purchase order is given, the maintenance approach has been decided upon, and the software design is started, system installation must be planned for. System installation can be performed by the user, minicomputer manufacturer, or third-party service company. Regardless of who performs the installation, decisions must be made on the method by which equipment is to be shipped, when and where it must be sent, and how it should be installed.

The manufacturer will usually provide installation service free of charge to the end user and at a cost of approximately 2 percent of system list price to

CUSTOMER NAME					P. O. NO.		**SERVICE REPORT**

Cawlco Inc.

RESS 193· Roxbury Drive, Beverly Hills · PHONE NO. 273 0110 · **No.** 878

PERSON REQUESTING SERVICE	CALL RECEIVED	TIME	DATE	CALL COMPLETED	TIME	DATE
C. Weitzman		1000	7-13-74		1610	9-13-74

JOB NO.	MODEL	CHARGE NO.	R.T.M.	SERVICE CODE
437	ZYD - 40	630970		

REASON FOR CALL: ZYD-40 not recording but a few entries from previous day's work

ACTION TAKEN: Cleaned capstan roller and adjusted roller tension on capstan shaft. Recorded a tape to check skew of ZYD-40

COMMENTS: Tape was not moving due to roller being dirty

MATERIAL USED					LABOR			
PART NO.	DESCRIPTION	QUAN.	UNIT PRICE	EXT. PRICE	TYPE	HOURS	RATE	PRICE
					REGULAR	.7	40	28
					TRAVEL	.5	4.0	2 0
					OVERTIME			
					STAND-BY			4.8
					TOTAL LABOR PRICE			
					REMOTE SERVICE CHARGE			
					18 MILES AT 15 ¢ MILE			2.70
			TOTAL MATERIALS					

FIELD ENG.

THE ABOVE DESCRIBED SERVICES WERE PERFORMED TO OUR SATISFACTION

CUSTOMER REPRESENTATIVE

DATE 9-13-74

NAME _____ TITLE Mgr

BILLABLE EXPENSES	98.70
OTHER	
SALES TAX	6.00
TOTAL AMOUNT DUE	101.70

ORIGINAL

Figure 7-9 Typical service report

DAY DWN	TIME DWN	DAY UP	TIME UP	HOURS DWN	CODE	REASON FOR CALL	CORRECTIVE ACTION	PART NUMBERS	QTY USED
266	1700	266	2130	4.5	SO	SELECTRIC PRINT BALL FAILS TO INDEX CORRECTLY.	ADJUSTED SELECTRIC.	104157	0
257	1515	258	1100	19.8	T1	THREE TERM. NG.	REPLACED MB, AND TWO MICRO SWITCHES.		0
258	1415	258	1545	1.5	S1	HUB ON MTU LOOSE.	TIGHTENED HUB ON MTU.		1
244	1449	244	1900	4.2	S1	SELECTRIC BALL DOES NOT MOVE.	REPLACED SELECTRIC.	104157	0
251	830	251	1330	5.0	T1	THREE TERM. PROBLEMS.	ADJUSTED KB'S AND REPLACED MB.	104772	1
258	1130	258	1330	2.0	T1	TERM. #7 OPER ID LIGHT OUT.	REPLACED BULBS.		1
260	1300	260	1530	2.5	S1	RE-INSTALL ORIGINAL SELECTRIC AFTER IBM REPAIR.	REPLACED SELECTRIC.		0
252	800	252	1230	4.5	T1	TERM. #17 & #13 LAMPS NO.	REPLACED LAMPS.	104772	0
256	820	256	1230	4.2	S1	SYSTEM WENT DOWN OVER THE WEEK	OBTAINED RE-GEN DUMPS, CLEANED CONTACTS AND RESEATED CARDS.		0
258	1130	258	1330	2.0	T1	TERM. #16 OPER. ID LAMP OUT.	REPLACED BULBS.	104772	0
258	1130	258	1330	2.0	T1	TERM. #16 LAMPS OUT	REPLACED BULBS.	104772	2
264	1000	264	1530	5.5	T1	THREE TERMS. DOWN.	ADJUSTED ALL THREE 2B'S		0
237	800	237	2300	15.0	T1	TERMINALS LOCKED OUT.	OPERATOR ERROR		0
245	800	245	1005	2.1	F1	TERM. #13 & 18 NG.	REPLACED ME69 & ADJUSTED KB.	8840	1
251	1000	251	1015	0.3	T1	TERM. #4 NG.	ADJUSTED KB.		0
251	1430	251	1515	0.8	F1	TERM. #18 DISPLAY NG.	ADJUSTED FLY/RETRACT SOLENOID.		0
256	800	256	1830	10.5	S1	HEADS NOT FLYING ON DISC.	REPLACED MICROSWITCHES AND ADJUSTED KB'S.		0
266	800	266	1700	9.0	T1	MANY TERM. PROBLEMS.	REPLACED CHAR DISPLAY LAMP ASS ASSEMBLY.	104732	1
267	630	267	730	1.0	T1	TERM. #5 NG.	ADJUSTED FOUR KB'S.		0
236	800	236	1700	9.0	T1	MANY TERM. NG.	REPLACED ME-3.	90852	1
242	810	243	300	18.8	S1	SERR #52	REPLACED SHIFT REGISTER.	11237500	1
242	900	243	100	16.0	T1	TERM #35 CHAR DECODE NG.	REPLACED MB.	104157	1
246	940	246	1045	1.1	S1	MTU DOWN.	ADJUST MTU AND REGENERATE SYSTEM.		0
250	830	250	2130	13.0	S1	DISC DOWN	REPLACED DISC WRITE DRIVER.		0
250	900	250	2200	13.0	S1	SERR #50	REPLACED DISC WRITE DRIVER	11238128	1
252	1145	252	1530	0.5	T1	TERM. #25 & #23 LOCKED OUT.			0
260	800	260	1210	0.4	S1	SYSTEM CRASH.	REGENERATED SYSTEM.		0
263	800	263	1700	9.0	B1	MANY TERM. PROBLEMS.	ADJUSTED 8 TERM. KB'S.		0
267	800	267	900	1.0	B1	DISC AND TERM. PROBLEM.	REGENERATE SYSTEM & ADJ. KB.		0
244	1200	244	1900	7.0	S1	SERR #60	SKEW OFF; READJUSTED, STILL NOT RIGHT.		0
239	800	239	1700	9.0	B2	PARITY AND TERM. PROBLEMS.	IES, TER. CONTROLLER, TERM. P/S, AND MB.	104157 104137 400535 104430	1 1 2 1
241	1400	241	2130	7.5	B2	TERM #13 NG.	REPLACED MB.	104157	1
242	1130	242	2230	11.0	S1	DISC PROBLEMS.	REPLACED SHIFT REGISTER 2.	11237500	1
242	1730	242	1800	0.5	T1	TWO TERM. NG.	REPLACED BOTH MB'S.	104157	2

Figure 7-10 Monthly service report summary

324

the OEM. Some manufacturers do, however, also provide free installation to the OEM. Often installation service includes free advisory support consisting of on-site software installation as well as technical counseling and system familiarization. The latter support is usually given free only for a period of 2 to 5 days after system delivery.

The user usually determines the method of shipment at the time he places the purchase order. When located close to the factory, shipment is usually made by truck. Where delivery times are critical, air freight is the most efficient way of transporting the hardware. The manufacturer will usually make the shipping arrangements with the shipping company. The manufacturer should be advised by the user of where the equipment is to be delivered, the time of day most convenient for delivery, and the size of the loading platform, the elevator, and the smallest door. (It is often more convenient for the manufacturer to rack-mount the equipment, perform check-out, and ship the equipment in the rack.)

Before delivery, the user must plan how to have the equipment installed. He is usually well advised to construct an installation diagram, which describes where each piece of equipment is to be placed in his facility. Great care should be taken to provide adequate access to the equipment for service. The installation diagram should also include cable runs and the location of electric outlets.

Large minicomputer configurations may require extra power to handle various power requirements such as special high voltage for disk drives and capability to handle surge current when power is turned on to all the equipment.

Additional points to consider are possible thermal, shielding, and grounding problems. Poor ventilation may cause the equipment to operate at excessive temperatures, resulting in lower MTBFs. Certain high-electrical noise environments may cause equipment failure resulting from voltage or current *spikes* on the line, and poor grounding procedures may cause damage to equipment from static electricity or other circumstances.

Other common causes for system malfunctions resulting from inadequate installation planning are the use of the equipment as a countertop for liquids such as coffee or soft drinks or for cigarette ashtrays which may be accidentally emptied into the equipment.

7.4 FUTURE SYSTEM GROWTH OR CHANGE

Planning the initial system should include considerations for future growth or change. Growth may consist of increased computerized tasks in a process control system, additional terminals in a business office, or news editing in addition to ad taking in a text-editing system. Change can consist of decline in system usage caused by a business slump or the future move of facilities to a different geographical location where perhaps the cost of the manufacturer's maintenance support is prohibitive.

Minicomputer System Modularity and Growth

Virtually all minicomputer manufacturers advocate and advertise modularity and expandability. However, the degree to which this can be gracefully accomplished varies widely.

The modularity referred to by most minicomputer manufacturers is often limited to the use of plug-in modules for logic and memory. In some cases, it also relates to I/O expansion and the use of priority interrupt and DMA channels in that these are offered optionally. Seldom does modularity relate to computing power beyond such standard options as hardware multiply/divide or, in some cases, floating-point hardware. In a few instances, a higher-speed memory can be substituted on a modular basis.

The most growth-oriented systems are based on the concept of the minicomputer family (see The Family Concept in Chapter 2). The family concept provides upwards software capability with additional computing power.

The use of user-microprogrammable minis provides a different kind of flexibility in that the system can be optimized for a different application from what it is originally used for. The disadvantage of altering the system firmware is, of course, instant incompatibility with most, if not all, existing software.

The most important growth considerations are generally related to cost. Cost in this case is the price of additional memory increments, expansion chassis, power supplies, communications adapters, peripheral controllers, etc. For OEMs, the cost is also related to the length of the discount period, the penalty incurred by changing the number of units originally signed for under a specific OEM discount, or the price advantage of increasing the scheduled number of units to be delivered under the OEM agreement. Some manufacturers provide a fixed discount regardless of the number of computers purchased, while others offer stepwise increase in discounts, depending on the number of units ordered and the scheduled time frame for deliveries.

Approaches to Design for Growth or Change

The three alternatives to system growth or change are to expand the existing system, get an additional system, or liquidate the existing system and obtain a larger (or smaller) system.

The expansion of an existing system can be done through the addition of various hardware modules, as previously discussed. However, where excess capability is available but no longer needed, the return of various modules to the manufacturer may be quite costly. An alternative solution is to sell the surplus modules to "used computer dealers," such as Time Brokers, Inc.,* or advertise the equipment in the trade journals such as *Computerworld* or *EDP Weekly*.

Use of two or more independent systems may be advantageous not only in terms of system redundancy but also when liquidating part of the system. A complete system usually commands a higher resale price than separate parts or modules. Where the original equipment is purchased with planned future liquidation in mind, it may be more attractive to select a less optional system from a large, well-known minicomputer manufacturer who has a well-established nationwide field service capability than to purchase a more sophisticated system from a small, less-well-known manufacturer who provides a recently introduced system with limited customer base and field service capability. The market for the more well-known mini is generally larger, not only because of more extensive support capability but also because of the large amount of software usually provided by the larger minicomputer manufacturer.

The third alternative, the exchange of a smaller system for a larger one, may be the most attractive solution for applications where the total system is leased and can be returned when the lease expires. Here again, the cost effectiveness of the approach is dictated by the particular application. Replacing systems where the user has a significant software investment may be quite costly, while, on the other hand, replacing a turn-key system in a business environment where the OEM provides full software support may be economically attractive if the older system can be replaced with a more powerful system for less cost.

REFERENCES

ELSPAS, B., M. W. GREEN, and K. N. LEVITT, "Software Reliability," *Computer*, January/February 1971, 21–27.

YOURDON, E., "Reliability of Real-Time Systems," *Modern Data*, January 1972, 36–42.

---

* TBI Equipment Division, Time Brokers, Inc., 500 Executive Boulevard, Elmsford, N.Y. 10523.

8

FUTURE MINICOMPUTER SYSTEMS

Much has been said about the state of the art in minicomputer processors, peripherals, software, and approaches to system implementation. As pointed out, differences exist in processor implementation such as in subunit organization (single- and multibus-structured minis), control section implementation (hard-wired and microprogrammable machines), and instruction set design. Other significant differences are found in available software, equipment reliability, and manufacturer support. Some minicomputer manufacturers provide a host of operating systems, compilers, utility routines, etc., while others offer little more than perhaps a loader, assembler, editor, and debugger.

"Hidden" differences usually exist in areas of system reliability and manufacturer support. Some manufacturers "cut corners" in the system assembly and quality control process. Two minicomputers made by separate manufacturers may have comparable, if not equivalent, performance features listed in their spec sheets. However, one of the systems may be shipped to the end user or OEM with minimal prior test or check-out procedures, while the second mini is subjected to exhaustive factory testing and extensive burn-in* procedures.

The second, equally difficult to determine, difference between minicomputers exists in the area of manufacturer support. Prompt and satisfactory response by the manufacturer to initial customer inquiries is not necessarily a sign of forthcoming, continued, time-saving, prepurchasing

---

* Burn-in is a method whereby components, subsystems, and total systems are run under simulated real-life conditions. Since most system hardware failures are experienced during the initial period of system usage (see Figure 5-21, the classical bathtub curve), the majority of marginal components that fail early in the system can be replaced in the factory prior to customer delivery.

support; on-time delivery according to date in confirmed purchase order; or adequate backup in case of equipment problems while still under warranty. However (speaking from experience), the reverse is quite often the case. Poor or slow initial response is commonly an indication of what can (or rather cannot) be expected once the purchase order is signed.

Inadequate customer support can be traced to the existence of an inordinately large number of minicomputer manufacturers, many of whom are either undercapitalized, have grown too rapidly, lack adequate sales, or are simply inexperienced in the business. The level of customer support is therefore not necessarily always related to the size of the minicomputer manufacturer.

Continued decline in the number of minicomputer and miniperipheral manufacturers paralleling the trend among large computer manufacturers will result eventually in a situation comparable to what has occurred in the domestic automobile industry: a few basic makes with infinite variation in model numbers and options. A fewer number of manufacturers but each with large resources may eventually result in increased quality and quantity of customer support. In addition, a reduction in the number of miniperipheral manufacturers will result eventually from the present trend among large minicomputer manufacturers such as DEC, Data General, Hewlett-Packard, and Varian, to increasingly develop their own peripherals in house.

Approaches to future minicomputer system design will also be influenced by the need to improve present systems and simplify required system support. Additional factors which will bring about improvements are the changing needs and growing sophistication of the user community as well as technical developments in related areas, such as circuit and memory technology, large computer machine design, and special-purpose military computer system engineering.

8.1 CHANGING NEEDS AND THE USER

The majority of today's minicomputer system users fall into two categories: the OEM or technically oriented end users who buy subsystem components and integrate them into a total system, and the less sophisticated end users who buy the total system as a complete turn-key product, including service and maintenance support.

The OEM usually looks for the most cost-effective components such as computer, peripherals, and communications equipment, while the sophisticated end user, who may be in the market for a single or limited number of computers, is concerned with the level and quality of software tools that will simplify system development.

In contrast to the OEM or the technically oriented end user, the user

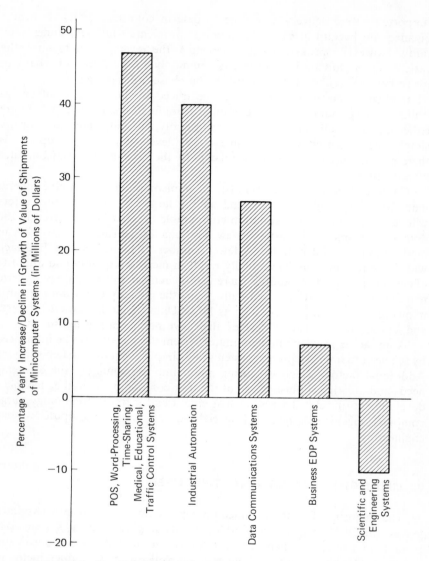

Figure 8-1 Yearly increase/decline in growth, in the 1970s, for value of shipments of minicomputer systems

lacking technical expertise in the computer area is mainly concerned with comparative cost savings of various new systems, transition time for converting from his present system to one of the new systems, the degree of training and the cost of personnel required to operate the system, and the cost of maintenance support for the estimated lifetime of the system. The needs of the various users can therefore be translated into requirements for improved, more reliable hardware and software, reduced maintenance, and simplified operability.

In addition, owing to ever-expanding application areas, increased demands are continuously put on the minicomputer system in terms of performance. What started out in the mid-1960s as a limited scientific and engineering tool for local batch processing must, in the future, meet increasingly more demanding real-time requirements.

The greatest growth market in the 1970s for minicomputers is anticipated in point-of-sale, educational, traffic control, text editing, word processing, type setting, patient monitoring and industrial, data communications and business EDP systems.* Paradoxically, however, the market for scientific and engineering systems is on the decline (Figure 8-1). This is explained by the fact that market growth is inhibited by high saturation because of a fairly stable population of research and development laboratories, which historically have been the largest users of scientific and engineering minicomputer systems.

8.2 TREND-SETTING DEVELOPMENTS BRINGING ABOUT CHANGES IN MINICOMPUTER SYSTEM DESIGN

Although industrial automation is only second largest in terms of growth increase, it is by far the largest of the five major application segments (Figure 8-1). The industrial environment is generally also the harshest of the environments that each of the five categories of minicomputer systems must operate in. The equipment must therefore meet more stringent requirements than minicomputer systems used in data communications, engineering, or business EDP. The future mini may therefore incorporate features presently available only in highly reliable minicomputers designed for military applications.

The cost of programming and software is also continually rising, while the cost of hardware is declining. One way of reducing programming cost is to increase the hardware in a particular system. It is obviously easier to program in a high-level language using a disk operating system with high-speed I/O peripherals than programming in assembly language, without auxiliary memory, with limited main memory and having access only to an ASR Teletype.

New developments in large-scale integrated circuit (LSI) technology coupled with novel computer architectures will make it possible to program

---

* Richard Matlack, "The Mighty Mini," *EE/Systems Engineering Today*, February 973, 114–116.

in a higher-level language without having to pay the penalty of inefficient usage of internal machine resources.

In addition, real-time applications such as patient monitoring, medical systems, and vehicle control, where a failure may result in loss of human lives, require the ultimate in reliability and dependability. The system should be able to detect errors when they occur no matter how infrequent. This is particularly true for errors which are of a transient nature, such as a dropped bit in an index register or the I/O interface. The system should be alerted to malfunctions, and an interrupt should be generated with a logout identifying the cause. It is important, from a systems point of view, to detect an error while the conditions leading to this error is still accessible for logging, thereby being able to isolate the failure. Finally, if and when a failure occurs, it is important to be able to return the system to operational status with a minimum of delay.

In applications where the system is operated in an office environment, it is highly desirable to have a simple-to-use system with a man-machine interface designed to minimize the period required for user training and system familiarization.

The following sections will consider some of the features which may, in the future, provide cost-effective solutions to the above problems.

The Militarized Mini-Improved Reliability for Severe Environments

The main design goal for militarized minicomputers is to optimize reliability. Militarized minicomputers are either machines developed for specific tasks by various military system manufacturers, such as Teledyne, Raytheon, Litton, and Hughes, or ruggedized commercial minicomputers which have been repackaged to meet more stringent environmental requirements than their commercial counterparts. The latter, although more general-purpose in nature, operate with extensive software that is available on the commercial peripheral equipment, so that new software can be developed in a non-military, support-facility environment at greatly reduced cost.

Ruggedness is achieved by several methods, varying from computer to computer. The Rolm 1602, which is compatible with the Data General Nova and therefore also called the Ruggednova, achieves ruggedness through the following methods:

- Each circuit board is attached to a thermally conducting metal frame (Figure 8-2).
- The integrated circuits (ICs) straddle the thermal frame, which serves two purposes: It stiffens the board and conducts heat away from the IC to the edge of the board.

- More expensive fork-type connectors are used instead of friction-type metal pads for better contact under vibration.
- An alignment block is inserted between connectors to provide additional support and prevent a card from being plugged into the wrong slot (Figure 8-2).
- Circuit boards are covered with a plate or "cookie sheet" to prevent oil canning or flexing of the board during vibration.
- Each card is clamped inside the computer chassis with a wedge. The wedge serves as a thermal connection between the board and chassis as well as a vibration and shock clamp.
- The Ruggednova is a closed box without a fan or coolant. This enables it to meet military electromagnetic interference specifications as well as to withstand dust, sand, and other severe environments.
- The power supply and all cards are coated with a material protecting the components from humidity and condensation.
- Ceramic, military-specified circuits are used instead of plastic integrated circuits for maximum component reliability as well as for operation under a wider range of temperatures.

The military mini is the only solution where a computer is required to operate in an environment requiring high system availability and where this high availability cannot be achieved through duplexing or the use of redundant systems because of environmental shock, vibration, and wide temperature extremes.

Figure 8-2 A typical ruggedized circuit board for the Rolm 1602 (Courtesy Rolm Corporation, Cupertino, Calif.)

Many industrial and commercial process control environments exhibit environmental conditions that are similar or identical to the severe military environments where militarized minicomputers are presently applied. By transferring the technology from present high-cost military minicomputers to their commercial counterparts, a large number of industrial processes, which presently do not use computers because of their high cost, can be automated.

Microprogramming, Stack-Oriented Architecture, and Other Features Reducing Future Programming Costs

Several of the more expensive, fourth-generation small computers or midis introduced in the early 1970s contain features which undoubtedly will influence minicomputer design in the future.

One of these systems is the 16-bit-word Hewlett-Packard System/3000,* which provides a hardware stack as part of its basic structure. As previously indicated (see Addressing in Chapter 2), a stack is a storage area where the last item stored in is always the first item taken out. Compilers can work efficiently with computers that are designed with a *push-down stack* architecture. It is much simpler for compilers to generate efficient programs for machines with the latter architecture than to use conventional multiregister architecture. The allocation of registers and temporary locations in memory is automatically solved when a stack is available. The combination of firmware and stack-oriented architecture makes it possible to optimize a system to execute machine code compiled from various high-level languages, such as FORTRAN or RPG. In fact, this concept has been implemented in the Microdata 3200.† This is one of the first minicomputers where a reloadable microprogram is available that implements a stack-oriented computer. Microdata has chosen microdata programming language (MPL), a subset of PL/1, a programming language developed by IBM, which incorporates features that are characteristic of FORTRAN and other higher-level languages. Unlike FORTRAN or PL/1, MPL is not machine-independent. [Owing to the large main memory requirements, PL/1 cannot be run in the existing minicomputers. This is presently true also for COBOL (common business-oriented language), designed for business-oriented problem solving.]

The concept of microprogramming and stack-oriented architecture is carried one step further in the larger-than-mini Burroughs 1700. Historically, computers have been designed to manipulate various fixed bit-length bytes,

---

* HP 3000 Computer System, *Reference Manual 0300-90019*, Hewlett-Packard Company, Cupertino, Calif., November 1972.

† Rod Burns and Don Savitt, "Microprogramming, Stack Architecture Eases Minicomputer Programmer's Burden," *Electronics*, February 15, 1973, 95–101.

words, double-words, etc. In spite of several schemes which utilize memory more efficiently through various encoding techniques or by grouping information according to time, where, for instance, in paged machines, information likely to be needed at the same time is kept on the same page, a large amount of memory space is wasted. Burroughs Corporation has therefore designed the B1700* to access and manipulate arbitrary-sized bit strings by hardware. Hence, all field lengths are expressable, and all memory is addressable to the bit. Variable instruction and operand lengths permit from 1 to 65K bits of data to be addressed with a single instruction. In addition to data compaction to the point where every bit is fully utilized, and because of the arbitrary field size, the B1700 uses two additional techniques to optimize memory storage utilization.

Huffman's algorithm† for minimum redundancy codes is used where most frequently used elements are represented by the shortest number of bit strings, while least frequently used elements are represented by the longest bit strings. The length of an encoded element varies inversely with the frequency of occurrence of that particular element.

In addition, fields which are needed most often in memory are collected into a common segment. Program profile statistics are recorded internally by the system. These statistics reflect what pieces of code spend the most time being executed. The fields in a program can therefore be organized according to dynamic frequency of occurrence. The previously described compacting methods make it possible to use higher-level languages such as COBOL, formerly not available in small computers.

In addition to the various compacting methods, the B1700 contains features such as virtual memory, multiprogramming, multiprocessing, and dynamic system configuration. Through the use of microprogramming techniques, processors, memory addresses, I/O channels, and peripherals are not uniquely coded into programs. These units can be brought on-line dynamically and used immediately without any reprogramming. Without a native machine language, this computer can execute every machine language using firmware, thereby yielding better performance for each application than a machine based on general-purpose architecture.

Under operating system control, programs written in several languages can thus run concurrently in a multiprogramming mix. Whenever the operating system transfers control from program to program, the B1700 will be able to change rapidly from a FORTRAN machine to a COBOL machine or RPG machine. The B1700 is at present one of the most advanced

---

* W. T. Wilner, "Design of the Burroughs B1700," *Proceedings, Fall Joint Computer Conference*, 1972, 489–497. W. T. Wilner, "Burroughs B1700 Memory Utilization," *Proceedings, Fall Joint Computer Conference*, 1972, 579–586.

† D. A. Huffman, "A Method for Construction of Minimum Redundancy Codes," *Proceedings of IRE 40*, September 1952, 1098–1101.

small computers being designed for language interpretation rather than general-purpose execution. Instead of the slow process of machine language programming, the user may select any higher-level language he wishes, thereby greatly reducing the cost of software.

Built-In Diagnostics and Error-Checking Features

Although most minicomputers provide some form of internal error-checking capability, none of them can match the number of such features offered by larger machine manufacturers. The most common minicomputer protective feature is memory block protection, where the user cannot write into a page or memory area that is protected. Some of the more powerful minis, such as the PDP-11/45, feature middle-of-a-word boundary addressing error checking, stack error checking, time-out error checking for addressing errors on the Unibus, and use of illegal or reserved instructions. A limited number of minicomputers provide memory parity checking, where one or two extra bits are added to each word for byte or word parity checking, respectively.

Future minicomputers will undoubtedly incorporate more sophisticated error-checking features that are presently available in midis, such as module errors, parity errors, and miscellaneous errors, some of which are summarized in Figure 8-3 for the Hewlett-Packard System/3000. Any of the errors listed in Figure 8-3 will produce an interrupt.

The Xerox 530 small computer* provides error checking with both operation protection and memory write protection. The protection system can be enabled, which will provide automatically a number of backup features, such as

1. If a privileged instruction is accessed from unprotected memory, the instruction is not executed.
2. If an instruction is accessed from protected memory and the immediately preceding instruction was accessed from unprotected memory, the instruction is generally not executed.
3. If an attempt is made to alter protected memory with an instruction accessed from unprotected memory, an interrupt will be triggered.

Even more sophisticated error procedures are provided by IBM Model 115, the smallest of the System/370 series machines.† The Model 115 main

---

* Xerox 530 Computer, *Reference Manual 901960A*, Xerox Corporation, El Segundo, Calif., October 1972.

† System/370, *Model 115 Facts Folder G520-2773-0*, 1st ed., International Business Machines Corporation, Data Processing Division, White Plains, N.Y., March 1973.

1. Module errors	Addressing of memory beyond the limit of physical main memory (Illegal Address)
	Attempt to address locations outside of a specific program or date area (bounds violation)
	CPU request for information from a module in memory which is not received within a predetermined time period (nonresponding module)
2. Parity errors	Error in parity from memory
	Parity error caused by either CPU or memory module
	Parity error in data or instruction being transferred between I/O channel and memory
3. Misecellaneous errors	Deletion of too much information from stack, resulting in stack underflow
	Calling of a nonexistent code segment or attempt to execute an instruction for which there is no valid code

Figure 8-3. Examples of some of the error conditions causing an interrupt in the Hewlett-Packard system/3000

storage corrects all single-bit errors and detects all double-bit and some multiple-bit errors. Furthermore, an interrupt is triggered to various malfunctions in I/O interfaces. These errors are subsequently localized using software diagnostic procedures.

Present and Future Developments in Man-Machine Interfaces

The present trend in minicomputer system design is to simplify the operational aspects, thereby minimizing required operator training. Many of the so-called intelligent terminals are programmed to guide the operator in a step-by-step fashion through the various operations, alerting the user to errors in format or data input. Similarly, the keyboards and function switches are arranged in a manner that makes them easily understandable.

New miniperipherals are presently being developed which will greatly facilitate the data I/O to the mini. An example of this is the voice recognition

Figure 8-4   CDC Plasma panel with 469 minicomputer (Courtesy Control
Data Corporation)

system presently available for use with the Data General Nova. This system,
developed by Threshold Technology, Inc., can recognize up to 100 words,
where the words must be spoken within about $1\frac{1}{2}$ sec, with a $\frac{1}{10}$-sec interval
between words. A new speaker can train the system simply by repeating
each word of the vocabulary 10 times in succession. Combining voice input
with voice output, the user will eventually be able to interact with the minicomputer system without using a keyboard, CRT, or hard-copy printer.

Where large amounts of source data entry are required, low-cost versions
of the diskette, introduced by IBM in 1973, will eventually replace paper
tape, cassette tape, and cards. More reliable plasma panel displays will also
replace presently used CRT displays, providing a more stable and legible
display image in a much smaller package. (Figure 8-4 shows an experimental plasma panel display developed by Control Data Corporation. The
display is interfaced to the CDC 469 militarized minicomputer shown at right
of the keyboard.)

8.3 THE MICROCOMPUTER AND ITS IMPACT ON
FUTURE MINICOMPUTER SYSTEM DESIGN

The micromini is the latest newcomer to the computer field. In the first
few years of its existence, the micromini's instruction times have come down
one order of magnitude, approaching those of minicomputers. The use of
LSI brings the cost of microcomputers more than one order of magnitude
below the cost of minicomputer CPUs.

It should be realized, however, that the micromini is only available at
present as an assembly of LSI circuit chips, each in a standard 16-, 24-, or

40-pin package containing a CPU, ROM to store microprograms and data tables, random access memory to store data and instructions, shift register for I/O, peripheral interface unit, etc. Their widest application is presently as programmable controllers for various peripheral interfaces, as controllers for point-of-sale terminals, as scientific calculators, and as various instrumentation equipment, by and large for OEM use. With few exceptions, the available software for microminis is either extremely limited or nonexistent.

Although the micro will offer competition to the mini processor, eventually forcing the cost of the CPU in the mini to come down even further, the effect of the micro will still be relatively limited, because of the high cost of main memory, peripherals, software, warranty, and sales-marketing support presently provided by minicomputer manufacturers.

It is quite possible, that circuit manufacturers such as Fairchild, Signetics, National Semiconductor, Intel, Rockwell Microelectronics, American Micro-Systems, Monolithic Memories, and others will eventually enter the microcomputer system field, providing the full range of software and system support in a manner equivalent to the present minicomputer manufacturers.

The following question therefore remains unanswered: Who will be the giants in the ever-expanding small computer business—the semiconductor houses, the minicomputer manufacturers, the large computer manufacturers, or all three?

REFERENCES

BURNS, R. and D. SAVITT, "Microprogramming, Stack Architecture Ease Minicomputer Programmer's Burden," *Electronics*, February 15, 1973, 95–101.

HIMMELFARB, M., "Minicomputers," *Digital Design*, February 1973, 18–26.

LAPIDUS, G., "MOS/LSI Launches the Low-Cost Processor," *IEEE Spectrum*, November 1972, 33–40.

SIDERIS, G., "Microcomputers Muscle In," *Electronics*, March 1, 1973, 63–64.

STONE, I. M., "The Changing Needs of Minicomputer Users," *Telecommunications*, January 1973, 37–51.

WEITZMAN, C., "Aerospace Computers and Peripherals," *Document TM-4743*, System Development Corporation, Santa Monica, Calif., July 1971.

———"Aerospace Computer Technology Catches Up with Ground Gear," *Electronics*, September 11, 1972, 112–119.

WILNER, W. T., "Burroughs B1700 Memory Utilization," *Proceedings, Fall Joint Computer Conference*, 1972, 579–586.

———"Design of the Burroughs B1700," *Proceedings, Fall Joint Computer Conference*, 1972, 489–497.

PROBLEMS
AND
EXERCISES

Problem 1-1

A Texas Instruments Model 980A Minicomputer is used as a remote terminal and concentrator with the following peripherals:

1	line printer, 365 lpm, 80 columns
1	card punch, 100 cpm, 80 columns
2	video terminal, 2400-bps bit-serial interface
1	high-speed paper tape reader, 300 cps
1	magnetic tape transport, nine-track, 800 bpi, 37.5 ips
6	Teletype Model-38 ASR, 110 bps
2	Teletype Model-37 ASR, 150 bps

The 980A is connected over a long-distance, full-duplex line using synchronous transmission to a large central data processing facility.

1. What is the minimum bandwidth required to sustain all peripherals and terminals for this line (assume bit-serial transmission and no buffering in the minicomputer)?

2. Assuming that the magnetic tape transport and card punch are not used on-line, what is the minimum bandwidth required for this line (again, assume bit-serial transmission)?

3. Assuming that the nine-track IBM-compatible tape transport is replaced by a single-track cassette recorder with 800 bpi recording density and 12.5-in./sec speed, what is the minimum required line bandwidth?

Problem 1-2

A small business is performing its data processing manually using clerks for accounting, inventory control, etc. The firm employs six people to perform these functions. Five of these receive a monthly salary of $1000, and the sixth person, a supervisor, receives $1500/month. The owner of this business is contemplating a computerized data processing service, but the inconvenience resulting from intolerable turn-around time and lack of in-house control coupled with high cost make it more beneficial to remain with the present system.

What are the cost benefits if the owner were either to lease a minicomputer turn-key system for $2000/month including applications software (5-year lease) or to develop his own system from "scratch." In either case he must figure on at least two people to operate the system. Assume an average salary of $1250/month for these two people. The total maintenance cost in either case is $500/month for both software and hardware.

Designing the system himself and using a consultant, the design cost will range from $5000 to $10,000. The cost of hardware with the lowest-cost system is $35,000, and software development is estimated at $60,000, with travel and miscellaneous cost items amounting to $1000. What are the benefits of changing to EDP, and which of the two alternatives is more attractive? State assumptions and explain selection rationale.

Problem 2-1

Three minicomputers are being considered for a navigational application on a commercial aircraft. The instruction execution times (in microseconds) are:

Computer	A	B	C
Add/subtract	1.4	1.8	2.3
Multiply	3.75	9.0	7.5
Logical compare	1.4	2.7	2.3
Shift (6 bits)	25.2	13.8	13.8
Logical AND/OR	1.4	1.8	2.3
Load/store	2.6	1.8	2.3
Conditional branch (jump)	1.4	1.8	2.6
Increment and store index	3.2	2.7	2.3
Move register to register (no memory reference)	1.4	0.9	2.3
Programmed I/O transfer	3.2	2.7	2.3

Depending on the particular applications class, some types of instructions are used more often than others. The most commonly used "mix" or instruction frequency for commercial applications is called the *Gibson Mix*.* In a navigational applica-

---

* Gordon C. Bell and Allen Newell, *Computer Structures: Readings and Examples*, McGraw-Hill Book Company, New York, 1971, p. 50.

tion, the following mix may be used to estimate the average instruction time of a particular machine:

Fixed, single-precision add/subtract:	25 %
Fixed, single-precision multiply:	25 %
Logical compare:	2 %
Load/store:	30 %
Increment and store index:	4 %
Programmed I/O transfer:	12 %
Other, miscellaneous:	2 %
Total:	100 %

Using this mix and assuming that everything else is equal, in what order of preference would you rank the computers?

Problem 2-2

One of the computers in Problem 2-1 will be used in a real-time application. A typical instruction mix, characteristic of a real-time application, follows:

Fixed, single-precision add/subtract:	16 %
Fixed, single-precision multiply:	5 %
Logical compare:	12 %
Logical shift (6 bits):	5 %
Logical AND/OR:	4 %
Load/store:	33 %
Conditional branch:	10 %
Increment and store index:	4 %
Move register to register (no memory reference):	5 %
Other:	6 %
Total:	100 %

In what order of preference would you rank the minis?

Problem 3-1

1. What are the most desirable and undesirable features (at least two of each) in a hard-copy terminal to be used in
   a. a library environment,
   b. a business environment.
2. What features are considered important in CRT display terminal selection (name at least three) to be used in
   a. newspaper text-editing systems,
   b. hospital, data base inquiry systems,
   c. sales order entry for salesmen in the field.

Problem 3-2

1. What are the advantages and disadvantages (at least three of each) of punched paper tape I/O?
2. How long does it take to transmit $1\frac{1}{2}$ pages (one page contains 132 characters per line, 63 lines) using full ASCII coded characters and asynchronous 300-bps transmission? Error rate is 1 per 10^5.
3. How long does it take to transmit $1\frac{1}{2}$ pages using USASCII coded characters for synchronous 4800-bps transmission over the same line? The transmitted data blocks are 10,000 bits long.
4. How many 80-byte records can be stored on a nine-track magnetic tape at a bit density of 800 bpi, using a $\frac{3}{4}$-in. interrecord gap? How long does it take to read the entire tape at the speed of 25 ips?

Problem 3-3

A 2311-like magnetic disk unit operates at 3600 rpm, with 200 tracks/surface and 10 surfaces. If average track length and bit density are 25 in. and 2000 bpi, respectively, what are the following values:

a. The average access time?
b. The total storage capacity?
c. The data rate per track read head?

Problem 4-1

1. How would you estimate the development cost (in general terms) of performing a system design using a hardware, firmware, and software approach?
2. What are the implications in terms of reliability for a systems approach based on hardwired control, firmware, and software?
3. What are the pros and cons of hardwired control versus microprogramming in terms of system maintainability and operability?

Problem 5-1

One of three computers is considered for an application. These three computers have their capabilities summarized in a table on page 345.

Compute the computer price/performance ratio for these systems based on the formula given in Cost Relationships in Chapter 5. The cost of system X is $6000; system Y, $6500; and system Z, $7000.

Problem 5-2

A computer is selected from one of the three described in Problem 5-1 to perform a large number of calculations for a real-time environment. Which of the three computers seems optimal and why?

Problem 6-1

A minicomputer system is designed to perform I/O, storage, processing, and control in a library. The records stored in this system are bibliographic, fiscal, and inventory. The total system is divided into several major library procedural

	X	Y	Z
Word size (bits)	16	16	16
Maximum internal storage (K words)	32	64	128
Number of bits in address field of single-word instruction	9	8	7
Number of general-purpose registers	16	8	7
Memory read/write cycle (μsec)	0.9	1.0	0.85
Real-time clock	Yes (2)	Yes	Yes
Memory protect	Std	Std	Opt
Power-fail safe	Yes	Yes	Yes
Hardware multiply and divide	Std	Opt	Std
Hardware floating point	Yes	No	No
Vectored interrupts	Yes	No	No
Stack processing	Yes	No	Yes
Microprogramming capability	Yes	No	No
Hardware program relocatability	Yes	Yes	Yes
Full set of logic instructions	No	Yes	No
DMA, programmed I/O	Yes	Yes	Yes
Memory ports	1	1	2
Off-line diagnostic software	Yes	Yes	Yes
Debugging routines	Yes	Yes	Yes
Fixed and relocatable loader	Yes	Yes	Yes
FORTRAN IV	Yes	Yes	Yes
ALGOL	Yes	No	Yes
BASIC	Yes	Yes	Yes
RPG	Yes	Yes	No
Real-time disk operating system	Yes	No	Yes
Batch operating system	Yes	Yes	Yes
Foreground/background processing	Yes	No	Yes

systems, such as administration and planning, serials control, cataloging, acquisitions of new books and periodicals, circulation, reference, and text editing. Thirty-two CRT terminals serve various functions, such as data input, data base inquiry, and text editing.

In text editing, the entire display screen, containing a maximum of 2000 characters, is transmitted to the minicomputer in a block mode at 2400 bps. The system must respond to the user within an average response time of 10 sec. The average time to type in a message at a terminal is $2\frac{1}{2}$ min. The system designer is contemplating the use of one of three types of disk systems:

1. floppy disk model A: average transaction time 4 sec (cost: $2000);
2. floppy disk model B: average transaction time 3 sec (cost: $3000);
3. 2315-like cartridge disk system: average transaction time 0.3 sec (cost: $8000).

Which disk will meet the system requirements at lowest cost?

Problem 6-2

Based on the accompanying configuration and data, compute the percentage utilization of the front-end processor for peak load. The cycle time of the 16-bit

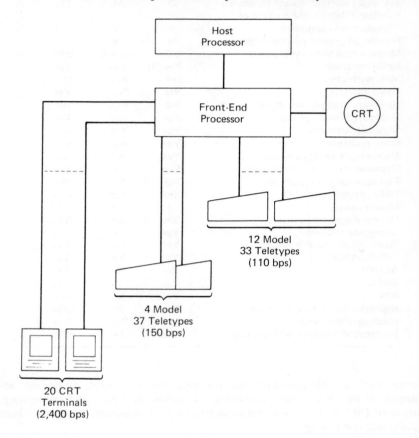

front-end processor is 1 μsec. The processor overhead is 2 cycles per word. The host processor can accept a maximum of 500,000 bytes/sec from the front-end processor. Line utilization is 10 percent for CRTs and 50 percent for Teletypes. The mini requires 400 μsec to process a character. The size of the refresh buffer for the CRT is 8K words, the refresh rate is 50 Hz, and the processor overhead is 4 cycles per word.

Problem 7-1

1. Calculate the probability of success, or the percentage chance that a mini-computer system will not fail, in a process control environment where the system will operate unattended for a period of 6 months or 4380 hr at a 10 percent duty cycle (it is turned off 90 percent of the time). The system

consists of a CPU, 16K of core, and a magnetic tape drive. Failure rate per million hours is 50 for the CPU, 70 for each 8K memory module, and 200 for the tape recorder.

2. What is the probability of success if a redundant 8K memory module and magnetic tape drive are added to the system?

Problem 7-2

What measures are available to improve the reliability and maintainability of a minicomputer system to be operated in a business environment (list at least five)?

Problem 1-1 (251 kbps, 9,424 bps, 20,491 bps)

Configuration diagram:

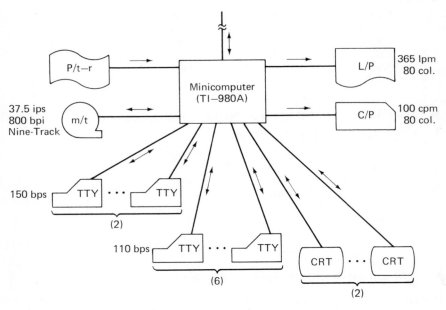

Paper tape reader	300 cps = 2400 bps
Magnetic tape drive	(8)(800 bpi)(37.5 ips) = 8 × 30,000 bps
	= 24,000 bps
TTY (M-37)	(2)(150 bps) = 2 × 15 cps = 2 × 120 bps
	= 240 bps

TTY (M-38)   (6)(110 bps) = 6 × 10 cps = 6 × 80 bps
                           = 480 bps
CRT-terminal   2 × 2400 bps = 4800 bps
Card punch   100 cpm = (100 cpm)(80 col/card)(8 bits/col)
                           (1 min/60 sec) = 1067 bps
Line printer   365 lpm = (365 lpm)(80 col/line)(8 bits/col)
                           (1 min/60 sec) = 3904 bps

1. Maximum data (bps) *into* mini   *out of* mini

m/t	240,000	240,000
TTY (37s)	240	240
TTY (38s)	480	480
CRTs	4,800	4,800
c/p	1,067	—
l/p	3,904	—
p/t-r	—	2,400
	250,491	247,920

▶ *Minimum line rate: 251 K-bps.*

2. Max data (bps) *into* mini   *out of* mini

TTY (37s)	240	240
TTY (38s)	480	480
CRTs	4800	4800
L/P	3904	—
p/t-r	—	2400
	9424	7920

▶ *Minimum line rate: 9424 bps* (use 9600-bps transmission rate).

3. c/t: (800 bpi)(12.5 ips) = 10,000 bps

c/t	10,000	10,000
TTY (37s)	240	240
TTY (38s)	480	480
CRTs	4,800	4,800
L/P	3,904	—
p/t-r	—	2,400
c/p	1,067	—
	20,491	17,920

▶ *Minimum line rate: 20,491 bps* (use 40.8K-bit transmission rate).

Problem 1-2 ($2950/month)

Alternative 1 *(stay with existing system):*

Clerks, accountants, etc., $1000/month (5):	$5000
Supervisor, $1500/month (1):	$1500
Total:	$6500/month

Alternative 2 (*lease system*):

> Lease hardware and software: $2000/month
> Operators (2): $1250/month
> Maintenance: $ 500/month
> _____
> Total: $3750/month

Alternative 3 (*purchase system*):

> Consultants: $ 10,000
> Hardware: $ 35,000
> Software: $ 60,000
> Travel and miscellaneous: $ 1,000
> _____
> Total: $106,000

Assume a 5-year life expectancy (very short).
System cost:

$$\frac{\$106,000}{5 \times 12 \text{ months}} = \$1800/\text{month}$$

> Operators (2): $1250/month
> Maintenance: $ 500/month
> _____
> Total: $3550/month

▶ Benefits:

$$6500 - 3550 = \$2950/month \quad \text{(savings)}$$

Purchase is more attractive since system value is >0 after 5 years. However, assuming that it takes 6 months to develop the system in-house,

Alternative 2 (*5 years*)

$$60 \text{ months} \times \$3750/\text{month} = \$225,000$$

Alternative 3 (*5 years*):

> 6 months to develop system: 6 × $1800 = $ 10,800
> 6 months of maintenance: 6 × $ 500 = $ 3,000
> 6 months to operate with existing system: 6 × $6500 = $ 39,000
> 54 months, purchased system: 54 × $3550 = $191,700
> _____
> Total: $244,500

The difference between alternatives 2 and 3 is therefore $19,500. It is assumed that the salvage value of the purchased system is equal to or more than this differential however.

Problem 2-1 (A, C, B)

	Weight	Computer A		B		C	
Fixed, single-precision add/subtract	0.25	1.4	0.35	1.8	0.45	2.3	5.8
Fixed, single-precision multiply	0.25	3.75	0.94	9.0	2.25	7.5	1.87
Logical compare	0.02	1.4	0.03	2.7	0.05	2.3	0.05
Load/store	0.30	2.6	0.78	1.8	0.54	2.3	0.69
Increment and store index	0.04	3.2	0.13	2.7	0.11	2.3	0.09
Programmed I/O transfer	0.12	3.2	0.38	2.7	0.32	2.3	0.28
Other, miscellaneous	0.02		—		—		—
	1.00		2.61		3.72		3.56
		0.98	2.56	0.98	3.65	0.98	3.50

▶ *Order of preference: A, C, B.*

Problem 2-2 (B, C, A)

	Weight	Computer A		B		C	
Fixed, single-precision add/subtract	0.16	1.4	0.22	1.8	0.29	2.3	0.37
Fixed, single-precision multiply	0.05	3.75	0.19	9.0	0.45	7.5	0.38
Logical compare	0.12	1.4	0.17	2.7	0.32	2.3	0.28
Shift (6 bits)	0.05	25.2	1.26	13.8	0.69	13.8	0.69
Logical AND/OR	0.04	1.4	0.06	1.8	0.07	2.3	0.09
Load/store	0.33	2.6	0.86	1.8	0.60	2.3	0.76
Conditional branch	0.10	1.4	0.14	1.8	0.18	2.6	0.26
Increment and store index	0.04	3.2	0.13	2.7	0.11	2.3	0.09
Move register to register	0.05	1.4	0.07	0.9	0.05	2.3	0.12
Other	0.06		—		—		—
	1.00		3.10		2.76		3.04
		0.94	2.91	0.94	2.59	0.94	2.86

▶ *Order of preference: B, C, A.*

Problem 3-1

    1a. *Desirable characteristics for library application:* quiet operation, upper- and lowercase characters, changeable font (IBM printball or similar), multiple copies, printing of preprinted forms. *Undesirable characteristics:* dot matrix characters (5 × 7), 80-column line width, special type paper (which fades), use of toner or other liquids that smell.

1b. *Desirable characteristics for process control environment:* high reliability, simple paper loading, current loop interface, rugged construction (non-mechanical keyboard). *Undesirable characteristics:* sensitive to power line and other electrical disturbances, sensitive to shock and vibration, use of a large number of mechanical parts requiring frequent adjustment.

2a. Local buffer, edit features, split screen, block transfer, computer-controlled cursor, 1500–2000-character display.

2b. Teletype mode operation, 500–1000-character display, high contrast display image, low audio noise level.

2c. Portable with carrying case; low weight; built-in coupler (magnetic and acoustic) Teletype mode operation; ASCII code; FDX, HDX switch; 100-, 150-, and 300-bps selector for various computer spigots.

Problem 3-2 (See Advantages; 7 min., 40 sec.; 29.2 sec.; 19 min., 12 sec.)

1. *Advantages:* Punch and reader can operate independently, message can be used for repetitive transmission, data retained for audit trails, permanent record, visual verification of contents, inexpensive. *Disadvantages:* Tape cannot be reused, bulky, awkward to handle, high maintenance cost for high-speed operation, punching usually slower than reading, noisy.

2.

$$1 \text{ page} = \left(\frac{132 \text{ characters}}{\text{line}}\right)\left(\frac{63 \text{ lines}}{\text{page}}\right)\left(\frac{11 \text{ bits}}{\text{char.}}\right) = 91,476 \text{ bits}$$

(1 start and 2 stop bits)

Transmission of $1\frac{1}{2}$ pages:

$$\frac{91,476 \text{ bits}}{300 \text{ bps}} \times 1.5 \approx 460 \text{ sec.} \qquad \text{(7 minutes, 40 seconds)}$$

(Note that with an error rate the 1 in 10^5, a maximum of two errors will occur. Since the transmission rate is 300 bps, less than 1 sec is lost on re-transmission of the two characters.)

3. In synchronous transmission, start and stop bits are not used. Hence,

$$1 \text{ page} = \left(\frac{132 \text{ char.}}{\text{line}}\right)\left(\frac{63 \text{ lines}}{\text{page}}\right)\left(\frac{8 \text{ bits}}{\text{char.}}\right) \approx 66,500 \text{ bits}$$

For a 4800-bps transmission rate with 10,000-bit blocks, the *net* data throughput is 3600 bps (error rate 1 in 10^5). Therefore, the time to transmit $1\frac{1}{2}$ pages is

$$\frac{66,500 \times 1.5 \text{ bits}}{3600 \text{ bps}} = 28.3 \text{ sec}$$

In 28.3 sec at 4800 bps, 135,600 bits ($= 28.3$ sec $\times$ 4800 bps) are transmitted. The message will thus be contained in 14 blocks (140,000 bits). The time to transmit 14 blocks is

$$\frac{14 \text{ blocks} \times 10,000 \text{ bits/block}}{4800 \text{ bps}} \approx 29.2 \text{ sec}$$

4.   Recording density: 800 bpi
      Record length: 80 bytes
      Interrecord gap: 0.75 in.
      Read speed: 25 ips
      Tape length: 2400 ft = 28,800 in.

The length of 1 record + 1 interrecord gap is 0.85 in.

▶ Number of records:

$$\frac{28,800}{0.85} = 33,858$$

▶ Read time:

$$\frac{28,800 \text{ in.}}{25 \text{ ips}} = 1152 \text{ sec} = 19 \text{ min, 12 sec}$$

Problem 3-3

                    rpm: 3600
        Tracks/surface: 200
              Surfaces: 10
      Bit/density (bpi):   2000
    Average track length (in.):   25

a. One revolution of the disk takes $\frac{1}{16}$ sec or 16.6 msec. The average rotational delay is one-half revolution, or 8.3 msec. Head positioning time is not given. Assuming a 60-msec average head positioning time, the average access time is 68.3 msec.

b. Total storage capacity is

$$\left(\frac{2000 \text{ bits}}{\text{in.}}\right)\left(\frac{25 \text{ in.}}{\text{track}}\right)\left(\frac{200 \text{ tracks}}{\text{surface}}\right)(10 \text{ surfaces}) = 100 \text{ Mbits}$$

c. Data rate per track read-head is

$$\frac{(25 \text{ in.})(2000 \text{ bpi})}{(16.6 \text{ msec})} = \frac{50,000}{\frac{1}{60} \text{ sec}} \text{ bits} = 300,000 \text{ bps}$$

Problem 4-1

	LSI	Firmware	Software
Cost (1)	* Significant reduction in production cost makes built-in macros cost-effective. High cost for recurrent manufacturing offset by low-cost production and hardware.	‡ Program-oriented microprograms can result in significant reduction in unit cost of hardware firmware vs. fixed instruction set. Future firmware cost equal to software cost.	‡ Cost of programming often a function of how well the hardware capabilities match programming requirements. Software cost for some programs nonrecurrent.

Problem 4-1 (Contd.)

	LSI	*Firmware*	*Software*
Reliability (2)	‡ Improvement of the overall system reliability by at least one order of magnitude (sharp reduction of external interconnections); highest level of reliability due to straightforward and relatively fast checking capability	† Slightly less reliable than hardware-only type systems since reliability partly based on software.	* Reliability of software is a function of program size and complexity. Difficulty in debugging all facets makes software least reliable of the three; not subject to physical failure once debugged.
Maintainability (3)	‡ Complete replacement of chip for single failure on gate level. Simplified diagnostics since more functions per chip allow isolation of problem to chip only; diagnostics can be built into chips.	† Micro-level diagnostic capability whether LSI, MSI, or discrete I/Cs are used; parity bit in ROM, special diagnostic microroutines.	* Software diagnostics time-consuming and many times impossible unless capability enhanced in hardware.
Operability (3)	* Higher speeds because of microminiaturization and advanced technology; once finalized, operability depends on design (may be special-purpose).	‡ Can be easily adapted to different problem-oriented environments; increased complexity in terms of user programming (difficult to program microprocessor). Generally very high operability.	† Operability constrained by speed, architecture, instruction set (limited number of machine codes), etc.

‡ High.
† Intermediate.
* Low.

Problem 5-1 (0.48, 0.60, 0.40)

$$P_h = \frac{\text{basic system cost (\$)}}{0.1M\{1 - [(W - F)/2W]\} + (20/T)(A_h + L_h + I_h) + 100N + 50R}$$

$$P_s = \frac{\text{basic system cost (\$)}}{500(D + B + L) + 1000A + 2000\,C + 50S}$$

where

	X	Y	Z
M (bytes)	64,000	128,000	256,000
F (bits)	9	8	7
W (bits)	16	16	16
R	16	8	7
T (μsec)	0.9	1.0	0.85
N (options)	4	3	3
A_h	100	75	75
L_h	50	100	50
I_h	50	50	100
D	1	1	1
B	1	1	1
L	1	1	1
A	1	1	1
C	4	3	3
S	100	0	100
$1 - \dfrac{W - F}{2W}$	$\frac{25}{32}$	$\frac{24}{32}$	$\frac{23}{32}$
$0.1M$	6,400	12,800	25,600
$0.1M\left(1 - \dfrac{W - F}{2W}\right)$	5,000	9,600	18,400
$A_h + L_h + I_h$	200	225	225
$\dfrac{20}{T}$	22	20	24
$\dfrac{20}{T}(A_h + L_h + I_h)$	4,400	4,500	5,400
$100N + 50R$	1,200	700	650
$\left\{0.1M - \left[1 - \dfrac{W - F}{2W}\right]\right.$ $+ \dfrac{20}{T}(A_h + L_h + I_h)$ $\left. + 100N + 50R\right\}$	10,600	14,800	24,450
$500(D + B + L)$	1,500	1,500	1,500
$1000A$	1,000	1,000	1,000
$2000C$	8,000	6,000	6,000
$50S$	5,000	0	5,000
$5000(D + B + L) + 1000A$ $+ 2000C + 50S$	15,500	8,500	13,500
P_L	$\dfrac{6,000}{10,600} = 0.565$	$\dfrac{6,500}{14,800} = 0.440$	$\dfrac{7,000}{24,450} = 0.286$
P_S	$\dfrac{6,000}{15,500} = 0.387$	$\dfrac{6,500}{8,500} = 0.765$	$\dfrac{7,000}{13,500} = 0.519$
$P\left(= \dfrac{P_L + P_S}{2}\right)$	$\dfrac{0.952}{2} = 0.48$	$\dfrac{1.205}{2} = 0.60$	$\dfrac{0.805}{2} = 0.40$

Problem 5-2 (X)

Desirable features:

	X	Y	Z
Memory protect	1	1	1
Power-fail safe	1	1	1
Hardware multiply/divide	1	1	1
Hardware floating point	1	0	0
Vectored interrupts	1	0	0
Real-time DOS	1	0	1
Foreground/background processing	1	0	1
Real-time clock	1	1	1
Total	8	4	6

Although Z has best price/performance ratio, X is better suited for real-time operation and to perform a large amount of number crunching.

Problem 6-1 (None, at 4,800 bps; Model B)

Number of terminals: 32.

Time to input one message from terminal: 2.5 min.

The average wait time is computed on the next page.

Note that data transmission to and from the CRT at 2400 bps (300 characters/sec) for 2000 characters is 6.7 sec. To meet the response time requirement with *any* disk, the transmission rate must be increased to **4800 bps**.

▶ At this rate, the floppy disk (model B) is acceptable:

Response time: $2.7 + 3.33 + 3.33 = 9.4$ sec < 10 sec

Problem 6-2 (73%)

Data transfer host to front end:

$$U_1 = 1 \times \left(\frac{2}{2}\right)\left(\frac{500,000}{10^4}\right) = 50\%$$

Terminal processing:

$$U_2 = \frac{1}{10}\left[\left(\frac{0.4}{10}\right)(20)(300)(0.1) + \left(\frac{0.4}{10}\right)(4)(15)(0.5) + \left(\frac{0.4}{10}\right)(12)(10)(0.5)\right]$$
$$= 2.76\%$$

Graphics display load:

$$U_3 = \frac{1}{10^4}\left[(8000)(4)(50)(1)\right] = 20\%$$

▶ $U_1 + U_2 + U_3 = 50 + 2.76 + 20 \approx 73\%.$

	Floppy Disk Model A	Floppy Disk Model B	2315
Average transaction time (sec)	4	3	0.3
Cost ($)	2000	3000	8000
ρ	$\dfrac{(24 \text{ messages/terminal-hr})(32 \text{ terminals})}{(3600 \text{ sec/hr})/4.0 \text{ sec}}$ $= \dfrac{768}{900} = 0.85$	$\dfrac{24 \times 32}{3600/3} = \dfrac{768}{1200} = 0.64$	$\dfrac{24 \times 32}{3600/0.3}$ $= \dfrac{768}{12{,}000} = 0.064$
L	$\dfrac{0.85(2 - 0.85)}{2(1 - 0.85)}$ $= \dfrac{(0.85)(1.15)}{(2)(0.15)}$ $= 3.25$	$\dfrac{0.64(2 - 0.64)}{2(1 - 0.64)}$ $= \dfrac{(0.64)(1.36)}{2(0.36)}$ $= 1.21$	$\dfrac{0.064(2 - 0.064)}{2(1 - 0.064)}$ $= \dfrac{(0.064)(2)}{(2)}$ $= 0.064$
$W\left(= L\dfrac{3600}{M}\right)$	$3.25\left(\dfrac{3600}{768}\right)$ $= 15.2 \text{ sec}$	$1.21\left(\dfrac{3600}{768}\right)$ $= 5.7 \text{ sec.}$	$0.064\left(\dfrac{3600}{768}\right)$ $= 0.3 \text{ sec}$ ~ 0
Average wait time (sec)	$15.2 - 4 = 11.2$	$5.7 - 3 = 2.7$	~ 0

Problem 7-1 (0.983, 0.991)

The reliability model is:

$$\text{CPU} \qquad \begin{array}{c} \text{8K} \\ \text{Core} \end{array} \qquad \begin{array}{c} \text{8K} \\ \text{Core} \end{array} \qquad \dfrac{m}{t}$$

$$\lambda = (50)_{cpu} + (70)_{8K\ core} + (70)_{8K\ core} + (200)_{m/t}$$

$$\lambda = 390, \qquad \text{MTBF} = \frac{1{,}000{,}000}{390} = 2560 \text{ hrs.}$$

$$t_{op} = (4380)(0.1) = 438$$

$$P = e^{-438/2560} = 0.9831 \text{ or } 98.3\%$$

$$\lambda = 50 + \frac{70}{2} + \frac{70}{2} + \frac{200}{2} = 220$$

$$\text{MTBF} = \frac{1{,}000{,}000}{220} = 4550 \text{ hrs.}$$

$$t_{op} = (4380)(0.1) = 438$$

$$P = e^{-438/4550} = 0.991 \qquad \text{or } 99.1\%$$

Problem 7-2

1. Tape or disk backup for files
2. Formal documentation
3. "Clean" operational procedures
4. "Controlled" environment
5. Adequate spare parts provisioning
6. Adequate training (personnel)
7. Off-line and on-line diagnostics
8. Fall-back procedures to nonautomated system
9. Equipment installed for ready access (front, sides, rear)
10. Fail-soft features in system (such as TTY backup for CRT)

INDEX

DATE DUE

SEP. 26.1974	AUG. 27.1975		
OCT. -8.1974	SEP. 25.1975		
NOV. 25.1974	MAR. -8.1976		
JAN. -6.1975	AUG. 26.1976		
JAN. 21.1975	JUL. -5.1977		
JAN. 23.1975	MAR. -3.1978		
FEB. 19.1975	SEP. 27.1978		
FEB. 20.1975	DEC. 18.1981		
FEB. 26.1975	MAR. 19.1982		
MAR. 10.1975	APR. 12.1982		
MAR. 12.1975	JUN. 10.1982		
MAR. 13.1975			
APR. -3.1975			
APR. 28.1975			
APR. 30.1975			
MAY 28.1975			
JUN. 11.1975			
JUL. -7.1975			